Abbreviations

Barrington, *Memoirs*	Jonah Barrington, *Memoirs of Ireland; comprising secret records of the National Convention, the Rebellion and the Union; with delineations of the principal characters connected with these transactions* (2 vols, London, 1835)
Barrington, *Rise and fall*	Jonah Barrington, *Rise and fall of the Irish nation* (Paris, 1833)
BL	British Library
Bolton, *Union*	G.C. Bolton, *The Passing of the Irish Act of Union* (Oxford, 1966)
CARD	Sir John and Lady Gilbert (eds), *Calendar of Ancient Records of Dublin* (19 vols, Dublin, 1889–1944)
Castlereagh corr.	Marquess of Londonderry (ed.), *Memoirs and correspondence of Viscount Castlereagh* (4 vols, London, 1848–9)
Cornwallis corr.	Sir Charles Ross (ed.), *Correspondence of Charles, 1st Marquess Cornwallis* (3 vols, London, 1859)
DNB	*Dictionary of National Biography*
Geoghegan, *Union*	Patrick M. Goeghegan, *The Irish Act of Union: A Study in High Politics, 1798–1801* (Dublin, 1999)
HC	*Journals of the House of Commons of the Kingdom of Ireland, 1613–1800* (19 vols, Dublin, 1796–1800)
KAO	Kent Archive Office
HMC	*Historical Manuscripts Commission*
NAI	National Archives of Ireland
NLI	National Library of Ireland
NLS	National Library of Scotland
PRO	Public Record Office (London)
PRONI	Public Record Office of Northern Ireland
QUB	Queen's University Belfast
TCD	Trinity College, Dublin

The Irish Act of Union, 1800

The Irish Act of Union, 1800

Bicentennial Essays

Editors

MICHAEL BROWN
University College, Dublin

PATRICK M. GEOGHEGAN
Trinity College, Dublin

JAMES KELLY
St. Patrick's College, Drumcondra

IRISH ACADEMIC PRESS
DUBLIN • PORTLAND, OR

First published in 2003 by
IRISH ACADEMIC PRESS
44 Northumberland Road, Dublin 4, Ireland

and in the United States of America by
IRISH ACADEMIC PRESS
c/o ISBS, 5824 N.E. Hassalo Street, Portland
Oregon 97213-3644

Website: www.iap.ie

British Library Cataloguing in Publication Data
The Irish Act of Union: bicentennial essays
   1. Ireland – History – The Union, 1800   2. Ireland – Politics and government –
1760–1820
I. Brown, Michael   II. Geoghegan, Patrick M.   III. Kelly, James, 1959–
941.7'801
ISBN 0-7165-2771-5 (cloth)
ISBN 0-7165-2772-3 (paper)

Library of Congress Cataloging-in-Publication Data
A catalog record of this book is available from the Library of Congress

Typeset by Carrigboy Typesetting Services, County Cork
Printed by MPG Books Ltd., Bodmin, Cornwall

Contents

Abbreviations — vii

Introduction — ix

1. The Historiography of the Act of Union — 5
   James Kelly

2. *The Injured Lady* and Her British Problem — 37
   Michael Brown

3. 'An Union for Empire': The Anglo-Irish Union as an Imperial Project — 50
   Thomas Bartlett

4. Political Anglicanism in Ireland 1691–1801: From the Language of Liberty to the Language of Union — 58
   Joseph Richardson

5. Ulster Presbyterians and the Passing of the Act of Union — 68
   Ian McBride

6. 'Like a Phoenix from its Ashes': United Irish Propaganda and the Act of Union — 84
   Manuela Ceretta

7. Dublin Castle and the Act of Union — 95
   James Quinn

8. The Failure of Opposition — 108
   James Kelly

9. The Irish House of Commons, 1799–1800 — 129
   Patrick M. Geoghegan

10. Dublin after the Union: The Age of the Ultra Protestants, 1801–22 — 144
    Jacqueline Hill

11. Completing the Union? The Irish Novel and the Moment of Union — 157
    Claire Connolly

Appendices

1. Members of the Irish House of Commons, 22 January 1799   177

2. Members of the Irish House of Commons, 1800   184

3. Irish MPs in the House of Commons of the United Kingdom, 1801   192

Notes   195

Notes on Contributors   233

Index   235

Preface

A number of debts have accrued in the preparation of this work. First, and most important of all, the editors wish to thank the contributors. We are also pleased to acknowledge the support of all who made the Act of Union Bicentennial Conference a success, especially the sponsors; the Bank of Ireland who provided the venue, and the Royal Irish Academy, which hosted a reception and the conference dinner. We would also like to thank the British Council and the Office of the Taoiseach for their support. We are also grateful to Dr Ciaran Brady, Dr David Dickson, Dr Patrick Kelly, and Dr Maurice Bric for kindly chairing sessions. Finally, a special mention to Professor Louis Cullen who assisted on the organising committee and chaired the opening session, and to Mr James McGuire who gave the conference consistent support and advised and helped throughout.

Introduction

The Act of Union remains controversial. Two hundred years after its passing it continues to excite and provoke, and its meaning and relevance elicit different responses from different people. The bicentenary of the Act was celebrated by some and ignored by others, and the Union remains a potent symbol of some of the divisions in Anglo-Irish history. Perhaps the most important result was that it created the United Kingdom of Britain and Ireland, and with it a new flag for empire, the Union flag. In recent years, there has been a revival in the critical scholarship on the subject, with one new monograph, two major collections of essays, a cluster of academic articles and a number of conferences. This volume draws in part from one of those conferences, but it also contains specially commissioned work which addresses areas previously overlooked. In many ways the recent historiography on the Union has avoided the narrow nationalist-unionist dichotomy of previous interpretations and the subject, which was once sorely underwritten, can no longer be said to be neglected.

The classic modern account of the Union is G.C. Bolton's *The Passing of the Irish Act of Union,* published in 1966.[1] An Australian historian, Bolton provided the first major reinterpretation of how the measure was enacted, rejecting the contemporary allegations of corruption. Setting the Union into the frame of a Namierite politics driven by familial linkages and the granting of political favours, Bolton successfully incorporated the narrative of the Union into both the Irish revisionist historiographic tradition and the world of British parliamentary history.

Bolton's monograph shaped understanding of the Union for thirty years for, other than a number of essays on eighteenth-century attitudes to the measure, it was not until the 1990s that historians began to re-examine the question.[2] In 1997, David Wilkinson published an important article '"How did they pass the Union"? Secret service expenditure' in the journal *History,* which reopened the controversy about the government's resort to bribery.[3] Wilkinson's work was based on files that had been lost for almost two centuries, which proved the existence of a secret slush fund amounting to £30,850 to help assist the Union pass through a recalcitrant parliament.

In the autumn of 1999, the second scholarly monograph on the Union was published. Patrick M. Geoghegan's *The Irish Act of Union: a study in high politics, 1798–1801* provided a new narrative account of how the measure was passed.[4] Self-avowedly traditional in his high-politics approach, Geoghegan broke new ground by linking the Union to broader attempts to secure Catholic emancipation. He further emphasised that the Union had a pan-British context, and that the collapse of Pitt's London administration was caused by the obstinacy of King George III on the issue of Catholic relief. The corruption argument was also addressed with the newly discovered secret service papers being placed in a wider imperial context.

With the bicentenary of the Act of Union, research into the issue accelerated and a number of important conferences were held to mark the event. One of the most important took place in Belfast in September 1999. There the Union was set in a European and imperial framework, with arresting contributions from J.G.A. Pocock, William Doyle and Christopher Bayly. Domestic concerns were also re-evaluated, with significant papers by Peter Jupp, A.P.W. Malcomson, James Kelly, Trevor McCavery, L.M. Cullen and Patrick M. Geoghegan. The proceedings of this conference were published in the *Transactions of the Royal Historical Society*, sixth series, 10 (2000).[5]

Two noteworthy conferences were also organised by Dáire Keogh and Kevin Whelan in 1999. These were held in Wexford and in Dublin and included a range of contributions on a number of different aspects of the subject, most notably its literary and cultural dimensions. A synopsis of the proceedings was published as *Acts of Union: the causes, contexts and consequences of the Act of Union* in 2001.[6] One of the most important features of this volume is the new work by younger scholars like Daniel Mansergh on the role of public opinion (a topic which he further explored in an article in *Eighteenth-Century Ireland*[7]) and Gillian O'Brien on the political backdrop to the Union. It also offers a colourful contribution by Nicholas Robinson on the Union caricatures and useful essays on the Anglo-Scottish Union of 1707 and the European crisis of the 1790s. The literature of the period is also studied, alongside some general summaries of the event itself.

The Act of Union Bicentennial Conference was held in the old Irish House of Lords, Dublin in June 2000, with G.C. Bolton present as the guest of honour at a special reception in the Royal Irish Academy. That conference provides the basis for this collection. Other papers, not published in this collection, were delivered by A.P.W. Malcomson, Peter Jupp, Gillian O'Brien, Dáire Keogh, Peter MacDonagh, and Gearóid Ó Tuathaigh.

While the *Transactions* volume places the Union in a wider imperial dimension, and *Acts of Union* provides a necessary cultural corrective, this collection aspires to provide an in-depth re-examination of many of the remaining contentious issues. The first essay, by James Kelly, examines how nationalists and unionists have considered the event, discussing all significant writing on the subject from Barrington to Bolton and beyond. What it establishes is, first, that the historiography of the Act of Union is longer and more obviously determined by political attitude than is true of perhaps any other issue in modern Irish history and, second, that an understanding of the historiography is revealing of the way the issue continues to be approached and interpreted.

The next two essays provide a conceptual framework for the rest of the volume. Michael Brown discusses the idea of union in political thought, and analyses the different types of union available to the British government in the wake of the 1798 Rebellion. By comparing the Union of 1801 to the Anglo-Scottish Union of 1707, he argues that, taken together, they mark an innovation in thinking about the concept of political unification that helps to situate both the subsequent Irish Catholic grievance and British imperial success. Thomas Bartlett takes up this latter theme in addressing how this issue was engaged with at the time of the Union's enactment. He contends that a central plank of the pro-union argument was to link its passage to imperial economic and political vitality. In discussing how the Union was intended as a gateway to empire, he contends that this argument was more influential than was previously thought.

Much has been written about Catholic responses to the Union and the government's strategy to persuade Catholics to support the measure, but the status of other denominations has been neglected. This volume helps fill that lacuna. Joseph Richardson provides an overview of Anglican attitudes towards unification with Britain. Focusing on the triumvirate of John Temple, William King and Richard Musgrave, he narrates the development of a Protestant 'language of liberty' in the eighteenth century. Ian McBride explores the question of Ulster Presbyterians and their response to the ending of the Irish parliament. He suggests that their quiescence on the matter, and their extensive engagement with the Volunteers, must be seen in the light of their desire to distance the community from the taint of republican radicalism. However, the community's tepid response to the Union's passage was not indicative of the de-politicisation process taking place on the radical wing of Irish political life more generally. For, as Manuela Ceretta's analysis of the response of the United Irishmen to the Union and their involvement in her discussion of the pamphlet campaign reveals, they addressed the subject in all of its parts.

One aspect of the ratification of the Union still in need of clarification is the mechanics of how the Union was passed. Three essays provide a reappraisal of the dynamics of the measure's ratification. James Kelly offers an analysis of opposition to the Union and of the various strategies adopted both in and out of parliament. James Quinn examines how Dublin Castle rose to the challenge of passing the Act of Union. It fell to Lords Cornwallis and Castlereagh to guide the measure through the Irish parliament while placating a restless country, and Quinn suggests that they deserve greater credit than they have received. Expanding on some of the themes previously encountered in his monograph, Patrick M. Geoghegan supplies a detailed account of how the Castle constructed a majority in the House of Commons. His figures for the parliamentary traffic in the period 1799–1800 provide the basis for a reassessment of the accusations levelled at the Dublin administration and a qualification of Bolton's assertion that the corruption involved achieved little out of the ordinary in easing the passage of the measure.

The volume concludes with two essays on the Union's short-term impact on Dublin politics and Irish cultural life. Jacqueline Hill charts the activities and responses of the ultra-Protestants in the two decades immediately following the measure, arguing that they played a crucial role in gaining recognition of the Orange Order from the higher echelons of British political life. Finally, Claire Connolly's examination of the way the Union was 'written-up' offers new perspectives into how Ireland was perceived in contemporary literature. As she suggests, the political, social and cultural failings of the Union were writ large in the literature of the period.

CHAPTER ONE

The Historiography of the Act of Union

JAMES KELLY

One consequence of the fact that the Act of Union has provided the main fault line in Irish politics over two centuries is the large number of historical accounts of its enactment. It has also meant that most histories of this event written during these two hundred years were penned to sustain a political outlook – unionism or nationalism – rather than to establish, describe and analyse accurately what happened. Significantly, a majority are nationalist in focus and approach. This may be testament in the first instance to the greater ideological emphasis that nationalists have attached to history, but it has also meant that the historiography of the Act of Union is first and foremost a case study of how it has been perceived by its opponents and critics. In comparison, the smaller number of unionist narratives has exercised less historiographical influence.

Despite the fact that most histories of the Act of Union were generated from within antipathetic political traditions, the interpretations offered are characterised less by variation in approach and emphasis than their number might suggest. Moreover, the common concern of their authors to sustain what are essentially political positions prompted the construction of narratives that invariably are incomplete, selectively evidenced and hermeneutically resistant to alternative readings. Jonah Barrington's *Rise and fall of the Irish nation* is probably the most influential such work,[1] since his informed polemic not only provided the interpretative framework that subsequent generations of nationalist historians adopted contentedly, but his conclusion that the Union was enacted as a result of 'bribery' also provided the key theme against which most unionist narratives have reacted. The role of patronage in ensuring the ratification of the Union was the subject of persistent comment while the measure was being agitated, but it was Barrington, in the 1830s, who placed it centre-stage historiographically. This proved irresistible to nationalists who contrived thereafter to discredit the Union by maintaining that it was imposed against the will of the 'Irish people' by recourse to 'corruption'.

This was a disputed conclusion, of course. Both its political proponents and modern historians contend that the patronage resorted to in 1800 to secure a majority for the Act of Union was within permissible parameters. This interpretation received its first historical articulation by T. Dunbar Ingram in 1887, but it was only in the 1960s that it was given an academic *imprimatur*.[2] G.C. Bolton's account of the passing of the Act of Union was the first major non-ideological history of the measure, and while it reflected a historiographical shift away from the partisan approach that had hitherto prevailed, the 'bribery and corruption' paradigm has not been entirely superseded though the terminology currently used is more neutral.[3] Indeed, the recent release of documentation appertaining to the allocation of money from the British secret service fund and the emergence of a 'neo-Romantic' nationalist interpretation of late eighteenth-century Irish history have served to reanimate it to a certain extent.[4] Nor is it surprising that this is so. Much more so than most events that the historian seeks to interpret, the Act of Union is not just a historical event; it is also a current political issue. As a result, those who attempt to engage with it must be alert to the fact that the inter-pretations they reach and the conclusions they offer are subject to political as well as historical interpretation. Taking this into account, the object of what follows is to trace and assess the historiography of the Act of Union. What it highlights is that the interpretation of the enactment of an Anglo-Irish union has undergone sudden as well as subtle shifts in emphasis that mirror and bear witness to methodological shifts in the process of historical recon-struction and ideological shifts in Irish society over two centuries.

I

The animated public controversy occasioned in 1799–1800 by the proposal to join the parliaments of Britain and Ireland in a legislative union did not survive the ratification of the Act of Union.[5] However, the measure was too pregnant with implication and the manner of its enactment too keenly contested for politicians on all sides not to conclude that an appropriately tuned historical account of the episode would serve a useful purpose.[6] Some opponents of the measure, in particular, felt strongly that 'the occult details of that proceeding' should be exposed and James Fitzgerald, who was dismissed from the office of prime sergeant in 1799 for refusing to support the Union, signalled his 'intention of writing its history'. He even prepared a 'prospectus of what he intended', but his desire for advancement, first for himself and, following his retirement from politics, for his son, collided with his authorial ambitions.[7]

Fitzgerald remained persuaded of the value of the undertaking, however, as he gave his 'prospectus' to Jonah Barrington, his fellow anti-unionist, in the hope that he might put it to good use. Barrington possessed the requisite skills.

The publication in 1809 of the first part of his *Historic anecdotes and secret memoirs of the legislative union* demonstrated amply his flair as a *raconteur* and his keen eye for detail, but none of the five parts published between that date and 1815 took the story beyond the achievement of legislative independence.[8] It was Barrington's intention to produce further instalments in which he offered his revelations on the Union, but none appeared in the late 1810s or during the 1820s. It has been suggested that this was the outcome of an agreement Barrington concluded with the Irish administration not to publish a history of the Union exposing government bribery in return for the liberty to leave Ireland to escape his debtors and, possibly, a charge of fiscal misappropriation. This cannot be substantiated.[9] It is clear, however, that neither officials on both sides of the Irish Sea in the early nineteenth century nor its general supporters had much appetite for a 'tell all' style account of the enactment of the Union lest it should generate a negative impression that would inhibit the acceptance of the measure in Ireland.

Conscious of this, and anxious to ensure that the failure in 1801 to deliver on the promise to concede Catholic emancipation did not alienate Irish Catholics, two substantial pro-union histories of the enactment of the measure were published in the early years of the nineteenth century. The first was Charles Coote's *History of the Union of Great Britain and Ireland*, which was printed privately for the author in London in 1802. A historian, who later achieved a measure of fame as the editor of a number of popular histories including Oliver Goldsmith's *History of England*, Coote described the measure as a logical response to the threat of 'disunion' posed by the 1798 Rebellion and the threat of annexation posed by France. Persuaded that a legislative union would prevent a 'return of commotion', and preferring to overlook the activities of its opponents and the 'intrigue' and 'corruption' involved in securing a majority of parliamentary votes, Coote's narrative offered little more than an extended account of proceedings in parliament. The exceptional coverage accorded events in Great Britain was indicative of the author's contention that the Union would advantage the empire because it would hasten

> the invigoration of the general government and the increase of imperial energy. The civil and social consequences of the measure will appear in the mutual participation of wealth and the comforts of life and the extinction . . . of animosity and rivalry, the advance of humanisation among the rude Irish, and the promotion of peace and order, and we may venture to predict that it will establish the prosperity of this great Empire on a firm basis, which will defy the assaults both of foreign and internal enemies.[10]

In contrast to Coote's imperial perspective, Francis Plowden's focus was trained on Ireland. Invited by the Addington administration in 1801 to write a history that would encourage Irish Catholics to embrace the Union despite the dashing of their hopes on emancipation, Plowden was ostensibly an excellent choice. An English Catholic, who had studied for the priesthood until the dissolution of the Jesuit Order in 1773 obliged him to opt for the law, he achieved a measure of fame in the 1790s as a Catholic activist and the author of pamphlets on constitutional and religious issues.[11] More pertinently, he had recently completed a text on 'the constitution of the United Kingdom of Great Britain and Ireland' and was persuaded that 'an incorporate union of the two kingdoms must be the greatest blessing to the British Empire', though his contention that this was only possible if its enactment was 'followed up by an indiscriminating adoption of all his majesty's subjects' was an important caveat.[12] The Addington administration was unaware of how firmly Plowden held this conviction when they promised him £300 to prepare a history, but they clearly harboured some reservations as Plowden busied himself gathering information. Equipped with a letter of introduction from Henry Addington that guaranteed him the co-operation of the chief secretary, Henry Abbot, Plowden was given access to all the 'printed papers'. However, he was not allowed access (on the prime minister's orders) to 'secret or confidential papers'. Furthermore, Addington determined that Plowden should not be allowed free rein to write as he pleased as the prime minister also made it known that he should not be authorised to publish 'as by government's authority and approbation without looking to its drift'.[13]

The prime minister's concerns were well placed, as Plowden was a man of independent judgement who did not take readily to instruction. This proved significant as Plowden observed during the two months that he spent in Ireland towards the end of 1801 that the Union was becoming 'daily less palatable to the people there', and that it was, by one opinion, already 'cordially detested by ninety-nine out of one hundred'. He was also persuaded, arising out of the discernible impact on public discourse of Sir Richard Musgrave's polemical *Memoirs of the different rebellions in Ireland*, that only 'a fair, impartial and authentic history' that 'counteract[ed] the effects of . . . Musgrave's and other *Orange* publications' would achieve the necessary object of 'reconcil[ing] the public mind in Ireland to the measure of union'.[14] With this in mind, he wrote energetically and duly submitted a manuscript of some 600 folios to the prime minister for approval in the spring of 1802.

Plowden anticipated that this was just a matter of form, but the expected endorsement was slow in coming. This troubled him, and his irritation escalated to anger as it emerged that the prime minister was more intent on retarding than on advancing its publication on the grounds that the author had not taken sufficient care to make it 'palatable to his employers'. Addington's wish was for an account that affirmed 'the utility and advantages of an incorporate union'. Plowden did not have a philosophical difficulty with this but he did not see that it necessitated that he should overlook the 'errors and faults' of the king's ministers and the promise to grant Catholic emancipation. The latter was a major point of difference. In view of the commitment he had given George III that he would not promote Catholic emancipation, Addington could not give his approval to the publication of a work that pronounced explicitly in its favour. For his part, Plowden was strongly of the opinion, as he informed Addington on 26 July 1803, that if ministers wished to 'promote union and affection in the sister kingdom' it was in their interest to face up to the mistakes that had been made in the past and embrace a conciliatory policy with respect to Ireland.[15] Most of all, this meant admitting Catholics to parliament, as he made clear in his history.

As a consequence of these unbridgeable differences, Plowden was left with little alternative but to publish his *Historical review*, which when it appeared in 1803 ran to two large volumes, without the anticipated government support. He followed it soon after with a pamphlet in which he provided a detailed account of his dealings with the government and a justification of his refusal to present 'an untrue and unfaithful history . . . to the public'.[16] His defence was cogent and his evidence well marshalled, but it ensured his history was greeted with suspicion by those who did not share his views on Catholic emancipation. This was ironic as Plowden encouraged his readers to look to the benefits a legislative union would bring. Indeed, he recommended they should acknowledge that it was a 'great political event' and work to make it a success:

> There can now be one disposition and one sentiment of every loyal subject upon it: an ardent desire, coupled with efficient exertion, to render it preventative of future evils, and accumulative of future blessings, improvements, and permanent prosperity to Ireland and the whole British Empire, now politically consolidated for those desirable ends.[17]

Plowden's observation that 'an incorporate union' was the only means by which 'the Irish nation could be effectually, though perhaps not instantly, relieved from the tyranny of an Orange ascendancy' that had fomented 'disunion, hatred, and religious acrimony' in the aftermath of the 1798 Rebellion was distinctly less comforting to unionists and attracted critical notice.[18] Yet, he was unrepentant. In a subsequent study of early nineteenth-century Ireland, he observed pointedly that though Catholics had favoured a union publicly and the Orangemen had opposed it, 'Catholic emancipation' had been sacrificed to the Orangemen's commitment to continued 'Protestant ascendancy'.[19]

Plowden was encouraged to reach this conclusion through his involvement with the cause of Catholic relief.[20] This apart, his account of the Union presents the arguments of both the unionist and anti-unionist side fully and without

the partiality and condescension identifiable in later works. He was under no
illusion that some MPs had 'basely sold what they sincerely thought to be the
interest of their country for . . . private gain' and that 'all means were devised
and attempted by both parties to gain proselytes to their respective opinions';
but he was persuaded that 'no political question was ever agitated with more
sincerity of conviction, as none admitted,' he acknowledged significantly, 'of
so much fairness or argument on both sides'.[21] He conceded that the 'general
voice seemed to reject' the idea of a union 'with indignation' in January 1799
but, he observed disapprovingly, 'the language' resorted to was 'of the boldest
kind, even bordering on defiance and sedition'.[22]

Though this might suggest that Plowden's work dealt in detail with public
opinion, his moderate political convictions and lack of access to official
correspondence caused him to produce a narrative that, like Coote's a year
earlier, was focused firmly and unapologetically on the institution of parliament. The result is not without value, though it is often little more than an
extended summary of what is to be found in the press (one of his main
sources of information) and in the published reports of debate in parliament.
Moreover, the serial summary of individual speeches that fills many pages wants
for a narrative dynamic. For instance, in his account of proceedings on 22
January 1799, Plowden minutely relayed the arguments for and against a union
although, by his own admission, 'talent, energy and independence prepon-
derated on the side' of the opposition.[23] On the positive side, this meant that
committed opponents like Jonah Barrington who averred that 'the foulest and
most unconstitutional means' were used to satisfy the wish of 'an indefinitely
ambitious minister' to effect 'the annihilation of his country' were afforded as
much space as active proponents like Sir John Blaquiere who maintained that
Roman Catholics had good reason to look positively upon the Union since,
'under the present order of things, [they] could never be accommodated . . .
without imminent danger to the Protestant establishment, both in church and
state'.[24] Subsequent debates in 1799 are not described quite so 'minute[ly]',
but the key occasions at College Green and at Westminster are all related at
great length.[25]

Plowden normally allowed himself few opportunities to venture opinions,
preferring, in most instances, to report the sentiments of MPs. One might
conclude on the basis of his decision to cite Arthur Moore's contention that
the administration was 'resolved to carry the measure of union by any, and
by every means, and to use all the engines and influence of power, and the
insidious practices of fraud and unfair dealing to bring about its completion'
that he was severely disapproving of their dependence on patronage. Yet,
Plowden merely observed of the extraordinary recourse to escheatorships
that 'many new members' were 'chosen in *lieu* of others who had retired

upon terms'.[26] At the same time, his later observation (in the midst of his equally detailed and balanced account of proceedings in 1800) that, shorn of his 'placement, pensioners and other influenced members . . . the minister had but slender grounds for triumphing in his majority' illustrates that he was not entirely non-judgemental. He likewise acknowledged the efforts of the opposition, Henry Grattan notably,[27] 'in disputing every inch of the ground' until the end.[28]

Compared with parliament, developments in the public realm are addressed sketchily. Plowden described the anti-union stand of the bar and merchants in December 1798, but he did not assess its appeal. He noted that 'public exultation rose to a great height on th[e] defeat of the ministry' in January 1799 but said little beyond observing that 'the popular journals were lavish in their panegyrics of the anti-unionists' and that 'printed lists of the voters were circulated . . . gratis' so that the public might know 'their glorious and virtuous defenders'.[29] The account offered both of the promotion of a legislative union in the summer of 1799 and of the continuing activity of anti-unionists is equally brief and disappointing. A reference to the intervention of 'military commanders . . . on pretence of preventing the intrusion and violence of the lower classes' elicited the observation that the intimidation of opponents was necessary to overawe 'the majority of the nation . . . hostile to the scheme of union' but no firm evidence was offered to sustain this.[30] His ostensibly disarming conclusion that accusations by anti- and pro-unionists that their opponents had recourse to 'the meanest artifices' and 'scandalous misrepresentations . . . were unfortunately but too well founded' was weak and evasive when, on the same page, he cited the marquess of Buckingham's contention of 24 September 1799 that 'popular sentiment in favour of union was rapidly gaining ground'.[31] Plowden's perception was that if the Union 'had not become generally popular, it had ceased at least to be generally unpopular'. Significantly, he implicitly attributed this to the readiness of Catholics to 'come forward' because of their dislike of 'the most violent opposers of the legislative union . . . the Orangemen and the real mal-contents or separatists'. However, he made no attempt to mask the fact that this was not the unanimous opinion of Catholics, citing Daniel O'Connell's criticism of 'this injurious, insulting and hated measure'.[32]

Plowden's concluding apostrophe that the Union should be welcomed 'by every true and loyal subject . . . as affording the sure means of conciliating the affections, consolidating the energies, and promoting the prosperity of every part of the British Empire', notwithstanding, his was not the 'unexceptionable' history he set out to write.[33] Nor was it the paean to the Union Addington desired, as the *Edinburgh Review* observed pointedly.[34] As a result, Plowden's *Historical review* was received most warmly by supporters of Catholic relief, of whom British and Irish Whigs were the most welcoming. Henry Grattan described the work as a 'manly and able production', while Earl Fitzwilliam applauded Plowden's attempt to 'produce principles of harmony, conciliation and good fellowship'.[35] It is difficult to know whether they were more impressed by Plowden's attempt to present a fair and balanced account or by his contention that the success of the Union depended on affording Catholics further civil rights. What is clear is that conservatives committed to uphold 'Protestant ascendancy' found the history objectionable on both counts, and their discomfort palpably exceeded the satisfaction registered in liberal circles.

Predictably, given his position as the leading conservative historical ideologue, Plowden's foremost critic was Sir Richard Musgrave.[36] Having previously accused Plowden of inciting 'disloyalty and insurrection', Musgrave first dismissed the history in the periodical the *British Critic* as a work of party designed 'to mislead the people of England'.[37] He followed this up with a detailed critique, only the last three of whose 175 pages addressed the Union, in which he dismissed Plowden's assertion that he was 'a sincere friend of the measure of an union' and denied that it was carried by 'fraud, force and bribery'. On the contrary, Musgrave maintained that it was approved because 'the best, wisest and most independent men in Ireland conscientiously supported the measure'; because it was favoured by the property of the country; and because 'the empty pride of national consequence at length yielded to the influence of cool deliberate judgement, and to a conviction of the deplorable situation to which factions, patriots and rebellion had brought the country'.[38] Never one to allow an opponent have the last word, Plowden prepared a detailed response refuting Musgrave's arguments, the primary effect of which was to fix him in the public mind as a political partisan, which ultimately was how his history came to be perceived.[39]

The controversy that greeted Francis Plowden's *Historical review* was a warning to all would-be historians of the Union of the difficulties of writing a history of this event that did not give offence. As a result, narratives like that presented by William Wenman Seward, whose *Political transactions of Ireland from the accession of King George III to the present time* was published in 1803, were constructed carefully to cause minimum offence. Seward, indeed, eschewed a linking narrative and relied wholly on contemporary documents. The information to be gleaned from the reports of public meetings, division lists, *précis* of proceedings in parliament, and the articles of the Union is not unrevealing, but his studied neutrality provides for poor history.[40]

Few authors were as self-denying as Seward, although few accounts of the Union were published in the quarter century following Plowden. Ironically, those that addressed the subject were influenced by his massive narrative and were prepared to concede that the manner of the Union's ratification left much to be desired. Stephen Barlow, who published his *History of Ireland* in

1814, is a case in point. Barlow's short account of the passing of the Act of Union echoes Plowden's longer narrative in several particulars, notably in conceding that the 'government was sedulous to multiply its partisans by a very liberal and comprehensive system of corruption', whereas 'the patriots were no less anxious to strengthen their cause by arguments and facts'. However, instead of making this binary thesis the core of his analysis, Barlow opted for a familiar narrative that focused on proceedings in parliament because it allowed him to look to future prospects rather than to dwell on past wrongs. He lamented that 'a question like that of a legislative union should have been embarrassed by party and local prejudices', but rather than explore the reality of how 'the viceroy . . . smooth[ed] the difficulties which opposed themselves to the measure', he emphasised the insubstantial basis for opposition in Ireland and the additional benefits that could accrue if the imperial legislature was 'wise enough to adopt a decided and manly policy'. Indeed, as far as Barlow was concerned, opposition to the Union in Ireland derived less from 'judgement' than from 'feeling'; less from a 'fair' assessment of its provisions than from 'strong local and personal prejudices'; and less from 'its prudence or policy' than from a sense of 'national honour'.[41]

Stephen Barlow's account is indicative of the prevailing confidence in the Act of Union during the early decades of the nineteenth century. Anti-unionist sentiment existed, but it was diffuse and disorganised, and it is significant that an attempt to organise an anti-union campaign in Dublin in 1809–10 did not bear fruit.[42] However, opposition to the Union grew in strength and vigour as the difficult economic environment that followed the conclusion of the Napoleonic wars reinforced the negative impact of the failure to concede Catholic emancipation before 1829. This prompted many in Ireland to conclude that a domestic legislature would be more advantageous. The most tangible political manifestation of this was Daniel O'Connell's campaign to repeal the Act of Union of 1830–31. This was short-lived, but it served to give repeal a legitimacy it had not possessed previously.[43] Moreover, in contrast to its advocates, who located their arguments in support of a union in the present, critics of the Union appealed routinely to history and to historians. Daniel O'Connell's speech in support of his motion for leave to bring in a bill for the re-establishment of a domestic legislature in Ireland on 22 April 1834 provides a powerful illustration of this.

O'Connell did not always attribute the information he cited in this long and impressive speech, but we know Francis Plowden was one of his main sources of information, not least for his own anti-union stand in 1799. More important for the perception of the Union and how the 'revolution' of 1782 was to be regarded in the future, O'Connell cited large extracts in support of legislative independence from the speeches of such prominent anti-unionists as Henry Grattan, William Conyngham Plunket and Charles Kendal Bushe. Their rhetoric informed his conclusion that 'the chief means' by which the Act of Union was 'consummated were intimidation, bribery, corruption, treachery and blood'. O'Connell glossed his allusions to 'intimidation', 'treachery and blood' by invoking the repressive security policy pursued in the 1790s which, he claimed dubiously, was contrived to set 'the Catholic against the Protestant, and the Protestant against the Catholic' and to foment a rebellion 'for the purpose of carrying the Union'. He justified his contention that the Union was secured by 'bribery' and 'corruption' by invoking Lord Grey's claim that 707,000 people had put their names to anti-union petitions compared with a mere '3000' who 'declared themselves in favour'; by pointing out that important interests were rewarded with pensions, peerages and promotions of various sorts; by claiming that 'upwards of £1,000,000' was provided without justification to 'purchase . . . Irish rotten boroughs' when no such compensation was provided in the Great Reform Bill; and by asserting that a total of 116 MPs who voted in its favour were the beneficiaries of government patronage.[44] O'Connell did not acknowledge any specific source for the last claim, but that it echoed Jonah Barrington, whose works he also consulted, suggests strongly that it came from that quarter.[45] What is indisputable is that the two men shared a hostile attitude to the Union that both informed and encouraged the emergence of a tangibly aggressive anti-union historiography from the mid-1830s.

II

Jonah Barrington's most important historical work, *Rise and fall of the Irish nation*, was first published in Paris in 1833. Comprising the *Historic anecdotes and secret memoirs*, in which he had previously related the 'rise' of the 'Irish nation' in 1782, and unpublished material informed by his own experiences of the 'fall' of the same 'nation' in 1800, it was the first attempt to write the history of the Act of Union from an avowedly opposition perspective. Barrington's credentials for undertaking such a task were hardly exemplary given his own dubious financial conduct while a judge of the Irish Court of Admiralty. However, he did possess an anti-union pedigree, having resigned his commission in the Lawyer's Cavalry Corps of yeomanry in January 1799 in protest against the measure and having stoutly criticised the 'corrupt and unconstitutional means' employed to win support in parliament in 1799 and 1800.[46] Moreover, he was possessed of a good (if selective) memory and a racy style, and he made ample use of both to produce a narrative of exceptional vivacity that registered an immediate impact. It was published in London in 1835 in the *de luxe* format of the *Historic anecdotes*, and cheaper editions bearing the title of the French edition were published in Dublin at irregular intervals thereafter.[47]

As its title indicates, Barrington's approach was the antithesis of Plowden's sober elaboration. This is epitomised by his concluding remark that the ratification of the Act of Union meant 'an independent country was . . . degraded into a province – Ireland, as a nation, was EXTINGUISHED'. Since he had alleged in his letter of resignation from the Lawyer's Cavalry that the Union amounted to a barefaced attempt 'to crush a rising nation' he was consistent on this point.[48] He was consistent too in attributing the Union to the malign ambition of William Pitt, but whereas in 1799 he was content to describe the prime minister as 'despotic', he maintained in 1833 that the Union was the culmination of a larger scheme devised and orchestrated by Pitt to 'annihilate the Irish legislature'.[49] Though less explicit on this point than O'Connell was to be in April 1834, Barrington linked the government's security policy in the 1790s to the Union on the grounds that it 'excited in many the fallacious idea that in the arms of England only Ireland could regain and secure tranquillity'.

As this suggests, Barrington's narrative of the enactment of the Act of Union was in many respects a story of heroes and villains, and anyone who supported or played a part in advancing the measure was automatically consigned to the latter category. Thus Cornwallis and Castlereagh demonstrated 'a disregard for every constitutional principle' throughout their political careers which, in Castlereagh's case, he summarised epigrammatically as follows: 'the commencement was patriotic, the progress corrupt and the termination criminal'.[50] Edward Cooke, the influential under-secretary, was described memorably as 'the private and efficient actuary of the parliamentary seduction'.

Barrington was adept at coining felicitously dismissive character sketches, and they both inform and enliven his narrative. The problem is that they are frequently inaccurate. In the case of well-known individuals like Lord Clare it is possible to distinguish insight from caricature, suggesting that in the case of lesser-known individuals his *bon mots* must be treated with great caution. For example, Barrington wrote that: 'Lord Tyrone, an automaton of Lord Clare, possessed plain manners, an open countenance, a slothful uncultivated mind, unsusceptible of any refined impression, or patriotic feelings; the example of his relatives gave him no stimulus beyond that of lucrative patronage'. This is eminently quotable; it is also irredeemably opinionated and partial. This might not be a problem if Barrington deployed his acerbic wit and ironic insights equally, but the leaders of the opposition generally escape lightly. As a result, the impression conveyed is that those who advocated the Union were morally unscrupulous and politically corrupt compared with its opponents, whose attachment to principle and courage is generally lionised. They are presented in an intrinsically heroic light as latter-day Davids challenging the might of the establishment Goliath.[51]

If Barrington's disposition to elevate the opponents of the Act of Union poses a serious question mark against the reliability of his narrative, the fact that he was a participant in the events that culminated in the enactment of an Anglo-Irish union ensures it will continue to be consulted. His account of events in the House of Commons in 1799 may not be as complete or as informed as that provided by Plowden but it is more atmospheric. While this cannot be said of his categorisation of the pro-union case as a blend of 'false reasoning, misstated facts, fallacious premises and unfounded conclusions', his description of the 'masterly severity' Lord Castlereagh employed in responding to George Ponsonby on 22 January 1799 gives life to that exchange. Likewise, one may not concur with his judgement that a request to Ponsonby on 25 January to write down his motion calling on parliament to stand by the constitution of 1782 'ultimately deranged the constitution of an empire, and annihilated the legislature of an independent nation', but his relation of the incident is revealing. So too is his assessment of the opposition's inability to capitalise on the events of 22/23 January as 'a retreat after a victory'.[52] Indeed, Barrington's analysis is at its most penetrating in his account of the parliamentary opposition and his conclusion that their weakness derived from their 'palpable want of political connexion', poor leadership, inadequate organisation, policy differences and tactical _naiveté_ as exemplified by their decision to opt for 'moderation' in the spring of 1799, remains persuasive.[53]

At the same time, Barrington was firmly convinced that the administration's recourse to 'all the weapons of seduction' was decisive in obtaining the votes necessary to secure the passage of the Act of Union. As he saw it, the administration had resort to 'every means of corruption' to 'carry a measure they had determined upon'. Thus they 'duped' the Catholics, won over susceptible MPs with lavish entertainment and the prospect of preferment, and deployed the military to discourage popular protest. They also 'bribe[d]' borough owners by compensating them for the loss of property, and secured signatures for petitions from 'every individual who could be influenced', even beggars, cottagers, tradesmen and felons.[54] The effects of this were manifest when parliament reassembled in January 1800. Persuaded by analysing the so-called 'red' and 'black lists' of how MPs voted on the subject of a union in January 1799 and January 1800, Barrington averred that Lord Castlereagh had 'palpably purchased' twenty-five votes in the run-up to the 1800 session. Since this was the equivalent of a majority of fifty in a division, which the 'government . . . never could or did obtain . . . on the principle of a union', Barrington concluded that 'public and actual bribery' rather than 'any change of opinion in the country, or any fair or honest majority' was the reason the Act of Union was carried.[55] This summation was not entirely consistent with his multi-factorial explanation of the weakness of the opposition offered earlier. But Barrington was so struck by the evidence of these lists and so eager to mitigate the refusal of the Irish parliament in 1800 to stand its ground that his account of events highlights 'bribery' and 'corruption' at the expense of such issues as military intimidation and the betrayal by Catholics (guided by their bishops) of their country, to which he had previously referred.

Barrington's 'fall of the Irish nation' was the most ideologically charged interpretation of the ratification of the Act of Union published to date. As such it exerted enormous influence on how the Union was seen in the nationalist circles that bought his book in large numbers. His contention that the Act of Union was purchased reinforced the view of the Union as unjust and unnatural. However, it was his equation of its enactment with the infliction of a 'death wound to the Irish nation' that gave his interpretation its ideological impetus.[56] When Barrington wrote or spoke of the Irish nation, he meant the 'Protestant nation'. However, his limited application of this term was ignored or lost sight of and he was enlisted, not just in support of the cause of repeal, but in the cause of the emerging Romantic nationalist sensibility that was attracted by his use of the language of nationhood. While Barrington might not have approved, Henry Grattan, whose re-entry into the Irish parliament in January 1800 was described by Barrington in reverential tones, would have had few qualms according to his son's emotionally charged account of the Act of Union in his influential biography of his father.[57]

Henry Grattan junior's expansive account of the 'life and times' of Grattan *pérè* is first and foremost an act of *filiopietas*. Yet, Grattan junior was also a politician in his own right and a determined advocate of repeal, and his account of the Act of Union, published in the 1840s, is direct testament to the impact on its emerging historiography of the growing enthusiasm in Ireland for repeal and of the embrace of Romantic nationalism. The emergence of the latter is typically identified with the revolutionary Young Irelanders, rather than with constitutional politicians like Grattan, but the personnel and ideological contours of physical force and constitutional nationalism overlapped, as Grattan junior's assertion that the Union involved the 'surrender' of 'even the forms of nationality' emphasises. Grattan junior was not entirely consistent in his interpretation of how this came about. On the one hand, he attributed it to the exploitative and perfidious attitude of England towards Ireland; on the other, he maintained that the Irish parliament no longer possessed any credit with the people as a result of the draconian security policy it had authorised during the 1790s. His emphasis on this point emulated Barrington, but whereas the latter argued that Pitt's strategy was about inducing 'Ireland to throw herself into the arms of the protecting country', Grattan junior avowed that it was about prostrating the country. 'When the insurgents were put down, the country was put down; for a government is certain always to convert its victory over a party, into a conquest over the people', he observed acerbically.[58]

The antipathy to government from London explicit in Grattan junior's narrative is one of its starkest features, and it provides a dramatic index of just how antagonistic to the Act of Union mainstream Irish opinion had become. As he presented it, a union was the ultimate strategic objective of British ministers and their Irish equivalents once legislative independence became a reality in 1782. They only waited until the early 1790s to embark on a 'horrid plot' to bring it about. Their motives for doing so lay in the familiar 'base designs' of economic jealousy and political domination inherent in Britain's attitude to Ireland. Grattan junior might have used this as the point of departure for a rhapsody on economic growth in Ireland during the eighteen years when the Irish parliament was legislatively free. He chose instead to emphasise the prospects that were interrupted because the enfeebled Irish legislature yielded to bribery and corruption on a grand scale in approving the Act of Union.[59]

His low opinion of the Irish parliament at the end of the eighteenth century and his views on the susceptibility of its membership to venality ('the House of Commons was fast growing into a House of Lords, as the House of Lords had grown into a court'[60]) notwithstanding, Grattan junior was quite emphatic that it *did not consent to its own abolition. No such thing; it refused its consent, and then by force was compelled to yield.'* Yet, he was short on detail as to how 'force' was brought to bear. He did mention that the government 'found it necessary to resort to all the means that stratagem, violence, intimidation and corruption could supply', but he added little to what Jonah Barrington had said a decade earlier. He reprinted the 'red' and 'black' lists *in toto*; reiterated Barrington's contention that *'twenty-five'* votes were 'purchased'; and alleged that the aggressive deployment of the military had been intrinsic to the task of securing a parliamentary majority in 1800.[61] The implication that patronage was the key to the administration's success in carrying the Union was affirmed when Grattan junior described the 'deluge of corruption' resorted to by the Irish administration. Convinced that 'the bench of bishops, the bench of judges, the bar, the revenue, the army, the navy, civil offices, military and naval establishments, places, pensions and titles, were defiled and prostituted for the purpose of carrying . . . this ill-omened union', Grattan junior concluded that the 'combination of force, fraud, violence, bribery and illegality' appealed to was unsurpassed 'in the annals of history'.[62]

This was absurd, but it was consonant with Grattan junior's perception that the government was determined that 'nothing should stop them in their efforts to accomplish' a union. Ironically, this was secondary to his primary purpose, which was to reveal the heroic effort made by its opponents, his father most notably, to prevent it. The story he told was familiar to readers of

Barrington, but Grattan junior relayed it with even more partisan pride. Thus, the efforts of the opposition to defeat what William Conyngham Plunket termed 'a system of black corruption' are repeatedly highlighted in a narrative that emphasises the 'great spirit and great ardour' of opposition spokesmen such as Plunket, James Fitzgerald, John Foster, Arthur Moore, George Ponsonby and Henry Grattan.[63] Similarly, Grattan junior's conclusion that public opinion was relentlessly hostile to the very idea of a union is supported by the presentation of an amended version of Lord Grey's disputed figures that the 7,000 people who petitioned in support of the Union were dwarfed by the '110,000 freeholders and 707,000 persons' who opposed it. In this context, it seemed safe for Grattan junior to claim that the 'great mass' of Catholics was 'adverse' and to explain away such supportive pronouncements as were forthcoming from that quarter by alleging that they were 'tampered with' or 'intentionally and basely deceived'. [64] His relentless anti-unionism climaxed with the assertion that Lord Clare or Lord Castlereagh 'deserved to die' for the crime they perpetrated against the Irish nation. It was a most egregious observation, but it was consistent with his approbatory citation of Richard Brinsley Sheridan's claim that the Irish parliament was worth dying for.[65]

The reality was that few felt so strongly at the time. As a result, Grattan junior's account of the resistance to the Act of Union presents the efforts of the opposition both inside and outside of parliament in too positive a light. This is particularly, but understandably, the case of his account of his father's return to the Commons in 1800.[66] This is entirely in keeping with Grattan junior's replication of Jonah Barrington's heroes and villains approach. The difference is that Grattan junior went significantly further in language and characterisation. One may seek to explain the difference between the two by reference to the fact that one wrote as a retired, the other as a practising politician, but a more tenable explanation is that political attitudes had hardened. Henry Grattan junior was part of an emergent Romantic nationalism that held that direct rule from Westminster was injurious to Irish best interests and incompatible with the country's destiny. Together, they provided an interpretation of the Act of Union that was not just hostile, it contributed to the developing sense of victimhood centred on the perception that the Union was imposed on the Irish nation which was an important element of nineteenth-century Irish nationalist rhetoric.

III

Perhaps because they could not advance a case of equivalent emotional intensity, the emerging unionist interest in mid nineteenth-century Ireland did not supply a history equivalent in scale or impact to that of Barrington or

Grattan junior. Such works as offered a unionist viewpoint were political rather than historical, and where they did offer a historical perspective it was supportive of a primarily political message. This can be illustrated by R.M. Martin's account of *Ireland before and after the Union*, published in 1848, which maintained that the Union had benefited the Irish economy. Martin buttressed his argument with a formidable array of selectively marshalled statistics, which he deployed to disprove the nationalist view that 'Ireland made the most extraordinary strides in commerce and manufactures during the period of what is termed "glorious independence"'.[67] According to him, 'what was *absurdly* termed the "constitution of Irish independence"' was a mere 'mockery' that 'the real friends of Ireland' realised 'must inevitably lead to a separation from England, or a legislative incorporation'. Concerned in the first instance to promote 'the substantial welfare of their country' rather than 'the fanciful prospects of interested partisans', they could only watch and warn as, despite the best efforts of 'the British parliament . . . to conciliate' Ireland, the 'country was torn . . . by factions and intestine feuds'. In one promiscuous listing, Martin instanced

> the Patriots, Agitators, Right-boys, White-boys, Peep-of-Day-boys, Conventions, Aggregate Bodies, Catholic Committees, Tarring and Feathering Committees, Defenders, Assassins, Houghers of Men and Houghers of Cattle Associations, Whig Clubs, St James' Delegates, Exchequer Street Delegates, National Congresses, Emancipators, United Irishmen, Reformers, Revolutionists, Societies of Peace and Societies of War.[68]

His point, which he reinforced with an account of pre-union Irish politics of exceptional bleakness, was that 'the insidious speeches, proclamations, and publications of pretended patriots' encouraged the preparation of 'plans of general insurrection' whose object was 'the creation of an Hibernian republic in an indivisible alliance with France' and that culminated in the 'dreadful massacres' perpetrated in County Wexford in 1798.[69]

Martin's analysis of the origins and nature of the 1798 Rebellion was manifestly indebted to Richard Musgrave; his rejection of the argument that England instigated the Rebellion 'in order to secure a legislative union' as an 'atrocious libel' was a response to Barrington and Grattan junior. In sharp contrast, Martin interpreted the Union as 'the only chance left for the peace, freedom and prosperity of Ireland', which was why it was favoured by 'the most respectable and wealthy Roman Catholics', approximately half the House of Commons 'and a large majority of the property and rank of the country'. It was, he propounded, a victory for 'reason, and a sound sense of mutual interests' that a union was ratified, and the experience to date demonstrated that it was of benefit to Ireland.[70]

Martin's interpretation of the Act of Union and of the factors that brought it about was so different to that of Jonah Barrington and Henry Grattan junior that they might as well have been describing different events. More significantly, their incompatible perspectives reflected accurately the deepening chasm between the dominant interpretations of the event as political alignments hardened. The nationalist interpretation promoted by Barrington and Grattan junior was given semi-canonical status in William O'Neill Daunt's *Catechism of the history of Ireland* which distilled and popularised their interpretation, identifing it as 'the duty of all Irishmen . . . to get rid of [the Union] as fast as they can'.[71] It is a measure of the pervasiveness of the nationalist interpretation that writers who did not define themselves as part of that tradition were influenced by its arguments, as is borne out by the widespread acceptance of the view that the Act of Union became law because of the government's resort to 'corruption'.[72]

The publication during the 1840s and 1850s of substantial amounts of the correspondence of Lord Castlereagh, Lord Cornwallis, John Beresford and the marquess of Buckingham provided material with which a more refined narrative might have been constructed but it was slow in coming.[73] Based on his reading of the *Cornwallis correspondence*, the unionist historian Goldwin Smith conceded that the Union was carried 'partly by corrupt means' but, contrary to Henry Grattan junior, he maintained that it was not 'among the most unpardonable instances of corruption'. He reinforced the unionist case by claiming that it had widespread support in Ireland and that it was the only option if Ireland was not to 'become the ward and vassal of France'.[74]

Though nationalist historians writing in the post-Famine period were aware that the printed editions of the correspondence of several of the principals allowed for the construction of more expansive and sophisticated narratives of the enactment of the Union, the interpretations they proffered continued to draw heavily on Barrington and Grattan junior. In his continuation of Abbé Mac Geoghegan's *History of Ireland*, Patrick O'Kelly related a familiar tale of how 'the unalloyed horrors of blood and carnage' of the late 1790s was exploited by Pitt to promote a union. The citizens of Dublin and elsewhere 'nobly exerted their influence in opposition', but the prime minister was not to be denied 'his iniquitous purposes'. The Catholic Church was 'tamper[ed] with'; patronage was readily forthcoming to 'assuage the love of titles and of gold' and to persuade 'traitors to their country [to] vot[e] away the liberties of Ireland'.[75] A later, expanded, version, 'compiled' by John Mitchel and published in 1869, drew heavily on Barrington, Grattan junior and Francis Plowden to advance the same interpretation in greater detail.[76]

This was also the perception of the former Young Irelander, Thomas D'Arcy McGee. Though he had abandoned physical force for parliamentary politics following his emigration to Canada, he continued to champion 'Irish emancipation' as the account of the Act of Union he provided in his *Popular history of Ireland*, published in New York in 1863, attests.[77] This is illustrated vividly by his description of Lords Clare and Castlereagh as 'public traitors' because they 'voluntarily offer[ed] their services to establish an alien and a hostile policy on the ruins of their own national constitution'. As this indicates, D'Arcy McGee was profoundly indebted to Henry Grattan junior, whom he also followed in defining 'force and fraud' as the 'two chief agencies by which the Union was effected' and in claiming that the Irish parliament was 'discredited' in the eyes of the people by its embrace of a 'fierce reactionary spirit' in the 1790s. This notwithstanding, neither the generous disposal of 'titles, pensions and money' nor the care taken to win over 'every description of people' – Catholics, Orangemen, Church of Ireland clergy, borough owners, reformers – with 'a particular set of appeals and arguments' was sufficient to secure its implementation.[78] The Irish administration was obliged to resort to extraordinary measures: 'Steps were immediately taken by the Castle to deplete the house of its majority, and to supply their places before another session with forty or fifty new members, who would be entirely at the beck of the chief secretary'. This was sufficient to ensure the Act of Union was ratified despite the fact that the number of signatories to pro-union petitions was eclipsed a hundredfold by those who took the opposite stand. McGee's main source on the enactment of the Union in 1800 was Jonah Barrington. McGee related this event in dramatic fashion with appropriate emphasis on the resistance of Grattan, but with the conviction that the 'counter revolution' that was the Union was accomplished by 'foul means' since it had no more than 'six or seven' genuine supporters in Ireland.[79]

D'Arcy McGee's book achieved wide circulation in Ireland following the publication of a British edition by Cameron of Glasgow in 1868. His recycling of Barrington and Grattan was all the more influential because it was this interpretation that the editor of the *Nation*, A.M. Sullivan, presented in his vastly popular *Story of Ireland*. First published in 1867, O'Sullivan's *Story* went through dozens of printings and several editions before the end of the century.[80] In truth, his account of the Union is an authorial travesty that has more in common with a badly plagiarised essay than an original work. This may be attributable to Sullivan's eagerness to attract a wide readership, but the sheer scale of his dependence on McGee and Barrington means his account of the Act of Union is intellectually uninteresting. It is important none the less, since his emphasis on the 'naked, unsparing, unscrupulous and unblushing corruption' resorted to to secure the ratification of the Act of Union, contrary to the avowed wish of the majority of the people of Ireland, affirmed the nationalist argument that the Act of Union possessed no legal or moral authority. It also popularised Barrington's contention that with the Union an 'independent country was . . . degraded into a province'.[81]

IV

The historiographical dominance of the nationalist view of the Act of Union helped in the promotion of the cause of Home Rule once it moved centre stage during the 1870s and 1880s. This put unionism under greater pressure to produce a defence of the episode that offered more than James Anthony Froude or William Ellis Hume-Williams were able to muster. As far as Froude was concerned, the Irish legislature after 1782 was 'the most mischievous parody of a representative legislature which the world' had 'ever seen'. He had no hesitation, as a result, either accepting or justifying Cornwallis's assertion that its abolition had been achieved by 'corruption'.[82] Hume-Williams was equally ready to absolve the appeal to 'lavish promises, . . . direct bribes' and 'martial law' on the grounds that a union was more palatable than 'separation'.[83] This was a tenable point of view, but Hume-Williams's defence of his position was too thin to satisfy many and by the mid-1880s, with Irish politics firmly fractured around the issue of Home Rule, unionists could no longer afford to cede the historiographical battleground to their opponents. Nationalists, by contrast, were determined to retain the interpretative initiative, with the result that a number of important histories of the Act of Union were published in the late 1880s and early 1890s. Each reflected an ideological perspective; their most striking common characteristics are their extensive use of sources and familiarity with the rules of evidence. This ensured that the accounts provided were more expansive and better researched than their predecessors. The most innovative was the unionist interpretation presented by Thomas Dunbar Ingram.

Ingram, who was educated at Trinity College Dublin and Queen's College, Belfast, trained as a lawyer and served for eleven years as professor of jurisprudence in the Presidency College at Calcutta prior to his return to Ireland in 1877. Unionist by inclination as well as by descent, it troubled him that the historiography of the Act of Union was so dominated by what he termed 'one-sided and extravagant books, like Grattan's *Life* or worthless publications such as Barrington's romances'. In response, he turned to the 'original sources' to establish what had happened. Persuaded by his reading of these that 'the Union was undertaken from the purest motives, . . . was carried by fair and constitutional means' and was accomplished 'with the hearty assent and concurrence of the vast majority of the two peoples that dwelt in Ireland', he published a revisionist account he called *A history of the legislative union* in 1887 that can be reasonably described as the first unionist and the first documented history of the passing of the Act of Union. Arising out of his conviction that 'all the charges against the government rested finally on the stories of Barrington or on the declamatory statements of the opposition during the sessions of 1799 and 1800', Ingram constructed his narrative from the rich selections of correspondence in print. He was thereby enabled to produce a book that not only offered a persuasive alternative to the received nationalist interpretation, it provided the proponents of the Union with an arsenal of historical arguments they could deploy in their defence of the Union and of unionism.[84]

Ingram was guided in his interpretation of the Act of Union by his perception that it was prompted by the necessary objects of securing the Anglo-Irish connection and protecting Irish Protestants. Since these were goals he approved of, he contrived to show that the pattern of late eighteenth-century Irish politics both legitimated and justified the Act of Union. For example, he cited the enfranchisement of Catholics in 1793 as an important factor as it paved the way for Catholics to dominate the Irish parliament and, over time, for the formation of 'a Catholic establishment and Catholic ascendancy', which might culminate in the undoing of 'the existing constitution in church and state', and 'a civil war' that Great Britain would be hard-pressed to subdue.[85] This analysis suggests that Ingram believed that once Catholics were given the vote 'Catholic ascendancy' would displace 'Protestant ascendancy' – an impression reinforced by his contention that even without Catholic enfranchisement parliamentary representation in Ireland was more generous than it was in Britain.

Paradoxically, Ingram was less disposed to defend the status quo in respect of the legislative changes agreed in 1782. Legislative independence, he argued, 'elevated' Ireland 'to the rank of an independent nation'. However, it did not preclude 'further measures which the legislatures of both countries might deem necessary for securing the permanence of connection between them'. The Act of Union was such a measure, and its ratification, Ingram claimed, 'secured for ever' Ireland's 'legislative independence'. This extended the normal definition of what constituted 'legislative independence' to breaking point, and Ingram weakened his argument further by maintaining that 'an incorporate union, in some shape or other, was inevitable' because of 'the requirements of the Empire'. In this context, he instanced the threatening behaviour of France in particular, but his reference to 'the hostility of the Catholic community' to Britain indicates that the security of the Protestant interest in Ireland was of greater import since 'Ireland could not exist an hour as a Protestant state without the support of England'.[86]

Ingram's reflexive Protestantism both colours and diminishes the useful arguments he advanced and the evidence he adduced in support of his contention that the Union was a logical response to the 'jealousies and dissensions' obtaining from 'the existences of two parliaments'. None the less, his account of the operation of the Anglo-Irish nexus during the 1780s and 1790s was better grounded in the realities of late eighteenth-century Irish politics than that offered by nationalists.[87] His account of the ratification of the Act of Union by the Irish parliament was equally well grounded. Sharply critical of nationalist historians who, he averred, 'avoid[ed] the development of events and the chronological order of occurrences' in favour of a 'patchwork' of facts whose gaps they filled up with 'unscrupulous declamation and glaring misrepresentation', he provided a detailed account of the high and low politics of its passage. This led him to the controversial conclusion that in 1799 there was majority support for the measure among Catholics and only minority support among Protestants.

Ingram maintained more tenably, though he echoed Barrington on this point, that the failure of George Ponsonby to press home his advantage on 24/25 January 'was the turning point of the whole contest' since several of those who had voted against a union at that time were far from unconditionally opposed. Obviously then, the orchestration of opposition was critical to the outcome, and Ingram was in no doubt that their effectiveness was diminished by the fact that they were a 'composite and discordant party united only in their opposition to the measure' who failed to prevent 'the country' being 'converted' to a union in 1799.[88]

In his analysis of the opposition, Ingram appealed to evidence that was ignored by previous authors. His general standard of research is impressive, particularly his delineation and discussion of the large number of pro-union addresses presented to Lord Cornwallis on his tours of Munster and Ulster, though his dismissal of the response orchestrated by the opposition in the spring of 1800 as 'feeble' is less than fair.[89] His assertion that the 'anti-unionists had recourse to a system of open and general bribery' likewise demonstrates his readiness to accept dubious evidence where it bolsters his case, and thereby to indulge in the same doubtful practices of which he accused his nationalist targets. At the same time, his chapter on Catholic support for a union is a significant improvement on previous accounts that embarrassedly glossed over the phenomenon or that gave disproportionate notice to Daniel O'Connell's stand in December 1799. Whether one can claim reasonably on the basis of declarations from four archbishops and thirteen bishops, peers and laity that Catholics gave it their 'hearty concurrence and co-operation' is problematic when, as Ingram acknowledged, 'they would have preferred full emancipation, unaccompanied by a union'.[90] However, the fact that such declarations were forthcoming reinforced Ingram's thesis that the Act of Union had popular support and that 'the battle was practically won' when it was presented for ratification to the Irish parliament in 1800.[91]

Like Barrington, but for different reasons, Ingram's account of events in the Irish parliament in 1800 is brief. Content to highlight the secure majority the administration possessed in the division lobbies and to play down Henry Grattan's intervention, the focus of the book shifts to a thematic assessment of the 'accusations' that the government had behaved corruptly. This occupies the final two chapters, and Ingram's analysis of the compensation paid to borough owners, the bestowal of peerages and the allocation of money to secure support is original and imaginative. His argument degenerates at times into special pleading, but the author's understanding of how patronage worked ensures it is possessed of authority even when it fails to convince.[92] Indeed, this can be said of the book as a whole. With Ingram's *History of the legislative union*, unionism had secured a historian who not just overturned the hitherto dominant nationalist interpretation of the Act of Union in several key respects, he presented a well-constructed historical argument as to why it was necessary and why it was supported. It is not without serious flaws, but it demonstrated clearly that the evidence could sustain an alternative thesis to that made popular by generations of nationalist commentators.

V

Ingram's *History* posed a challenge to nationalists to provide an equivalently well-documented account of the origins and ratification of the Act of Union. The first such work, also published in 1887, came from the pen of the nationalist MP for South Donegal and professor of constitutional and criminal law at King's Inns, J.G. Swift MacNeill, who had already a number of historical titles to his credit.[93] Entitled *How the Union was carried*, it too drew heavily on Cornwallis's and Castlereagh's correspondence, parliamentary debates and other printed primary source material but, unlike Ingram, it broke little new ground interpretatively. Rather, it affirmed the traditional nationalist contention that the Irish parliament was abolished as a result of 'fraud and violence unparalleled in the history of the world'. MacNeill contended that it would not be possible ever to establish 'the full measure of [the] . . . iniquity' perpetrated against Ireland at the time of the Union because 'the authors of that measure have purposely destroyed the evidence' but he was content to note that 'the Irishman believes, and truly believes' this was so.[94]

Having set the Union within a familiar nationalist frame of reference, MacNeill drew on the 'expurgated' correspondence that was available to sustain his contention that 'an intolerance of Irish prosperity' and a desire to enrich itself provided the main motive for Britain to pursue a union. Through selective citation, he was able to adduce several authorities in support of this conclusion. His narrative acquired greater authority when he explored the government's handling of Irish affairs in the 1790s. Guided in part by Henry Grattan junior, MacNeill argued that Lord Fitzwilliam's dismissal, and the rejection of the reformist strategy he favoured, was the signal for the commencement of 'a system of horrors' that demonstrated that the 'English government had intentionally stimulated the Irish people into rebellion, in order to pave the way for the Union'. MacNeill thus explicitly disagreed with Goldwin Smith's argument, and he rehearsed familiar episodes from the late 1790s to sustain his contention that the people were 'so frightened . . . they would readily consent to a union'.[95] MacNeill's use of evidence to demonstrate this is highly revealing. He resorted readily to the nationalist practice, criticised by Ingram, of adducing the sentiments of opponents, such as Lord Moira, Richard Brinsley Sheridan, Henry Grattan or, on occasion, Daniel O'Connell, to prove a point. His recourse to Castlereagh's and Cornwallis's correspondence was equally selective; they were appealed to to support the claim that 'corruption' was utilised to secure the ratification of the Act of Union. As this suggests, MacNeill used historical evidence to present the Union and its principals in the most negative light. Thus, in the longest chapter in the book, entitled 'Some of the means by which the Union was carried', and which carries discrete subsections bearing titles such as 'Dismissals from Office', 'Abuse of the Place Bill', 'Compensation to Patrons', 'Sale of Peerages', 'The Bribing of Members' and 'The Duping of the Roman Catholics', the familiar and the not so familiar are juxtaposed to affirm the second element of MacNeill's general thesis that the Union was carried by corruption.[96] He even reiterated O'Connell's old canard that only 3,000 people signed pro-union petitions compared with the 707,000 that put their names to petitions against the measure.[97]

MacNeill's detailed and annotated statement of the traditional nationalist view that the Act of Union became law due to 'intimidation and corruption' reflected the general satisfaction with this interpretation within nationalist Ireland in the late nineteenth century. This was emphasised by the MP, Justin Huntley McCarthy, whose eccentric account of the Union attributed its ratification to 'bloodshed and bribery'. He also quoted Thomas O'Hagan's verse to the effect that the Union was passed 'By perjury and fraud / By slaves who sold their land for gold, / As Judas sold his God'.[98] This popular doggerel probably did more to inform nationalist consciousness at the popular level that the Union was secured through a combination of intimidation and corruption than any work of history, but there was no let-up in the eagerness of nationalist commentators to affirm this message in prose. The most substantial such contribution in the last decade of the nineteenth century came from W.F. Dennehy.

William Francis Dennehy was a journalist and writer on historical subjects who became editor of the *Irish Catholic* in 1888. Like many nationalists he was disturbed by T. Dunbar Ingram's claim that Catholic support was important in securing agreement for the Act of Union and, eager to set the record straight, he published a series of sixteen articles on its passage in his magazine in which he addressed the episode. Mirroring the contemporary enthusiasm for documented narratives, Dennehy quoted extensively from 'the actual words and writings of the chief actors'. This gave his work a vivid quality, with the author trying to expose 'the unparalleled conspiracy by which Ireland was deprived of her ancient legislature and her constitution violated'. The series created such an impression that a collected edition was published as *The story of the Union told by its plotters*.[99]

As its title attests, Dennehy's account echoed the nationalist conclusion that the Act of Union was the culmination of a 'diabolical plot . . . carried into execution with . . . thoroughness and . . . unscrupulousness'. Such a scenario needed villains and, resorting to language that was only slightly less intemperate than that of Henry Grattan junior and Justin Huntley McCarthy, Dennehy liberally disparaged those who had any part in promoting its acceptance. Thus, John Beresford was described as 'bigoted and corrupt', Lord Castlereagh as 'glib and treacherous', Edward Cooke as 'one of the chief disbursers of "blood money"', Thomas Lewis O'Beirne as 'unfortunate and misguided' and so on. Likewise, those who accepted ministerial patronage were 'hireling wretches', while the Irish parliament was 'bad, bigoted, and . . . corrupt'.[100]

Dennehy's penchant for dismissive character assessments was reinforced by quotations selected to sustain the perception that the Act of Union was the outcome of terror, intimidation, duplicity, deceit, corruption and bribery.[101] He engaged in this practice though he was knowledgeable of the principles of good historical practice. For instance, his use of primary source material was as extensive as Ingram's, and the quotations that pepper his text are footnoted accurately. More significantly, he was aware that 'no greater mistake can possibly be made than for the people of one generation to judge the actions of their predecessors of another period by the standard of the ideas which prevail in their own time'.[102] The problem was that he did not heed his own advice and apply this commendable principle impartially. He appealed to it to defend the Catholic hierarchy against criticism for supporting the Union and agreeing to the veto on ecclesiastical appointments but signally declined to apply the same standard when the question of explaining the position taken by Protestants was at issue.

As this implies, Dennehy's priority was to justify the stand taken by the Catholic leadership and, thereby, to counter the effects of Ingram's lengthy exposition of the support Irish Catholics gave to a union. Dennehy, by contrast, maintained that the support was a reaction to the opposition of the Orange Order and a reflexive gesture on the part of those who identified the

Union as 'their only protection against a faction seemingly intent on their defamation and destruction'.[103] More significantly, he insisted 'that the hearts and minds of the majority of the Catholic priesthood and laity of Ireland, as of their fellow-countrymen of all creeds, were sound on the great question at issue'. This was hardly consistent with the weight of evidence but, determined that Catholics should not be identified as pro-union, he defined its Catholic supporters as a small elite guided by the earl of Kenmare, whom he dismissed with characteristic decisiveness as 'a corrupt trafficker'.[104] This was a harsh judgement, but Dennehy made no bones about where he stood: 'Nothing – no lapse of time, no vote of any parliament, or of any constituency – can ever make the Act of Union anything but a deed of rebellion, a triumph of traitorism, unsanctified and invalid in the eyes of every loyal and honest Irishman'.[105]

If Dennehy's attempt at a Catholic nationalist history of the Act of Union must, like the orthodox nationalist version provided by Swift MacNeill and, to a lesser extent, the unionist narrative of Dunbar Ingram, be adjudged to have overstepped the boundaries of historical credibility in its eagerness to affirm its ideological position, the closest this fertile period in the historiography of the Act of Union came to acquiring a balanced interpretation was in the final volume of W.E.H. Lecky's *History of England in the eighteenth century*, published in 1890.[106] Ostensibly, Lecky was poorly equipped to provide a balanced account since in the second edition of his influential *Leaders of public opinion*, published in 1871, he had described the Act of Union 'as not only a great crime, but . . . a great blunder'. Moreover, his odyssey from Home Rule to moderate unionism and his wish to disprove James Anthony Froude did not suggest that he was possessed of the necessary distance to tackle a subject that wanted for a non-partisan history.[107] Lecky was not to provide it, but he came closer than anyone else.

In the conclusion to his 300-page exploration, Lecky ventured the opinion that, while it would have been legitimate for the British government to pursue the option of a union if Ireland was at risk of 'being conquered by the party of disloyalty', the defeat of the 1798 Rebellion invalidated this argument. As a result, Lecky concluded, the decision to press for a union was entirely made in England. More than that, the 'measure was an English one, introduced prematurely before it had been demanded by any section of Irish opinion, carried without a dissolution and by gross corruption, in opposition to the majority of the free constituencies and to the great preponderance of the unbribed intellect of Ireland.'[108] There was a basis here for a hostile account of the origins and ratification of the Union but Lecky did not allow this critical conclusion dim his capacity to provide a thorough description of all aspects of the measure that is impartial in its judgements and visibly fair in its reading of the evidence. The sense of confidence this generates in the text is reinforced by Lecky's moderate tone, which is in sharp contrast to the semantic extremism of a majority of published accounts since Barrington. As a consequence, Lecky's conclusions that the Irish administration engaged in 'a shameless traffic in votes' and that 'the majority which ultimately carried the Union was not an honest majority expressing honest opinions' are all the more striking. Most pertinently, it was his ability to set the Act of Union in its wider context, to track the broad contours of support, and to offer a perspective on trends as well as events that gives his account a quality possessed by no other nineteenth-century narrative. It remains valuable for this reason, though its interpretations, conclusions and assumptions can be questioned in many aspects.[109]

The publication within a four-year period between 1887 and 1891 of documented accounts of a unionist, nationalist and broadly non-partisan nature represented a significant milestone in the historiography of the Act of Union, not least because each sought to present its findings according to modern historical rules. It is true that their main source of evidence was the correspondence published in the mid-nineteenth century, but several authors extended their search beyond what was to be found in these collections and in the printed reports of proceedings in parliament. Dunbar Ingram, for example, scoured contemporary newspapers for reports of public meetings upon which he based his assessment of public opinion.[110] He also sought to examine the pamphlet literature but was frustrated by his inability to secure access to a large collection of such work. Lecky, meanwhile, was the first to recognise the value of archival research in the collections of the Public Record Office, British Library and Irish State Paper Office. This more thorough approach to the collection of evidence permitted the preparation of fuller and more complete accounts of the Act of Union. The problem was that, Lecky possibly excepted, the narratives that ensued were tailored to reflect a political point of view. As a result, though knowledge of how the Union was enacted increased, understanding of the forces that made the Union possible was still limited because, like most history written in Ireland during this period, most analyses of the ratification of the Act of Union were coloured, if not actually determined, by the political perspectives of their authors and the readership at which they were aimed.

VI

Lecky's approach and method indicated that there was scope for a history of the Act of Union that was not an extension of the ideological perspective of its author, but little work of this kind was produced in the following half century. One interesting contribution published in the early twentieth century that sought, at least implicitly, to bridge the ideological chasm that existed on the issue was prepared by John Roche Ardill. A clergyman of the

Church of Ireland and the author of the well-received *Forgotten facts of Irish history*, he chronicled the ratification of the Union through documents. Ardill's willingness to allow the material speak for itself makes it difficult to pin down his politics, but the disproportionate space devoted to Catholic support suggests that he had an agenda other than historical reconstruction.[111] However, the collection of letters, resolutions and other extracts he assembled offers a useful if not a comprehensive perspective on the passing of the Act of Union.

Ardill's attempt to rise above partisan controversy was replicated by the novelist Emily Lawless in her popular history of Ireland that went to three editions and many printings between 1887 and 1923. This is epitomised by her description of the money provided to borough owners who lost the right to nominate MPs as 'compensation' and her advice to readers 'to put the ugly word "bribery" out of our thoughts'.[112] Lawless did not exonerate Lord Castlereagh (he, it is alleged, engaged in the 'repellent' task of eliciting support with no 'reluctance') but her account of the episode is non-judgemental and non-sensationalist. Moreover, her non-combative approach was reinforced by the impact of Lecky's contention that, in so far as the British government and the Irish executive abused its power to bring about a union, it was in respect of its recourse to patronage.

Though allegations of the abuse of patronage were a feature of all accounts of the Union from Plowden on, most nineteenth-century nationalist accounts followed Barrington and Grattan junior in alleging that the government fomented rebellion in 1798 in order to create the conditions that would make it possible. This was unproven, but it took Lecky to demonstrate that it was untrue and, following him, 'bribery and corruption' had no rival as the primary explanatory trope of nationalist historians. Thus, according to George Sigerson, in work on 'the last independent parliament of Ireland' published during the first two decades of the twentieth century, Pitt's intentions in pursuing a union may have been honourable, but the means chosen 'to carry them out were ill-chosen, unscrupulous and vile'. He was specifically critical of the fact that 'the government employed the resources of the nation and the powers of the crown to upset the decision of parliament by corrupting the representatives of the people'.[113]

Robert Dunlop reached the same conclusion in 1922: 'There is no need to mince words. Bribery and corruption were time-honoured or time-dishonoured methods of tuning the Irish parliament' and the majority that accepted the Union in 1800 was purchased by these means.[114] Edmund Curtis concurred: he acknowledged that the experience of rebellion and the fear of radicalism 'cowed' the 'lower classes', but he maintained that a parliamentary majority was secured by 'buying out the "fee-simple of Irish corruption"'.[115] Stephen Gwynn was more disposed to entertain traditional nationalist claims that 'the English Government desired the Rebellion as a necessary precursor to union' in his 1923 *History of Ireland*, but he too explained its ratification by reference to the fact that the House of Commons 'was by corrupt means induced to vote its own extinction'.[116] Irish-America was offered similarly simplistic fare. According to George Creel, the Union was approved after 'a campaign of corruption absolutely unparalleled'; Charles Johnston attributed its ratification to 'unlimited bribery'.[117]

Such an analysis of the Act of Union carried more weight when the architects of the corruption were identified. This was not a matter that detained Robert Dunlop and Edmund Curtis who attributed the Union to William Pitt's wish to strengthen the empire, but few were as temperate in their assessments.[118] E.A. D'Alton, a Catholic clergyman, unhesitatingly blamed Pitt and Lord Castlereagh. Unwilling to accept Lecky's conclusion that Pitt had not 'provoked the Rebellion of 1798', he ascribed the ratification of the Union to the 'forces of corruption' that were marshalled at the behest of the 'imperious' Pitt by the 'cold . . . callous and heartless' Castlereagh whose primary attributes he defined as 'treachery . . . duplicity and hypocrisy'.[119] The Irish-American cleric, M.J. McKenna, was even more splenetic; whilst the disposition to offer a more reasonable portrait from within the nationalist fold was rejected as unwarranted 'whitewashing'.[120] In truth, it seemed unlikely that any attempt to present a more historically accurate portrait of Castlereagh or of the ratification of Act of Union during the first half of the twentieth century would be acceptable to Irish nationalists. Significantly, the 'bribery and corruption' paradigm was dominant in the simplified histories of the Union prepared for the classroom at primary and secondary level in the Irish Free State as well as for popular consumption. Equally importantly, the impression fostered, as instanced by James Carty's *Class-book of Irish history*, was that 'all classes and creeds of the Irish people were [so] extremely hostile to this project' bribery 'on an enormous scale' was necessary to secure its passage.[121]

Given the pervasiveness of this reading of the Act of Union within the Catholic-nationalist community, there was little room for an alternative point of view and few attempts were made to offer one. Perhaps the most notable effort came from the pen of Sir James O'Connor, 'a loyal son of the Catholic Church', who proffered the United Irish diagnosis 'that nothing was to be expected from the Irish parliament, and that the only remedy was in bringing it to the ground'. However, whereas the United Irishmen were confident that a republic would be an improvement, O'Connor apprehended 'the cure might have been worse than the disease'. He was acutely conscious that 'the strategic position of Ireland in relation to Great Britain' meant that England could not tolerate that Ireland should be 'a constant menace' to its security. O'Connor was one of the few writers to accord this strategic question attention. He also argued that a union was justified since it 'lessen[ed] the chance of insurrectionary projects' in Ireland, enhanced the likelihood of Catholics being accorded full civil and political rights and improved the country's economic prospects. Given O'Connor's confessional allegiance, it was logical that he should highlight the level of Catholic support for the Union and the 'real opposition' of Protestants. He conceded that in order to secure approval for the Act of Union, the government had recourse to a 'scale of . . . corruption [that] staggers modern conceptions', but this had to be seen in the context of the fact that 'the opponents of the Union were not behind in their attempts at bribery'. Their role in the corruption of the Irish parliament apart, O'Connor argued that 'the obloquy' thrown at Pitt and Castlereagh was unjustified since by any reasonable definition the Union was 'a perfectly fair bargain'.[122]

This was a conclusion unionists had no difficulty accepting though their participation in the historiographical debate on the subject continued to be overshadowed by the sheer volume of nationalist commentaries. Their modest number notwithstanding, the unionist interpretation of the Act of Union advanced by Dunbar Ingram was expanded in several respects in the decades following the publication of his book. Thus Lord Ashbourne, in *Pitt: some chapters in his life and times*, provided a well-documented account of Pitt's contribution,[123] and Caesar Litton Falkiner offered 'sympathetic portraits' of Lord Castlereagh and Lord Clare that diverged sharply from the insistently critical stereotypes produced by nationalists.[124] Unionist general narratives were less forthcoming, though Goldwin Smith, returning to a subject he had last addressed in 1865, offered a brief account in 1905 in his study of *Irish history and the Irish question* that described the Union as a logical response to a threatened French invasion. He also maintained that it was preferable to the corrupt 'sectarian ascendancy and oligarchy' that was party to the 'murderous and ruinous conflict of political parties, social classes, and religious sects' that gripped Ireland in the 1790s. As this suggests, Smith was eager to defend 'the purity of Pitt's motives' and those of his colleagues. He acknowledged that the process of securing a majority was 'not edifying' but he defended the government against the accusation of 'bribery'. The money that was expended was directed, he argued, towards the legitimate task of compensating for loss of property.[125]

J.R. Fisher published a more thoroughly researched account of eighteenth-century Irish politics incorporating new information deriving from the private papers calendared by the Historical Manuscripts Commission in 1911. The author's understanding of the workings of the Irish political system in the eighteenth century enabled him to avoid some of the more familiar errors and to present the Union as a logical outcome of earlier trends, but the exploration offered of the enactment of the Union is disappointingly brief. Moreover, it is too intent on rescuing Castlereagh's reputation from 'abuse'. 'Corruption' is admitted though its impact and import are queried, and the use of secret service funds justified in terms of campaign expenses.[126]

VII

The incorporation of evidence from recently published collections of primary material was a positive feature of Fisher's work, though his account was identifiably partisan for all that. The construction of a narrative that was both well documented and impartial in its assessments was not possible in the absence of an approach to historical reconstruction that put present-centred attitudes to one side and that appealed to contemporary documentation as the ultimate arbiter of interpretation. This process accelerated in Ireland in the 1930s, but the Union only attracted notice slowly. The first significant effort was R.B. McDowell's pioneering dissection of the arguments used by both the pro-and anti-union interests in the propaganda battle that accompanied the larger political struggle on the issue.[127] As a logical exposition of the hopes and fears articulated by both sides it was a welcome departure from the prevailing 'bribery and corruption' approach, but it is narrowly focused thematically and evidentially. None the less, the Act of Union attracted no further attention in the short term, so when J.C. Beckett came to write his classic text, *The making of modern Ireland 1603–1923*, in the early 1960s he was obliged to appeal to W.E.H. Lecky and J.R. Fisher for basic information. Beckett was too sophisticated to parrot their views, but the account he offered bears witness to their influence. He endorsed Lecky's rejection of the nationalist argument 'that Pitt deliberately fomented rebellion in order to bring about union' and supported him in attributing its passage to 'argument, bribery [and] intimidation', whilst he was guided by Fisher in his analysis of Castlereagh's character. As this suggests, Beckett's narrative is driven by a desire to explain the attitude of various interests to the Union rather than by a political point of view. For instance, he adjudged (correctly) that the opposition to the Union was weak in 1800, its extravagant rhetoric and attempt to organise petitions notwithstanding. Significantly, his observation that, while the compensation paid to borough owners 'might be regarded as a form of bribery, . . . it was paid irrespective of the political conduct of the recipient' can be seen to herald the commencement of the process, most closely identified with G.C. Bolton, of normalising the recourse to patronage.[128]

The publication in 1966 of Bolton's study of the passing of the Act of Union was a landmark in Union historiography since it was the first full-length modern scholarly attempt to explain its ratification based on a consideration of the extant archival record. Bolton's approach and method reflected that promoted by Lewis Namier, which had much in common methodologically with the 'scientific' history taught in the universities in Ireland. As a result, it was warmly welcomed in academic circles and it soon became the standard text on the subject.[129] Bolton's most striking conclusion was that the patronage appealed to by Dublin Castle as part of its campaign to retain the support of normal loyalists and to persuade waverers was within the boundaries permitted in the eighteenth century and that it was wrong to attribute the Act's ratification to corruption. No less importantly (though it attracted less notice), Bolton also expanded the context in which the engagement of Irish opinion with the Union was assessed by systematically tracing public as well as political opinion at a regional as well as at the national level. In the process, he further revealed the extent to which both its proponents and opponents appealed to those familiar barometers of public opinion – petitions, pamphlets and public meetings – to elicit support.[130]

As the least obviously partisan and most thorough account extant of the Act of Union, Bolton's work had an immediate impact and it was soon commonplace for historians describing the Act of Union either to make no reference to the subject of corruption or to cite Bolton in support of the view that what took place was acceptable.[131] It also became normal to explain Pitt's decision by reference to his rational desire to sustain a secure Anglo-Irish connection.[132] Edith Mary Johnston, for example, in 1974 accounted for the initiative to secure a union as 'the product of exhaustion rather than evolution' and accounted for the majority in its favour as the result of the skilful application of 'every stratagem of management and weapon of propaganda'. Ten years later, R.B. McDowell offered a similar analysis though he conceded that securing a majority involved 'trying to gratify the crudely personal objectives of many peers and MPs'.[133] Not everyone was convinced. Corruption continued to feature prominently in some textbooks and works of synthesis.[134] Roy Foster, meanwhile, contrived to have it both ways in his history of modern Ireland by acknowledging that there 'was much agonizing over what was, and was not, correct practice in purchasing support'.[135]

Foster's observation that there was no clear contemporary standard by which one can assess whether the Irish administration's appeal to patronage to secure support for the Union was acceptable underlines the difficulty this issue poses. Perhaps influenced by this, R.B. McDowell all but ignored the matter in his widely consulted *Ireland in the age of imperialism and revolution* in favour of an extended distillation of the arguments advanced by the pro- and anti- side.[136] This remains of abiding interest, though it was criticised by reviewers for not embracing Bolton's findings in a more explicit manner.[137]

That McDowell chose not to do so is a fair measure of the ascendancy of Bolton's interpretation in the two decades following its publication. Some other work was published, but it was mainly of the nature of elaboration on themes neglected, overlooked or just omitted by Bolton. Among the works that qualify for inclusion in the latter category are Bolton's own survey of the 'British reaction' and Hereward Senior's careful outline of the response of the Orange Order.[138] In addition, this author has explored of the changing appeal of a union to British and Irish opinion in the seventeenth and eighteenth centuries, from which it is clear that the Anglo-Irish Act of Union possesses a longer and more significant genesis than previously allowed.[139] Homer Calkin produced a brief overview of the Union 'pamphlet war' in 1978, while John Biggs-Davison and George Chowdharay-Best demonstrated that the spirit of partisan history had not died by publishing an updated unionist narrative in 1984, which maintained the Union had majority support, disputed the allegation that bribery was necessary to secure its passage and pointed to the existence of a 'Catholic unionist tradition'.[140]

VIII

The modest impact that this exploration of Catholic unionism registered underlined the transformation that had taken place in the historiography of the Act of Union over the previous half century. It was clear at the same time that there was more to be said on the subject than was contained within the covers of Bolton's study and the bicentenary has provided a useful stimulus. Yet, the historiography of the Act of Union remains one of the most controversial areas of Irish history, and is likely to remain so for at least as long as the Union exists. To concede this is not to argue for the impotence of history when faced by such an issue, but to emphasise how vital it is that historians are aware of the ideological implications of the questions they ask and the answers they offer. An awareness of the historiography may help in this. Without it, historians are more likely to plough well-worn interpretative furrows. In the case of the Act of Union, due attention must be paid to its origins as well as to the manner of its enactment and to the support for the measure that existed. So far, insufficient attention has been accorded the fact that over 100 MPs, a majority of peers and large sections of Irish opinion were prepared to endorse a union before the Irish administration indicated its readiness to reward its supporters. How come there were so many? Likewise, what was the appeal of the measure in Great Britain? Answering these and other questions is as important as providing a correct narrative of events between 1798 and 1801. One thing is certain, there is unlikely to be unanimous agreement, but the differences should not be as sharp as they have been for most of the 200-year historiography of the Act of Union.

CHAPTER TWO

The Injured Lady *and Her British Problem: The Union in Political Thought*

MICHAEL BROWN

In 1800, the idea of a union between states was hardly new.[1] Notably, the Anglo-Scottish parliamentary Union of 1707 supplied a precedent for the Irish Act of Union. However, the idea of union was a complex and varied one, which requires examination if the purpose of the British administration in the late 1790s is to be understood. Indeed, what constituted a union was the product of much consideration in the early modern period.

UNION IN EARLY MODERN POLITICAL THOUGHT

Union, as typically understood, took two broad forms, depending on the origin of that unification. First, the vagaries of dynastic politics, and the close blood ties that bonded the European monarchies occasionally resulted in the monarch of one polity inheriting by death or marriage the crown of another. This produced the rather complex political configuration termed the multiple kingdom, or confederation.[2] Secondly, unification might be forced upon a kingdom by its failure to defend itself in warfare. This military conquest resulted in what shall be here termed unification by dominion.[3] Although in early modern thought this was commonly termed union by incorporation as it involved the combining of two once distinct polities, the implications of conquest ought to be distinguished from the union of parliaments by consent or treaty, here termed a union by incorporation.

The British Isles in the seventeenth century provide examples of both variants of union. First, the Scottish royal family, the Stuarts, succeeded to the thrones of England and Ireland through the failure of Elizabeth Tudor to produce a direct heir. This generated a multiple monarchy in which all three kingdoms kept a distinct parliament, however weak those of Ireland and Scotland may actually have been. The *Interregnum* between 1649 and 1660 is an example of the second type. Cromwellian military successes ensured that

Ireland and Scotland were subdued and the political union of these islands was imposed from on high by an English parliament.[4]

While the *Interregnum* has been cited as the first example of a full political union between the three major political communities on the archipelago (Wales was never more than a principality), that is not how it was understood at the time. The model of a multiple kingdom was just as familiar to the protagonists as that of the dominion. For example, the French absolutist state, which in the eighteenth century was considered the political unit par excellence, had a number of internal tax borders and local judicial assemblies or *parlements*.

One must also remain aware that Ireland's inclusion in a multiple kingdom was problematic for Ireland was actually declared to be a kingdom by an English monarch, Henry VIII, in 1541. This was itself the chosen solution to the ambiguous status of the island in the holdings of the early Tudors – underlining the fact that the multiple kingdom model was thought of as a typical form of political union in the period.

A further ambiguity surrounding Ireland's constitutional status derived from Poynings' law. Enacted in 1494, this regulated the introduction and passage of bills in the Irish parliament, and wrote into the constitution the belief that Ireland was a dependency. It underpinned the contention that Ireland was a colony of England.[5] It suggested that England could determine the constitutional shape of Irish political life as it was predicated upon the absence or illegitimacy of any previous political institutions. This assertion was deeply upsetting to those settlers who had committed themselves to a life in Ireland and who described themselves as the 'English in Ireland', and therefore as holders of the rights and privileges of other Englishmen. While the Declaration of the Kingdom ought to have ameliorated this condition, Poynings' law remained fully effective until 1782, and the colonial character of Irish political life aggrieved the élite throughout this period. It is this sense of grievance that found definitive expression in William Molyneux's *Case of Ireland . . . truly stated* of 1698.[6] As Molyneux wrote: "tis manifest that the great body of the present people of *Ireland*, are the progeny of the *English* and *Britains*, that from time to time have come over into this kingdom; and there remains but a mere handful of the ancient *Irish* at this day; I may say, not one in a thousand . . . '.[7]

INJURING IRELAND: 1707

The sense of grievance that agitated the 'English in Ireland' was deepened by the unification of the parliaments of Scotland and England in 1707. As Jonathan Swift allegorised it, Ireland was little more than a jilted lover, who having submitted to the lascivious desires of her rich and handsome neighbour, had too late discovered that he had determined upon marrying another. The 'injured lady' of his imagining protested in vain that her suitor (England) had breached his promise of matrimony, forsaking a good match for a brazen hussy of another faith (Presbyterianism) and of little fortune.[8]

> As to her person she is tall and lean, and very ill shaped; she hath bad features, and a worse complexion; she hath a stinking breath, and twenty ill smells about her besides; which are yet more insufferable by her natural sluttishness; for she is always lousy and never without the itch. As to her other qualities, she has no reputation either for virtue, honesty, truth or manners; and it is no wonder, considering what her education has been. Scolding and cursing are her common conversation. To sum up all; she is poor and beggarly, and gets a sorry maintenance by pilfering wherever she comes.[9]

The Union of 1707 was unusual for it was neither a union of two monarchies, accomplished in 1603, nor a union by conquest; the Restoration of 1660 had reintroduced the three-kingdom structure. Nor was it the colonisation of a land without formal politics. What the Union of England and Scotland involved was a negotiated merger of the two parliaments of Westminster and Edinburgh. It generated another model for political unification wherein the members subscribe to, and shape, the rules. It was termed union by incorporation.

The motives for unification among the parliamentarians in Edinburgh were clear. The 1690s in Scotland experienced a series of crop failures due to bitterly cold conditions.[10] Food scarcity repeatedly reached famine proportions. Moreover, the endeavour of the political nation to expand the economy through imperial ventures had ended in ignominious failure. The Darien scheme, which involved founding a Scottish colony on the isthmus at Panama, collapsed in a flurry of famine and typhoid, taking an estimated twenty-five per cent of Scottish liquid capital with it.[11]

The desire for economic success led Scottish magnates to conclude that an Anglo-Scottish union was desirable if it was accompanied by free trade with England and its dependencies. Article four of the Treaty of Union expressly granted: 'That all the subjects of the United Kingdom of Great Britain shall from and after the Union have full freedom and intercourse of trade and navigation to and from any port or place within the said United Kingdom and the dominions and plantations thereunto belonging.'[12]

The English also saw the Union as a desirable outcome for reasons of state. The English polity was unsettled by the prospect of the death of a childless monarch, Queen Anne, precipitating a political crisis wherein the English chose a Protestant monarch and the Scots installed a Roman Catholic. International relations, with a Catholic threat emanating from an aggrandising French monarch, also demanded that the threat posed by the

Jacobite line be nullified. When the Scots forced the English hand, by threatening to legislate for the succession independently of England, union was chosen as the means out of the impasse.[13]

The Union of England and Scotland was passed in Edinburgh on 16 January 1707 by 110 votes to 67. As its first article stated, the Union gave birth to a new political entity, which replaced the kingdoms of England and Scotland. Henceforth: 'the two kingdoms of Scotland and England, shall upon the first day of May next ensuing the date hereof, and forever after, be united into one kingdom by the name of Great Britain.'[14] The second article clarified the nature of the succession to this newly created throne. It resolved the fears of the English polity that Scotland might choose a distinct, possibly even a Stuart, monarch for the northern throne, asserting that:

> the succession to the monarchy of the United Kingdom and of the dominions thereunto belonging after her most sacred majesty, and in default of issue of her majesty be, remain and continue to the most excellent princess Sophia electoress and dutchess dowager of Hanover, and the heirs of her body, being Protestants . . . and that all papists and persons marrying papists shall be excluded from and for ever incapable to inherit possess or enjoy the imperial crown of Great Britain, and the dominions thereunto belonging or any part thereof.[15]

Finally, the nature of political representation was clarified by the third article which proposed that 'the United Kingdom of Great Britain be represented by one and the same parliament to be styled the parliament of Great Britain.'[16] The technicalities through which the parliaments of Scotland and England were to be merged was left to separate legislation. However, article twenty-two of the Union provided for the admission of forty-five commoners and sixteen peers from the Scottish political nation into the newly composed parliament of Great Britain.[17]

Crucially, article eighteen declared that the Scottish legal system, grounded in the Roman law tradition, was to remain distinct from the English common law system. As the treaty explained:

> the laws concerning regulation of trade, customs and such excises, to which Scotland is by virtue of this treaty to be liable, be the same in Scotland, from and after the Union as in England; and that all other laws, in use within the kingdom of Scotland do after the Union, and notwithstanding thereof, remain in the same force as before (except such are as contrary to or incon-sistent with this Treaty) but alterable by the parliament of Great Britain.[18]

Akin to this legal independence was the religious settlement. Importantly, the Scottish people were predominantly of Presbyterian persuasion. While the treaty of Union did not engage with the thorny issue of religious uniformity, the Scottish parliament passed an 'Act for securing the Protestant religion and Presbyterian church government.' This safeguarded the Presbyterian character of the Scottish church: 'Her majesty with advice and consent of the said estates of parliament doth hereby establish and confirm the said true Protestant religion and the worship, discipline and government of this church to continue without any alteration to the people of this land in all succeeding generations.'[19]

The effect of the article concerning law and the subsidiary act concerning religious observance was to differentiate the Union of 1707 from the other available forms of union. The Union of 1707 was not a union of dominion, for Scotland had neither been militarily defeated nor its institutions superseded by their English counterparts. Nor was Scotland a colony for it was recognised as a vibrant, equal and legitimate state. Nor, despite the designs of some of its opponents, notably Andrew Fletcher of Saltoun, did the Union solidify and extend the confederation of states that was characteristic of the Stuarts' holdings.[20]

Fletcher, a Scottish MP, envisioned such a configuration in his *Account of a conversation*.[21] He speculated that the unification as enacted would ensure the prosperity of London and the desolation of the provinces. Instead, he projected a league of confederated statelets. He proposed twelve cities in which defence and justice could be situated. This would negate the threat posed to the polity, wherein 'the three kingdoms of Scotland, England and Ireland . . . are yet in their present condition exposed to the fate of a single battle, if a great army of enemies could be landed near London.'[22] He specified the cities of 'London, Bristol, Exeter, Chester, Norwich, York, Sterling, Inverness, Dublin, Cork, Galloway [*sic*] [and] Londonderry' as potential sites for the distribution of sovereignty and argued that, far from denigrating the great city of London, it would benefit the polity as a whole.[23] He contended that:

> if the people of Yorkshire or Devonshire were not obliged to go further than York or Exeter to obtain justice, and consequently had no occasion to spend money out of those counties, how soon would we see another face of things in both? How soon would they double or treble their present value? That London should draw the riches and government of the three kingdoms to the south-east corner of this island, is in some degree as unnatural, as for one city to possess the riches and government of the world.[24]

Despite Fletcher's fears, the Union of 1707 kept a series of distinctly Scottish institutions alive and enabled civil society to flourish in Scotland throughout the eighteenth century. The Union underwrote and protected Scotland's cultural identity while merging its political authority with that of its most powerful neighbour. As such, it was an incorporating union, in which equal and distinct members treated so as to create a series of shared institutions to direct activity. Thus, Scotland and England negotiated a series of political establishments, enabling them to compete as a unit internationally in trade and empire. In other realms, notably in law and in religion, they remained distinct.

This is to treat of the Union of Scotland and England at a reified level. In doing so, there is a danger of occluding the sense of imposition felt by many within Scotland and the financial inducements that marred the passage of the bill. The nationalist myth of a Scottish political nation 'bought and sold for English gold' has some substance.[25] While the stark assertion of William Ferguson that the Union of 1707 was one of the great eighteenth-century fix-ups is an exaggeration, scholars have shown that the selective payment of arrears did play a part in shoring up the Union's support.[26] Although the recipients were owed payment for past services, the distribution of some £20,000 indicates that political sympathies were considered pertinent when adjudicating claims. The marquess of Queensberry received £12,000, while the bulk of the remainder went towards members of the Squadrone party whose support was considered critical to the success of the Union.[27] That certain payments, for example to Lord Elibank, Lord Forbes, or the Squadrone member Campbell of Cessnock, amounted to as little as £50 did not lessen the sense that the Union negotiations were burnished with the grease of corruption. Riots in Edinburgh and Glasgow in late 1706 expressed vividly popular disillusionment.

The coercion that aided the bill's passage was equally unsubtle. The riots in Edinburgh and Glasgow against the Union appeared to foreshadow armed insurrection. When the Cameronians – a faction of militant Presbyterians – joined with the Jacobites and threatened military action, the government moved to negate the threat. The marquess of Queensberry manoeuvred the Scottish standing army to the outskirts of the capital, while English troops were moved up to the Scottish border. Troops stationed in Ireland were moved northwards, to enable easy access to the disaffected south-west of Scotland. The implication was that the English were prepared, with the assistance of pro-union politicians in Scotland, to impose a military solution. Had this occurred, the outcome would have been dominion not incorporation.[28]

THE INJURED LADY'S GRIEVANCE

Despite the corruption and coercion that underlay the Union of England and Scotland, to onlookers in Ireland it appeared to be a done deal.[29] As early as 1703, the prospect of an Anglo-Scottish union was causing consternation among Ireland's political elite. The archbishop of Dublin, William King, joined forces with the MP for Swords, Robert Molesworth, to back the idea of a legislative union with the English houses of parliament. The *Journal of the Irish House of Commons* reports how, on 11 October, Molesworth notified the Irish Commons that a committee of the whole house, appointed to consider the state of the nation, had resolved 'that her majesty be most humbly moved, that through her princely goodness and wisdom and favourable interposition, her subjects of this kingdom may be relieved of the calamities they now lie under, by a full enjoyment of their constitution or a more firm and strict union with England.'[30] Although nothing came of this resolution, the passage of the Union of Scotland and England, completed in 1707, prompted a reappraisal of Irish circumstances. In 1706, when the measure was being debated in Scotland, Francis Annesley wrote to King explaining that:

> It is much to me that no one step is taken by the people of Ireland, to be admitted into the Union, where are all your mighty patriots? Sleeping, when they should or at least offer at doing good for your poor nation; those who would have served them must not stir, they are so much under their displeasure and those who ought to be active are only so for their private interest, not for any good to their kingdom.[31]

Subsequent to its passage in 1707, the Union appeared to Irish eyes as a given in the political firmament, rather than as the bastardised political compromise of Scottish *mythe d'historie*. What the Union of Scotland and England implied, as Swift's commentary suggested, was that the Scottish political nation was constitutionally superior to the political nation gathered in Dublin. Scottish MPs at Westminster had direct input into the political life of Ireland, while the Irish had no commensurate input into the politics of Scotland. In effect, the Union of 1707 served to highlight and to exacerbate the ambiguities and incoherence within Ireland's constitutional condition.

THE INJURED LADY'S PROGRESS

The constitutional relationship between Britain and Ireland generated a series of specifically political crises during the eighteenth century. The relationship with Britain could have developed towards any of the models outlined above. Ireland could have subsided into a clear-cut colonial acquisition; it could have re-asserted the confederal model of the multiple kingdoms; theoretically, a war between the two polities might have broken out resulting in either dominion or independence. Each of these variations generated a crisis during the century.

The Declaratory Act of 1720, which legislated in favour of Westminster's legislative supremacy over Ireland, was in keeping with the concept of Ireland as a dependency. It further watered down the confederacy created by the Declaration of the Kingdom of 1541 in favour of a colonial model. It under-wrote Poynings' law, reiterating the subordinate position of the parliament in Dublin.

With the rise of the Patriot movement, events began to favour the confederal model. The effect of Grattan's Parliament of 1782 was to amend Poynings' law and to repeal the Declaratory Act. In achieving parliamentary independence, Grattan and his colleagues were declaring that the parliament of Ireland was on an equal footing with that in London. They were asserting that the Irish relationship to Britain was one of equal partners – two independent kingdoms that happened to share the same monarch. Thereby, the Patriots, from Charles Lucas to Henry Grattan, could square the circle of local patriotism and loyalty to the House of Hanover. Both were dependent upon a confederal system of multiple kingdoms. As Grattan enquired of his audience in the Irish House of Commons in 1782:

> Are the American enemies to be free, and these royal subjects [the Irish] slaves? Or in what quality does his majesty choose to contemplate the Irish hereafter? His subjects in parliament or equals in congress? Submission therefore will not do: there remains then but one way; assert the independency of your parliament.[32]

Having denied the claim of English superiority over Ireland, on the grounds that 'England has no title to that power to make laws for Ireland; none by nature, none by compact, none by usage, and none by conquest', Grattan proposed a motion that expressed the confederal nature of his vision.[33] It requested that

> a humble address be presented to his majesty of our most sincere and unfeigned attachment to his majesty's person and government. To assure his majesty, that the people of this country are a free people that the crown of *Ireland* is an imperial crown; and that the kingdom of *Ireland* a distinct kingdom, with a parliament of her own, the sole legislature thereof. To assure his majesty that by our fundamental laws and franchises, laws and franchises which we, on the part of the nation do claim as her birthright the subjects of this kingdom cannot be bound, affected or obliged by any legislature, save only by the king, Lords and Commons of his majesty's realm of *Ireland*.[34]

Crucially, the motion concluded with the assertion that the Irish parliamentarians wished

> to assure our majesty that next to our liberties we value our connection with *Great Britain*, on which we conceive, at this time most particularly, the happiness of both kingdoms intimately depends, and which as it is our most sincere wish, so shall it be our principal study to cultivate and render perpetual.[35]

In 1798, faced with the recalcitrance of the British polity to treat Ireland fairly, certain elements of the populace, largely in the north and south-east, sought to achieve political independence. As Wolfe Tone extolled in his *Address to the people of Ireland*:

> It is then for unequivocal independence that every patriotic Irishman ought to struggle; and prostituted, as has been the name of patriot, to vanity and self-interest, Ireland still contains many generous hearts and firm spirits that can feel, with true enthusiasm, the value of the blessing they would risk their lives to purchase for their country. Glowing with resentment for injuries, and indignantly marking the strides of injustice, one spark of hope would light the glorious flame that leads on to a certain victory.[36]

Drawing on French republican ideas, and the writings of Tom Paine and other English radicals, the United Irishmen forced the British polity into a military response. Had the Rebellion come close to success, the options presented to the British polity would have been to release Ireland from the relationship, or to subdue it militarily. This would have resulted in independence or dominion.[37]

THE INJURED LADY'S SETTLEMENT

In this narrative, 1801 can be seen as the application of the Scottish model of unification on to an Irish political nation. As early as June 1798, William Pitt's advisers were using the Scottish Union as a blueprint in the drafting of a proposed Irish union.[38] Moreover, the parliaments that merged with that at Westminster were notable for their activity rather than their sloth. The Scottish parliament in the 1690s and 1700s had experienced a new lease of political power as a result of the Glorious Revolution and, more specifically, the abolition of the Lords of the Articles – an executive committee for drafting Scottish legislation – in 1690.[39] This new freedom enabled them to force the issue of the succession. The Irish parliament of the 1780s and 1790s was no less active in the wake of parliamentary independence. Indeed, the Irish parliament passed more legislation in the 1790s than in any other decade and the bulk of this came towards the close of the period.[40] Just as with the Scottish Union, the Union of 1801 was a merger of two distinct parliaments and, interestingly, emerged from a similar blend of corruption and coercion.

The coercion is most evident in the heavy-handed way in which the United Irishmen were dealt with. This set the tone for the debate on the Union, with the political nation well aware that the British polity was not prepared to countenance Irish radicalism. Nonetheless, the deal had to meet the demands of the politicians, and, as this was not initially the case, the first suggestion of a union ran into the sands in 1799.

The scale and consequence of corruption surrounding the eventual passage of the Act of Union has been the subject of extensive debate.[41] The discovery of secret service papers detailing illegal expenditure has shed important light on this matter, but it remains unclear as to whether it swayed the vote decisively. Reluctant minds were certainly convinced by fiscal remuneration and the question of compensation for boroughs was central to the thinking of some MPs. In this, as in so much else, the pattern is similar to that found in Scotland at the start of the eighteenth century.

As in the Anglo-Scottish Act of Union of 1707, the Irish Act opened with three articles which defined the nature and import of the legislation. First, the Act declared that: 'the said kingdoms of Great Britain and Ireland shall, upon the first day of January, which shall be in the year of our lord one thousand eight hundred and one, and for ever, be united into one kingdom, by the name of the United Kingdom of Great Britain and Ireland.'[42] Secondly, the Act made secure the rules appertaining to the succession of the crown, and made clear the Protestant nature of the crown, declaring

> the succession to the imperial crown of the said United Kingdom, and of the dominions thereunto belonging, shall continue limited and settled in the same manner as the succession to the imperial crown of the said kingdoms of Great Britain and Ireland now stands limited and settled, according to the existing laws, and to the terms of union between England and Scotland.[43]

Finally, as in the Union of 1707, it clarified the nature of political representation, stating 'that the said United Kingdom be represented in one and the same parliament, to be styled "the parliament of the United Kingdom of Great Britain and Ireland."'[44] Subsequent clauses outlined the merger of the parliamentary bodies and legislated for the choosing of Irish commons and Lords to sit at Westminster. This was a break with the Scottish precedent, where this was legislated for after the passage of the Union itself.

The Scottish model was again apparent in the clauses dealing with the commercial, legal and religious consequences of unification. As in Scotland, the merger of the two parliaments combined with free trade relations between the two jurisdictions. Although many of the commercial restrictions on Irish trade with the British Empire had been lifted before 1800, article six ensured that:

> His majesty's subjects of Great Britain and Ireland shall, from and after the first day of January one thousand eight hundred and one, be entitled to the same privileges, and be on the same footing as to encouragements and bounties on the like articles, being the growth, produce or manufacture of either country respectively, and generally in respect of trade and navigation in all ports and places in the United Kingdom and its dependencies.[45]

Article eight declared that the legal system, as in Scotland, was to remain *in situ*. Although this did not involve so dramatic a cultural bifurcation as the difference between common law and Roman law, the declaration was still significant. It ensured that:

> all laws in force at the time of the Union, and all the courts of civil and ecclesiastical jurisdiction within the respective kingdoms, shall remain as now by law established within the same, subject only to alterations and regulations from time to time as circumstances may appear to the parliament of the United Kingdom to require.[46]

This recognition of the cultural specificity of Irish legal institutions underpinned the thinking concerning the nature of union as a whole. The power given to Irish legal precedent was in line with that granted to the Scottish legal system in 1707 and differentiated the Union from the imposition of British rule upon Ireland. The Union of 1801 was not, therefore, in the terms of political theory, an example of a confederation, a colony or a dominion (despite the defeat of the United Irishmen in 1798). Instead, the Union is best understood as the entry of Ireland into the political association of Great Britain, wherein the rules were again debated and reformulated. It was, as was the case with Scotland, a union of incorporation.

It was the first occasion since 1541 that the government of England or subsequently that of Britain had treated Ireland as a political entity of equal stature; the union of the 1650s had been predicated upon English military superiority. Moreover, it was the first time since 1541 that the Westminster élite had tried to settle the question of Ireland's fundamental status rather than engaging in makeshift measures provoked by specific events. The Union involved British recognition of Ireland's importance to its own future and that Ireland could not be treated in a cavalier manner.

THE INJURED LADY'S UNWANTED RELATIVES

One last question remains unanswered. The crucial logistical difference between the Scottish and Irish unifications is that the Scottish model preserved the traditional religious structure supported by the majority of the people. Ireland was predominantly Roman Catholic in orientation. However, article five of the Anglo-Irish Act of Union proposed that:

> the churches of England and Ireland, as now by law established, be united into one protestant episcopal church to be called 'The united church of England and Ireland'; and that the doctrine, worship, discipline and government of the said united church shall be and shall remain in full force for ever, as the same are now by law established for the church of England; and that the continuance and preservation of the said united church of

England and Ireland shall be deemed and taken to be an essential and
fundamental part of the Union.[47]

It may appear logical that the British polity was anxious to exclude the
Roman Catholics from the newly formed polity, thereby maintaining the
intrinsically Protestant character of the state. This would certainly be in line
with thinking about the religious content of British identity as described by
Linda Colley.[48] She has argued that the war with France drove the Scots and the
English to conceive of Britain as a pan-Protestant polity. The Union of 1801 was
thus an attempt to bolster Anglican control over the recalcitrant Roman
Catholic Irish. However, this was not the case. Leaving aside the vexed issue of
the Presbyterian attraction to radical French ideas, and their participation in the
Rebellion of 1798, Pitt and his government were, long before the Union became
viable politically, committed to ameliorating the Catholic position.[49] Granted,
their motivation was also to control the Roman Catholics, but their tactic was
appeasement, not arbitrary government. The British government's conviction
that the Roman Catholics needed to be pacified rather than controlled resulted
in a series of Catholic relief measures.

The Relief Acts came in two bursts, between 1778 and 1782, and between
1792 and 1793. These removed most of the penal impositions on the Roman
Catholic populace, ensuring that they could take leases of 999 years, inherit
property as Protestants did, acquire land, teach in schools, act as guardians to
children, become lawyers, hold civil and military offices and receive university
degrees. This last benefit was underlined in 1795 by the constructive measure of
opening the Royal College of Maynooth.

However, it was the Irish Anglicans who presided over the parliament in
Dublin and they demanded the continuing exclusion of the Roman Catholic
majority from the political nation – just as it was their ancestors at the end of
the seventeenth century who enacted the penal legislation in the face of,
albeit mild, opposition from Westminster.[50] Indeed many members of the
Irish Anglican élite perceived union as a means of ensuring the continuance
of Protestant hegemony in Ireland. They were prepared to merge with the
Westminster parliament so long as the Union was not combined with
Catholic emancipation. In this, crucially, they found an ally, not in the prime
minister, William Pitt, but in the monarch, George III.

This division between London and Dublin makes sense of the pro-union
stance of much of the Catholic hierarchy. The Union offered the Roman
Catholics an *entrée* into Great Britain, and an opportunity to do down the local
establishment. The trend, it must be remembered, was in favour of increasing
religious tolerance – at least within the echelons of high political life in London.

This configuration illuminates the divisions that emerged in the debate
surrounding the Union. Both Anglican and Catholic opinion were split over

the consequences of the Union, with anti-union opinion being grounded on the fear of Catholic emancipation and of Protestant hegemony, and pro-union opinion being founded on the desire for Protestant hegemony and for Catholic emancipation.[51] This split, apparently confessional in nature, was not clearly drawn on confessional lines. Pitt, for one, was decidedly in the pro-union and pro-emancipation camp, believing that, without Catholic emancipation, they might gain the country but lose the people.

In the event, Pitt and the Roman Catholic hierarchy were to be disappointed. The Union is passed, but the attempts by the London government to forward a bill favouring Catholic emancipation foundered upon the twin rocks of Irish Anglican fury and the British monarch's obstinacy. To the rather shaky mind of George III, the concept of Catholic emancipation was anathema. He stood by his coronation oath as defender of the faith and believed that, far from binding the Catholics to the throne, emancipation was the first step on the road to American-style independence.

The intellectual commitment of William Pitt to his ecumenical vision of the British Empire, and his failure to bring it into being in Ireland led, as Patrick Geoghegan has shown, directly to his fall from power in the first months of 1801.[52] Pitt understood that the British system of government, which he was trying to extend into Ireland, would not work if the majority did not have access to it. As with the Presbyterians in Scotland, the Irish Catholic majority had to be included in the polity. Without them, the loyalty and trust upon which the system relied would be threatened.

In retrospect, Pitt was correct in this analysis. The failure of the Union to be accompanied by Catholic emancipation helped to polarise Irish political life around confessional identities. The division between Catholic and Protestant had shown signs of weakening in the 1780s and early 1790s. The development of Catholic Whiggery – pro-union, pro-Hanover and pro-Rome – makes clear that there was no political affiliation intrinsic in Irish confessional differences which, given the correct circumstances, might not have been altered. Union may have resolved some of the problems within Ireland's constitutional status, but the 'injured lady' still had a problem with her British neighbour. The system of unification that had been applied, with a reasonable degree of success, in Scotland was never fully extended into Ireland.[53] The failure to grant emancipation resulted in the continuation of the sectarian character of Irish political life and the continuing dysfunctional nature of the Irish polity, prone to outbreaks of violence and divided over the nature of its political identity. It presaged the rise of Daniel O'Connell both as emancipator and as repealer. In effect, it helps to explain the peculiarly religious twist given to nationalist politics in Ireland in the nineteenth century.

CHAPTER THREE

'An Union for Empire': The Anglo-Irish Union as an Imperial Project

THOMAS BARTLETT

Ireland's position within the old British Empire (1600–1783) was profoundly ambiguous.[1] The country was, admittedly, 'England's oldest colony', but she had been held rather than wholly governed since the twelfth century. Moreover, since 1541 Ireland had constituted a kingdom in her own right and, in addition, from medieval times had possessed a parliament consisting of a House of Commons and a House of Lords. Consequently, as a kingdom with a parliament, Ireland was marked off decisively from every colony acquired subsequently by England, all of which retained their colonial status, and could only boast of assorted assemblies, councils and courts, none of which had parity with a parliament. Ireland's proximity to England was also a complicating factor: as an island lying closely off a larger island, itself located just off continental Europe, her geographical position meant that the eighteenth-century colonial stereotypes (extreme temperatures, exotic produce, curious animals, slavery, distance from the mother country) were conspicuously lacking there. To paraphrase V.T. Harlow's question, was there a place for a colony on the doorstep of the mother country? Moreover, if Ireland was not a colony, could two kingdoms, adjacent to one another, and under the one king, co-exist in the one empire?

There was yet a further difficulty: unlike other colonies in the Atlantic world, Ireland's population in the eighteenth century resolutely resisted simple categorisation into coloniser and colonist. Religion, not national origins (or skin colour), was the great divide; but this was not a simple bi-polar, Catholic/Protestant, division, for the presence of large numbers of Presbyterians (possibly a majority of Irish Protestants by 1750) was a hugely complicating factor. Furthermore, the empire was by no means static in the eighteenth century, but was instead growing in importance, both materially and culturally. Ireland did reasonably well out of imperial trade, and there is some evidence that there was an appreciation of further benefits which could flow from a closer imperial association. It may be noted also that there was resentment that Ireland was not gaining sufficiently from her involvement in the empire. At least one strand in the separatist impulse in Irish nationalism can be traced, notably in Theobald Wolfe Tone's writings, to the conviction that while Irish blood was vital in winning colonies, Ireland herself derived little recognition or acknowledgement of her sacrifice. Tone seems to have imagined that an Ireland separate from, and independent of, England would be able to found her own colonies abroad.[2]

The eighteenth century witnessed a huge territorial expansion of the empire: Canada and India, with their ethnically and religiously mixed populations, were two massive acquisitions gained as a result of the Seven Years' War (1756–63). However, the need to garrison these far-flung possessions placed huge strains on existing military resources, and the consequent need for large numbers of new recruits to be drafted into the armed forces of the crown placed question marks against traditional exclusionary policies. Put bluntly, Irish Catholics had been regarded by Dublin and London as 'the enemy' up to the 1760s; thereinafter, they were viewed (at least in London) as a reservoir of recruits whose leaders' goodwill might be well worth purchasing through timely concessions on the penal laws.[3] It was anybody's guess what effect this new departure would have on the rigidly segregated Irish political world. The expansion of the empire, then, placed a strain on Anglo-Irish relations, but so too did its contraction. With the secession of the thirteen colonies and the setting up of the republic of the United States, Ireland's position in the empire was quite fundamentally altered. For British politicians, the loss of the thirteen colonies concentrated attention on how not to lose Ireland; while the loss of thirteen assemblies in the New World left the Irish parliament dangerously exposed within the empire. Shorn of its sheltering sister-institutions in the American colonies, the Irish parliament's anomalous position after 1783 was laid bare and, despite its new powers (extorted during the American war), a huge question mark was placed against its future. By the end of the century, Ireland's role in the empire, and Irish attitudes towards that evolving empire, had changed dramatically. Similarly in London, under the impact of all-out war with revolutionary France, an imperial strategy was being formulated, one which would place a premium on central direction, unified authority and a unified general staff, and one in which there was no place for an 'independent' Irish parliament, querulous and quarrelsome.

Yet, while a legislative union was increasingly viewed by the prime minister, William Pitt, and his advisers as the preferred solution to Britain's Irish problem, all talk or indeed thought of union with Britain had to be dismissed as premature, for there was no real possibility of the Irish parliament voting itself out of existence. By the 1790s, the burgeoning self-confidence of the Protestants of Ireland, the enhanced importance of their potent symbol of identity, the Irish parliament, and their growing identification with Ireland

and Irishness meant that there was no prospect of their giving up that institution. Admittedly, the Catholic Relief Act of 1793 had advanced substantially the cause of union in both countries – for the inability of the Irish parliament to defend the Protestant interest had been then exposed mercilessly and certainly from that date on there had been an identifiable pro-union lobby in both England and Ireland: but the primary difficulty had, nonetheless, remained – the consent of the Irish parliament would not be forthcoming.[4]

At a stroke, the 1798 Rebellion changed the prospects for union, and British ministers and their Irish allies hastened to seize the opportunity that offered. The unionist moment had finally come: but it might have passed, and there was no question of leaving the matter until quieter times prevailed. It was vital to act, wrote one unionist, 'while the terror of the late Rebellion is fresh', and George III signalled his agreement for 'using the present moment of terror for frightening the supporters of the Castle into a union'.[5] Accordingly, the new lieutenant, Lord Cornwallis (alongside his chief secretary, the Irish-born Viscount Castlereagh) was entrusted with a dual mandate: first, to crush rebellion, then to put through a legislative union.

What was a union between Ireland and England supposed to accomplish? As Pitt saw it, his proposed union gave the perfect riposte to those who had in the United Irish Rebellion sought separation; and to that extent union was to be promoted as a key instrument of counter-revolution, a vital strategic imperative which would draw England and Ireland closer and closer together so as to frustrate those Irish Jacobins and their French allies who had sought to prise them apart. In addition, on a constitutional level, union was seen as the final solution to those problems that had – in Pitt's view – bedevilled Anglo-Irish relations since 1782 (if not since 1692, when an Irish parliament had first begun to sit regularly). In particular, Pitt was to stress the profoundly unsatisfactory nature of the 'Constitution of 1782', the wilful failure to reform it in the 1780s and, hence, the ever-present danger of a clash between two 'independent' legislatures – a clash, he claimed, only narrowly averted at the time of the Regency crisis, when the Irish parliament had intervened in the appointment of a regent during George III's incapacity. Furthermore, Pitt claimed that it was only in a united parliament that the Catholic question could be solved in such a way as to gratify the political ambitions of Irish Catholics without endangering the position of Irish Protestants. Indeed, it was only in a united parliament that certain knotty problems – to do with tithes or education or payment of priests – could be effectively tackled.

There were other benefits which, Pitt assured fellow MPs, could stem from union: Ireland would gain commercial advantages, money would flow into the country and there would be an infusion of 'English capital, English manners [and] English industry' so that Ireland would prosper from union with England as much as Scotland had done since her Union of 1707.[6] So far, so commonplace, for such arguments, by and large, had been well-rehearsed over the previous decade; but Pitt, and those who thought like him, also stressed the advantages which Ireland *and the empire* would derive from a closer incorporating union; and this 'imperial' theme in the debates over the Union may be worth extended treatment.

I

Hitherto, empire, whether as term or concept, had scarcely entered into the lexicon of those in favour of union. A unionist pamphlet published in 1751 was typical in that there was no mention of an imperial dimension. Instead, the author of *A proposal for uniting the kingdoms of Great Britain* stressed the general utility of a union and claimed that it would pluck Ireland out of the obscurity in which she then languished: 'At present, Ireland hath no character, nor even a name in the affairs of Europe'.[7] In so far as empire was cited, the term appears to have denoted a mere trade arrangement: but herein lay a difficulty, for by the 1790s Ireland could be said to have obtained as much commercial advantage as she could from 'our plantations in America' (as the Irish customs officials termed them) and from other colonies further afield. It should be remembered that in 1780 restrictions on Irish trade within the western empire had been removed and that, by 1793, Ireland had access to the lucrative East Indian trade.[8] It was a major worry for those British politicians, anxious to promote the idea of union in the years 1798 to 1800, that Britain had few commercial advantages left to offer in return for Irish agreement. This was in marked contrast to that trading partnership within the empire held out to the Scots in 1707, an offer that had played a major role in inducing them to support the Anglo-Scottish Union.[9] However, the fact that Britain had little left to give in terms of access to imperial trade did not mean imperial matters as such were ignored in the Union debates. On the contrary, the prospect of a strengthened empire, the notion of an imperial partnership and the idea of 'an union for empire', were held out to Irish Protestants as key inducements to give up their parliament.

The imperial theme was set from the beginning. For Lord Cornwallis, the essential backdrop to union was 'the general cause, which engages the empire' and the compelling need to strengthen the empire in the face of French aggression.[10] For Castlereagh, too, a union would 'consolidate the strength and glory of the empire'; though he rather went on to spoil matters by tactlessly raising the question of Ireland's 'imperial contribution', and claiming that Ireland's colonial trade was a matter 'not of right but of favour' – both touchy subjects with Irish MPs.[11] Other Irish pro-unionists took up this theme of a union for empire, though here the emphasis was on the threat posed by an independent Irish parliament to imperial unity. Thomas Conolly, for example, pointed out that 'two independent legislatures in one empire [were] as absurd and monstrous as two heads on one pair of shoulders.'[12] Meanwhile the young lawyer, William Smith, argued that only a legislative union could ensure 'that ONE empire shall no longer be exposed to the risk of wavering languidly and inertly between the dissentient systems of two parliaments'.[13]

It was, however, William Pitt, in the British parliament who spelled out in detail what might be called the imperial argument. For Pitt, the ongoing war with France was 'the most important and momentous conflict that ever occurred in the history of the world'; the fate of the British Empire hung in the balance; a union with Ireland (that 'mighty limb of the empire') would increase 'the general power of the empire . . . to a very great extent by a consolidation of the strength of the two kingdoms'. Pitt held out the exciting prospect of the creation of an entirely new assembly, one that would be neither British nor Irish but instead would be a 'general imperial legislature', an institution which, 'free alike from terror and from resentment, removed from danger and agitation, and uninflamed by the prejudices and passions of that distracted country', would adjudicate impartially and disinterestedly on those vicious issues that had riven Ireland for years and had left her so exposed to French intrigues.[14]

Pitt's remarks were echoed by his colleagues. Henry Dundas, minister at war, identified the prevalence in Ireland of 'new doctrines, so dangerous to the existence of all regular governments, consequently so dangerous to that of the empire', as making a union necessary, and he forecast that after union 'the voice of Irishmen . . . would be heard, not only in Europe but in Asia, Africa and America'.[15] The former Irish chief secretary, Sylvester Douglas, a Scot, dismissed the argument that post-union Ireland would suffer a loss of constitutional status by arguing that 'Ireland, by an union, no more becomes a *province* in any offensive sense of the word, than Great Britain: they both become provinces, or component parts of one whole and integrated empire'. Unconsciously echoing Tone, Douglas pointed out that currently 'Ireland cannot either plant a colony or establish a foreign settlement'.[16] He and Dundas agreed that union would give Ireland both a new role and a new voice in the empire.

Another Scot, Lord Minto, made the conventional point that a union with Ireland would afford 'an occasion of real and efficient force to our present empire, as a navel [*sic*] and military power', but he then went on to consider the wider imperial dimension. The only connection Ireland had with England was an imperial one and that it was this 'imperial connexion which makes Ireland a member of the noblest empire of the globe'. In his view, the proposed Union was simply building on that foundation. 'For what, after all', he asked rhetorically, 'is this imperial connexion in the necessity of which we are all agreed? If it be anything more than a name and if it afford any substantial advantage, does it not consist in securing a conformity or rather a perfect uniformity and unity in the counsels of the two countries on affairs of imperial concern?' Again in terms that recalled Tone's strictures on Ireland's poor imperial performance, Minto then depicted the harsh reality of Ireland's current imperial role:

> Ireland cannot by the utmost success of the war acquire an acre of new territory to the Irish dominion. Every acquisition made by the forces of the empire, however great her share may have been in the danger or exertion, accrues to the crown of Great Britain. If an island were taken by regiments raised in Ireland and composed wholly of Irishmen and by ships manned altogether by Irish seamen, that island is a British conquest, not an Irish one.

He promised that all this would change following union: for Ireland's inability to acquire overseas dominions was an argument in favour of separatism; for Minto, it was a key attraction of union. After union, concluded Minto, 'Ireland is still Ireland, while a new scope is given to the pride, and a larger opened to the patriotism, of every Irishman'.[17]

Beyond the walls of the Irish and British parliaments, pro-union pamphlet writers took up and elaborated this theme of a union for empire. Archibald Redfoord wrote of the 'powerful tendency [of union] to give the British Empire strength and stability,' and he reassured doubtful Protestants that it would be a 'Protestant empire', one which would have an overwhelming majority of Protestants within 'the imperial state'.[18] Or, as another writer had it: 'By an union, the majority of the empire will be Protestant and they have the right and the power to fix the national religion'.[19] The improbably named 'An Orangeman' stressed the career opportunities at the heart of the empire that would open after union: 'Is not Irish genius equal to the task of imperial government' he asked, before going on to point to the glittering examples of Burke, Sheridan and Barré, imperial statesmen all: 'Where would we have heard of them, had they remained at home to wrangle in the little infantine squabbles of a local legislature?'[20] In short, declared an anonymous author, '[union] is pregnant with immense, unequivocal and permanent imperial advantages' and it was only the 'reformists, republicans, and separatists of this town' who refused to support it.[21]

II

So common – and it appears, so attractive – was this theme of empire in the general Union debate, that those opposed to union were forced to make an attempt to rebut it. They did so in two ways. First, anti-unionist writers stated that English prejudice against the Irish was both inveterate and deep-rooted. At a basic level, anxieties were expressed that Irish orators would be unable to gain a hearing for themselves in the London legislature. An Irish gentleman, wrote 'Molyneux', 'smell[ing] of the turf of boggy Ireland . . . would be ashamed to exhibit the Irish brogue in the British senate'.[22] In this regard, the cautionary example of Henry Flood, was cited: an Irish Demosthenes when speaking in the Irish parliament, yet at Westminster, whither he had removed himself in the 1780s, he suffered the humiliation of concluding 'a very able and eloquent speech amidst the yawns and coughs of an English senate'.[23]

More substantially, English antipathy towards the Irish, it was claimed, was simply too great to be overcome: 'We are a savage, immoral, ill-mannered race . . . I well know such are the sentiments', wrote one pamphleteer, 'which the low and the vulgar of your country entertain of the people of Ireland'.[24] 'I am well aware of the rooted prejudices, I had almost said hatred' wrote another 'that lodges in the breast, of some Englishmen towards Ireland'.[25] The English 'have been taught to hate and despise [us] from their infancy' argued Denis Taaffe, so much so that even the 'very liberal' Englishman cannot but consider the Irish as 'semi-barbarous, destitute of industry, punctuality, and honesty'.[26] Such naked prejudice on its own, it was pointed out, would stop Irishmen taking up the promised role in imperial direction.

Secondly, and in a more sophisticated way, some anti-unionist politicians and writers claimed that union would ultimately prove fatal for empire. Admittedly, John Foster, the principal opponent of union in the Irish parliament, based his arguments against union on the grounds that it would prove a bad deal for the Irish economy, and he denied that any British parliament could be trusted to defend the interests of Irish Protestants. But even Foster was forced to confront the 'imperialists': contrary to what was promised, post-union Ireland would not be at the heart of empire, he maintained, but instead, 'we shall become a colony on the worst of terms'. There was a further threat: 'exclusive of all its injuries to Ireland, [union] is big with danger to the old fabric of the British constitution, and if it falls, the empire goes with it, and they and we and all of us fall down.'[27] Foster was concerned that the 100 Irish MPs who were to go to Westminster would overset the balance of the constitution because they would constitute little more than ministerial cannon fodder.

Others forecast disaster for the British Empire, for Irish anger at this 'provocation' (union) might turn the people towards France. 'Would not, might not, the measure of union drive the people of Ireland (which God avert) to seek protection from our natural enemies, even under a republican form of government?'[28] Another author claimed that union could never solve

Ireland's religious problems but 'on the contrary [would] prove the means of final separation'.[29] Taking the longer view, Charles Ball found the outcome of union easily predictable: '[it] would ultimately involve this country in the next greatest calamity that could befall it – a total separation from England'; and this in turn would lead to the break-up of the empire.[30]

III

Notwithstanding arguments such as these, the anti-unionists lost the debate and the Union was passed. Of course, many factors help to explain the passing of the Irish Act of Union, and these have been well canvassed in the two hundred years since its enactment. What may be said is that, when linked to empire, the unionist case was certainly an impressive one; the offer of 'an union for empire' struck a chord with the politically involved classes, and to an extent forced anti-unionists on to the defensive. Grattan's famous peroration against the proposed Anglo-Irish trade / defence treaty of 1785 – 'perish the empire live the constitution' – could not be dusted down and re-deployed in 1799;[31] surely a sign that empire was held in much higher regard in 1800 than it had been even fifteen years earlier.

In the event, while few of the promises held out by unionists were realised in the hundred years after 1800, the Union did in fact prove to be a gateway to empire. Throughout the nineteenth century, and beyond, Irishmen and Irishwomen entered enthusiastically into the business of empire whether as merchants, soldiers, settlers, missionaries, doctors or administrators. The empire was religiously blind, at least where Irish Protestants and Irish Catholics were concerned, and both would quickly become eager imperialists, the latter group taking especial pride in the heroic deeds of Irish soldiers and the heroic self-sacrifice of Irish priests and nuns. Throughout the nineteenth century, the empire offered career opportunities – male and female, clerical and lay – that were simply not available in Ireland. Indeed, from the 1830s on, what was called 'the colonial patronage' was explicitly drawn on to meet the career aspirations of the Irish Catholic middle classes who clamoured for tangible benefits from emancipation.[32] Undeniably, the Catholic Irish nation were to have major problems with the Protestant British state in the nineteenth century; but an appreciation of the benefits of empire, meant that Irish protests tended to be circumspect. Both the repeal movement and the Home Rule movement explicitly denied any intention of disrupting the empire. We may conclude that throughout the nineteenth century, the bond of empire was at all times stronger than that of union.

Political Anglicanism in Ireland 1691–1801: From the Language of Liberty to the Language of Union

JOSEPH RICHARDSON

The century beginning with the victory at the Boyne (1690) and culminating with the concession of legislative independence in 1782 has been seen traditionally as the golden age of the Anglican political nation in Ireland.[1] Indeed 1782 heralded the triumph of Irish Anglicanism as a political force. Yet, by 1801, the political nation had relinquished its legislative sovereignty won a mere nineteen years before. This suggests a catastrophic collapse in political Anglicanism between the publication by Archbishop William King of the *State of the Protestants of Ireland under the late King James's government* in 1692 and Sir Richard Musgrave's *Memoirs of the different rebellions in Ireland from the arrival of the English* in 1801.[2] We will compare the versions of political Anglicanism they promulgated and the context in which they were published.

WILLIAM KING'S POLITICAL ANGLICANISM

James II's defeat on 1 July 1690 at the Boyne signalled the success of the Williamite cause in Ireland. By 10 December 1690, King was preaching a sermon at St Patrick's Cathedral proclaiming the day as 'the day of thanksgiving for the preservation of his majesty's person, his good success in our deliverance, and his safe and happy return into England'.[3] This sermon was King's first explicit expression of his political theology and relied on the notion of special providence, analysing in detail the evidence of God's direct intervention to save his chosen people.

King asked his congregation to reflect upon two things: 'the depth of the contrivance and design against us, from which God has graciously pleased to deliver us; all the princes . . . as profess the Reformed religion being struck at by it'; and 'the miraculous concurrence of providences [*sic*] for our deliverance in breaking this design so deeply laid and vigorously prosecuted.'[4] The design in question he summarised briefly: "'Twas in short to destroy you and your religion and enslave all Europe under the tyranny of the French king.'[5]

In King's eyes, providence linked the political struggle all over Europe against a Catholic, absolutist, French tyranny. But 1690 was not the end of Protestantism's struggle. J.C.D. Clark has recorded the persistent vitality of a form of providentialism and divine-right theory from the reign of James II to the end of the eighteenth century.[6] While the Tories had used it in its simplest form against the Whigs, emphasising the king's godly right to rule, the post-1688 theory was shorn of its short-lived Catholic theocratic overtones:

> from articulating a practical and innovatory programme, the doctrine became an affirmation of allegiance and Anglican religious identity . . . Paradoxically, therefore, . . . divine indefeasible hereditary right actually won adherents after 1688 and 1714, and Whigs were drawn to defend the . . . hereditary claims of William III, Anne, and George I, or to use the doctrine of the 'divine right of providence', identifying God as 'the great disposer of Crowns'.

Providence was still 'the age's leading concept of natural and historical causation.'[7] The significance of King's sermon lies in the fact that it illustrates a powerful point sometimes overlooked in the analysis of the Glorious Revolution. Theology, specifically the theology of the established church, managed to acquire the dominant role in the explanation of the Revolution to the public.

King gave his considered opinion of the Jacobite regime in the form of a history of his church's persecution under King James II. King's goal in the *State of the Protestants* was to demonstrate that James had rebelled against the *concessio* of rights made by the kings of England that had become part of the immemorial rights of the subject and the settled constitution of the kingdom. On a larger scale he had to illustrate a simple subtext, that the Anglican establishment equated to and embodied society's political philosophy as interpreted through historical precedent and natural law, and that James II's regime, on the other hand, embodied an arbitrary and foreign system. In doing so, King set out to show that James was the true rebel who overthrew the ancient constitution and rendered himself liable to sanction.[8] Within the first five pages, King set out his hypothesis; the rest of the book consists of points of evidence brought forward to prove his contention.

On the first page King made his most important intellectual move. He elided any distinction between the high Anglican definition of revelation and natural law:

> it is granted by some of the highest assertors of passive obedience, that if a king design to root out a people or destroy one main part of his subjects

in favour of another . . . they may prevent it even by opposing him with force; and that he is to be judged in such a case to have abdicated the government of those whom he designs to destroy contrary to justice and the laws. This is Grotius' opinion in his book *De jure belli et pacis*, Lit. 1, Cap.4, §11 . . . 'if a king be carried with a malicious design to the destruction of a whole nation, he loses his kingdom, which if grant [ed], since a will to govern and to destroy cannot consist together, therefore he who professes himself an enemy to a whole people doth in that very act abdicate his kingdom: but it seems hardly that this should enter into the heart of a king who is not mad, if he govern only one people: but if he govern many, it may happen that in favour of one people he may desire the other were destroyed'.[9]

King co-opted Hugo Grotius, the Dutch jurisprudent, as an authority for his judgement. Grotius had created a doctrine of natural law that made revelation philosophically normative. He had also asserted the legitimacy of resistance *in extremis*.[10] Bringing together natural law and revealed law, as defined by Anglicans, allowed King to assert that James had rebelled against the natural law when he attacked the church. The actions of Anglicans were thus actions in self-defence. Making James the rebel placed all the moral opprobrium on him. As Patrick Kelly has stated:

> the *State of the Protestants* was not primarily written as a narrative of events, since the author's main purpose was to show that in offering resistance to James II Irish Protestants had not been guilty of an arbitrary abandonment of their sworn allegiance to their lawful sovereign, but had acted from a justified motive of self preservation against a ruler who had already abandoned his entitlement to their allegiance through planning their destruction as a people.[11]

Gilbert Burnet saw King's book as the definitive interpretation of the Glorious Revolution.[12] Indeed, the book went into several editions.[13] King's work, though, fitted into a much older, broader, politico-theological rhetoric, which defined Anglicanism as the language of liberty.

As far back as Charles II's restoration in 1660, similar warnings about the threat of universal monarchy had been made, as Steven Pincus has made clear.[14] Although the Dutch were England's enemy in 1664, Pincus's argument shows that, by the 1670s, the threat of universal monarchy was perceived to come chiefly from the French. In the light of this, King's opinions of James's defeat and the later defeat of Louis XIV cannot be understood merely as a product of the Irish experience. Rather, they must be seen as part of a wider Anglican fear of Catholic world hegemony, brought about through war and trade, leading towards a single religious and political dispensation. Anglicanism equated with liberty. It was the religion of a free people and allowed them the exercise and expression of their liberty.

King's language of liberty was not necessarily a language of national self-determination. As James Kelly has shown, King was prepared to contemplate parliamentary union with England in the early eighteenth century, especially when the Anglo-Scottish Union occurred in 1707.[15] It must be said, though, that he was sceptical of the value of union because of his mistrust of English officials' motives. Kelly has described how the progress of Anglo-Scottish negotiations created envy in the Irish Anglican political class more generally. The envy was turned to bitterness when England refused Irish demands for a union on similar terms. Thus was born Swift's image of Ireland as the 'injured lady'.[16]

SIR JOHN TEMPLE

King's *State of the Protestants* was written in a political idiom which had a particular resonance for Anglicans in Ireland. As we have noted, King's work was divided into an initial thesis followed by detailed and comprehensive evidence. Musgrave repeated King's use of this format in 1801, just as King had followed the earlier example of Sir John Temple.

Temple had written an account of the massacres of Protestants which had occurred during the 1641 Ulster Rising.[17] The rising had been triggered by the attempt of Charles I's government to use Irish troops in the interlocking disputes between the king, his parliament in Westminster and the Presbyterians of Scotland.[18] Gaelic Catholics rose in Ulster claiming royal support. Although this was untrue, Charles I never dispelled the suspicions of his Anglican and dissenter subjects on the matter. The course of the Rising and the murder of Protestants in Ulster demonstrated two points clearly to Anglicans. In the first place, they were exceedingly vulnerable to their Catholic neighbours and, in the second, Catholics, Gaelic Catholics especially, indulged readily in sectarian massacres. When the Old English Catholics of the Pale joined the Rebellion it became countrywide and led to the establishment of the Confederation of Kilkenny. The Confederation proved to Anglicans that Catholics of whatever cultural background would always side with each other to subvert the state and despoil the Anglican subject of his liberties. Catholicism was a religion of rebellion, sedition and oppression. Toby Barnard has shown that the experience of 1641 and the lessons drawn from it were not lost on the political establishment.[19] The annual religious commemoration of the events of that year warned the Anglican political nation of its precarious position and reinforced its title to political power as the sole possessors of true religion and defenders of liberty.

Temple's work established the paradigm employed by King and Musgrave. It combined a forensic approach, the documentation of massacres and injuries, with a politico-theological rhetoric of causation. Temple began by disclaiming any talent for his task and hoped that the 'unquestionable truth of what I set down in a plain and brief narration' would cover these blemishes.[20] He then claimed to have read all the original and authentic documents concerning the Rebellion.[21] Notwithstanding his desire to treat the Rebellion, Temple felt obliged to express the Anglican belief in the moral, political and cultural superiority of the society created by those who adhered to the church established by law. Gaelic history was a fabrication of fabulous myths not worthy of being dignified as history.[22] Gaelic political mores were savage, power was arbitrary and succession to authority occurred through the sword.[23] He rehearsed the traditional historiography of England's first encounter with the Gaels, emphasising the invitation of Dermot MacMurrough to the Anglo-Norman barons to come to his aid.[24] Acutely conscious of the disparity between the two cultures, even on first encounter, Temple recounted how the 'beastly manners and customs' of the natives had corrupted the English.[25] Having established the historical scene, he then returned to the Rebellion of 1641 and attributed it to the machinations of two groups: popish lawyers and priests. The former tried to confuse parliament with legal chicanery into repealing Poynings' law the latter encouraged rebellion as a great Catholic cause. The clerics asserted that killing a Protestant was no more sinful than killing a dog, that Protestants had to be extirpated and that protecting them was unforgivable.[26]

Temple crafted a mix of cultural, political and religious judgements into a potent political syllogism. Catholicism was equated with native origins and native origins with savagery. Therefore, Catholicism was savage. According to Temple, priests and popish lawyers were merciless in their pursuit of the extirpation, first, of Protestant rights under the law and, then, in the extirpation of the Protestants themselves.

After the Boyne, the Anglicans established secure control of the political life of the kingdom of Ireland, but a constitutional anomaly and the pressures of inter-island politics exposed a fundamental contradiction within the new establishment. King's work had equated Anglicanism and liberty, thus all Anglicans partook of the same rights whether resident in Ireland or England. This was not the case in law. Poynings' law had subordinated the Irish legislature to the King in council while the Declaratory Act of 1720 had asserted the constitutional dependence of Ireland to the British legislature by claiming that London's upper house had final appellate jurisdiction for Ireland. Irish Anglicans were not therefore the equals of their English co-religionists.

SIR RICHARD MUSGRAVE

Musgrave's work follows the paradigm set by Temple and King almost exactly. He went to great lengths to explain why he published his book in 1801. Jim Smyth has demonstrated why such a justification was necessary: anti-Catholicism had lost its appeal with senior politicians.[27] On one side, Musgrave wished to refute the assertions of various Catholic and English authors, while placing the late Rebellion (1798) in the proper context of its historical antecedents. However, Musgrave was conscious of the intellectual subtext underlying the events of the last decade of the eighteenth century. He averred, 'I take [it] upon me to assert that the Protestant religion is the only bond of union between the two kingdoms.'[28] He also stated that the Orange Order was the result of Ulstermen organising to protect themselves against massacre and to oppose the repeal of the penal laws.[29] From the beginning, Musgrave's interpretation pitted Anglicans and dissenters together against Catholics in direct contrast to the alignments which had emerged in England. However, it was the Anglicans alone who had the moral qualifications for government. The established church was 'the most loyal, liberal and humane body of people in Ireland.'[30] Musgrave was arguing himself back into the mentality of King. He was transforming himself into the king's Englishman in Ireland with the added corollary that the Anglicans of Ireland alone could be trusted with power.

Musgrave then made a contradictory move. He began by laying the ground for his case that the rebellions that punctuated Ireland's history were the result of religious bigotry.[31] He claimed, however, that the odium for the penal laws rested with the government in London because before 1782 Ireland's legislature was unfree. After independence the Dublin parliament repealed many of the penal laws. Liberal Irish Anglicans removed the burdens on the papists, not London. This dichotomy ran through the whole of Musgrave's thinking in his *Memoirs*. He sought to play the religious card while simultaneously pitching for the claim that the Anglican position was 'liberal and humane'.[32]

The introductory discourse to his history shows his debt to his predecessors Temple and King. He understood that only one solution was possible:

> Two separate sovereign powers, civil and ecclesiastical, cannot co-exist in the same state, without perpetual collision, producing discord and rebellion; and that the only remedy for the calamities attendant on such a state is, either the extinction of one power, or the milder procedure of incorporating it with the other. The latter mode has been adopted in Ireland, abstract reasoning must approve, and experience will demonstrate, the measure to be founded in the truest wisdom.[33]

Musgrave knew that political Anglicanism could not exist credibly in a legislatively independent kingdom of Ireland and thus he felt wisdom demanded
union. He also favoured the union of the established churches. This allowed
the Anglicans of Ireland to claim membership of the majority religion in the
United Kingdom of Great Britain and Ireland, thus reinvigorating political
Anglicanism as a viable political creed.

To reinforce the claims of political Anglicanism he examined Catholicism
as a political philosophy and found it wanting. A standard disclaimer prefaced
his attack. While he was not anti-Catholic,

> the pope's infallibility and supremacy, his dispensing power, exclusive
> salvation, and other points . . . are subversive of society; and its pliability,
> so much boasted of by doctors [John Thomas] Troy and [Thomas] Hussey,
> must alarm every loyal subject, when they asserted in their pastoral letters,
> that it was equally suited to a monarchy, an aristocracy or a democracy.[34]

The contemporary threat of Catholicism was not something new. The native
Irish were uncivil: 'their Brehon laws were calculated to make them savage
and keep them so'; no-one enjoyed secure rights to property or life itself.[35]
Their government was unstable since one king succeeded another only after
war – no law regulated succession. According to Musgrave, 'it was a peculiar
favour from heaven to send a civilised people among them'.[36] While an
incomplete submission of the natives took place, the restraint on their
habitual licentiousness, caused by the imposition of English laws, goaded
them into continual rebellion.

For Musgrave, the English and Irish peoples did not coalesce to form one
nation and the Reformation increased the antipathy between the two
groups.[37] This analysis ignored the Old English, whose English nationality
and Catholic religion disrupted the stark dualism of Musgrave's model. The
Reformation turned Catholic clergymen, educated on the continent, into the
leaders and propagators of bigotry. Following the paradigm of King and
Temple, Musgrave delineated the history of Catholicism's fostering of bigotry.
The survey began with Pope Gregory VII and Emperor Henry II at Canossa,
then moved to Innocent III and the foundation of the Inquisition. This latter
institution was erected solely to defend the pope's wealth and sovereignty.[38]
When 'reason reassumed her empire', that is, after the Reformation, it was
used as a form of police to extirpate heresy. Catholics received indulgences
for combating heretics in war.[39]

The church sought to destroy family loyalty and social harmony by absolv-
ing Catholics from oaths to excommunicated people. Catholic sons were not
bound to their Protestant fathers or wives to their husbands. Catholics

preached rebellion. [40] Bishops were traitors: 'from this time the bishops became the spies and centinels [sic] of the Roman Pontiff; and, in order to insulate their affections, to detach them from the state to which they belonged, and to engage them in the interest of the Holy See, he enjoined celibacy on the popish clergy.'[41]

Musgrave's underlying paranoia emerges clearly with the characterisation of celibacy as a papal policy to separate priests and bishops from the state. Perhaps it hints at a fundamental Erastianism informing Musgrave's thinking. Certainly it would seem to indicate a suspicion of the clergy as a separate caste. Catholic doctrines of exclusive salvation had caused rebellions all over Europe and the pope's incitement had been the chief cause of bloody rebellion and massacre in 1641.[42] This ended the catalogue of papal crimes justifying the publication of his book. Political Anglicanism had come full circle back to the paradigm of 1641.

Why then did Musgrave return to the rhetoric of 1641 and 1690 in 1801? How was it serviceable after 1800? After the Act of Union, the Catholic menace to the Irish parliament was no longer the threat it could have been. Even if Catholics did have the franchise they were unlikely to dominate the new United Kingdom parliament. Now, however, Irish politics was based on a franchise defined by property, not religion. The London executive had clearly linked union to emancipation and while emancipation had had to be sacrificed to gain the votes of MPs and peers, the situation changed again in the new parliament. Irish Anglicans had sacrificed an increasingly unsustainable control of the Irish parliament for the comfort of Protestant numbers in Westminster. However, after 1 January 1801, Westminster decided what were the best interests of the new United Kingdom, in which Catholicism was an increasingly influential regional power bloc. Therefore, Irish Anglicans were being forced to redefine themselves. Musgrave took refuge in the rhetoric of Temple and King. It allowed him to emphasise anew the civilising mission of Anglicans in Ireland and to warn of the political threat Catholic politics represented in Westminster. Musgrave's work was an admonition against Catholic emancipation. It looked to the future, yet employed the rhetorical resources of the past to further political Anglicanism's objectives in a new British order.

CONCLUSION

Musgrave's justification for his *Memoirs of the different rebellions in Ireland* was the same as William King's and John Temple's – to defend the rights of Anglicans to the establishment of their church and to demonstrate its place as the true religion. In comparison with King's highly intellectualised treatment of political Anglicanism, co-opting Hugo Grotius effortlessly, Musgrave's work is less a defence or exposition of political Anglicanism than a diatribe against Catholicism. His whole approach bespeaks an absence of deep intellectual understanding of the role of Anglicanism as both the true church and the expression of English liberties. Again the comparison with King is illuminating; when King wrote his book Louis XIV embodied a readily identifiable, absolutist Catholicism which, by default, situated Anglicanism as the language of liberty. King was also building on a common British understanding of Catholicism as a hegemonic empire. For Musgrave, though, the effects of 1782, 1789 and 1798 were more compelling.

There is a great irony in the fact that the apotheosis of the Anglo-Irish ascendancy in 1782 was its undoing. The ninety years or so from the Battle of the Boyne saw the flowering of an Anglican culture which made Dublin the second city of the first British Empire, yet it all collapsed within nineteen years of legislative independence. One of the reasons may well be that the opportunity of converting substantial numbers of Catholics to the estab-lished religion was frittered away during the eighteenth century.[43] Implied in this criticism, though, is a nationalist subtext which sees the mass of people as vital to the political nation. This is, however, anachronistic. Ireland was a typical *ancien régime* state bound together by overlapping and contradictory bonds of blood, religion and patronage.[44]

Irish Anglicans bridged the gap between both islands but in doing so had to speak two different languages. In England, they spoke the language of Anglicanism as a language of liberty, the language of English sovereignty. In Ireland, that was not available to them because Poynings' law did not allow the effective replication of the king-in-parliament as the *locus* of sovereignty. This made the Irish Anglicans custodians of an English political mission, not a sovereign people. In Ireland, they spoke a language of civilisation and reason. As Musgrave asserted, the Gaels were to be understood as brutish and chaotic requiring the restraint of firm government, while both Catholics and dissenters followed unreasonable religions. Anglicans were, Musgrave claimed, 'liberal and humane'.[45] The year 1782 was an attempt to speak the language of liberty in Ireland. It failed because the civilising mission had remained unfulfilled. By the end of the eighteenth century, the Anglicans of Ireland realised that the language of liberty could not be made to work in Ireland. But for Musgrave, Anglicanism was the only thing holding the islands together and its importance as a binding force received only added emphasis from the French Revolution and its Irish manifestation in 1798.

The 1798 Rebellion defined the individual as a citizen with natural rights who was subject to a secular republic in which no religion had official position. In doing so, it eliminated the confessional boundaries demarcating

Irish life. Crucially for Musgrave, it allowed the entrance of Catholics and dissenters into political institutions and denied the claim of Anglicans to a privileged position. The civilising mission of Anglican Ireland became redundant.

It should come as no surprise that in 1800 the Anglicans of Ireland committed political suicide. They were already dying, only union could save them and their political language. The surprise comes rather from the fact, as Patrick Geoghegan has shown, that such great effort had to be expended by London in procuring their survival.[46]

CHAPTER FIVE

Ulster Presbyterians and the Passing of the Act of Union

IAN McBRIDE

At the beginning of July 1798, as rebellion gave way to white terror, Lord Clare outlined the obstacles he anticipated in passing a union. The primary difficulty he foresaw was what he referred to as 'our strong national love of jobbing'. The political élite, Clare predicted, would not willingly forgo the spoils system that underpinned government majorities in the Irish Commons, though he was hopeful that the venality of Irish politicians would be outweighed by apprehensions for 'the safety of our persons and estates'. In a passage which is worth quoting at some length, the lord chancellor provided a detailed consideration of the likely political response:

> I think the general feeling of the landed interest is in favour of the measure, and when the advantages of it in a commercial point of view are understood, I suppose the commercial interest of the country would then be generally and strongly for it. The Catholics will, I make no doubt, oppose it with violence as will the northern republicans, and therefore before the measure is avowed, it will be essentially necessary to have a strong British military force here . . . The Speaker [John Foster] will, I believe, be against the measure, and I know the archbishop of Cashel [Charles Agar] will oppose it vehemently. Lord Shannon, I think, sees the necessity which presses for it, and I am pretty confident that the general feeling of the House of Lords is in favour of it. Our proprietors of boroughs which would not be represented will demand compensation. If this should be practicable, I make no doubt a great many of them will acquiesce.[1]

This passage reminds us of the oligarchic assumptions of the *ancien régime*, a world where politics was still a matter of 'jobbing' and where boroughs constituted a type of property, for which their owners might reasonably expect compensation. Since public affairs were the preserve of a narrow landed class, the government's priority was to enlist important members of the Irish 'cabinet'. Catholics and the 'northern republicans' could be treated as a problem of public order. Yet, arguably, it is this last group, the Presbyterian radicals, who constitute the most interesting – and certainly the most obscure – section of public opinion at this time. The dissenters of the north had provided the backbone of the Volunteer movement from 1778, spearheaded the campaigns for parliamentary reform in 1783–85 and 1792–93, and supplied ideological direction and manpower to the United Irish movement from 1791 to 1797.[2] In the wake of the 1798 Rising, however, they seem to have reciprocated Clare's inattention to them by remaining uncharacteristically reticent during the Union debates.

Little is known about Presbyterian attitudes during the years after 1798. Clare's conception of the Act of Union as an event in high politics has been endorsed by the small number of modern historians who have examined it. Until recently, the only serious modern study was G.C. Bolton's *The passing of the Irish Act of Union*. While Bolton offered some subtle observations on the role of public opinion in guiding eighteenth-century political morality, his focus was on the parliamentary arena. Similarly, Patrick Geoghegan's acclaimed study of the Union, whilst it deals expertly with the Catholic question, has nothing to say about the problem of Protestant dissent. Only one entry for 'Presbyterians' can be found in the index, directing the reader to Cornwallis's estimate that Presbyterians and Catholics together composed about nine-tenths of the population.[3] Even as a demographic statistic, however, Presbyterians were rarely visible during the bicentenary conferences held to commemorate the Union, when the subject was often discussed solely in terms of the relationship between the British state and Catholic Ireland.

A brief excursion into the partisan historiography that appeared during the Home Rule period yields equally disappointing results. The political crises of 1886, 1893 and 1912 provoked vindications of the Anglo-Irish Union, including two fairly substantial works, Thomas Dunbar Ingram's *A history of the legislative union of Great Britain and Ireland* (1887), and J.R. Fisher's *The end of the Irish parliament* (1911). Both works contend that support for the United Irish movement in Ulster was shallow and that Presbyterian radicalism was distinct in its ideological origins and driving impulses from Catholic disaffection. In the north, according to Ingram, the 1798 Rising was little more than 'a flash in the pan', caused by over-excitement about the French Revolution, while the southern rising assumed 'the mixed complexion of a religious war and a *jacquerie*.'[4] Accordingly, he was able to take at face value the pro-union declarations that greeted Cornwallis on his northern tour in October 1799.[5] J.R. Fisher, editor of the Liberal *Northern Whig,* likewise insisted on the absence of nationalist sentiment amongst the Ulster revolutionaries.[6] He too had little to offer on Presbyterian attitudes towards the Act of Union, but he implied a rapid shift of loyalties following 1798. Wexford, claimed Fisher, had cured the Presbyterians of their 'magniloquent loquacity', pointing out that two leading United Irishmen of Presbyterian origin, Hamilton Rowan and Samuel Neilson, had been converted to the Union – a questionable assertion echoed by many unionists since.[7] This essay will attempt a more detailed reconstruction of Presbyterian political sentiments during these turbulent years.

I

How was the proposal for legislative union received in the north? The evidence is fragmentary, difficult to interpret and stubbornly resistant to generalisation. With the alternative political structures of the Volunteers and the United Irishmen destroyed, expressions of public opinion were confined to the formal political world of parliamentary representation, grand juries and county meetings of gentlemen and freeholders. It is not always clear whether MPs reflected the views of their constituents or if, on the contrary, the electorate was held accountable to the landed élite. Nevertheless, as Bolton discovered, the electoral geography of the northern province can be divided into two broad tendencies.[8] In the constituencies of Counties Londonderry, Antrim and Down, where Presbyterians predominated, the MPs tended to be pro-union (five out of six). The unionists, despite initial opposition, also won the battle for resolutions and petitions, though the pattern was complicated by divisions in County Down, crystallised by the influence of the marquess of Downshire. The contrast with the border counties of southern Ulster, where Protestants and Catholic communities were balanced more equally, was marked. Counties Armagh, Cavan, Monaghan, Fermanagh and Tyrone returned two anti-union MPs each. Significantly, this split mirrored the divisions manifest at the Dungannon reform convention of February 1793, attended by delegates from Antrim, Down, Donegal, Londonderry and Tyrone.[9]

How can we account for this divergence? The concentration of opposition in south Ulster is not difficult to explain. Armagh was the home of Charlemont, the 'Volunteer earl', for whom patriotism and Protestantism remained indissolubly linked. Perhaps the greatest danger to the government in the region, however, came from the Orange Order. Its extensive organisation, the vertical ties between gentry and tenantry in mid-Ulster, and the affiliation of heavyweight 'ascendancy men' such as John Foster, Sir John Parnell and George Ogle to the Dublin Lodge, posed a grave threat. It is important to emphasise that union was intended to be – and was perceived as – an assault on the loyalist 'junto' which had directed policy under Earl Camden. To many hard-line defenders of Protestant ascendancy, who believed that they had saved Ireland for the British crown, the conciliatory policy adopted by

Cornwallis towards the rebels was an outrage. Paradoxically, however, their access to establishment circles constituted the Orangemen's weakness, for like the champions of Protestant ascendancy generally, they found it difficult to sever connections with an administration they had habitually supported. Anxious to avoid a schism, the leadership of the Grand Lodge approved a resolution on 5 January 1799 supportive of a policy of neutrality on the Union question. Despite a series of northern mutinies in 1800, after three Dublin lodges invited their brethren to declare against 'the extinction of the Irish nation', there was little the disaffected Orangemen could do without the sanction of more prominent members.[10]

The behaviour of the north-east is more puzzling. To suggest, as Bolton appeared to, that support for the Union took root in conditions of security, does not take us very far.[11] After all, it was precisely this area that posed the major threat to the ascendancy regime before 1798. James Patterson has highlighted government anxieties over continuing republican activity among lower-class Presbyterians of Antrim and Down for several years after 1798, particularly during the winter of 1798–99 when it was believed that the French were preparing for invasion at the Texel and Brest.[12] A year after the 'turn-out', General Nugent reported that the three counties of Antrim, Down and Londonderry were still gripped by 'a spirit of discontent'.[13] Indeed, Dublin Castle continued to receive reports of arms raids, pike manufacturing, the assassination of loyalists and the activities of outlaw rebel leaders, such as George Dickson and Thomas Archer, during the winters of 1798–99 and 1799–1800. In January 1800 it was reported that 12,000 rebels were in arms at Ballymoney, under the masonic banner of the Knights of the Black Garter.[14] A key to political attitudes in this north-eastern crescent was suggested in a letter from the earl of Londonderry to his son, Viscount Castlereagh, in December 1798. In the course of a generally upbeat assessment of gentry opinion in County Down, Londonderry commented that 'most of those who were actuated with a strong reforming spirit entertain such a dislike and antipathy to the present subsisting parliament of the country, that they will not be very adverse to any change that will rid them of so very corrupt a legislature'.[15] As with the Orange Order then, reactions to the abolition of the Irish legislature turned on the survival of the old 'Irish cabinet', whose resistance to change many people in Ireland – and in Britain too – held responsible for the outbreak of the Rebellion. Among the liberal gentry and middling sorts, the attitude towards Union was not so much enthusiasm but acquiescence.

Some further light is shed on the matter by Cornwallis's tour of the north in October 1799, which convinced the lord lieutenant that a favourable disposition towards union was making 'rapid progress' through the province.[16] His most notable success was at Belfast, where he was entertained by the corporation and merchants of the town.[17] Other sources agree that Belfast – or at least its propertied inhabitants – supported the abolition of the Irish legislature.[18] Yet such optimistic assessments, usually discovered in ministerial papers, must be treated with caution. Reservations were expressed among the cotton manufacturers and West India traders who feared British competition.

Cornwallis had boasted that 'the cry for union' was unanimous throughout Antrim and Derry and that he was presented with addresses at Antrim, Coleraine, Limavady and other towns, signed not only by the corporation but by the 'principal inhabitants'.[19] One item on this impressive list came from the provost, corporation and inhabitants of Strabane, a strongly Presbyterian area that lay within the estates of the marquess of Abercorn. But for a more accurate picture of opinion there, we must turn to the correspondence of the chief agent on the estate, who described how he had secured the address from 'the respectable people of the town', but not without 'a vast deal of trouble and anxiety to myself, for the bulk of the people are unfriendly to union'.[20] Elsewhere too, as we have seen, there were signs of a split within the Presbyterian community along social lines, which suggest that carefully staged declarations of loyalty may have concealed continuing disaffection among the lower orders.

If the Orange Order offered one institutional base for anti-union sentiment, another potential platform for opposition of a more 'patriotic' tone was the General Synod of Ulster, which annually gathered together the clergymen and elders of the majority of Presbyterian congregations in the north. Like the Order, the Synod maintained a public stance of benevolent neutrality towards the Union, but its fourteen presbyteries were divided and it may be that a majority were actually hostile to the proposal. Personal political allegiances were complicated by confessional and institutional interests, moreover, since the extension of the United Kingdom entailed not only legislative but ecclesiastic union. Presbyterians, regionally concentrated and tightly organised, enjoyed a more favourable legal position than the thinly scattered congregations of English nonconformity. Most obviously, the Irish Sacramental Test, prohibiting Protestant dissenters from offices under the crown, had been repealed in 1780; in England, by contrast, petitions for the repeal of the Test and Corporation Acts had failed in 1787, 1789 and 1790. There were further concerns too, concerning the status of dissenting schools and marriages. Even the most solid supporters of union, such as the Rev William Bruce of Belfast, the dominant force in the autonomous Presbytery of Antrim, harboured apprehensions on this score. In England, Bruce feared, Irish Presbyterians were 'either unknown, or looked upon as an obscure sect of schismatics'. The imperial parliament, he feared, would find it difficult to confer any benefits on Irish dissenters that it withheld from their English counterparts.[21]

In the aftermath of rebellion both the General Synod and the Presbytery of Antrim came under the tenuous control of conservatives who sought to rebuild a stable relationship with the British government. The lynchpin in this conservative strategy was Viscount Castlereagh, who was linked to Ulster Presbyterianism by family background, electoral interest and his early political credentials as a Northern Whig. Within the Synod his chief ally was Robert Black of Derry, whose position as agent for the *regium donum* – the annual grant paid by the state to the Presbyterian clergy – had allowed him to build up a personal power-base within the church. Among his closest allies were the Rev Thomas Cuming of Armagh and the Rev Alexander Craig of Lisburn, both of whom were relatives by marriage. These three were able to dominate the proceedings of the Synod's meeting in August 1798, a thin house, owing to the disturbed state of the country. Unsurprisingly, perhaps, addresses of loyalty to the king and the lord lieutenant were agreed unanimously and a pastoral letter to the Synod's congregations was drafted extolling the virtues of the British constitution and warning against the dangers of French intervention. More controversially, the Synod was obliged to admit that some of its members had been 'implicated in seditious and treasonable practices' and it called on each presbytery to investigate the conduct of its ministers and probationers.[22] The following year it was concluded that, a 'comparatively small number' had been implicated in the insurrection, and the Synod's reputation for loyalty to the Hanoverian monarchy was therefore still intact.[23]

This public confidence should not be allowed to disguise the difficulties faced by Presbyterian leaders after the Rebellion. During the 1790s, a number of prominent clergymen had acquired notoriety by chairing public meetings, serving on the various committees of the United Irish system, assisting political prisoners, and contributing propaganda to the *Northern Star*. Sir Richard Musgrave's *Memoirs of the different rebellions in Ireland* (1801) emphasised that most Presbyterians outside Antrim and Down had remained loyal, but it also contained abundant information on the activities of radical clergymen such as Sinclare Kelburne, Thomas Ledlie Birch, William Steel Dickson and Samuel Barber.[24] Commentators sympathetic to Catholic emancipation were tempted to shift the blame for rebellion on to dissenting agitators: the Catholics, it was maintained, had taken up arms for negative reasons – 'that they may not be insulted and oppressed', while Presbyterianism was 'the organ of positive rebellion.'[25] Indeed, the political record of the Presbyterian clergy and pro-bationers was far from respectable. In the Presbytery of Bangor, which had a particularly radical reputation, two members (James Porter and Robert Gowdie) had been executed, three (James Hull, John Miles and David Bailie Warden) had been banished to the United States, whilst one (William Steel Dickson) was a state prisoner at Fort George.[26]

By reading between the lines of the Synod's minutes and by drawing on the few sources, it is possible to reconstruct some of the conflicts that followed the Rebellion. In 1799, Cuming made an attempt to deprive the widow of the Rev James Porter, author of the famous radical satire *Billy Bluff* (1796), of the annuity to which she was entitled under the terms of the Widows' Fund.[27] Furthermore, the Synod passed a resolution designed to exclude two of their number from the *regium donum*, William Steel Dickson and John Smyth, who were 'still in confinement', having been 'implicated in treasonable or seditious practices'.[28] These measures reflected the ascendancy of a loyalist circle eager to assert their dominance over the organs of Presbyterian government. Five years later, when the post of clerk to the Synod became vacant, Robert Black campaigned vigorously on behalf of his brother-in-law, Thomas Cuming. The rival candidate, the Rev Nathaniel Shaw, was stigmatised as the 'friend and concealer' of the Rev James Townsend, the second-in-command at the battle of Ballynahinch, and his election, Black argued, would be fatal to the attempt to demonstrate the Synod's 'return to order and decency'. Not surprisingly, Cuming was elected by a large majority, but Black's correspondence with William Bruce reveals his fears concerning the strong United Irish sympathies that still existed among the elders.[29]

This internal power struggle was also reflected at the local level, where the traumatic experience of the Rebellion and its repression had torn apart a number of Presbyterian communities. It is important to stress that congregations were divided long before the turn-out. In Saintfield, County Down, for example, the radical preacher Thomas Ledlie Birch had informed Wolfe Tone in 1792 that his neighbourhood had been converted to the United Irish agenda, yet the formation of a breakaway congregation in 1796 was partly attributable to his pro-Catholic sympathies.[30] Many families also withdrew from William Steel Dickson's congregation around the time of the Dungannon convention, to which he had acted as unofficial chaplain.[31] In July 1798, his congregation at Portaferry published a declaration of loyalty in the *Belfast News-Letter* regretting that 'they had been drawn to the brink of a precipice by artful and ambitious men' – presumably a reference to their notorious minister; their connection with Dickson was eventually dissolved.[32] Much less is known of the other state prisoner, Rev John Smith, who returned to his Kilrea congregation, although the session records show that he too was attacked by loyalist Presbyterians.[33] At Larne, James Worrall, who was confined briefly in Carrickfergus gaol in 1798, lost some of the most influential families from his congregation, though one was persuaded to return after he read a recantation of his political opinions from the pulpit.[34]

It was a profound embarrassment for the advocates of 'order and decency' when William Steel Dickson was released from Fort George in January 1802.

Dickson had been identified in the report of the House of Lords committee on the Rebellion as the adjutant-general of the rebel army in County Down and, although he had never been brought to trial, the truth of the charge was widely accepted. Following his liberation, Dickson received a call from the congregation of Donegore, but the members of the congregation were threatened with the loss of their share of the *regium donum* if they proceeded.[35] Soon after, however, Dickson accepted a call from Second Keady in County Armagh. This small, newly established congregation was later refused a share of the *regium donum* on the technical grounds that it had been erected after the royal bounty had been restructured and augmented as part of the Union settlement. Dickson, however, interpreted the decision as a personal insult, and not without some cause. At the Synod of 1805, when a memorial from the Second Keady congregation was rejected for the second time, Dickson bitterly reopened the question of the Synod's treatment of both the state prisoners and of James Porter's widow in 1799.[36]

In 1812, Dickson published a long account of his imprisonment containing a vitriolic attack on 'the *pious* and *loyal* servility of a small, but, latterly, a dominant party' in the Presbyterian church.[37] A brief pamphlet war followed, and over the next two years speeches were made at the Synod attacking and defending the book, until Dickson was granted a partial victory with the passing of a resolution vindicating his complaints about the 1799 minutes. Interestingly, seven of the twenty-two ministers who expressed support for Dickson had also been implicated in the Rebellion.[38] Robert Black's discomfiture in this matter foreshadowed his later defeats over the question of the Synod's relationship with Belfast Academical Institution, a new college that had close links with former United Irishmen.[39] It also serves as a useful reminder that we should not overestimate the reaction against radicalism that took place after 1798. During the following decades, the language of opposition would be tempered by fears of renewed disorder and the need to distance itself from Jacobinism. As late as the 1830s, the Belfast radicals were vilified in election squibs as 'the '98 set'. Yet, Presbyterian political attitudes remained almost instinctively anti-government in character.[40]

Of more immediate interest is Dickson's vituperative book, *A narrative of the confinement and exile of William Steel Dickson* (1812), which suggests something of the state of feeling that prevailed within the General Synod during the passage of the Union. 'I am fully convinced', he declared, 'that not one in ten were active in, or really approved of, things then done. The day was a day of terror. . . . They were made to believe, that they were a *suspected body,* and that exertions must be made to remove that suspicion.'[41] Interestingly, whilst Dickson attempted to discredit the statements of the government informers Magin and Hughes regarding his military appointment, he avoided any overt denial of his involvement in the organisation of the insurrection. Given his generally defiant tone, it is no surprise to find Dickson lamenting that his native land had been reduced to 'a dependent province, and its five millions of inhabitants sold, at their own expense, to a foreign government'.[42] That these sentiments were more widely shared is demonstrated by an unpublished history of Irish Presbyterianism drafted by the Rev William Campbell in 1803. Campbell had preceded Robert Black as the Synod's negotiator with Dublin Castle and had opposed Presbyterian support for parliamentary reform and Catholic relief during the 1780s. It is all the more remarkable, therefore, that his account of the 1790s describes an essentially loyal, industrious community driven into insurrection by the withholding of reform and by the reign of terror enforced after 1796. 'As to the Rebellion that was raised in Ulster', he wrote, 'it was the act not of the body of Presbyterians, but only of a part made mad by unexampled oppression: which appeared to have been contrived by the prevalent faction . . . to ruin the nation and make way for the Union'.[43]

II

Although patchy, the primary evidence reviewed above suggests a much more complex picture than that presented by Ingram or Fisher. It seems likely that a majority of Presbyterians continued to subscribe to an antiministerial position, with continuing disaffection particularly strong amongst the lower classes of Antrim and Down. With the radicals in disarray, however, and the moderate reformers bereft of any coherent strategy, the initiative was seized by those, like Bruce and Black, who adhered to the Castlereagh line. In order to make sense of these conflicting and ambivalent attitudes towards the Union we need to examine the longer-term trajectory of Ulster politics in the late eighteenth century.

To begin with, we should be cautious in categorising Presbyterians as loyalists or rebels, for this distinction does not do justice to the diversity of attitudes which they held across a series of issues. Even in Belfast, the Society of United Irishmen met with opposition from its inception, from moderates who identified with the more traditional programme for parliamentary reform adopted by the Northern Whig Club. Their differences crystallised at a town meeting convened on 28 January 1792 to draw up a petition for Catholic emancipation. In contrast to the 600 supporters of the United Irishmen, 253 citizens stressed their commitment to the cause of reform, but dissented from the petition on the grounds that premature enfranchisement would lead to instability.[44] Amongst the minority were many of the most respected reformers in Belfast, such as Dr Alexander Haliday, the Rev

William Bruce and Henry Joy, the editor of the *Belfast News-Letter*. Their position was soon echoed in Derry, where the Rev Robert Black called for reform by 'ARGUMENT, PETITION, REMONSTRANCE, *but not by force*'.[45] However, the Belfast schism on the Catholic question, illuminated in Tone's journal and newspaper sources, has distorted our understanding of Presbyterian politics before 1798. As ideological debate accelerated against the background of revolution and war in Europe, concern with the Catholic question was displaced by questions of property and the maintenance of social order, which in turn yielded to clashes over the repressive measures taken by government from 1796.[46]

A similar spectrum of opinion was found in the Ulster countryside, where continuing support for constitutional change was tempered by growing unease at social unrest. The survival of a broad strand of reformist opinion was illustrated by the response to the imposition of the oath of allegiance and the raising of yeomanry corps in 1796–98. Many moderates objected to the oath on the grounds that it sanctioned the abuses of the unreformed system and required them to uphold the 'unconstitutional' laws passed since 1793. According to a loyalist pamphlet published in 1797, the conviction that taking the oath was incompatible with support for reform 'is now become a prevailing sentiment among the lower orders of society throughout the north'.[47] At the same time, recruitment for the yeomanry was opposed by northern liberals who still clung to the volunteering ideal whilst stopping short of republicanism. When two Belfast units were eventually raised, a number of the new recruits reassured the town that they had not forsaken 'the rights and liberties of *all* the people of Ireland'.[48] Elsewhere, too, yeomanry corps declared for reform and emancipation.[49] Ultimately, then, in the face of social and political upheaval, many liberal middle-class Presbyterians were prepared to defend a government whose political philosophy they rejected, and whose policy of repression they abhorred. Well might Martha McTier pity the dilemma faced by the 'honourable man who must either decline arming against a foreign foe or swear to support the present government'.[50]

A second complicating factor in determining Presbyterian allegiances at the time of the Union derives from the shape of the Rebellion itself. It is well known that the risings in Antrim and Down were belated and unco-ordinated. Part of the explanation lies in the violent counter-insurgency measures undertaken by General Lake in 1797 and in the arrest of important figures in the upper echelons of the United Irish system which left younger, less experienced and less influential men in charge. Such action continued until the eve of the Rising itself. This disorganisation cannot be wholly attributed to state repression, however; part of the explanation lies in a spectacular failure of nerve on the part of the Ulster leadership. At the provincial meeting of 29 May 1798 only two of the twenty-three colonels from Antrim supported the call to rise, the others preferring to wait for news of a French landing or success in the south.[51] According to James Hope, most of the officers 'either gave secret information to the enemy or neutralised the exertions of individuals as far as their influence extended'.[52] This lack of discipline may have been exacerbated by the fact that the focus of United Irish military strategy had shifted to Dublin, leaving the north to act out a supporting role.

The divisions within the republican ranks, the growth of disillusionment, and the lack of discipline among the rank and file provided one framework within which the defeats at Antrim and Ballynahinch were interpreted. This is not to deny that patriotic deeds, heroic resistance and martyrdom all featured in stories of the events which the Presbyterians of Antrim and Down remembered as 'the turn-out'.[53] According to the publisher and poet William McComb, many 'rude' ballads were composed after the death of Bessie Gray and in cottages maps were hung up representing the battle scene with the heroine mounted on a pony and bearing a green flag.[54] Other radical activists such as Henry Joy McCracken, the Rev James Porter and Henry Munro were immortalised in popular songs. Yet the record of hesitation, timidity and betrayal inhibited the valorisation of the rebel defeat and directed attention towards 'the men who flinched and fell away'.[55] When Presbyterian clergymen came to record the rich oral traditions of their congregations in the late nineteenth century they found many stories of cowardice: the folklore of 1798 centred less on patriotic martyrs than on those who had feigned sickness or injury to avoid turning out.[56]

In addition to this demoralisation, the disabling of republicanism in Ulster was hastened by counter-insurgency operations, which embraced the burning of several towns and villages, the indiscriminate destruction of property, torture, floggings and the grim theatre of public execution. On 2 July 1798, the Rev James Porter was hanged in view of his meeting-house. A member of his congregation who was a carpenter had been compelled to erect the scaffold and other hearers were forced to attend and witness the execution.[57] When the Rev Robert Magill, who was ten years old in 1798, came to write an account of the Rebellion in Broughshane his overriding memory was the executions and floggings afterwards and 'the awful spectacle of the heads of rebel leaders displayed in Ballymena with their hair waving in the wind'.[58] Nor were these scenes confined to Antrim and Down. Following a brief turn-out at Maghera, the dissenting meeting-house was occupied by the Tipperary militia, the minister fled to America and two elders – suspected rebels Watty Graham and Billy Cuddy – were hanged and beheaded in the town.[59] Among the witnesses to these events was the ten-year-old Henry Cooke, who later wrote of that year that 'impressions were left in my mind that I have never forgotten'.[60]

Yet, the loyalist reaction to the Rising in the north was much more complicated than a catalogue of atrocities would suggest. After his arrival in mid-June, Cornwallis ordered a pardon for all rank and file rebels who surrendered their weapons and took the oath of allegiance. As Michael Durey has observed, Cornwallis's relatively lenient policy favoured the Ulster rebels more than their compatriots elsewhere.[61] Of the thirty-eight rebels who had their sentences reduced to banishment overseas, all but three came from the north, a high proportion of them Presbyterian ministers or licentiates. These findings reflect the geography of violence during 1798 and attest to the willingness of Dublin Castle to consider pleas for leniency on behalf of Presbyterian radicals. Once again, the web of familial and friendship connections between influential Presbyterians and the Stewarts of County Down proved vital. Convinced that there was no natural basis for the brotherhood of affection in the north and that the 'religious complexion of the rebellions in the south' had cured the Presbyterian radicals of their separatism, Castlereagh was confident that the Synod of Ulster could be brought under government control.[62] With the exception of leaders like Steel Dickson, his policy was one of 'acting against the Catholic rather than the Presbyterian members of the union'.[63] Though the differences between north and south should not be overestimated, it seems that the Presbyterians were better connected than their Catholic allies, and in this respect the Northern Whigs were crucial.

Thus, John Campbell White, the Belfast physician and active United Irishman, wrote in October 1801 from Baltimore, where he had established a successful medical practice. He expressed his gratitude to Henry Joy for 'handsome and polite interference' on his behalf with Viscount Castlereagh.[64] Dr Haliday wrote to Castlereagh direct on behalf of the Larne clergyman James Worrall, who had been arrested on 23 June 1798. Worrall's political views, Haliday insisted, were limited to parliamentary reform and Catholic emancipation; he had been persecuted by local loyalists for his independent political stance.[65] Even the Rev Thomas Ledlie Birch, a high-profile republican, was saved from the scaffold through the influence of his brother, a loyalist, a yeoman, and a friend of the Stewarts.[66] What is surprising is just how many of the Ulster rebels managed to reach some kind of accommodation with the authorities, many of them young men who claimed they had been propelled into leadership positions at a late stage, and carried away by youthful idealism.

As we have already seen, radicalism, although dispersed, was never entirely extinguished. The United Irish system, painstakingly built up in the mid-1790s, did not just vanish. Yet, by the time of Robert Emmet's Rebellion, the remnants of republicanism in Ulster had been overshadowed by displays of ostentatious loyalty. In August 1803, James McClelland reported from Carrickfergus that County Antrim was quiet, commenting that '[t]he lower orders of Roman

Catholics may not be well-affected, but this does not matter as long as the Presbyterians are loyal'.[67] In Londonderry, meanwhile, Brigadier General Hart recommended that the local dissenters be enrolled in armed corps. '[A] total change seems to have taken place in the minds of the Presbyterians', he reported; 'they seem endeavouring to outdo each other in their expressions at least of a determined loyalty . . . in which it is generally believed they are now really sincere'.[68] Interestingly, one of the candidates the Derry Presbyterians had recommended for their lieutenant was an ironmonger named Samuel Moore, whose father had been proclaimed a rebel and fled to America. A few months later, Dr Snowden Cupples, the Orange vicar of Lisburn, observed that '[t]hose who were deeply engaged in the last rebellion & most anxious to make a common cause with Catholics have now the greatest dread & suspicion of them'. To his surprise, he found that Presbyterians would only serve in yeomen corps where Catholics were refused admission.[69]

For repentant republicans, the yeomanry was the obvious route to rehabilitation. Henry Joy noted that a number of former United Irishmen were commissioned as officers of the Belfast Volunteer Infantry in August 1803, seizing 'the present opportunity of *renouncing* the follies of their former career'.[70] Allan Blackstock has found waves of ex-radical Presbyterians joining the yeomanry after 1798 and 1803; he has estimated that in the year of liberty the Presbyterians already accounted for somewhere between 5,000 and 7,000 of the 18,000 Ulster yeomen.[71] In a sense, they were renewing the old public band tradition that stretched back to the plantation; it is important in this respect to note that the yeomanry, as Blackstock has shown, was not simply the Orange Order in uniform, but appealed to the old Volunteering tradition.[72] Having said that, it is also true that some Presbyterians were willing to take the Orangeman's oath. It was observed that, as the Order expanded, some of its most violent recruits were erstwhile republicans trying to compensate for their previous errors by establishing their anti-Catholic credentials.[73] One Anglican magistrate noted that Presbyterians joined the Orange Order to 'screen themselves' and take revenge on their '*quondam* associates of a different persuasion'.[74]

Castlereagh's prediction – that the Wexford Rebellion would help to dissolve the United Irish coalition in Ulster – is confirmed by many other sources. What is often forgotten, however, is that there was also a wider international context to the reorientation of Presbyterian politics. The United Irishmen had sprung up in the wake of the French Revolution, in an age of reform, as the Belfast Society put it, 'when unjust governments are falling in every quarter of Europe' and, equally importantly, 'religious persecution is compelled to abjure her tyranny over conscience'.[75] Admiration for the utopian experiment of the new republic was accompanied by a fascination with the dismantling of the French confessional state, hence the interest shown by the *Belfast News-Letter* in the admission of Protestants to political office in France.[76] For many Presbyterians this mood of Enlightenment optimism shaded off into a more defined body of millenarian ideas, as events on the continent were interpreted in the light of the books of Daniel and Revelation. The common link between most of the millenarian writers reprinted by the *Northern Star* – Pierre Jurieu, Robert Fleming, Christopher Love, John Owen, Christopher Goodwin, Alexander Peden, James Bicheno, Richard Brothers – was that they had linked the rise of the Antichrist not only with Rome but with the French monarchy. Although millenarian speculation did not entirely cease, Bonaparte's expedition to Egypt, his concordat with Rome and his assumption of imperial status made it difficult to reconcile support for France with radical principles.[77] 'Long before 1803', Linda Colley has written, 'the French had ceased to be viewed, even by many radicals, as liberators and exemplars for the unreformed states of Europe.'[78]

III

There were many compelling reasons, then, for Ulster Presbyterians to avoid public debate in the years after 1798. In defeat, the rebels of Antrim and Ballynahinch cast themselves in a series of roles, or at least accepted the roles prescribed for them by others. We have encountered foolish champions of civil and religious liberty whose eyes were opened by Wexford, congregations who were seduced by designing clergymen, enthusiastic youths thrust into positions of leadership by popular clamour and communities forced into armed revolt by an oppressive government. Presbyterian attitudes to the 1798 Rising were shaped in the knowledge that the Rebellion had in practice been a predominantly southern, Catholic affair; the controversy surrounding Musgrave's *Memoirs* consequently turned on the relationship between Catholic Ireland and the British state. Meanwhile, the reaction against Jacobinism, revealed most clearly by the entrance of propertied Presbyterians into the yeomanry from 1796, continued. Constitutional reformism was not completely subsumed by loyalism, as historians have sometimes supposed, but the moderates, helpless in the face of events, found it hard to articulate an independent position. By way of conclusion, however, we should draw our attention to two exceptional cases, where the pervasive silence surrounding Presbyterian politics after 1798 was broken.

The first is Dr William Drennan, the poet and veteran radical, who had been living in Dublin since 1789. During the Union debates of 1799–1800, Drennan produced three remarkable pamphlets protesting against the extinction of Ireland's parliament, which anticipated the full-blown romantic nationalism of the nineteenth century. 'Whether garrisoned as by a pale, partitioned as a lordship, degraded as a province, or cajoled as a kingdom', he wrote, 'the national mind of Ireland has still remained unconquered'.[79] Like other patriots, Drennan questioned whether the College Green parliament, which exercised political power on behalf of the people, had the authority to dispose of that trust. However, he went further than others, arguing that not even the Irish people themselves had the right to barter away their country. Ireland, he wrote, was 'by right divine, entailed to the latest posterity, not to be docked by any fiction of law'.[80] Yet Drennan was unusual in this respect. The concept of the 'nation' during the eighteenth century referred primarily to a community of laws and institutions, rather than an organic entity whose genius had been distilled in its language and customs.[81] Although the distinction becomes rather artificial if pressed too far, the political thought of the United Irishmen is still better described as Enlightenment republicanism than Romantic separatism: it was not an assertion of self-determination grounded upon ethnic or cultural difference, but an assault on *ancien régime* pillars of monarchy, aristocracy and church in the name of a non-sectarian republic.

If the idea of a republic has to be divested of later, nineteenth-century connotations, then so too does the idea of union, or at least the modern understanding of unionism as an alternative to nineteenth-century nationalism. It is now fashionable to view the events of 1798–1801 as the completion of a process of state formation begun under the Tudors, which saw the three kingdoms of England, Scotland and Ireland incorporated into a single polity. Yet it is worth noting that, beyond the adoption of a few pan-British symbols, no attempt was made to assimilate all the inhabitants of the two islands into a single British nation. Indeed, the obvious precedent, the Anglo-Scottish Union of 1707, was founded upon a recognition of Scottish difference – in ecclesiastical establishment, in legal system and education, all of which were distinct from, and in many ways directly opposed to, those of England. In the long run, the United Kingdom did not lead to the triumph of a unitary British identity, but permitted the continuation of more limited regional and national allegiances.

The second exception is William Percy's *Irish salvation* (1800), the only pamphlet published in Belfast on the Union issue. This dialogue between a farmer and a schoolmaster argued that Ireland, as a result of internal divisions and external weakness, could not exist independently, but must be linked to either Great Britain or France. A United Kingdom, as 'Mr. Teachwell' explained, offered the benefits of greater prosperity, as the Scottish example had demonstrated. Yet, the chief aim of the Union, he declared, was to provide a new framework within which Catholic emancipation could be reconciled with Protestant security. He then returned to the perplexing fact that the Irish were 'a mixed divided kind of people' as the result of what he rather delicately described as *'former wars* in barbarous superstitious periods'.[82] For some of the lower orders, for whom the dialogue was intended, this appeal may not have held much weight. As Lord Clare had observed, popular disaffection was ultimately held in check by the British military presence. Yet, this does not provide a full explanation of Presbyterian acquiescence in passing of the Union. Even Drennan, the impassioned defender of legislative independence, spoke in private of 'the old corrupt, incoherent connection which is called by Grattan and Giffard "The Irish Constitution"'. Although many decades would pass before industrialisation, evangelicalism and Catholic resurgence would combine to crystallise a new sense of Britishness, there is little evidence that Ulster Presbyterians mourned the passing of the discredited assembly that we now call 'Grattan's parliament'.

CHAPTER SIX

'Like a Phoenix from its Ashes' United Irish Propaganda and the Act of Union

MANUELA CERETTA

'There is already a living argument in the face of every United Irishman in Ireland. The gloom of the past discomfiture has been exchanged for the smile of anticipated success. You know they are ready to run riot with joy.'[1] With these words Thomas Goold, a friend of Edmund Burke and a former Irish MP who wrote against the Union, commented on the United Irishmen's involvement in the propaganda war that preceded the Act of Union. Goold's testimony was just one of many indications that United Irish propaganda against the Union gave rise to considerable anxiety in official circles. The Dublin Castle under-secretary, Edward Cooke, felt it necessary to attack the views of the Catholic United Irishman William James MacNeven in his pro-union pamphlet.[2] Moreover, on 19 December 1798, the MP and leading Orangeman, John Claudius Beresford, wrote to the chief secretary, Lord Castlereagh, that the Union has given to 'the almost annihilated body of United Irishmen new spirits, and the society is again rising like a phoenix from its ashes'.[3] In particular, Beresford considered the anti-union pamphlet written by Denis Taaffe,[4] a Catholic priest who claimed to have fought in Wexford in 1798 and was clearly sympathetic to the ideals of the United Irishmen, a 'pretty specimen' of the troubles the movement was making.[5]

The reaction to the Act of Union was described by James Bentley Gordon, Anglican clergyman and author of the *History of the Rebellion: Ireland in 1798* (1801), in terms similar to those used by Theobald Wolfe Tone to delineate the impact of the French Revolution in Ireland. Just as Tone noted that the 'French disease' had divided the nation 'into two great parties',[6] Gordon wrote: 'the nation became divided anew into two parties: the unionists and the anti-unionists, in each of which were indiscriminately ranged royalists, croppies, Orangemen and Catholics'.[7] Like the debate on the French Revolution, the question of the legislative Union between Britain and Ireland was both extensively debated and deeply polarising, even at times among those of the same party, sect or movement.

However, the extent of the debate on Union, amounting to about 300 pamphlets, only partially explains why the United Irishmen were so deeply involved in it, despite their recent failed attempt at revolution.[8] Given that the Union was the most momentous constitutional change in Ireland since the Glorious Revolution, it encompassed questions of fundamental importance for the United Irish movement, such as political independence, Catholic emancipation and the problem of the relationship between the autonomy of the Irish parliament and the liberty of the Irish citizens.

I

Even before the foundation of the Society of the United Irishmen the idea of union had been treated as a matter of considerable importance by persons who later became members of the movement. The radical Presbyterian polemicist William Drennan, in a letter dated 1785, claimed that the only true options Ireland had were, in reality, 'a commercial treaty', 'union' or 'disunion', and added: 'I hope in God that a short time will show the expediency, necessity and sublimity of the last choice, without which Ireland will never become a great or a happy people'.[9] In November 1790, Wolfe Tone and the small committee of the College Historical Society set up in Trinity proposed to discuss whether 'a union with England would be of advantage to this country'.[10]

Aside from these early allusions, there are numerous references to a union in the writings of the United Irishmen, both as individuals and as members of the society, long before the intense debates of 1798–1800. In *Idem sentire, dicere, agere*, the anonymous prospectus containing the first idea of founding the United Irishmen, written by Drennan in June 1791, we see among the issues to be confronted by Drennan's 'brotherhood of affection', the question of whether there is 'any middle state between the extremes of union with Britain and total separation, in which the rights of the people can be fully established and rest in security'.[11]

In September 1792, Captain Edward Sweetman, who formally became a United Irishman two months later, linked with typical United Irish rhetoric the Catholic question, the liberty of the people of Ireland and the prospect of union. Speaking on behalf of the electors of the Catholic convention, he put the attainment of civil and political rights for the Catholics and the creation of a nation made of citizens as the only alternative to a country inhabited by slaves and at the mercy of England. He warned Protestants:

> if you refuse that mercy, and withhold this justice, you should prepare for a union: Things cannot remain in their present situation; you must either give freedom to the Catholic or abdicate it for yourselves . . . A union will

be advantageous to the Catholic . . . The Catholic would not be raised to
the Protestant, but the Protestant would be levelled down the Catholic,
and sunk into a slavish acquiescence in the will of a country accustomed to
despise him.[12]

A month later, the Dublin Society of the United Irishmen, in a letter
addressed *To the Friends of the People, at London*, dated 26 October 1792, made
clear that the object of the movement was 'a real representation of the Irish
nation' in parliament, but the letter specified that the parliament in question
was 'an Irish parliament' and in order to eliminate any doubt the Society
wrote: 'As to any union between the islands, believe us when we assert that
our union rests upon our mutual independence. We shall love each other, *if
we be left to ourselves*'.[13]

Repeatedly in 1792, in 1793, and even more after Fitzwilliam's dismissal in
1795, the United Irishmen showed clearly their awareness that Pitt and the
British government had not abandoned the project of union, heralded by the
introduction of the commercial propositions in the mid-1780s.[14] The measure
with which the 'country will be lost indeed'[15] was prophesied in March 1793
by Drennan, who in March 1795 let his brother-in-law know that 'the report
of this day is that Catholic emancipation is to be the price of an union'.[16] On
4 May 1795, during the discussion of the Catholic bill introduced by Grattan,
the future United Irishman Arthur O'Connor addressed the House of
Commons with the following words: 'you who shall vote on this night for the
rejection of this bill will appear in the eyes of the Irish nation, not only as a
man voting in obedience to the British ministers, against the voice of the
people, but as a man voting for an UNION WITH ENGLAND.'[17] In 1796, the
United Irish propagandist William Sampson asked in his *Advice to the rich*: 'Do
you think you are not driving on to a UNION with England, and that upon a
footing which will make you poor indeed?'[18]

The United Irishmen were not only aware of the prospect of the Union, but
were also quite apprehensive about the means which a British government
would use to obtain it. Aware that in time of war security considerations could
be used to justify almost anything, they suspected that the British government was deliberately attempting to provoke a crisis in Ireland to prepare
the way for a union. In fact the possibility of revolution in Ireland seems to
have convinced Edmund Burke, formerly an opponent of union, that even
this 'bold experimental remedy' might be 'justified, perhaps called for, in
some nearly desperate crisis of the whole empire.'[19] Drennan, for example,
was adamant that union would sooner or later be presented as a necessary
measure to prevent republican revolution. In September 1796, he claimed
that the fear of an invasion 'will be an excellent pretext for putting the
country into a sort of barracks and garrisoning it with Englishmen,

preparatory, perhaps, to a forced union'.[20] Drennan believed that this crisis would be the pretext with which Pitt would attempt to carry the Union, and he evaluated in this light the repressive measures against the United Irishmen begun in 1793. Sampson considered the dismissal of Fitzwilliam and 'the subsequent treatment and provocation' as evidence of the government's intentions and later recalled that with the *Advice to the rich* he 'endeavoured to show, that the government were stimulating the nation to rebellion for that end [Union].'[21]

In the opinion of the United Irishmen, repression, revolution and union were the steps that the government was trying to make to obtain, in Drennan's words, a 'forced marriage' and would have the effect 'of turning fornication into adultery'.[22] His views were echoed by Arthur O'Connor, who described the Union as a measure that would 'everlastingly reduce' the country 'to the state of an abject province'. Sampson summed it up as a 'COLONIAL UNION' useful to cement 'a despotism . . . by means of a strange soldiery and standing army';[23] while MacNeven claimed that under the Union the Irish would have been governed 'as a conquered people, deprived of the power to change the system of legislation according to the times and needs'.[24]

II

Despite this early awareness of the project of union, it was only in the final years of the century that members of the United Irish movement began systematically to debate the Union, in pamphlets and anonymous handbills that can be attributed to them with a certain degree of confidence. Apart from the exception of Samuel Neilson, who wrote from the prison of Fort George in Scotland in June 1799, that

> I see a union is determined on between Great Britain and Ireland. I am glad of it. In a commercial point of view, it cannot be injurious; and I can see no injury the country will sustain from it politically . . . If I had possessed the means, I would have published my sentiments on this subject in a short nervous pamphlet; so deeply I am impressed by its national utility,[25]

the United Irishmen declared themselves against the Union, sometimes repeating or clarifying ideas already expressed, sometimes expounding new arguments. What stimulated and broadened their reflections, without changing their fundamental features, were the main arguments used in favour of the Union, in particular, the claims made by Pitt, called the 'British Machiavel'[26] by Taaffe, and the thesis advanced by Edward Cooke in his pro-union pamphlet, which in MacNeven's opinion showed 'ignorance and insolence at every line'.[27]

From an examination of the arguments employed in the pro-union pamphlets, it is easy to recognise some very old topics, but there are also new ones that appear to have been written purposely to cope with United Irish propaganda of the 1790s. Among the old arguments used by Pitt, in his speech of 31 January 1799, was that of presenting the Union as an easy task to accomplish: 'England speaks the same language and her laws, customs and tradition are the same as Ireland, but carried to a greater degree of perfection'.[28] Not only did Pitt display an air of superiority that the United Irishmen cannot have appreciated, but he used exactly the same words in favour of the Union that almost one century before were adopted by the republican thinker Henry Maxwell. In 1703, in fact, Maxwell declared that the 'happy wedding'[29] of the two parliaments would have been easy to create, because the language, the tradition and the laws of the two countries were identical.[30] As Maxwell had done at the beginning of the century, Pitt chose to ignore the fact the language and the traditions of the two countries were not identical. He did not take into public consideration the plurality of which the people of Ireland was made, echoing the Orangeman who wrote in 1799 of 'the Protestant as the nation'.[31]

In briefly mentioning another old Protestant commonplace – the role of 'divine providence' in saving the country – Pitt turned to something that for centuries had been considered a pro-union argument: the desirability of having a Catholic minority in the realm.[32] This was a thesis that he had defended more forcefully some years previously in a letter where he described the Union as a guarantee for the 'Protestant interest' because it would create a Protestant majority in parliament and a Catholic minority in the empire.[33] A similar sectarian arithmetic was also used by Edward Cooke in his famous pamphlet in 1798, when he noted that the proportion of Catholics to Protestants under the Union would change to 3 to 14,[34] and by the loyalist propagandist Sir Richard Musgrave, who noted that 'In a menacing tone, the papists have told us for some years "we are 3 to 1". With the Union, we may retort "we are 11 to 3"'.[35]

In engaging with the United Irishmen, who made their appeal to the nation, Pitt's rhetorical strategy was to appeal to the empire. On behalf of the empire, Pitt wrote that 'a mistaken sense of national pride is so likely to operate in judging the Union.'[36] Instead of persisting in seeking an independence that Ireland would be unable to maintain it had to be acknowledged that union 'tends to the general prosperity of the empire', 'will benefit every member of the empire', is 'calculated to produce mutual advantages to the two kingdoms', and will give to Ireland 'its due weight and importance as a great member of the empire'.[37]

Cooke used the same argument, affirming that in evaluating the measure people should not reason in 'terms of national dignity and national pride.'[38]

The word 'nation', that in Thomas Goold's opinion had an almost 'magic force' in the hands of the United Irishmen, had become a dynamic political weapon.[39] In the past, the word nation had been an instrument for broadening or underlining already existing divisions in Irish society. First, it was used in its political meaning and attributed only to Protestants, and second it was used in its plural form to describe the anomalous situation of Ireland. The United Irishmen gave a new meaning to an old word, convinced as they were that the word nation could be declined only in its singular form. Founding the concept of nation on individual rights and public interest they took possession of it and of other related political ideals such as popular sovereignty, liberty and political participation. From Pitt's point of view, America and France had already proved that the ideal of the nation was a dangerous weapon, and for this reason it had to be destroyed by recourse to the concept of the empire.

However, the logic of the empire brought with it a cultural dimension, as illustrated by Pitt's quotation given above which spoke of England's laws, customs and traditions being 'carried to a greater degree of perfection' in their country of origin.[40] To be part of the empire meant to be blessed by British civilisation and, through proper conduct, this was a blessing to which the Irish could aspire. Pitt, for example, noted that Irishmen 'deserved' the name of 'Britons' for the part they played in the suppression of the 1798 Rebellion.[41] Edward Cooke went a step further, arguing that the time had come for the Irishmen to acknowledge reality and to proclaim 'our defects in civilisation and policy'.[42] With an imaginative metaphor, Cooke supported his idea of the Union as a civilising mission saying:

> if any person has a son uneducated, unimproved and injured by bad habits and bad company, in order to remedy these imperfections, would it not be his first endeavours to establish him in the best societies and introduce him into the most virtuous, the most polished and the most learned company? . . . What can any sanguine Irish patriot wish for his country, but that its inhabitants should attain the same habits, manners and improvement which made England the envy of Europe?[43]

Like Pitt, Cooke referred to a key topic of traditional Protestant rhetoric, that the Catholics offered allegiance to a foreign king, but, unlike Pitt, he supported this claim with an appeal to the powerful lesson of history.[44] The cultural and political inferiority of Ireland was, he claimed, the product of its 'disgraced' history, made of conflicts, massacres and divisions within Irish society that nobody, not even those bathed in Enlightenment optimism such as the United Irishmen, could deny. To these arguments, dominated by the logic of the empire, by the necessity of a Catholic minority, by the exigency of protecting the Protestant interest and the need to preserve 'the Protestant religion and establishment as a fundamental article', the United Irishmen responded vigorously, claiming to uncover a false or perverse thesis advocated by the supporters of union.[45]

III

First, the United Irishmen argued that the empire was simply a mask under which England concealed her interests and claimed that union with Britain would have 'annihilated Ireland for the good of the empire'.[46] Several years previously, in *Idem sentire, dicere, agere*, Drennan had excluded from the right of membership of the brotherhood of affection 'those that are bound down by obedience to that wizard word *empire*, to the sovereignty of two sounding syllables'.[47] At the beginning of the 1790s, Tone wrote: '*the good of the empire*! Let us substitute "England" for "the empire" and see if it be not nearer the fact and truth'.[48] In MacNeven's opinion, 'the disastrous but instructive consequences of the subjection to a foreign power' should clarify to the Irishmen 'the measure of their duties toward Great Britain.'[49]

In the place of empire the United Irishmen looked to a world composed of nations. For the United Irishmen, a nation had a political dimension; it was the product of a shared civil and political condition and was capable therefore of encompassing all Irishmen whatever their religion, culture and language. Applying the categories of political contractualism not only inside political society but also outside, they claimed that the so-called empire was just an 'English necessity' that should be replaced by sovereign nations and by a 'law of the nations'[50] to protect the weakest ones. Such contractualist theories served to deny any claims against Irish independence grounded on precedent. Dispensing with this precedent, the United Irishmen argued that 'every connection between free and independent nations should be of its own nature a voluntary act; and . . . connections that are not voluntary, are chains';[51] they added that 'the connection between nation and nation is cemented and strengthened by its being placed on the basis of justice and reciprocal benefit. It is a bond founded on interest; and when that is violated, all bond of connection is broken.'[52]

Second, there were also those who dispensed both with the logic of empire and of nation and treated the Union in terms of sectional interest. As the Catholic archbishop of Dublin, John Troy, reported after a meeting of influential Catholics on 24 December 1798, 'the general opinion . . . was that the Catholics as such ought not to deliberate on the Union as a question of empire but only as it might affect their peculiar interest as a body'.[53] The dangers of such a sectional approach were highlighted by William James MacNeven who warned Catholics 'not to exchange the liberty of Ireland for the Catholic liberty'.[54]

As the United Irishmen did not consider Catholic emancipation as a 'Catholic grievance but the grievance of the nation',[55] so they regarded liberty not as a Protestant, Catholic or Presbyterian concern but as a national concern. The problem for them was to create, obtain and maintain a 'national freedom'[56] in debates with those who defended the idea that liberty had religious distinctions. This commonly-held view was made clear by the earl of Clare, the lord chancellor, who in a speech on the Union to the House of Commons claimed that every attempt to weaken the connection between the two countries was a threat to 'Protestant liberty'. Clare warned Protestant MPs that:

> the only security for your liberty is your connection with Great Britain, and gentlemen who risk breaking the connection must make up their minds to a union. God forbid I should ever see that day; but if ever the day on which separation shall be attempted may come, I shall not hesitate to embrace a union rather than a separation.[57]

Third, the United Irishmen, in attacking the very idea of British civilisation, broadened the range of their propaganda to encompass cultural factors. In the pamphlets written in response to Cooke and the Union there are some of the few charges levelled by the movement against the destruction of the Irish language, the abuse of the cultural differences and Anglocentrism. Commenting on the effects of colonisation on Irish culture, Denis Taaffe had the Anglo-Irish John Paddy ask England:

> Have we not faithfully and assiduously co-operated with you in devising such laws as might reduce them to a state of poverty, barbarity and ignorance . . .? Could you contrive more effectually to accomplish this, than by the suppression of printing and instruction in the national language? Well knowing that before a whole people can master a strange idiom, and renounce their vernacular tongue, many generations must pass away.[58]

This manoeuvre was again presented as operating under the guise of a civilising mission. Taaffe accused England and her ally, the Protestant ascendancy, of undermining the cultural identity of Ireland, but he also reflected on their abuse of religious and cultural differences. He made clear that the supposed superiority of the Protestant religion and of the English language was a matter of convenience: 'black men, and white men, and red men will answer the purposes of the old tyrannical policy, *divide et impera*, as well as religion'.[59] For the same reason Taaffe, ignoring or pretending to ignore the part played by Protestantism in forging British identity, asked: 'what then has entitled Protestants to the disgraced partiality of British policy, and qualified them to be the undoers of the land of their birth?'. His answer was: 'the single circumstance of being the minority'.[60] Equally, Drennan, in his *Letter* on the Union addressed to Pitt, criticised the Anglo-centrism of Irish society, though without proposing to substitute it with a Hiberno-centrism. He invited his country men 'instead of looking at the world through Britain, to look at Britain through the world'.[61]

In arguing against the shrewd appeal to the past made by Cooke and against the politics of fear that had served governments so well throughout the eighteenth century, the United Irishmen drew attention to the *divide et impera* strategy. They noted that – not surprisingly – this strategy was at work in the propaganda in favour of the Union, where it was inconsistently presented as a benefit for every sect of the society and as a benefit incompatible with the well-being of the other sects.[62] But apart from that, they made clear that the massacres evoked by Cooke were not the product of an 'unnatural union' among incompatible persons but were the fruit of the *divide et impera* strategy. Carrying on a theme previously addressed in the early 1790s, they did not try to forget the past but attempted to interpret it differently, putting forward new explanations to those facts that they could not deny. They asserted that 'nations as persons are the product of education'.[63] This enlightened opinion could have paved the way to a different future but it also could have formed a solid barrier to make it different from the past. The United Irishmen were convinced that even if hate was a 'stranger to the country it had infected', as MacNeven wrote, it could be instilled.[64]

If in the past, religion was called down 'from heaven to sow discord on earth',[65] iin the present, it was the alliance between the ascendancy and Orangemen that continued to have the same perverse effect. Convinced of the existence of collusion between government and Orangemen, the United Irishmen were acutely aware of the disastrous consequences it could have on Irish society;[66] but they were not prepared to accept union as a remedy for neutralizing both the ascendancy and Orangeism, notwithstanding the authoritative opinion of an impartial observer of the Irish situation, William Ogilvie. The Scottish thinker was in fact convinced that the very existence of the Orangeism was a reason in favour of the Union. To counter the claims of Orangemen (whom he termed 'state criminals') who opposed the Union because they were convinced they had 'an *exclusive right* to public professions and salaries', Ogilvie maintained that a fusion of the British and Irish parliaments was the best way to destroy the privileges claimed by the Orangemen, arguing that only under a legislative union would it be possible to concede emancipation to Catholics without putting the ascendancy in danger.[67]

For their part, instead of the Union of the Irish and British parliaments, the United Irishmen put forward the concept of union among Irishmen and exhorted their countrymen: 'hope not from any union but *your own*' and 'embrace as a friend, and a brother, every man of any sect or party (whatever his past errors) who shall take arms in his country's cause, and make *her* [Ireland's] *interest his religion*'.[68]

In United Irish opinion, hate could be injected through historiography and social practice. Historiography never let Irishmen forget the memories of the past and it never seriously tried, in the opinion of the United Irishmen, to establish the true motivations of the conflicts that had 'disgraced' Irish history.[69] Social practice also played its part in broadening the divisions of Irish society. Drennan wrote in 1795:

> our eyes and ears by custom grow callous to what our heads and hearts condemn. The remembrance of civil war is still perpetuated from year to year, by the puerility of a flower or a ribbon; and we see hatred, and unforgiveness, commemorated and sanctioned, with the parade of a procession, or what in this case, may be called the savage sociality of a public dinner.[70]

In a similar vein, the United Irishman Thomas Russell observed that 'there was no national spirit in Ireland – on the contrary the anniversary of those events which led to degradation of were celebrated, strange as it may appear, by Irishmen with martial pomp and festivity'.[71]

Despite the evidence that the people were not inclined to forget or reassess the past – as shown by the Armagh outrages and the growing number of increasingly triumphalist Orange parades from 1796 onwards – the United Irishmen were not prepared to accept union even as a remedy for the divisions of the society. Such an opinion had been put forward in 1776 by the impartial voice of Adam Smith who wrote in the *Wealth of Nations*, that 'without a union with Great Britain, the inhabitants of Ireland are not likely for many ages to consider themselves as one people'.[72] In contrast, the United Irishmen argued that the only way to destroy those 'brazen walls of separation' that prevented the 'separate nations' of Ireland from 'mingling' and kept them 'convened' as an 'incoherent mass of dissimilar materials, uncemented, unconsolidated like the image of Nebuchadnezar'[73] was the union of the people of Ireland under the common name of Irishmen, as the words written by an anonymous United Irish propagandist show:

> Now my countrymen, let me exhort you to persevere in forwarding that UNION on which depends your eternal welfare, and which all the powers of hell with which your enemies are invested, shall never be able to dissolve. On your UNION depends your victory over tyranny and oppression; – In your UNION lies all strength, importance and foundation of your future happiness. Then let the UNION be always uppermost in your thought; let all animosity between parties or individual cease; forgive trifling injuries, and heart and hand become ONE PEOPLE.[74]

IV

The content and the exhorting tone of the writings of the United Irishmen are quite indicative: *a* people had still to become a reality and they still needed to be convinced to make the effort to constitute themselves as a nation. The events of the second half of the 1790s did not cause the United Irishmen to change their mind, but they did dampen their optimism and deeply damaged their faith in their countrymen. Despite the 'loaves and fishes'[75] distribution and the political manoeuvres employed by the government to secure support, the movement was convinced that the Irish people must accept a large part of the responsibility for the passage of the Act of Union. As Drennan wrote, in his last public letter on the Union, a letter that he considered his 'political will and testament',[76] it was not the 'British Machiavel', nor the perverse principles of the ascendancy nor the Orangemen who were solely responsible for the Union. The Irish people themselves with their old prejudices and fears were to blame for it, because they were 'not yet been able to become members of the same body, having the same friends and the same foes.'[77]

These words reflected the disillusionment of the leadership of the United Irishmen who looked on in despair as the Union was opposed only by small, self-interested groups, and the majority of Irish people meekly acquiesced in its passing. Such an outcome underlined the failure of United Irish propaganda against the Union and, more generally, the failure of the United Irish nation-building project as a whole.[78]

CHAPTER SEVEN

Dublin Castle and the Act of Union

JAMES QUINN

The Dublin Castle administration, which was charged with passing the Act of Union, was a small-scale bureaucracy, dominated by a handful of crucial personalities. Among the most important of these were the lord chancellor, the earl of Clare, who piloted the measure successfully through the House of Lords, and who as lord chancellor kept the opposition of the Dublin bar within bounds.[1] His anti-Catholicism was an important factor in shaping the eventual settlement, and did much to convince conservative Protestants that union was not a conspiracy by papist sympathisers to subvert the Protestant ascendancy. Clare's efforts were complemented by those of Edward Cooke, the hard-working and efficient Castle under-secretary. Cooke was well-schooled in the nuts and bolts of parliamentary management, and his efforts in building up a government majority in the Commons and as a pro-union propagandist were of the utmost importance in passing the measure. But, ultimately, the main burden of accomplishing the Union fell upon the two highest-placed officials in Dublin Castle – the lord lieutenant, Charles Marquess Cornwallis, and the chief secretary, Robert Stewart, Viscount Castlereagh – and it is their roles that are treated in detail here.

I

In some ways, Cornwallis and Castlereagh were an unlikely pairing. Cornwallis was fifty-years-old and a military and administrative veteran when appointed viceroy of Ireland in June 1798; he had already refused the position a year previously and, on this occasion, he took it with great reluctance. At twenty-nine, Castlereagh was a relative political novice, and was not Cornwallis's first choice as chief secretary. But, as events unfolded, the two worked well together and developed a lasting respect for each other. They had many qualities in common: both were dedicated and disinterested public servants, committed to imperial ideals. They shared a horror of violent revolution and sought a solution that would bring peace to Ireland and security to the empire. Both were also reserved men – Castlereagh, in particular, struck many as cold and aloof – and had little time for the flattery and blandishment that was often required to woo the Anglo-Irish gentry. John Beresford, for example, an experienced and wily political observer, thought them both ill-suited for a task in which personal persuasion would play such an important role.[2]

But, whatever Beresford may have thought of him, Cornwallis had the confidence of the prime minister, William Pitt. His successful period as viceroy of India, where he led British armies to victories in the Mysore wars and reformed the British administration, marked him out as a statesman who combined military skill with administrative acumen. Therefore, when the outbreak of rebellion in May 1798 provoked a major crisis in Ireland, Pitt, already preoccupied with fighting a war on several fronts against France that was not going well for Britain, sought to secure his troublesome western flank once and for all. Having finally lost patience with the Irish administration, he saw Cornwallis as the man to restore order in Ireland and accomplish what he believed to be the only solution to the problem of Anglo-Irish relations – the legislative union of the two kingdoms.

Cornwallis arrived in Ireland on 21 June 1798. Before any great schemes of constitutional reform could be undertaken, the country had to be pacified. The back of the Rebellion had been broken at Vinegar Hill on the day before his arrival, but the difficult task of mopping-up pockets of rebel resistance remained. Realising that there was no point in driving rebels to complete desperation and encouraging last ditch resistance, Cornwallis decided on a policy of firmness and lenity to restore order. He concluded an agreement with the imprisoned United Irish leaders, agreeing to spare the lives of those sentenced to death in return for general information about their conspiracy and the exile of the entire leadership. The rank-and-file who remained in the field were offered a pardon if they surrendered their arms and the indiscriminate reprisals being carried out by the military were halted. Crown forces were brought under proper military discipline, and courts martial were properly constituted and their proceedings recorded and forwarded to the lord lieutenant.[3]

To Irish loyalists, whose blood was up after the events of the past months, such a policy was akin to capitulation to the rebels and they were quick to denounce the new viceroy as 'Cropwallis', a weak English liberal, whose ignorance of Ireland and sympathy for papists and rebels risked the hard-won victory of recent months.[4] Cornwallis, for his part, was astounded by the ferocity and bigotry of Irish loyalists and believed that, if given their head, they would drive much of the country into rebellion and make his task of pacification impossible.[5]

Cornwallis arrived in Ireland with instructions from Pitt to conclude a legislative union, but he was slow to raise the question, not wishing to offend local sensibilities by precipitate action.[6] However, the French invasion of August and September highlighted Ireland's vulnerability and gave additional impetus to the government's desire to settle the Anglo-Irish question. By mid-September, Cornwallis began to consider how Ireland could be made an asset to Great Britain rather than a 'useless and almost intolerable burthen'.[7] He believed that Irish Protestants had been so shaken by recent events that they would readily consent to a union.[8] But, before the government publicly broached the issue, rumours of its intentions leaked out and created considerable concern among groups such as borough proprietors, members of the Irish bar and the Dublin populace generally who saw their interests as being endangered. The fact that the debate had begun without the government having published its plans for union allowed the anti-union side to exploit the fears and uncertainties of those who would be most affected. In particular, many men of property were worried that no detailed plans for compensation had been spelled out. Moreover, since the bar generally opposed the measure, the anti-union side could call on skilled polemicists such as Charles Kendal Bushe, William Conyngham Plunket and John Philpot Curran, and anti-union newspapers and pamphlets dominated the propaganda war in the latter months of 1798.[9]

The Castle attempted to recover the initiative with pamphlets such as Edward Cooke's, *Arguments for and against an union*, published in December 1798, and approached the opening of parliament in the new year with reasonable confidence.[10] However, such confidence was soon shown to be misplaced and, on 23 January, the Commons voted by a narrow majority to remove a paragraph advocating union from an address to the lord lieutenant. It was the opposition's finest hour. They had taken the fight to the Castle and stymied their plans to bring forward a union in that parliamentary session. For the Castle, it was a sobering setback and showed the extent to which they had underestimated the magnitude of the task facing them. Cornwallis, in particular, bore the brunt of the blame for this defeat and was heavily criticised by several leading members of his own administration, including pro-unionists such as Clare, Beresford and Cooke. Cooke was particularly scathing: 'Lord Cornwallis is nobody – worse than nobody . . . his silly conduct, his total incapacity, and self-conceit and mulishness have alone lost the question'.[11] The ultra-Protestant MP and lawyer, Patrick Duigenan, claimed that Cornwallis had become 'not only an object of disgust, but of abhorrence' to Irish loyalists. He was accused of ignoring the concerns of the Irish gentry and of gratuitously offending powerful figures such as John Foster and Lord Enniskillen. The agreement he had negotiated that spared the lives of the United Irish leaders and his attempts to restrain loyalist zeal in suppressing the embers of rebellion were also cited as important factors in discouraging the country gentlemen and alienating them from his administration.[12]

The question of the Castle's security policy was a crucial one: constitutional change does not occur in a vacuum and attempting to carry a union in a seriously disturbed environment would have been doubly difficult. In such circumstances, the government would have faced charges from the opposition that they sought to exploit the fear and panic caused by the Rebellion and even the practical matter of getting landlords to leave their estates to attend parliament would have been difficult.[13] In his early months in office, therefore, Cornwallis's energies were directed primarily at calming the country rather than promoting union, to such an extent that even Castlereagh criticised him for devoting more time to military than civil matters.[14]

In his early months, Cornwallis was primarily concerned with mopping up the Rebellion, checking military excesses and preventing a campaign of indiscriminate coercion that would have only prolonged rebel resistance. Though some loyalists could see nothing but leniency in his actions, Cornwallis was adamant that his was a judicious policy that applied leniency or firmness as the circumstances demanded. His reply to some of his critics in London, who criticised him for sparing the lives of United Irish leaders, was that, if he had sufficient evidence, he would have gone ahead and hanged them all, but he realised that without such evidence most would probably escape punishment. Since the agreement offered the Castle a convenient means of getting rid of a large number of troublesome agitators, who otherwise would have been detained indefinitely without charge, Cornwallis believed that he had secured a good deal for the government. This was a view shared by Cooke and Clare, who were the shrewdest hard-liners in the Dublin administration.[15]

Similarly, it was pointed out to Cornwallis's critics in the Commons that when severity was called for, he did not flinch from exercising it: between September 1798 and February 1799, 380 rebels were tried by martial law, of whom 131 were capitally convicted and ninety hanged. His response to pleas for clemency for Theobald Wolfe Tone was to strike out the additional punishment of beheading after hanging, but the hanging itself was to go ahead.[16]

Cornwallis was lenient only in comparison with the croppy-hunting, shooting and flogging elements of the ascendancy that took such relish in the white terror that followed the Rebellion. He was essentially a humane and prudent man, at a time when such qualities were in short supply. Moreover, orderly military habits were in his blood: he believed that an army without discipline was merely a rabble and the uncontrolled and indiscriminate nature of the counter-insurgency campaign he encountered in Ireland horrified him. In seeking to bring order and humanity to suppressing the Rebellion, Cornwallis had considerable support, even if those who advocated more extreme measures generally made more noise. Most level-headed observers recognised that his policy of firmness and leniency contributed to the pacification of the country at a considerably smaller cost than a campaign of outright coercion. For example, the duke of Leinster, a committed anti-unionist, noted that Cornwallis's 'humane conduct here merits the applause of every honest, independent man'.[17] But, fairly or not, Cornwallis was saddled with a reputation for excessive leniency towards rebels and sympathy towards Catholics – rumours abounded that he had taken a Catholic mistress – and some observers believed that he had so compromised himself in the eyes of Irish Protestants that they would oppose whatever policy he put forward.[18] The marquess of Buckingham claimed that 'there does not exist one grain of confidence in the talents of Lord Cornwallis, who has thrown away the greatest game that ever was put into the hands of man'.[19]

Much of this criticism of Cornwallis was predictable. The Irish cabinet was used to dominating viceroys and the power they had exercised for the previous decade had induced considerable arrogance. Men such as Foster and Beresford believed they were indispensable to the running of the administration and, when it was clear that Cornwallis had decided to disregard them, the sudden loss of their power and influence came as a shock. They had, after all, seen off important figures such as Fitzwilliam and Abercromby, and they regarded Cornwallis as just another well-intentioned meddler. But, in this case, they underestimated both Cornwallis's character and the level of support he had in Whitehall and, when they found that he was here to stay, their criticism contained much of the pique of disappointed men.[20] Even Buckingham, himself a critic of Cornwallis, noted 'every one loud against Lord Cornwallis, some with reason but most without any'.[21]

For his part, Cornwallis soon recognised that he could only avoid such criticism by subordinating himself to the Castle cabinet and persisting with coercive and anti-Catholic policies. He was not willing to do this, not least because he believed their influence was founded on corruption and that they were 'detested by everybody but their immediate followers'.[22] In general, he found the business of dealing with Irish politicians – with their insatiable demand for patronage and their dextrous ability to change their minds – thoroughly dispiriting and he made little effort to disguise his contempt for their selfishness and duplicity, complaining regularly of his situation.[23]

II

Both Cornwallis and Castlereagh have been justly criticised for their complacency in the months leading up to the defeat of January 1799.[24] Castlereagh, whose responsibility it was to build up and keep together the government majority in the House of Commons, betrayed his inexperience at parliamentary management and badly miscalculated the level of the government's support. He was also a mediocre parliamentary speaker whose speeches were unlikely to inspire his supporters or convert his opponents. He also appears to have miscalculated the mood of the House, stressing Irish dependence on Great Britain to an extent that showed little regard for the pride of the assembly he was addressing.[25] The Castle also erred in failing to define the detail for the proposals of the Union – a state of affairs that allowed the speculations of anti-unionists to thrive. Not surprisingly, Irish country gentlemen were cautious about voting for a union when they were uncertain about how such a measure would affect them. Borough owners notably were particularly concerned at the prospect of surrendering their property without adequate compensation.

Castlereagh put the defeat down to the carelessness of some government supporters in encouraging their members to attend and the ferocity of the opposition of many country gentlemen. But he was confident that such opposition was founded more on self-interest than principle and that anti-unionists could be turned.[26] He quickly identified the amendments that the government would have to make to their original proposals. The initial intention had been to select one member from each of the thirty-two counties and the eighteen largest towns, with the remaining fifty members being chosen from boroughs, in order to keep the abolition of boroughs to a minimum. But Castlereagh belatedly realised that such proposals were extremely unpalatable to the powerful county interests – who carried a weight far beyond the sixty-four seats they actually represented – since reducing the county representation to one seat would diminish their influence and involve them regularly in expensive electoral contests. However, if the plan was amended so that the counties continued to return two members, the value of these seats would be enhanced and county members would be more likely to fall in behind the government. He also concluded that borough proprietors could not be expected to vote away their interests without being suitably compensated and that some compensation for property owners in Dublin might assist the measure.[27]

The defeat of January 1799 dispelled the complacency that had gripped the Castle, and only now did it take seriously the advice that Edward Cooke had given some months earlier – that the Union ' must be written up, spoken up, intrigued up, drunk up, sung up and bribed up'.[28] Imbued with a real sense of purpose, it set about constructing a majority, adopting a new ruthlessness in dealing with anti-unionists and nakedly using its power over patronage as the lever with which to carry the measure. Prominent officials who had not supported the Union were dismissed and fence-sitters were warned that neutrality would no longer be tolerated. The two most prominent victims of the purge were John Parnell, the chancellor of the exchequer, and James Fitzgerald, the prime sergeant.[29] It was made clear that the primary qualification for continuing to hold office was support for the Union and that this policy had the full support of the British government.[30]

Cornwallis drew the lesson from the defeat in the Commons that it was impossible to pass a measure which was opposed by such strongly entrenched private interests and for which so little public support had been expressed.[31] Even in a legislature as undemocratic as the Irish parliament, such an important measure could not be carried in the face of overwhelming out-of-doors opposition. Since the opposition had won the battle for public opinion in the months before January 1799, the government set about mobilising popular support to give the impression that the Union was not being carried against the will of the country. Pro-union publications were systematically and widely circulated and declarations and petitions were sought to convey an impression of grassroots support to embarrass county MPs who had voted against the Union.[32] As part of this campaign, Cornwallis undertook tours, to the south in July and August and the north in October, to gauge the public mood and enlist public support. He declared himself highly satisfied with his reception.[33]

In the end, the battle for public opinion was undecided: each side pointed to its own petitions as being the most genuine, claiming that those of their opponents had been secured by bribery and intimidation. John Foster, for example, poured scorn on Cornwallis's lack of success in obtaining addresses from open constituencies on his progress through Ireland and insisted that 'the real sense of the kingdom is against the measure'.[34] For its part, the Castle claimed that, whatever about the numbers for or against the Union, the property of the country was solidly pro-union. More recently G.C. Bolton estimated that 'a minority of articulate public opinion favoured the Union, a rather larger group, perhaps half as many again, opposed the measure, and the rest were apathetic'.[35]

Whatever the precise state of affairs, the Castle did not have to win the battle for public opinion. It did not need, and never seriously sought, a democratic endorsement of the Union. All it needed was a sufficient level of public support to neutralise anti-unionist, out-of-doors protests and make the popular attitude towards union an open question. It could then concentrate on winning over those particular interests which would help to give it a parliamentary majority, a far easier task than attempting to persuade the nation as a whole. Good general that he was, Cornwallis saw no need for a mass assault on the enemy front-line when he could concentrate his forces on their weak points.

The Castle generally showed considerable nervousness about popular opposition, never trusting, for example, to dissolve parliament and call a general election on the question of the Union: Cornwallis noted that government could gain no advantage from such a step.[36] It was enough to have union voted through parliament and to draw the sting of public protest by pointing to its own level of public support. The Castle had no desire to risk the political ferment that a widespread debate might produce. Cornwallis's tours were more an attempt to reassure the faithful than to produce converts – he deliberately avoided areas of staunch anti-unionism – and he even instructed government supporters to obtain pro-union declarations without convening public meetings.[37] The more confined the debate the more easily the whole business would be managed and it is significant that the Castle generally looked benignly on public apathy towards the Union in the country at large.[38]

One of the groups it did concentrate its attentions on was the Catholic population. Cornwallis's initial intention was to couple union with Catholic emancipation, in the belief that if the government should 'make a union with the Irish nation, instead of making it with a party in Ireland' it would settle the entire Irish question once and for all.[39] However, he was aware that it would be opposed by important figures such as Lord Clare and that such disagreement could fatally split the pro-union camp and endanger the entire measure.[40] Clare visited London in November 1798 to argue against linking emancipation and union and received assurances, apparently from Pitt, that this would not happen. Faced with this difficulty, Cornwallis decided to proceed cautiously, as the Fitzwilliam debacle had shown the danger of raising Catholic hopes only to dash them. He reluctantly came to the opinion that union and emancipation should not go together but he insisted that the legislation should not contain any clauses that would prevent Catholic relief in the future.[41] Leading Catholic nobles such as Fingal and Kenmare and the archbishop of Dublin, Dr John Thomas Troy, were prepared to give their tacit support to union on this basis.[42] Tacit support from the Catholics was what the Castle really wanted, as overt Catholic enthusiasm for the Union would have aroused Protestant suspicions and increased opposition from that quarter.[43]

Yet, Cornwallis persisted in his belief that a final settlement of the Catholic question should follow union and indicated his support for emancipation to his Catholic contacts. Without making any specific promises, he left them with an impression that their claims would be dealt with sympathetically in the near future. Also, throughout these negotiations he treated the Catholics with great courtesy, something they had received precious little of from Dublin Castle in the past decade. He was a man that Catholics leaders felt they could trust and his sympathetic and courteous attitude in winning Catholic goodwill for the Union was, in the end, to be an important factor in its passing.

Although concerned about civilian public opinion, the Castle was rather more worried about the part that a militarised public opinion might play. Even at the end of the century, the shadow of the Volunteers loomed large.

The bloodless and moderate revolution they had helped to accomplish in 1782 stood in stark contrast to the savage violence and extremism of 1798. Many Irish Protestants looked back with nostalgia to the part played by the Volunteers in winning legislative independence and Cornwallis had reason to be fearful that the 60,000 strong yeomanry might attempt to represent themselves as the heirs to the volunteering tradition and the defenders of the independence won in 1782. From his earliest days in Ireland, Cornwallis regarded the yeomanry with trepidation. They reminded him of the loyalists of America, whom he recalled with horror; worse, he thought the Irish yeomen 'much more numerous and powerful, and a thousand times more ferocious'.[44] Ominous noises emanated from many yeomanry corps who believed themselves to be largely responsible for defeating the Rebellion in 1798, and who considered that the abolition of the Irish parliament was a poor reward for their efforts. Some spoke of laying down their arms and others of resisting the government by force.[45] For this reason, Cornwallis responded with firmness to the marquess of Downshire's attempts to harness the support of the Down militia against the Union, fearing that if it set a precedent whereby anti-union aristocrats were allowed to mobilise the support of military formations under their influence, the Castle's work in neutralising public opinion would have all been for nothing. The sanctions taken against Downshire were severe; he was dismissed from his regiment and from the governorship of the county, and removed from the office of registrar in the court of chancery and from the privy council. This put paid to any ideas that other magnates might have had of enlisting military support, and prevented any kind of rerun of 1782. Cornwallis considered this a decisive moment, claiming that 'by this act of vigour I have saved the country and carried the Union'.[46]

After the defeat of January 1799, the government took the prudent decision not to broach the question of union for the remainder of the parliamentary session.[47] Instead, it concentrated its efforts outside parliament, in order to pave the way for a successful vote in a subsequent session. Leading interests were appeased and anti-union officials dismissed and the message went out that the only route to advancement was through support for the Union. In effect, it followed the course of action outlined by John Beresford: 'proceed with caution and coolness, and you will carry your point . . . . Leave the business of an union, now impressed on the minds of the people, to work as it may, and when it is brought forward, it will be so with more advantage'.[48] Moreover, the government avoided introducing contentious legislation in the hope of preventing the formation of a solid opposition. It postponed some important but controversial measures such as the introduction of an income tax and legislation to enlist Irish militiamen into regiments of the line. Even a plan to station a number of Russian regiments in Ireland was shelved lest government be accused of attempting to dragoon the country with Cossack hordes.[49] This single-minded focus on passing the Union also largely explains why controversial measures such as a reform of the tithe system or state provision for the Catholic clergy were not introduced. Such measures were complex and potentially divisive and the Castle recognised that legislating for them could incur significant delay and aggravate opposition to the Union itself and generally distract from the main business at hand. Passing the Union took precedence over everything, and it was important, as Cornwallis put it, 'that nothing should be at present attempted to sour the public mind'.[50]

In building up its parliamentary majority, the most effective means adopted was granting places to anti-union or neutral MPs and replacing them with newcomers who would vote for the Union.[51] This meant that few MPs who had voted against the Union in 1799 faced the embarrassment of voting for it a year later. Of course, the ruthless manner in which government employed the extensive patronage at its disposal and the large amounts spent on compensating borough owners, left it open to charges of corruption, then and later. Since the publication of G.C. Bolton's *The passing of the Irish Act of Union* these charges have been put in their contemporary context and the role of corruption had been downplayed.[52] In passing the Act of Union, there was no drastic departure from the political culture of the day. Government traded jobs for votes as it normally did and compensated property owners as it was expected it would. It was a simple fact of eighteenth-century political life that borough owners were not prepared to vote away the privilege of nominating MPs without satisfactory compensation. In a political culture deeply sensitive to the rights of property, any attempt to abolish boroughs without compensation would have been denounced as expropriation. It has also often been observed that the magnate who benefited most from borough compensation was the staunchly anti-unionist marquess of Downshire, just as the official who benefited most from compensation for the abolition of his office was John Foster, Speaker of the Commons, and the Union's most tenacious opponent.[53] As Patrick Geoghegan has pointed out, the only step that was unusual was the fact that the government resorted to using over £30,000 in secret service funds to reward supporters of the Union, prevent defections to the anti-unionists and buy parliamentary seats.[54] But, it is hardly surprising that in persuading a proud and ancient legislative assembly of 300 members to consent to its own abolition, government had to trespass beyond the normal conventions of the day.

Cornwallis found many of these measures distasteful. Dirtying his hands in the marketplace of Irish politics, and having to deal with Irish politicians, whom he regarded as bigoted, avaricious and untrustworthy, made him deeply unhappy. Several months into this trading and cajoling he wrote:

The political jobbing of this country gets the better of me: it has ever been the wish of my life to avoid all this dirty business, and I am now involved in it beyond all bearing, and am consequently more wretched than ever. I trust that I shall live to get out of this most cursed of all situations, and most repugnant to my feelings. How I long to kick those whom my public duty obliges me to court! If I did not hope to get out of this country, I should most earnestly pray for immediate death.[55]

Only his belief that the continued existence of the British Empire required the carrying of the Union gave him heart to carry on.[56]

Distasteful though he may have found it, Cornwallis stuck to his task. Although his personal reserve did not always gain the warmth of Irish magnates, because of his integrity they knew where they stood with him and, in the morass of wheeling and dealing that went with the Union, it was important to have such a point of stability. The determination with which he sought to deliver his promises after the Union had passed, in the face of strong opposition from Whitehall which believed that the Castle had been rather too profligate in promising places and peerages, showed that this reliance on his integrity was not misplaced.[57]

For his part, Castlereagh suffered from less squeamishness about the methods used to accomplish the task in hand and went about constructing a pro-union majority in the Commons with great determination. As Lecky noted, he 'pursued his course with quite business-like composure . . . [and] believed that he was corrupting to purify'.[58] It was his assured performance in carrying the Union that marked him out as a politician of the first rank. After a somewhat shaky start, he grew into the role of parliamentary manager until he could effectively answer veterans such as Grattan and Foster. By the passing of union, he had come to be regarded as 'master of the House of Commons'.[59] By this time, Cornwallis observed that his obvious efficiency had largely mitigated the unfavourable effect caused by his coldness of manner. Castlereagh also showed an assured hand in dealing with the financial and commercial points of the Union, displaying a willingness to listen to commercial interests and to modify his original proposals in line with the representations made to him, which greatly facilitated the smooth passage of union legislation.

III

When parliament resumed in January 1800, the Castle had done its work well and a majority had been constructed, even if Cornwallis had a low opinion of the sincerity and reliability of the unionist majority. The lord lieutenant thought many of them 'knaves' and 'fools' and was uneasy about the prospect of holding them together.[60] But, once government had won over a respectable measure of public opinion, had managed to convince the Irish Commons that it would persevere until the Union was passed and had indicated that it would compensate borough proprietors, it was always likely to prevail. It also helped that they were facing an opposition divided between those whose saw themselves as protecting Irish liberties and those who saw themselves as upholding the Protestant ascendancy and which, whatever the rhetorical talent at its disposal, could put forward no constructive alternative to the proposals for union, other than to maintain a status quo that had invited invasion and rebellion and could only be maintained by the continuance of severe coercion. Nor could the opposition seek to exploit differences between Dublin and London. Although relations between Cornwallis and Portland were at times strained, ultimately the Castle and Whitehall saw union as the prime goal and worked together to achieve that end. With Pitt instructing the Irish administration to persevere and allowing it to promise almost anything that was required to accomplish the measure, the final verdict could be in no real doubt. Having recognised that the government had gained the upper hand, many anti-unionists were not prepared to alienate themselves irrevocably from government by engaging in pointless opposition. Lord Auckland had forecast that, in these circumstances, 'rattism' would quickly erode the opposition minority and, true enough, the rats slowly but surely deserted the anti-unionist camp.[61] In the end, the final legislation carrying the Union was passed with comfortable majorities in a subdued House of Commons and received quietly in the country at large.[62]

In assessing the performance of the Castle's leading players in these months, it has to be said that the task facing them was a considerable one, given the entrenched interests that they had to overcome, but, given the resources available to them, it was one that they should have been well able to accomplish. In the months leading up to the rejection of union in January 1799, neither Cornwallis nor Castlereagh particularly distinguished themselves, but the response of both men to defeat was impressive. Their strategy of concentrating their resources and attention on particular interests was shrewd and effective. For a year they worked relentlessly to win over these interests, only bringing forward union when they were certain of victory. Both men displayed qualities of tenacity and considerable political skill and even Lord Chancellor Clare, though he was sceptical at first that Cornwallis was capable of carrying the Union, eventually conceded that 'he has on the whole been the man, of all others, best selected for the crisis'.[63]

In the end, the passing of the Union was something of an anti-climax. Edward Cooke commented on how quietly it was received, even in Dublin.[64] But the anti-climatic nature of the final debates on the Union to some extent obscured the magnitude of what had been accomplished. Within a year, a parliament that had existed for over 500 years was persuaded to agree to its own extinction. Ironically, among the instructions that the Castle had received from London was that the Union should not be a means of introducing any radical measure of parliamentary reform. Yet, carrying the Act of Union itself was a step of breathtaking radicalism.[65] During the debates on the reform of the Irish parliament in 1797, one member summed up the mood of the Commons when he maintained that, although it was perhaps true that the Irish parliament needed some reform, 'it was bad policy to thatch a house in a hurricane'.[66] Just over a year later, with the storm still raging, the British government concluded that the bill for renovations was too high and decided to pull down the entire edifice. In Cornwallis and Castlereagh, they found two unlikely but effective levellers.

CHAPTER EIGHT

The Failure of Opposition

JAMES KELLY

Though the opponents of the Anglo-Irish Union failed to achieve their purpose and prevent the measure's enactment, a majority of the histories of this event written in the two centuries since its ratification present their efforts in a positive, not to say flattering light.[1] This can be largely explained by the fact that, because a majority of the histories of the Act of Union were written for a nationalist audience, they were ideologically predisposed to interpret the actions of the Union's opponents in a heroic light and to interpret its ratification, in the words of Henry Grattan junior, as a triumph for 'force, fraud, violence, bribery and illegality'.[2] The smaller number of unionist historians, by contrast, have emphasised public support for the measure and the frailties of the parliamentary opposition.[3] Modern scholarship is less obviously partisan, but the focus on patronage in most accounts has meant that the opposition has received less than its share of attention.[4] The object of this essay is to look at the opposition anew to establish, first, how the inchoate coalition of interests that combined to oppose an Anglo-Irish union in 1798–99 drew on traditional patriot anti-union sentiment,[5] and neo-conservative hostility to constitutional change to prevent the Irish administration from presenting the measure. It aspires, secondly, to show how the opposition's inability to maintain the momentum generated in the winter of 1798–99, poor tactical decision making, uninspired leadership and inability to match the organisational vigour of Dublin Castle meant that they were unable to prevent the ratification of the Act of Union in 1800.

I

When the terms of an Anglo-Irish union were being considered in the corridors of power in Dublin and London in the autumn of 1798, the parliamentary and extra-parliamentary interests that had traditionally opposed the political agenda of the Irish executive, and who had secured legislative independence sixteen years earlier, were ill-circumstanced to resist its implementation. The military defeat in 1798 of the alliance of United Irishmen and Defenders that had aspired to create an independent Irish republic and the eagerness of its surviving leaders to diminish their role in and the import of their revolutionary strategy thereafter ensured no overt opposition from a quarter that had previously dismissed a legislative union as a 'plan of subjugation'.[6] Nor, despite the popular politicisation promoted by the United Irishmen during the 1790s, was 'the great mass of the people' disposed to protest. The judgement of one military observer that they gave 'the question of union' little thought did not receive general endorsement, but it is entirely consistent with the fact that the politics of the Act of Union were conducted entirely within traditional political structures.[7]

Within these structures, the role of opposition in parliamentary politics was played in the 1790s by the Whig-patriots, but they were only slightly less ill-positioned than the radicals to meet the challenge of resisting a legislative union due to a combination of ill-conceived strategic decisions and personal difficulties. The most debilitating of these was the withdrawal of Whig-patriot MPs from the House of Commons in May 1797 and their refusal to offer themselves for re-election the same year in protest at the draconian 'law and order' strategy promoted by the Irish administration and supported by a majority of representatives. As a consequence, the ranks of what Jonah Barrington tellingly termed 'the old opposition . . . did not exceed fifty' after the 1797 general election, and their weak and demoralised condition was emphasised in the spring of 1798 when a meeting of the Whig Club 'adjourned without proceeding on any business for want of members'.[8] To compound their problems, Henry Grattan's supposed association with a number of leading United Irishmen prompted allegations that he was a member of that society or that he was au fait with their plans for a rebellion. These were unfounded, but the perception was sufficient to discredit him in the eyes of many and to encourage him, for political as well as for health reasons, to spend a lot of time outside the country during the late 1790s.[9] The vacuum at the head of the Whig-patriots was ostensibly filled by George Ponsonby who re-entered the House of Commons in 1798, but Ponsonby's credibility was also diminished since, like Grattan, he and his family 'party' were perceived by die-hards to have 'contributed to raise' the country in rebellion. As a result, Ponsonby, no less than Grattan, maintained a low profile politically.[10]

The chequered recent fortunes of its leading orators diminished the capacity of the Whig-patriots to mount a vigorous campaign of opposition to Pitt's scheme for a 'permanent settlement' that secured the Anglo-Irish 'connection' in 1798–99.[11] Yet because their political touchstone – the 'constitution' of 1782 – was seen to encapsulate the dignity of 'Protestant Ireland', the observation of Lord Castlereagh in July 1798 that he could identify 'no strong disposition in the public mind to favour' a union suggested that any attempt to bring it into being would meet with strong resistance.[12]

There was little evidence of this in the autumn of that year, though speculation that an Anglo-Irish union was being contemplated was a matter of
common conversation by mid-October.[13] Well-placed denials that this was the
case persuaded important sections of public opinion against accepting that a
union was, the *Dublin Evening Post* observed, 'an admitted fact' throughout
November, but Lord Charlemont, the *éminence grise* of Whig-patriotism, was
uneasy. Prompted by rumours to broach the matter with Lord Castlereagh in
mid-October, he was persuaded by the acting-chief secretary's evasive
response that it was the case.[14] Eager to frustrate a scheme that would nullify
legislative independence, his dearest political achievement, Charlemont
wasted no time alerting his political friends, Lord Pery, Lawrence Parsons,
James Stewart, Francis Dobbs and William Conyngham Plunket, but the
administration's refusal to concede publicly that a union was in contemplation
discouraged activity. Parsons's observation in early November that 'having
heard nothing further respecting this detested union, I begin to indulge . . .
hopes that it will not be attempted' illustrates just how inhibiting was the
prevailing uncertainty.[15] This mood could not be sustained, the best efforts of
the Castle press notwithstanding, as the administration actively embarked in
late November on lobbying support among the political élite, and it was
commonly avowed by the beginning of December that 'the Union is most
certainly to be brought forward'.[16] Sir Richard Musgrave, who was persuaded
by his 'fears for the Protestant religion and the Protestant state' to become
a 'warm advocate for the Union', was quietly confident that the measure
would be 'carried', but few shared his optimism.[17] The dominant view on the
pro-union side was that the weight of public opinion, though currently silent,
was hostile, and that its 'opponents . . . only wait for government to take the
first step' to spring into action.[18] It was this prospect that prompted Edward
Cooke to offer his frequently cited advice that if an Anglo-Irish union was to
be obtained 'it must be written up, spoken up, intrigued up, drunk up, sung-
up, and bribed up'.[19]

   The irony was that the opponents of a union believed they faced an
equally imposing challenge if they were to resist the measure successfully.
Assessing the mood of the country in late November, the liberal *Dublin
Evening Post* observed nervously that the government had carefully and
deliberately chosen 'this moment of affright and despair, of tired strength
and mutual suspicion' when 'the public tone and spirit [were] relaxed,
fainting and exhausted . . . and patriotism [was] disgusted, [and] frightened
from the field by the horrid forms that usurped her name' to press the
measure.[20] If union was to be resisted, it was incumbent upon the opposition
both to rally public support to their cause and to conduct itself with skill and
energy in parliament.

As the final weeks of 1798 rolled by and the Irish administration did not seek, beyond inaugurating a 'pamphlet war' in which it was thoroughly outgunned, to rally public opinion to its side, it became apparent that the pro-union and anti-union interests were employing fundamentally different tactics. The administration's strategy, based on the premise that its interests would be best advanced by the personal approach and by optimising the terms of the Union, centred on persuading potential supporters that it was in both their and Ireland's interest to see an Act of Union on to the statute book.[21] The opponents of a union, by contrast, sought to raise a public outcry against the abolition of their parliament. Reports, however exaggerated, that 'the whole country is against' were encouraging in this context, but the opposition had yet to make an impression by early December when Richard Musgrave observed contentedly that 'the Union, tho' much talked of, has not occasioned as much agitation as I expected'.[22] It was clear to the Irish administration by this date that 'the principal opposition' was to be expected from Dublin, and the convergence of vested economic and ideological interests that was required if the opposition was to achieve its aim and prevent the measure was formally signalled on 9 December when a full meeting of the bar resolved that 'a LEGISLATIVE UNION of this KINGDOM and GREAT BRITAIN is an INNOVATION, which . . . would be HIGHLY DANGEROUS and IMPROPER'. The wording was the handiwork of William Saurin, a leading advocate and commanding officer of the Lawyers' Corps of yeomanry, but of greater consequence was the fact that the meeting brought together anti-unionists of a variety of political hues.[23]

According to Edward Cooke, the earliest advocate of a bar meeting was William Conyngham Plunket who was brought into parliament by Lord Charlemont. Plunket did so in the confident expectation that a strong anti-union stand from this quarter would encourage others, but it is significant that the moving spirit behind the meeting of the bar in early December was not the liberal Plunket but the conservative William Saurin. This can hardly have been pleasing to Whig-patriots like George Ponsonby and John Philpot Curran, but what made the occasion more than ordinarily impressive was the readiness of individuals across the political spectrum to support the declaration that was presented, as, in addition to Ponsonby and Curran, Jonah Barrington, William Duquery, Charles Kendal Bushe, Peter Burrowes and Francis Dobbs were also forthcoming.[24] It was, as the extensive coverage given the event underlined, a decisive moment, and its importance was highlighted by the fact that constitutional issues were afforded as much priority as professional concerns. Moreover, it was confidently expected that the example set by the bar would be imitated by the rest of the country.[25]

This was, as time was to show, more than a little optimistic, but the bar meeting did generate some momentum behind the anti-union campaign.

One index of this is provided by the 'paper war' stimulated by the publication in late-November of Edward Cooke's ostensibly impartial *Arguments for and against an union*. Cooke's object was to persuade the unsure and undecided to support the measure, but his intervention proved counterproductive and a veritable wave of responses and rebuttals, a substantial proportion of which were authored by lawyers, eclipsed his contribution.[26] While this illustrated, as the administration had anticipated, that the legal profession would be 'averse to a union', the impetus behind what the *Dublin Evening Post* lauded as 'the manly and spirited' manifestations of anti-unionism in the 'metropolis' in the winter of 1798–99 was actually provided by neo-conservatives.[27]

In the wake of the 1798 Rebellion, as Irish Protestants wrestled with the contention that those who had taken up arms had done so with the intention not just of establishing an independent republic but also of effecting their extirpation, familiar arguments in support of an undiluted 'Protestant ascendancy' were received with particular favour. For those who were drawn by the certainties inherent in such rhetoric, an exclusively 'Protestant constitution' had enormous appeal, and many recoiled instinctively against the radical constitutional innovation that a union implied.[28] Their unease was indicated publicly by their participation in the meeting of the Irish bar on 9 December 1798. Attempts shortly afterwards to persuade the Aldermen of Skinner's Alley, an influential, 'numerous' and 'loyal' metropolitan pressure group, and the Orange Order to commit themselves to the opposition cause were frustrated by conservative proponents of a union such as Patrick Duigenan, but it was only a temporary set-back.[29] Within a week the most important voice of metropolitan opinion, Dublin Corporation, had pronounced against a union, and the anti-union cause was boosted further by a similar declaration by a previously unheralded assembly of bankers and merchants. The political implications of the latter are difficult to estimate, but both John Claudius Beresford, who was MP for the city, and James Digges LaTouche endorsed the bankers' action.

More significantly, the action of the Corporation stirred municipal trade organisations. The impact of the intervention of an individual guild or commercial body was modest. However, the readiness of so many to do so, and the decision of the Aldermen of Skinner's Alley to revisit the issue on 9 January 1799 and to pronounce, in the presence of John Claudius Beresford, their dismay that any attempt should be made to diminish their 'PRESENT happy constitution', is indicative of the rising tide of economic as well as neo-conservative opposition in the capital.[30] The fact that the freeholders of Dublin county, the freeholders and freemen of Dublin city and the electors of the boroughs of Swords and Trinity College Dublin expressed their disapproval in only slightly less forceful terms offers further testament to the strength of popular anti-unionism in Dublin and its environs.[31]

The situation elsewhere was less encouraging. The influence of John Foster in County Louth, John Ball and Edward Hardman in Drogheda, Lawrence Parsons in King's County and Sir John Parnell in Queen's County ensured anti-union declarations from gatherings of local freeholders and freemen. These were reinforced by similar declarations from counties Meath, Westmeath, Carlow, Monaghan and from Galway city.[32] This was not entirely unimpressive but, considering the importance of the matter at issue and the example of Dublin, it was less than overwhelming. This conclusion is reinforced by the inability of Charlemont's son, Lord Caulfeild, to elicit a hostile declaration from County Armagh, but the 'neutrality' of Ulster opinion was less disquieting than the readiness of some in Munster, Cork most notably, to welcome 'an union . . . grounded upon just and equitable terms'.[33]

Of potentially greater import was the lack of concord across the spectrum of anti-union interests. The patriots and neo-conservatives that constituted the anti-union cause were at one in believing that a union was not to Ireland's advantage, but they agreed on little else and they existed in largely discrete and ideologically antagonistic spheres. This gave little cause for concern in the winter of 1798–99, as popular anti-unionism was first and foremost an expression of metropolitan neo-conservatism, then in the ascendant politically in the capital. The ideological thrust of the anti-unionism emanating from most meetings of freeholders reflected traditional patriot politics, and this was true also of their political representatives. How these two incompatible political outlooks would cohere should the campaign against an Anglo-Irish union be prolonged was problematic. This was not expected, as the Whig-patriots chose to follow the course advocated by Francis Hardy, MP for Mullingar, and determined that 'opposition should be made . . . on the general question at once'.[34]

II

Francis Hardy was persuaded that this was the way to proceed by his recollection that this strategy had paid dividends in 1785, when the matter at issue was William Pitt's attempt to bring Britain and Ireland together in a commercial union.[35] Unfortunately the documentation that would allow for a confident reconstruction of the preparations the opponents of a legislative union made for the meeting of parliament on 22 January 1799 does not exist. What information can be gleaned suggests that the momentum generated by popular opposition, combined with strategic errors on the part of the Irish administration, enabled them to maximise their support base in parliament.

This was an impressive achievement because early soundings of members' intentions seemed to favour the administration.[36] However, the opposition's position improved in the run-up to the meeting of parliament and, on the eve of the opening of the parliamentary session, Edward Cooke conceded that 'the opposition can muster 100 certain, if they assemble'.[37] This represented a significant improvement on their vote in recent sessions, though it was less than the 113 indicated at the beginning of the year. If, as this suggests, the votes of a sizeable number of MPs inclined towards opposition were there to be won, the chief secretary's observation that the opposition sought and secured pledges from more than 100 MPs demonstrates not just that they were well organised but that they were more thorough in eliciting promises of support than the administration. It was certainly the case that, combined, the heightening 'clamour out-of-doors', the administration's inability to reassure worried 'borough proprietors', and the 'lukewarm' disposition of many otherwise reliable 'agents of government' meant that the opposition approached the session in reasonably stout heart.

At the same time, differences within their ranks between 'younger members, who were for starting from the post', and senior figures, like Lord Pery, who advised that they should 'not . . . fight or divide on the address, but wait . . . for a more specific proposition', cautions against over-embroidering their capacity to pursue a successful parliamentary campaign. This is reinforced by the fact that there is no evidence to suggest that the opposition disagreed with the governmental assessment that the best they could expect was a large 'minority' that would 'make it difficult to carry the measure'.[38] None the less, worrying noises emanating from the ranks of normally dependable borough proprietors like Lords Ely and Downshire; Speaker Foster's inspiring example; the impression created that Sir John Parnell 'retired' from the chancellorship of the exchequer rather than vote for a union; and the realisation that between twenty and thirty members in the administration's interest would be absent on the commencement of the session made it clear that they were unlikely to have a better opportunity to exceed even their own optimistic expectations.[39]

When members of both houses of the Irish parliament gathered on Tuesday, 22 January 1799 for the opening ceremonies of the annual session, the opponents of an Anglo-Irish union did so determined to go on the offensive. They still needed a specific target, and the administration sought not to offer them one by acceding to the advice of ministers that the speech from the throne should not mention a union. Rather, MPs were invited to consider 'the most effectual means of maintaining and improving a connexion, essential to their common security, and of consolidating as far as possible, into one form and lasting fabric, the strength, the power, and the resources of the British Empire'. This did not appease the opposition and, convinced, as Sir John Parnell observed, that this was an attempt to introduce a union 'by a side-wind', they determined to make their disapproval known.

However, before members could debate this weighty matter, George Ponsonby threatened to throw the administration into disarray by moving that Lord Castlereagh should vacate his seat since he was not a legal member of parliament. Ponsonby's contention was that, since Castlereagh had been reappointed chief secretary by Lord Cornwallis, he was subject to the terms of the amendment to the Place Act passed in 1798, which provided that an MP who accepted 'a place of profit from the lord lieutenant' should vacate his seat.[40] This prompted a poorly recorded exchange that 'occupied the house some hours', but the attorney general's assertion that Castlereagh had remained in secure 'possession' of the office from his initial appointment by Earl Camden and therefore that the 1798 act did not apply registered sufficiently strongly with MPs to safeguard the chief secretary's position. In point of fact, Ponsonby's contention was correct, but his argument was deficiently made. He would have made a stronger case, and increased the prospects of his securing a positive outcome, if he had shown that Castlereagh served in an 'acting capacity' between March and November 1798 when Thomas Pelham's poor health caused him finally to resign and Castlereagh was formally appointed Irish chief secretary.[41] Ponsonby's poor preparation thus enabled the administration to brazen out Castlereagh's failure to comply with the law with some ease, and Ponsonby's willingness to withdraw his motion, 'rather than delay any longer the main business of the night', represented the end of the matter.[42]

This 'main business' gave the administration no relief as the opposition resisted Lord Tyrone's attempt 'to move an address of thanks to his majesty for the most gracious speech . . . from the throne' on the grounds that to do so would be tantamount, as one member put it, 'to giving a pledge to adopt a legislative union'.[43] This was questionable, but with the Whig-patriots to the fore, the leading opposition MPs all spoke vigorously against a union. Their main performer was George Ponsonby, who made 'a very able and eloquent' attack on the principle of a union and, as a preliminary to this, presented an amendment to the address affirming the 'undoubted birth-right of the people of Ireland to have a resident and independent legislature'. This amendment was lost by one vote, after nineteen hours of animated debate, but the energy and emotion displayed by a succession of opposition speakers, Whig-patriot (William Conyngham Plunket, Jonah Barrington, Francis Dobbs and Francis Hardy) and conservative (John Claudius Beresford and George Ogle), palpably exceeded that of their opponents.[44] The failure to prevent the address being approved by two votes (105 to 107) was a caution against euphoria, but the outcome was an undeniable success for the opposition. Castlereagh conceded as much when, in response to Ponsonby's expression of his intention of 'fixing an early day for a debate on the principle', he 'intimated his intention . . . not to persist any further in the measure at present'. However, because he refused to pledge 'not [to] renew the question this session', the opposition determined in the words of the recently dismissed prime sergeant, James Fitzgerald, to 'put an end to it' immediately.[45]

When the House of Commons gathered on 24 January 1799 to consider the proposed address to the king prepared by the committee appointed for that purpose, they targeted the presence in the address of a paragraph 're-echo[ing] that part of the speech which recommends an union'.[46] It was an obvious response to a transparent attempt by the administration to regain the initiative and, guided by Lawrence Parsons who took the lead on this occasion, a succession of leading Whig, patriot and other dissentient voices (Francis Dobbs, James Moore O'Donnell, R.L. Edgeworth, George Ponsonby, John Parnell, James Fitzgerald, James Browne, Arthur Moore and Jonah Barrington) convinced a majority of members to agree to expunge the offending paragraph by 109 votes to 104 after a 'fierce debate'.[47]

Emboldened by this, and by 'the accession of three friends who had arrived in town', the opposition sought to press home their advantage. George Ponsonby moved a resolution affirming 'that this house will ever maintain the undoubted birth-right of Irishmen, by preserving an independent Irish parliament of Lords and Commons resident within this kingdom, as settled and approved by his majesty and the British parliament in 1782'. It was a bold attempt to block further discussion of a union, and, while it appeared for a moment that members would agree, the reluctance of a number of country gentlemen 'to bind' themselves 'for *ever*' prompted a belated change of heart and Ponsonby withdrew his motion rather than risk its defeat.[48] It was an appropriate action, as the loss of the motion would have restored the initiative to the administration. At the same time, there was no masking the fact that this outcome represented a setback for the opponents of a union. Sir Henry Cavendish, an expert on parliamentary procedure, compared it to 'a retreat after a sudden victory' and, while this military image may seem inappropriate, Jonah Barrington's lyrical description of the 'sudden transition from exultancy to despondency' indicates that some of the opponents of a union agreed.[49]

The administration, naturally, sought to capitalise on this unexpected stroke of good fortune. Lord Cornwallis went so far as to suggest that the opposition 'party' was 'partially dissolved'. He did not expect 'prosecuting the measure of union with success in the course of the present session', but he was hopeful that the opposition would not be able 'to assemble numbers with any effect on general topics'.[50] It became apparent within a few days that this was indeed the case. Castlereagh consoled himself meanwhile with the observation that 'the opposition of the country gentlemen . . . turns more upon points of personal interest than a fixed aversion to the principle of union', but he made no attempt to conceal the fact that the administration had been humbled and that he had been outmanoeuvred. 'I did not apprehend that the question would have been fought on the address', he confessed to the duke of Portland on 28 January.[51]

In the light of this admission, it was inevitable that the administration's deficient preparations should attract critical notice. But it is significant that the piquant criticism of Sir Richard Musgrave that 'each individual member should have been tried before the measure was openly avowed by government', and that '£200,000' if appropriately applied 'would have silently prostrated all opposition' was not endorsed by ministers.[52] Indeed, in contrast to August 1785, when the Irish administration had experienced a similar reversal, there was little criticism or recrimination within government, and the firm and ready assurances forthcoming from London 'that nothing that has happened ought to occasion any alteration in the intentions we had formed, or any deviation from the plan which it was in our contemplation to pursue' not alone steadied the Irish administration, it put pressure on the opposition to sustain their anti-union activity.[53]

This did not register with most of the opposition in late January 1799, as they revelled in the applause of the public. Indeed, it was tempting, amidst the celebrations, for them to overlook the fact that a union had not been abandoned, as the *Dublin Evening Post* warned, but they had few grounds for anxiety then as public endorsement of their actions was readily forthcoming.[54] This took the form, primarily, of addresses of thanks to 'the glorious and virtuous' 111 MPs that had voted not to accept a union on 25 January. Specific addresses were also presented congratulating John Foster, Sir John Parnell and James Fitzgerald.[55] This appeased but did not satisfy Lord Charlemont, who did not hesitate to make known his opinion that the victory, 'though glorious', was 'not decisive'. He urged his correspondents to action on the grounds that 'the silence of the country' is the only argument administration can bring forward'.[56] However, his advice fell largely on deaf ears and within a number of weeks the tide of anti-unionist declarations began to ebb, and the momentum began to drain slowly from the opposition cause. This was symbolised by the fact that among the various schemes mooted to promote the anti-union cause in the spring of 1799, the suggestion that there should be a 'public memorial' honouring the peers and commoners that opposed a union in parliament fell by the wayside. More significantly, support for a legislative union was boosted by a number of factors, of which the publicity afforded William Pitt's 'impressive' and 'judicious' speech introducing the measure at Westminster was the most significant.[57] Since ministers had already decided, because the level of 'agitation is so great in Dublin and in various parts of Ireland at present', that 'the question cannot be entertained until the next session', the opposition was not greatly exercised by this. For many, indeed, their fondest wish was simply to return to political normality.[58]

III

Though the duke of Portland's description of George Ponsonby's failure to secure approval for his motion on 25 January as a 'total rout' is characteristically inflated, the experience chastened the opposition in the House of Commons.[59] The fact that the administration chose 'to conciliate and reunite those who show any inclination' did not help their cause. Moreover, because Lord Castlereagh refused to commit the administration not to introduce the measure later in the session, the opposition was obliged to remain on the alert. They made a number of attempts during February 'to consolidate their party', and to build morale by hosting dinners, at which the guest list featured those who had opposed a union, and by courting Speaker Foster. They even took up a collection to help defray Foster's debts, though it is not clear how much was raised or if it ever reached its intended recipient.[60] Whatever the outcome, neither these efforts nor the attempt in late February by 'the leading anti-unionists . . . to induce their whole party actively to oppose' bills legalising the exercise of martial law and 'the more speedy suppression' of rebellion appealed to 'country gentlemen'. Cornwallis was relieved; he reported contentedly to the home secretary on the last day of February that 'all attempts to form a party against government, with a view to overturn this administration, had entirely failed'.[61]

The incapacity of the opposition to capitalise upon the antipathy to a legislative union to forge a larger and more coherent party interest obliged them to moderate their parliamentary ambitions. None the less, they persisted with an anti-union strategy. This was far from vigorous, but it achieved its primary purpose, which was to provide the Irish administration with no justification for springing union legislation on parliament. Significantly, however, they registered few successes and scored a number of own goals. For example, an attempt on 15 February 'to get Foster into a committee' to allow him 'to make an inflammatory speech against an union and to abuse Mr Pitt' failed by twenty votes.[62] Three weeks later, James Fitzgerald presented a bill proposing that in the event of a regency 'the exercises and administration of the regal powers of the imperial crown of Ireland should be vested in . . . the person or persons in whom the administration of the regal powers of the imperial crown of Great Britain shall be vested'.[63] Fitzgerald's object was to neutralise the argument that the regency crisis of 1788–89 demonstrated the need for an Anglo-Irish union, but it backfired badly, as Castlereagh happily observed:

By throwing the labouring oar entirely upon the opposite party, we have obtained a complete admission of the danger resulting from the present principle of connection and of their inability to move it, without altering and surrendering up their final and immutable settlement of 1782.[64]

Perhaps it was this realisation that prompted John Foster to avail himself of the opportunity of a committee stage debate on Fitzgerald's bill on 12 April to make his a long anticipated anti-union speech. Foster certainly did not hold back. He ranged far and wide over the subject in a four-hour oration that lifted the 'droop[ing] hearts' of some anti-unionists, but which elicited strong criticism in pro-union circles. More importantly, as Bishop Euseby Cleaver of Ferns noted, Foster's intervention did not leave 'the cause of union weaker in the House of Commons than he found it'.[65]

As this suggests, there was uncertainty within the ranks of the opposition before the end of spring 1799 as to their ability to resist a union should it be revived. James Fitzgerald conceded privately on 1 March that at 'the next attempt the Union will be carried'. Ironically, Fitzgerald had no difficulty in justifying his own actions as an MP who 'never will attach myself to any party', though his decision to press his regency bill, following so soon on George Ponsonby's misjudgements on 22 and 25 January, was symptomatic of the opposition's disunity and poor strategy.[66] At the same time, their failure to sustain a strong campaign of public opposition during the spring of 1799 was probably more consequential since, as the public declarations of support for Foster and Fitzgerald emphasise, the public would have welcomed their leadership.[67] The extent of their strategic *naiveté* is underlined by Jonah Barrington's admission that the opposition explicitly determined that '*moderation* was . . . the proper course for a loyal opposition' deriving from the conviction that they had 'virtually negatived' the 'proposal for a union' in January.[68] The complacency to which this also attests certainly contributed to the opposition's failure in by-elections in the 'populous' and 'independent boroughs' of Newry and Galway in February, and to their inability to secure appropriately worded addresses at the spring assizes.[69] Most serious of all, it allowed the Irish administration gradually to generate a degree of public momentum behind a union. This commenced tentatively at first, but it was sufficiently promising by the beginning of the summer for supporters of a union to observe contentedly, not just that they were 'gaining ground with respect to the Union' but, that their 'adversaries . . . are daily losing ground in the provinces'.[70] Lord Charlemont consoled himself by observing that 'no anti-unionist, to my knowledge, has vacated his seat', but age and ill-health prohibited him from anything other than exhortation and from hoping that the Herculean effort of the administration 'to accomplish their designs' would fall short.[71]

That Lord Charlemont, a veteran of so many opposition campaigns, could appeal to nothing more substantial emphasises not just the weakness of the opposition's position, but also their lack of direction. The problem, as Jonah Barrington defined it, was that they had

> no great leader whom they could collectively consult or obey – no systematic course determined on for their conduct – no pre-arranged plan of proceeding without doors, or practical arrangement for internal debate; their energies were personal, their enthusiasm graduated, and their exertions not gregarious. Every man formed his own line of procedure.[72]

There was speculation within the Irish administration in mid-February that John Foster had 'placed himself at the head of the anti-unionists'. But this was never likely because the opposition was 'united on no question but that of the Union'; they were not, to cite Barrington once more, even in agreement on 'the measure of that opposition'.[73] As a consequence, the 'anti-unionists' were, and remained, an ad hoc 'political connexion' rather than a coherent 'party'. The practical implications of this were highlighted by 'their radical difference of opinion on the Catholic question' since it ensured that the attempt by George Ponsonby to forge a link with Catholics was destined to fail because, the speculation of pro-union Catholics notwithstanding, it was unacceptable to John Foster.[74] Arising out of this, Lord Cornwallis plainly exaggerated when he described the opposition as 'formidable in character and talents'. They were strong enough, as the 'brisk skirmish[es]' they precipitated through April and May attest, to take on the Irish administration in the House of Commons, but they were incapable of producing victories which, luckily for them, was not necessary to 'render . . . the prosecution of the measure in parliament impracticable'.[75]

This outcome naturally pleased anti-unionists, some of whom continued to apprehend that the administration might seek to take advantage of the 'progress' they had made 'in parliament' to spring the measure on them late in the session.[76] This apart, matters continued to work against them during the summer months as the impact of individual negotiation, dismissals, compensation for borough owners, changes to the personnel of the House of Commons and the dissemination of unionist propaganda improved the prospects of an Anglo-Irish union taking place.[77] The most visible manifestation of the changing fortunes of the pro- and anti-union interests was the growing number of union addresses emanating from all corners of the kingdom.[78] Pro-union propaganda was less than entirely effective, but there is no evading the conclusion that the opposition surrendered the initiative they had in the public sphere, with the result that the government's argument that the options for Ireland were 'union or separation' registered with increasing force.[79]

As this suggests, the most striking features of the opposition to an Anglo-Irish union in the summer of 1799 are its languor and effeteness. Thus Lord Cornwallis was given free rein to rally support during his successful tours of Munster in July and August and Ulster in October, though the primary effect of this was to isolate Dublin, outside of which, Cornwallis observed, there was little likelihood of strong opposition.[80] The lord lieutenant's confident pronouncement in July that 'it would . . . be impossible to excite any popular commotion against the Union' outside Dublin reflected both the increasing optimism of the Irish administration as the 'Union . . . daily gain[ed] ground' and the almost total absence of a popular anti-union campaign during the summer and autumn of 1799.[81] Liberal newspapers like the *Dublin Evening Post* continued to carry anti-union comment during this time, but it diminished in scale in parallel with the decline in anti-union activity of opposition politicians. A number, notably Thomas Osborne, Jonah Barrington and Capel Molyneux, did publish declarations hostile to a union, but their primary motivation was electoral.[82] In an attempt to sustain the anti-union cause, the *Dublin Evening Post* sought to discredit the tide of favourable pronouncements from freeholders, freemen, Catholics and others that filled most newspapers during the summer and autumn by highlighting any evidence of impropriety brought to its notice, but the impact of this was modest.[83] The difficulties facing the anti-union cause were vividly revealed on 19 July when an attempt to grant the freedom of Dublin to William Saurin 'for the spirited manner in which he came forward and delivered his sentiments against the destructive measure of an union' failed for want of support.[84]

IV

Having surrendered the initiative in the parliamentary, public and propaganda spheres and, thereby, aided the Irish administration forge a solid and expanded phalanx in the House of Commons, anti-unionists faced an uphill struggle if they were to repeat in 1800 what they achieved in January 1799. Obviously, this would not happen without the reanimation of the anti-union campaign, and there were signs during the autumn that this might yet occur as the quietude of the summer gave way to more lively press comment and reports that plans were being hatched to establish 'an anti-union newspaper'. However, the first real sign of intent was not forthcoming until 19 October 1799 when Dublin Corporation agreed an anti-union resolution.[85] Even then the response was slow, and it was not until November and December that the grand juries of Dublin city and county and the freeholders in County Roscommon produced further declarations to warm applause.[86] The publication on 9 December of the first issue of an explicitly anti-union newspaper,

The Constitution, or Anti-Union, helped since it dovetailed with expanded anti-union comment elsewhere to raise the opposition's profile in the run-in to the new session. The *Anti-Union* relied heavily on the liberal wing of the Irish bar for copy, but its impact on public and political opinion was modest. A relieved John Lees observed on 20 December that 'scarcely anything has appeared deserving notice in the anti-union newspaper that has not been refuted'.[87]

Despite its uninspiring content, the *Anti-Union* made a significant contribution to the visible reinvigoration of the opposition to an Anglo-Irish union in the weeks before the opening of the 1800 session. This prompted anti-union declarations from gatherings in counties Leitrim, Limerick, Galway, Tipperary, Monaghan and Westmeath; from a rump of middle-class Catholics in Dublin and unsuccessful attempts to do likewise in Tyrone, Donegal and Fermanagh.[88] It was unmistakably less impressive than a year earlier, but it did ensure that a union was once again the 'general topic' of conversation as MPs gathered for the opening of the session on 15 January 1800.[89] Given that the administration calculated that the opposition would not muster above 100 members, and that the Castle (with some twenty to thirty friends absent) reckoned their own vote at near 150, the prospects for the opposition looked slim. At the same time, the fact that the opposition's ranks had solidified since mid-December, when their number was put at no more than eighty-two, indicated that, for all their expectation of 'a large majority', the administration could not afford to take the opposition lightly.[90]

Though pertinent documentation is again remarkably thin, it is clear that the parliamentary opposition's strategy for the 1800 session was the same as it was for 1799; they sought to take the contest to the administration. Critically, they no longer had the benefit of surprise, but the anticipated return of Henry Grattan to the House of Commons gave them some cause for optimism. In practice, events were to reveal just how much ground the opposition had ceded to the administration in the twelve months since MPs had last debated the issue. This was revealed on 15 January when, in a repetition of what had transpired on 25 January 1799, Lawrence Parsons moved an amendment 'declaratory of the resolution of parliament to preserve the constitution as established in 1782' in the debate on the address to the king. A long and animated war of words ensued which, despite the choreographed re-entry of Henry Grattan to the Commons' chamber, went against the opposition by the margin of forty-two votes – 138 to 96. It was a result that demonstrated amply that there was little prospect of the opposition being able to defeat the measure in parliament, since their vote was down on January 1799 and the administration's ranks were set fair to increase as vacant seats were filled.[91] It emphasised the gravity of the tactical error the opposition had made in the spring of 1799 when they effectively ceded the public arena to the administration.

Acutely conscious of the magnitude of what was at stake, and anxious to improve their precarious situation, the leaders of the opposition gathered on 20 January 1800 at the Dublin home of the second Lord Charlemont (his father had died the previous August) to consider their next move. Since they were, as they had been in 1799, an 'ill-assorted mixture', they possessed few options, but, conscious that the die was cast for the session if a substantial number of MPs were not persuaded to alter their vote, they determined to try to bring this about by the time-honoured tactic of appealing to the country. With this in mind, a circular was prepared and signed by three of the opposition's leading eminences – Lord Downshire, Lord Charlemont and William Brabazon Ponsonby – on behalf of thirty-eight county MPs urging men of influence throughout the country to get up petitions against a union for presentation to the House of Commons. Their object was to procure moderate anti-union declarations from more than the eighteen or nineteen counties Castlereagh claimed had pronounced in favour of a union, and they identified the early session recess as a timely opportunity to set this process in train.[92]

However, even at this moment of crisis, there were clear signs of friction within the opposition camp. The most manifest was the resentment felt by 'loyal anti-unionists', John Foster most notably, at Grattan's return. But ill-feeling was also generated by the decision of 'a cabal' of anti-union lawyers 'not to employ' unionists; by the negative publicity arising out of the establishment of 'an anti-union stock purse', that may have raised as much as £100,000, for the purchase of seats and other purposes; and by the 'abuse' of supporters of a union in newspapers such as the *Anti-Union*.[93] There were differences too over the tactics the anti-unionists should employ. Speaker Foster's disposition to favour 'moderation out of doors' was so strong that he declined to sign the circular of 20 January in support of a petitioning campaign though he was present at the meeting at which the decision was taken. Furthermore, the advocacy by radicals like Peter Burrowes of an appeal to the yeomanry, which may have contributed to the appearance on 20 January of a handbill 'calling on the yeomanry to rise in arms and save the country', alarmed moderates who were horrified that such radical gestures should even be contemplated.[94]

With the active support of the popular press,[95] which needed no convincing that the survival of the Irish parliament depended on the public's response, the opposition were galvanised into urgent action. They reinforced their voting ranks in the House of Commons through the purchase of seats for Peter Burrowes and Thomas Goold, while £4,000 was made available to John Philpot Curran to do likewise.[96] However, their main focus in the spring of 1800 was getting up petitions. As the bastion of popular anti-unionism,

Dublin was held up as 'the patriotic example'. Significantly, the declarations forthcoming from that quarter in January 1800 were less obviously reflective of ideological concerns than those approved in the winter of 1798–99. Dublin Corporation set the tone with a series of resolutions (agreed on 17 January) and a petition (agreed on 31 January) in which it expressed its 'abhorrence of the indirect modes which have been adopted to carry into effect the measure of a legislative union', and drew attention to the impoverishment, the loss of 'chartered rights' and the 'surrender of the birthright of Irishmen' it involved.[97] The city's guilds endorsed this line of argument. John Beresford described the resolutions approved by the guild of merchants on 15 January as 'very strong', and, while this is a reasonable assessment, the resolutions originating with the guilds also reflected more traditional patriot and corporate concerns than was the case a year earlier. They had more general appeal as a result – a conclusion affirmed by pronouncements by the grand jury, and by the freemen and freeholders of the city that a union could not possibly advantage the kingdom.[98]

Public endorsement for this position was less forthcoming outside Dublin,[99] but this did not inhibit anti-unionists when parliament resumed on 3 February. They had successfully 'raised a powerful clamour against the measure in many parts of the kingdom and put the capital quite in an uproar'. There was even a whiff of violence in the air, as the mood of the public was manifestly more volatile than it had been on 15 January when the large crowds that filled 'the streets about the houses of parliament' had observed 'good order'. A worried administration apprehended tumult, but though there were a number of minor incidents on 5 February, there was no serious disorder.[100] This came as a great relief to officials, as some MPs had shown signs of weakening in the face of public pressure and a number had even briefly jumped ship. Encouraged by this, some within the ranks of the opposition concluded optimistically that they could overturn the administration's majority in the Commons, but once the Castle interest registered a number of solid divisions, and the impact of the news of Lord Downshire's dismissal struck home,[101] the nervousness that was so apparent in early February soon dissipated.

The opposition was outnumbered 158–115 on 6 February upon the question of 'taking his majesty's message into consideration for a legislative union with Great Britain'. This was one of the largest recorded divisions in the history of the Irish House of Commons, and it set the tone for what was to follow. Twelve days, and a number of further reverses later, the House of Commons approved 'the preliminary resolution to the articles of union', which encompassed the 'principle' of the measure, by the slightly larger margin of 161 votes to 115, following a debate that is better known for the duel it precipitated between Henry Grattan and Isaac Corry.[102] It was a decisive moment and, realising the futility of insisting on a division on every resolution, the opposition henceforth determined to choose their ground more carefully.[103]

Consonant with this, the opposition intensified their efforts 'to bring forward the mass of the people' in the knowledge, as Edward Cooke observed, that 'any attempt to move government without a general cry of popular discontent is folly'.[104] The preparedness of Catholics in Longford and Louth in January to endorse the anti-union stand of Daniel O'Connell, and the unwillingness of many Orange lodges to adhere to the directive of the Grand Lodge of Ireland and 'continue silent' suggested this was still possible.[105] More importantly, reports from around the country indicated that anti-union interests were busy preparing petitions for presentation to parliament, and twenty-five counties and eighteen corporate and commercial interests had done so by the end of February.[106] This notwithstanding, the campaign against the Union was disappointing because the public discontent it generated was not sharp enough to cause MPs to alter their voting pattern. This was underlined on 4 March when George Ponsonby brought forward a motion respecting 'the sense of the nation upon the subject of an union'. It was 'the opposition's great question' and the fact that the debate was finally adjourned on the motion of the chief secretary, 155 to 107, merely emphasised, as Edward Cooke observed piquantly, that the opposition had made 'no impression' on the government phalanx since the opening of the parliamentary session.[107] No less crucially, the fact that addresses supportive of a union were presented from gentlemen and freeholders from counties Meath, Westmeath, Down and Mayo and from Catholic and Protestant freeholders of County Kilkenny emphasised that the proposed Act of Union was not without its supporters.[108]

Despite the modest impact they had registered to date, the opposition persisted with their attempt to excite public resistance by contriving in March 'to fix upon the most unpopular points of the measure' in the hope that they could thereby 'inflame the country'. With this object in mind, they 'excited great alarm among . . . manufacturing and commercial interests' by claiming that the growing cotton industry in Ireland would be overwhelmed by British imports. They also contrived to excite alarm about the security of the exemption from the tithe of agistment sanctioned by the House of Commons in 1735, but the prompt intervention of Lord Castlereagh succeeded in preventing the opposition from capitalising on the genuine concern felt on both points.[109] This served to allay the concerns articulated within the Irish administration in late February with the fact that the opposition was 'united' and 'steady to each other'. This remained the case, not least because the opposition dined together on a regular basis during the session. Their main resort was Atwell's Commercial Buildings Tavern in Cope Street, but smaller groups met in private in the houses of Lord Charlemont and Capel Molyneux, and it was as a result of such encounters that they reached the tacit understanding with the Speaker to be in the Commons' chamber daily at 4 pm when he 'counts the house'.[110] Such practices helped the opposition's campaign, but they did not mean that they were 'united in any general system of embarrassing government', and a succession of reversals and defeats in the division lobbies on a variety of issues including the question of compensation during the mid-weeks of March convinced them that there was no advantage to be obtained pressing every resolution to a division. They effectively gave up contesting the passage of the Union resolutions on 21 March. As a result, they completed their passage through the Commons within a few days and they had received the sanction of the House of Lords by 28 March.[111]

The ratification of the Union resolutions narrowed both the options and the prospects of the opposition successfully resisting the proposed Anglo-Irish Union. They resolved to soldier on, and perceiving that the spring assizes provided them with their last opportunity to rally public opinion, they determined that petitions should be got up for presentation direct to George III. This bothered Pitt, who instructed the Irish administration to secure 'counter-declarations' in order to demonstrate that the people of Ireland were not 'against the measure'.[112] Precipitated, as a result, into a further test of public opinion on a legislative union, the opponents and proponents each contrived to rally support. The anti-unionists, who had most to gain, had a motivational advantage on their rivals and this enabled them to secure a substantially larger number of petitions. In some instances, the support generated by anti-union interests was highly impressive. There were as many as 5,000 signatures from freemen, freeholders, merchants, traders and manufacturers appended to the Cork petition. However, neither this nor further petitions from counties Sligo, Fermanagh, Kings, Cavan, Roscommon, Longford, Dublin or elsewhere influenced Cornwallis who concluded that 'if any change has taken place in the public mind, it appears to have been in favour of the measure'.[113] This is questionable since the strong manifestations of popular anti-unionism visible through April and May encouraged its parliamentary opponents to make a final stand against the Union bill in the House of Commons.

The re-entry of John Philpot Curran and the prominent stand taken by Henry Grattan served to enhance both men's posthumous reputations, but they did little for the anti-union cause other than demonstrate the determination that was the most sterling feature of the opposition's unavailing effort's to resist an Anglo-Irish union in 1800. They did so, moreover, against an unfavourable backdrop as a botched attempt to assassinate George III prompted an unexpected surge in popular loyalism in late May–early June.[114] This facilitated the final passage of the Act of Union and its acceptance by sections of the public. The result of a by-election in County Londonderry in which a pro-union candidate triumphed over the anti-union nominee of the Ponsonbys suggested this was likely in any event. But of equal significance are the statements attributed to a number of opposition MPs who observed as soon as the Act of Union received the royal assent that they not only accepted the decision but would encourage others to do likewise.[115] This was not the attitude of everyone; Capel Molyneux, for example, still adhered twenty-two years later to the commitment he entered into in 1800 not to 'attend, levee, ball or dinner at the Castle until its repeal should take place'. The historian Francis Plowden also encountered strong anti-union sentiment on a visit to Ireland in 1801.[116] One cannot claim on the basis of either that repeal existed as a political issue from the moment the Act of Union came into effect, but perhaps there is less discontinuity between the opposition manifested in 1798–1800 and the later repeal movement than is sometimes suggested.

V

It can be argued that the failure of the Irish opposition to an Anglo-Irish union was neither unexpected nor surprising. Crucially, after starting off so well in the winter of 1798–99, they could not sustain the momentum that brought them success. It is true that they contributed to their own difficulties by making important tactical errors at crucial moments, but the opposition in the eighteenth-century Irish parliament had seldom been able to sustain successfully a campaign against the combined interests of the British government and Dublin Castle, and the late 1790s were no different. Moreover, the changes made to the terms of the Act of Union in 1799 and 1800, the provision to compensate borough owners for loss of property, and the extensive recourse to patronage and to propaganda to ensure a majority also favoured the Irish administration second time round. But, perhaps the most critical factor was the conclusion of many Irish Protestants that their personal and political interest was more likely to be secure within an Anglo-Irish union than within a separate Irish kingdom or Irish republic, which were the alternatives presented to them. It took many Irish Protestants time to reach this conclusion, but it is surely significant that the decisive contribution to opposition made by Protestant neo-conservatism in the winter of 1798–99 was not replicated in 1799–1800.

Nonetheless, one should neither underestimate the significance nor the impact of the opposition to the Act of Union. The combination of patriotism and neo-conservatism that successfully resisted a union when it was first proposed may have represented an unlikely coalescing of interests, but it was sufficient to prevail over a disorganised and somewhat complacent

administration, and to ensure that the terms of the measure were significantly altered. The problem for the opposition, and it was a habitual problem
throughout the eighteenth century, was that they could not bind the
combination of indignation, self-interest and principled resistance that fuelled
their campaign in the winter of 1798–99 into a coherent political organisation.
If they had done so they would have transformed Irish Protestant as well as
Anglo-Irish politics.

The fact that, as in the mid-1750s, late 1760s and mid-1780s, the Irish
Protestant élite in 1799–1800 acceded, though not without resistance, to the will
of the British government and on this occasion acquiesced in the abolition of
the Irish parliament mirrors the rise in support for a legislative union that
gathered in the 1790s, and the realisation of a majority of Irish Protestants that
when it came to their security the Anglo-Irish connection was essential. In the
circumstances of the late 1790s, when the options were 'union or separation', a
majority chose the former, frequently after extracting a price, because this was
the more palatable alternative. In this context, the fact that the opposition to
the Act of Union failed is less surprising than that they showed so well for so
long. That they did is testament to the strength of the attachment of Irish
Protestants to an Irish parliament, and to the conviction of the Irish Protestant
élite in their right to rule. However, when obliged to choose between a
domestic legislature and a secure Anglo-Irish connection, a majority opted for
the latter. This ultimately is why the opposition in Ireland to an Anglo-Irish
union failed.

CHAPTER NINE

The Irish House of Commons, 1799–1800

PATRICK M. GEOGHEGAN

William Hazlitt, the nineteenth-century critic, once described John O'Keeffe as the 'English Molière'. He was incorrect on both counts; the Dublin-born playwright was neither English nor talented, but he was intensely patriotic and after 1800 wrote a number of songs and poems condemning the Act of Union. O'Keeffe was an exact contemporary of Henry Grattan, and wrote in his memoirs that he used to play football with the young patriot leader in College Green.[1] In his twilight years, O'Keeffe wrote a nationalistic poem, which ended with a scathing critique of the Union:

> Our mansions desolate! Our comforts fled!
> In hearts now alien, patriot spark is dead.
> Lords of our flowery Isle, to their disgrace,
> Barter'd my rights for title and for place.
> William our king! Thou'art good, we thee implore,
> To College Green our parliament restore!

Only a fragment of this work remains; O'Keeffe destroyed most of it and modestly asserted that while this would satisfy 'the thousand friends of the Union' there would be 'millions' of people with a different opinion.[2] Perhaps unsurprisingly, the work, like O'Keeffe himself, is now all but forgotten.

The destruction of the Irish parliament, which O'Keeffe so lamented, has been the subject of much recent scholarship. However, relatively little has been written on the workings of the Irish House of Commons between 1799 and 1800, or about how the composition of the house changed dramatically during these years due to the influence of 'title' and 'place'.

UNITING THE PARLIAMENTS

In 1799, the Irish House of Commons was composed of 300 MPs representing 150 two-seat constituencies. These were divided between county and borough seats. A further distinction can be made between the constituencies that had an 'open' electorate and those that did not. The most prestigious seats were those returned by the thirty-two 'open' county constituencies, most of whom had substantial numbers of freehold voters. The other 118 constituencies ranged from those boroughs that were called 'cities' or 'towns' and which were at the disposal of a corporation or a patron, to boroughs that could be secured or purchased from a proprietor; finally there was the University of Dublin. A.P.W. Malcomson, in his groundbreaking work on the period, has calculated that of the 107 borough constituencies all but ten were 'closed'; this increased the attractiveness and prestige of the eighty-six 'open' constituency seats.[3]

When the prime minister, William Pitt, and his foreign secretary (and former Irish chief secretary), Lord Grenville, worked on a plan for union in early June 1798 they considered allowing Ireland 150 seats in the House of Commons of the United Kingdom.[4] This figure was calculated in terms of the ratio between Ireland's and Britain's population, following the precedent of the 1707 Anglo-Scottish Union. The number of 150 MPs was extremely convenient, as it allowed for the preservation of all the existing Irish constituencies with one rather than two members. After much deliberation, in the summer of 1798 Pitt decided to lower the proposed Irish representation. By August, he had come to feel that the figure of 150 Irish MPs was too high, and he resolved to reduce the number to 100, although he was wary that this might 'stir too much the principles of parliamentary reform'.[5] To choose these 100 MPs Pitt suggested returning one member from each of the thirty-three [*sic*] counties (perhaps mistakenly adding Carrickfergus or Drogheda), with a further member from each of the seventeen 'most considerable cities and towns' in other words, the seventeen largest 'towns and cities' that already returned members to the Irish parliament. The remaining fifty seats could then be chosen from the existing 100 constituencies (that is, the ninety-six boroughs, the two manors, the University of Dublin and the other county and town[6]), with each constituency returning one rather than two MPs. The prospect of 100 Irish MPs entering the British House of Commons did not rest easily with many people in England. Lord Liverpool feared for the effect it would have on the parliamentary system, while Lord Sheffield was even more blunt. He felt that eighty 'wild Irish' was 'rather too much', and insisted that seventy-five would be sufficient, as 'the present House of Commons is very trumpery and bad enough. I do not think any of our country gentlemen would venture into parliament if they were to meet 100 Paddies'.[7]

Before the Union first came before the Irish House of Commons a number of interesting suggestions were made for choosing the 100 MPs. The marquess of Buckingham, twice lord lieutenant for Ireland, sketched some proposals that he sent to his brother, Lord Grenville. These involved returning one MP from each of the existing 150 constituencies and then balloting 100 from this number to sit in the House of Commons. The unlucky fifty would then be given responsibility for various administrative duties in Ireland.[8] While the government gave a cautious support to this scheme, it was hardly practical, and was never likely to be adopted. The chief secretary, Lord Castlereagh, circulated a more acceptable proposal in January 1799, which allowed for two MPs from the cities of Dublin and Cork, one MP from each of eight other towns, and one MP from each of the thirty-two counties. The remaining seats could then be filled by returning one MP from half of the remaining 108 constituencies, with the existing fifty-four ordinary boroughs returning members to the next parliament. In other words, these boroughs would only be represented at alternate parliaments, a proposal which would certainly have been confusing if it had been adopted. The scheme had not been thought out very carefully, as the figures did not add up: it allowed for only ninety-eight Irish MPs at Westminster, a reduction of two on the proposed total that would have satisfied neither Ireland nor Lord Sheffield.

The Union bill that passed successfully through the Irish House of Commons in 1800 encompassed ideas floated in August 1798 and allowed 100 Irish MPs to sit in the lower house of the parliament of the United Kingdom. However, the constituencies that provided these 100 seats were radically different in the final version of the measure. Under article eight, section three, it was decided that sixty-four 'commoners' would be returned for the counties and thirty-six MPs for named boroughs. In this way, each county would continue to be represented by two members. The remaining thirty-six seats were calculated by halving the representation of Carrickfergus, Drogheda and the University of Dublin, one member from seven named 'towns', nine members selected from seven named 'cities', and one member from sixteen other boroughs.

The method for deciding which Irish MPs would sit in Westminster from 1 January 1801 was complex. The sixty-four members for the thirty-two counties, and the four members for the cities of Cork and Dublin were deemed returned, like all of the existing MPs in the British House of Commons, without any other election or selection process. However, the remaining thirty-two MPs had to be chosen from boroughs that had previously returned twice that number to the Irish House of Commons. Rather than have a general election to resolve the problem, it was decided in article eight, section seven, of the Act of Union to leave the matter to fate. The sixty-four MPs were instructed to meet in the chamber of the Irish House of Commons before 1 January 1801 where the clerk of the crown, or his deputy, would write down the names of the members on separate pieces of paper. These papers were to be folded and placed in separate glasses. The papers would be picked randomly by the clerk, giving each candidate a fifty per cent chance of success; the first name out would take the seat. After the thirty-two MPs were so chosen the clerk would give a certificate to each of the successful candidates and make a return 'of the said names' to 'the House of Commons of the first parliament of the United Kingdom'. In this way, a ballot system would decide which Irish MPs were to join their fellow countrymen at Westminster.

All eventualities were covered in the Union articles regarding the workings of this ballot. If a member died before the drawing of lots was made the other candidate was returned automatically. There was also a provision for one of the candidates withdrawing from the contest: in this case, the other candidate was duly returned. If both candidates withdrew, or died, a provision was included for a by-election to take place. Given the arbitrariness of this arrangement high-profile casualties were inevitable. Isaac Corry, the Irish chancellor of the exchequer, lost out to John Moore, at Newry Borough, although he was soon returned for the safe seat of Dundalk which was at the government's disposal. In Clonmel neither John Dennis nor Stephen Moore decided to contest the seat and William Bagwell was brought in to represent the borough. Elsewhere, Frederick Trench balloted successfully against William Gregory to become MP for Portarlington, while William Talbot's name was picked for Kilkenny City; for the following decade this seat was controlled by an arrangement between the earl of Ormond and the Cuffe family. A number of aspiring politicians with an eye on Westminster entered the Irish parliament after the Union debates so that they could join the imperial legislature. One such person was John Knox who succeeded Richard Fortescue Sharkey as MP for Dungannon in late 1800; he never took his seat in London. He drowned at sea before the new parliament met, although his death was not known for some time, and the seat remained vacant for most of the year.

Since Nicholas Westby, MP for Wicklow, also died in late 1800 this meant that there were only ninety-eight, instead of one hundred, Irish MPs available to take their seats in the House of Commons of the united parliament when it first met in 1801. Of these ninety-eight members, fifty-one had supported the Act of Union, forty-six had opposed it, while one, Arthur Gore, MP for Donegal, did not vote on the question.[9]

By retaining thirty-three boroughs the government saved approximately £400,000 in borough compensation as well as preserving the option of keeping safe seats for supporters. The fact that all the MPs for the counties were returned automatically meant that these seats retained their prestige, and special status in the country. It also saved those members from the perils of a lottery, and the embarrassment of having to find a new seat before 1 January 1801. Dublin City and Cork City were the only other constituencies to retain their two seats. For those MPs with Westminster ambitions in constituencies that were downgraded to one seat it soon became a matter of some interest to see who would contest the remaining thirty-two seats. Things were worse for the MPs for Charleville, County Cork; Middleton, County Cork, and Clogher, County Tyrone, who did not even have the luxury of a lottery; their seats were automatically abolished. It seems that support for the Union was no protection as five of the six MPs for these constituencies voted for the measure in 1800.[10]

After the passing of the Union, there remained the pressing question of what to do with the old parliament house. The provost of Trinity College Dublin recommended turning the chambers into lecture-halls but this was rejected by the government because it was feared that the students would get into disturbances with the Dublin citizens when crossing the road between the two buildings.[11] One proposed way around this obstacle was a suggestion to build a tunnel between Trinity and parliament house so that the students could not get into any trouble. In the end, however, the Bank of Ireland intervened and purchased the parliament house for £40,000 in 1802.

THE PASSING OF THE UNION

With the discovery of 'lost' secret service papers, that prove the illegal use of a covert slush fund by the government to pass the Union, it is worth re-examining the membership of the Irish House of Commons between 1799 and 1800. When the Irish parliament met on 22 January 1799, to hear the king's address and have an unscheduled debate on the Union, 293 of the 300 seats were filled. Two of the empty seats were for the county of the town of Carrickfergus, and Wicklow County. In the former, the earl of Belfast had succeeded to the peerage as marquess of Donegal, and the seat remained vacant for the remainder of the year. In the latter, the death of William Hoare created a vacancy that was only filled by a relative on 8 February 1799. A further two seats were empty because the MPs stepped down to represent other constituencies (John Metge moved from Banagher, King's County, to Tallagh, County Waterford; while Francis Hardy moved from St. Johnstown, County Longford to Mullingar Manor, County Westmeath). At the start of the parliamentary session on 22 January 1799 it was announced that three more seats were vacant, and writs were issued for Ardee (Atherdee), County Louth; Mullingar Manor, County Westmeath; and Callan, County Kilkenny. The sitting members, Charles Ruxton, William Doyle and Charles Kendal Bushe, had all accepted escheatorships (a sinecure worth thirty shillings a year).

Much of the 'neo-corruption argument' has centred on the use of the fighting fund to persuade unprincipled members to change sides, or troublesome members to vacate their seats and allow a pro-union candidate to take their place. However, it is also worth examining how much transfer activity took place in the Irish House of Commons in the eighteen-month period when the Union was debated. The *Journals of the House of Commons* show that most of the movement occurred in closed boroughs; the most prestigious 'open' constituencies experienced almost minimal change. In total, there was no change in 225 of the 300 seats, with these members representing the same constituency for the final two years of the Irish parliament; seventy-five out of 300 seats changed members between 22 January 1799 and 7 June 1800.[12]

In a few constituencies where there was movement there are instances where the same seat changed members more than once. Some of the seventy-five changes were enforced by death or by an MP succeeding to the peerage. Two members died in 1799; Robert Ross (Newry) and Sir John Blackwood (Killyleagh). Six died in 1800; a high figure given that the session lasted only seven months. These were Hugh Howard (Athboy); Charles King (Belturbet); Hugh O'Donnell (Donegal); William Montgomery (Hillsborough); Charles Powell Leslie (County Monaghan) and Daniel Gahan (Wicklow). One MP vacated his seat because he was raised to the peerage in 1799 as Lord Viscount Kingsborough (County Roscommon), while five vacated their seats for the same reason in the 1800 session. However, as only one of these changes occurred before 7 June 1800, the final day in which the Union was debated (Lord Viscount Caulfeild (County Armagh)), the other four are not included in the total of 225.

After the opening of the parliament, in January 1799, twenty-three MPs vacated their seats during that session and were not returned for the same constituency. In total twenty-nine writs were issued, but in some cases the same member was re-elected, or the writ was issued before the Union debate on 22 January. It should be noted that some members received genuine offices in this period and resigned their seats under the terms of the Place Act to seek re-election; as they were returned for the same constituency, they are not included in my calculations for changes in the representation. The twenty-three changes are accounted for by two MPs dying, one being raised to the peerage, seventeen vacating their seats by accepting escheatorships, and the remaining three accepting other nominal offices or sinecures. The parliamentary traffic in seats increased dramatically in 1800. In that year, sixty-three MPs vacated their seats and were not returned for the same constituency. In total, seventy-seven writs were issued, but again, some were returned for the same constituency and are therefore not included in this analysis. The sixty-three changes can be accounted for by six MPs dying, five being raised to the peerage, thirty-seven accepting escheatorships and the remaining fifteen accepting other nominal offices or sinecures.

It is difficult to list precisely the names of the MPs who voted for and against the Union in 1799 and 1800. There are two sets of published lists, but both are dangerously unreliable. The first, and most famous set, are Jonah Barrington's notorious 'red and black lists', which he published in the second volume of his *Historic memoirs* in 1832.[13] Many names are excluded from this work, however, and it contains other significant errors. The second set can be found in John Roche Ardill's *The closing of the Irish parliament* which was published in 1907.[14] These lists also contain many errors, including the wrong names for constituencies and inaccurate details about members, thus distorting many of the calculations and conclusions.[15] There were many lists for 1799 published at the time, and these are quite accurate, allowing for some new calculations about how the Union passed through the Irish House of Commons.

'RENEGADES' AND 'RETREATERS': THE BATTLE IN PARLIAMENT

The government won the battle in parliament in 1800 because they were more ruthless than their opponents, they had more resources at their disposal and they had a better strategy that included Catholics and Protestants within its terms. G.C. Bolton lists four means by which the government was able to gain a Common's majority:

> Rebellious or abstaining members from supporting groups could be won over. Direct converts might be made from the anti-unionist ranks. The neutrals . . . could be recruited to the ministerialist side. Alternately, neutral or hostile borough members might be persuaded to sell their places, perhaps at a profit, to a friend of the government.[16]

The two groups that will be examined here are the second and the fourth category, the 'direct converts' and the MPs who vacated their seats to allow 'a friend of the government' to replace them. The first group is what Jonah Barrington termed the 'renegades', the anti-unionists who deserted the opposition in return for peerages, patronage or direct payment. The second category can be termed the 'retreaters', the MPs who were not prepared to vote for a union, but were open to persuasion about vacating their seats in return for some reward, even if it meant allowing a unionist to take their place. While Bolton admitted that much trading took place, he was sceptical about the swirling allegations of corruption, insisting that the appeal to patronage and borough compensation by the government was an acceptable part of late-eighteenth-century practice. Given the dearth of available evidence to the contrary, Bolton's historical methodology cannot be faulted. However, recent scholarship has centred on the discovery of new archival material which shows the allocation of secret service money to an illegal government fund to assist the measure.[17] The seduction of private interests during the period was far less clear-cut than Bolton has claimed and there remains much work to be done on the detail of how the Union passed in the Irish House of Commons. One central argument of Bolton's work in particular has not been questioned: his calculation of how many MPs converted to the government's side during the Union debate. Bolton cautiously put the figure at twelve, excluding members who were believed to be hostile, but abstained, in January 1799. This number he then dismissed as being 'so small as to be almost insignificant in a House of 300 members'.[18]

Even accepting the figure of twelve MPs changing sides between January 1799 and 1800, this represents over ten per cent of the anti-union vote in January 1799. The fact that the government was able to persuade just over one in ten of its opponents to change sides within twelve months is surely significant and certainly suggestive. The conversion of twelve members to the Union side ensured that there were twelve fewer votes for the opposition, so it marked a total gain in parliamentary terms of twenty-four for the government. This is not to say that all of these members were bribed or corrupted. Many new arguments had been made during 1799 in favour of the Union, borough compensation had been conceded, and the support of the Catholics had been enlisted, so there were plenty of genuine reasons for the 'renegades' to convert.

Certainly, the motives of the MPs who changed from the government to the opposition side in the same period have never been questioned in the same way. This seems to reflect the prejudices of the people doing the calculations, with opposition converts praised for their principles, but government converts condemned for their venality. James Butler, the MP for County Kilkenny, supported the Union when it was first debated in the Commons, but by 1800 had become convinced that it would be bad for Ireland.[19] William Blakeney (Athenry) and Thomas 'Buck' Whaley (Enniscorthy) also changed their positions in the same period.[20] The exploits of the Bagwells are a notorious case in point. The head of the family, John Bagwell, who was also known as 'Old Bags' and 'Marshal Sacks', opposed the Union with his son, William, in January 1799 and brought another son, Richard, into the house a few months later to add to his influence. Now with three votes at his command, he made terms with the government after representations from the Castle through the ubiquitous Jonah Barrington. But still not satisfied and sensing a brilliant opportunity, Bagwell then offered his votes back to the opposition. He informed the Castle in February 1799 of his family's desertion unless they were paid £10,000 to better the £9,000 offered by the opposition. Cornwallis was disgusted, and refused any further deals insisting that 'the objects he solicited were promised'. Realising that they had overplayed their hand and that they risked losing everything, the Bagwells skulked back to the government side before it was too late.

While it is impossible to work out precisely the number of 'renegades' during the Union debates, there is some evidence for conversion to unionism on a larger-scale than Bolton has indicated.[21] It is possible that the figure was as large as twenty, and higher if one includes the MPs who were known to be hostile but abstained in January 1799.[22] The most interesting of these is Alexander Hamilton, who became such a fervent supporter of the Union that he conscripted his two infant nephews as unionists as well as 'the embryo which his sister was then carrying'.[23]

The role of the 'retreaters' in the passing of the Union and the misuse of the Place Act in securing a majority is also worthy of consideration. The Whig opposition had tried for many years to secure approval for a bill 'securing the freedom and independence of the House of Commons', failing in 1764, 1766, 1767 and 1777, but finally achieving some success in 1793. In that year, a Place Act was passed that ensured that MPs who accepted an office or place of profit under the crown after 31 December 1793 must automatically vacate their parliamentary seat and seek re-election. This was amended in 1798 to include offices, or places of profit granted by the lord lieutenant, chief governor or acting chief governor, to close any loophole and the bill received the royal assent on 4 June 1798.

This gave the Castle a mechanism for allowing MPs to vacate their seats, similar to the Chiltern Hundreds in Britain. The lord lieutenant could grant a member a nominal office, sinecure or escheatorship for one of the four provinces and his seat would fall vacant upon acceptance. The MP could then withdraw from parliament, rather than seek re-election, and allow someone else to replace him. To prevent corruption, the vacating member had to promise the lord lieutenant 'that no cash transaction was involved',[24] but this rule was sidestepped and circumvented between 1799 and 1800. During the passing of the Union, the House of Commons experienced a massive turnover and the Place Act was the means by which the change was effected. Even committed opponents of the Union made use of the legislation. For example, William Burton, MP for County Carlow, opposed the Union but allowed one of the borough seats he controlled to go to a unionist. Seats were sometimes referred to as 'borough stock' and many proprietors agreed with the sentiments of Lord Portarlington, who, in 1798, had referred to seats as 'certain commodities I have to dispose of'.[25]

Perhaps the most intriguing consequence of the passing of the Place Act came during the first debate on the Union, on 22 January 1799. The opposition, led by George Ponsonby, used the legal implications of that act to launch a surprise ambush on the government. When Lord Tyrone attempted to propose the traditional vote of thanks after the king's address, Ponsonby rose to his feet and declared that 'according to his information' there were at that time 'aliens and strangers . . . usurping seats in that house'.[26] He then questioned the validity of the seat of one MP in particular who was sitting in the chamber. The government were taken by surprise by this sudden attack on an unexpected flank, and were even more disturbed when they discovered that the member that was being challenged was their leading minister, Lord Castlereagh. Ponsonby argued that by accepting the office of chief secretary to the lord lieutenant, Castlereagh had vacated his seat under the 1793 legislation and the 1798 Amending Act and that he had been obliged to seek re-election. The relevant articles of the legislation were read into the Commons' records, and there was much embarrassment for the young Castlereagh.

The attorney general, John Toler, intervened, claiming that Castlereagh had been appointed in March 1798 by Camden, before the amending act had been passed, and so did not fall within its terms. Two hours of heated debate took place on the question, which did nothing for morale on the government benches, but everything for the opposition, who cheered at Castlereagh's discomfort. In the end, Ponsonby withdrew his motion to allow for a debate on the Union and the question was allowed to drop. The opposition probably accepted they had exhausted this delaying tactic and historians have largely ignored it. In retrospect, it seems Ponsonby was correct in his accusations from a legal standpoint and that the attorney general was being more than a little disingenuous.

While it was true that Castlereagh became chief secretary in March 1798, this was only in a temporary capacity, because of the illness of Thomas Pelham. He continued in this position under the new lord lieutenant, Cornwallis, in June 1798, but the crucial fact is that it was Pelham who was reconfirmed as chief secretary to the new viceroy in that month and not Castlereagh. Cornwallis and Whitehall made various attempts to find a permanent replacement for Pelham throughout that summer and autumn and it seemed Castlereagh would be made chancellor of the exchequer. In the end, Cornwallis was persuaded of Castlereagh's abilities and he was formally appointed his chief secretary in November 1798.[27] Therefore, this was the correct date of his appointment as chief secretary and, because it was in the autumn, he should have fallen within the terms of the amending act. Legally, therefore, he had vacated his seat and a writ should have been issued for a by-election. Either oblivious to the legal ramifications of his appointment, or unwilling to risk a difficult by-election in County Down with the new parliamentary session approaching, Castlereagh did nothing, with consequences that were embarrassing, and almost very damaging, for the unionist cause. The government had risked losing their leader in the chamber, their crucial minister, for the entire debate in the Commons at the very time they needed him most. They would find the Place Act a more convenient ally in the months ahead.

CHANGES IN BOROUGH REPRESENTATION 1799

Twelve borough seats were vacated in 1799 and filled with a new member the same year.[28] Three saw a family member replace the outgoing MP and might therefore be considered as 'no change'. Of the remaining nine, one was vacated as a result of a member dying (Robert Ross; Newry), and an anti-unionist took the seat. Six of the remaining seats went to members who would support and vote for the Union. The anti-unionists therefore made only two gains in borough representation in the entire year: Robert Shaw (St Johnstown, County Longford) and Henry Luttrell (Clonmines), compared with six for the unionists – Savage (Callan); Aldridge (Carysfort); Sharkey (Dungannon); Pakenham (Longford); Ormsby (Gorey); and Johnson (Roscommon).

Barrington records an interesting anecdote about Luke Fox, the MP for Clonmines, County Wexford, whose patron was Lord Ely. Apparently, he was terrified to vote either against the government or against his patron. When he was cornered during the first debate on the Union, he instead insisted that he had vacated his seat. He was soon granted the escheatorship of Ulster and he was replaced on 15 May 1799 by Henry Luttrell (Lord Carhampton) who himself resigned his seat in early 1800. Fox returned to the Commons as MP for Mullingar Manor, County Westmeath, and was sworn on 8 February 1799. He voted for the Union in 1800. Bolton dismissed the story of how he vacated his seat as a 'yarn' and insisted that Fox had accepted an escheatorship on 9 January 1799.[29] While it is true that Fox had fallen out with Ely and was on his way out, the reality is that the escheatorship was only announced in the Commons on 28 January and Fox's seat was not included among the warrants that were issued on 22 January. Therefore, he was still sitting in the Commons during the Union debates and if he was indeed forced to say how he was going to vote he could have claimed, quite legitimately, that he was about to vacate his seat. Whether the government had made terms with him, as Barrington alleged, is unknown.

CHANGES IN BOROUGH REPRESENTATION 1800

The first half of 1800 saw an unprecedented marketing of boroughs. Some constituencies changed both their members in the early months of the year; one constituency (Thomastown, County Kilkenny) even changed members a second time. Two boroughs (Callan and Carysfort) that changed one member in 1799 underwent further change in 1800. Henry Luttrell, a virulent anti-unionist, vacated his seat in early 1800 and was replaced by a pro-union MP. The significant statistic is that in thirty-three boroughs in 1800, representing sixty-six seats, a total of 106 different people were returned for parliament within the space of six months (see the table on p. 142 for full details). The nature of this 'traffic' can best be illustrated by examining it in practice in two instances.

CASE STUDY ONE: CLOGHER, COUNTY TYRONE

The two MPs for Clogher in 1799 were Thomas Burgh and the mercurial Jonah Barrington. As the latter was the great critic of the corruption that accompanied the passage of the Union it is worthwhile examining the changes that occurred in his own constituency during the Union debate, 1799–1800. Both Burgh and Barrington vacated their seats early in the 1800 session. Burgh became one of the commissioners of account on 17 January, while Barrington accepted the escheatorship of Munster on the same day. In their place came Lieutenant General William Gardiner and Richard Annesley, who were both sworn in on 3 February 1800. Both replacements were committed supporters of the Union and selected for that purpose.

The fact that Barrington was prepared to vacate his seat so early on in the session, after just one debate on the Union, casts serious doubts on his later claims of heroism. Indeed, he even implicated himself in some questionable activity in his own *Memoirs* when he admitted, without any embarrassment, to having acting as an agent for the Castle in finding out the terms of an anti-union MP.[30] As a contemporary noted perceptively, Barrington had 'the same notion of blushing that a blind man had of colours'. The government won the division after the debate of 15–16 January by 138–96 and Barrington seems to have decided that the entire battle was lost. Indeed, he later conceded that the government showed more spirit than the opposition in 1800, and by vacating his seat and leaving the parliament at that time he certainly showed little character himself.[31]

In his annotated 'red list' of members who voted against the Union in 1799 and 1800 Barrington boldly included his own name as someone who 'refused all terms'; his fellow representative, Thomas Burgh, did not even get a mention.[32] However, the replacement of Barrington and Burgh with two pro-union MPs did not go smoothly. There was a problem with the candidacies of Gardiner and Annesley and the election was controverted. A committee of the Commons investigated a petition by Charles Ball and John King, and it reported on 29 March that their request was not 'frivolous or vexatious'. Although the committee insisted that Gardiner's and Annesley's elections had not been 'procured by corrupt means', their names were erased nonetheless and Ball and King took the seats in their place; they were sworn in the same day. Annesley was another member-for-hire, prepared to serve wherever he was needed. He was MP for Blessington, County Wicklow in 1799 but vacated the seat on 20 January 1800 by accepting the escheatorship of Munster. He returned to the house in February, as MP for Clogher, until his election was nullified. Another seat was found for him, because he was so obliging, and he replaced General John Cradock as MP for Middleton in the final months of the parliament; he was sworn in on 8 May 1800.

CASE STUDY TWO: THOMASTOWN BOROUGH, COUNTY KILKENNY

The most activity in any single constituency occurred in Thomastown, County Kilkenny. At the start of 1800, the two MPs were George Dunbar and James Kearney. Both men vacated their seats in March: Dunbar became a gentleman at large to the lord lieutenant (6 March), while Kearney accepted the escheatorship of Munster (28 March). Dunbar was replaced almost immediately with Charles William Stewart, who was the chief secretary's twenty-one-year-old half-brother and who is now best remembered for editing the *Castlereagh correspondence*. Stewart, who had been a soldier since the age of fourteen, was sworn in as an MP on 18 March.[33] Kearney was replaced more slowly. It was not until 8 May that the seat was taken by the wandering William Gardiner. Both he and Stewart were brought in as supporters of the Union. General Gardiner had already been a recent MP in the Irish House of Commons, having been sworn in on 3 February 1800 as a member for Clogher, County Tyrone. He was, however, deemed 'not duly elected' shortly afterwards, and a new member took the seat. The same day as Gardiner was sworn in, Stewart accepted the escheatorship of Ulster and resigned his seat after only fifty-one days. This was to allow him to contest the vacant seat at County Londonderry, which he did successfully, becoming MP for the prestigious county seat on 29 May. Another replacement at Thomastown had to be found swiftly and Major General John Francis Cradock was enlisted for the position; he was sworn in on 19 May. Cradock was another of the military men (like the 1798 veterans, General Gerard Lake and General George Nugent) who entered the House of Commons in 1800 to support the government and they were very willing to help their commander-in-chief, Lord Cornwallis, in passing the Union. Cradock had re-entered the House of Commons on 20 February 1799 as MP for Middleton, County Cork, but vacated the seat on 12 April 1800 by accepting the office of gentleman at large to the lord lieutenant. That he was willing to return to the Commons a little over a month later, and with only three weeks of union debates remaining, shows just how persuasive the Castle administration could be, and just how concerned they were with preserving their majority.

TABLE

Name of constituency	Number of MPs in 1800
Ardfert (County Kerry)	3
Athenry (County Galway)	4
Athlone (County Westmeath)	3
Ballynakill (Queen's County)	4
Bannow (County Wexford)	4
Belfast (County Antrim)	3
Blessington (County Wicklow)	3
Carrick (County Leitrim)	3
Carysfort (County Wicklow)	3
Castlebar (County Mayo)	3
Clonmel (County Tipperary)	3
Clonmines (County Wexford)	3
Dingle (County Kerry)	3
Dunleer (County Louth)	3
Enniscorthy (County Wexford)	3
Enniskillen (County Fermanagh)	3
Fore (County Westmeath)	3
Gowran (County Kilkenny)	3
Granard (County Longford)	3
Kells (County Meath)	3
Kilbeggan (County Westmeath)	3
Killyleagh (County Down)	3
Knocktopher (County Kilkenny)	4
Longford (County Longford)	3
Maryborough (Queen's County)	3
Monaghan (County Monaghan)	3
Newtownards (County Down)	3
Philipstown (King's County)	4
Portarlington (Queen's County)	3
St Johnstown (County Longford)	3
Thomastown (County Kilkenny)	5
Tuam (County Galway)	3
Tulsk (County Roscommon)	3

106
MPs for 33 boroughs

Even taking just two constituencies, Thomastown and Clogher, it is possible to witness an extraordinarily complex series of manoeuvres as both sides competed to win the battle in parliament. In the end, the concatenation of events allowed General Cradock to switch from Middleton, County Cork, to Thomastown, County Kilkenny, while Richard Annesley moved from Blessington, County Wexford, to Middleton, County Cork, via an unsuccessful stint representing Clogher, County Tyrone.

REPRESENTING IRELAND

The parliamentary traffic in the Irish House of Commons between 1799 and 1800 was more congested than at any other time in the entire century. The Castle was determined to ensure that the Union passed, no matter what, and gradually built up an unbeatable majority in the lower chamber, which was then guarded jealously for the remainder of the session. Success was achieved through a complex strategy of deploying patronage and secret service money, while at the same time guaranteeing borough compensation and enlisting the support of the borough patrons and the Catholic hierarchy. The tactics in parliament, after the fiasco of January 1799, were cold, clinical and ultimately very effective. The numbers of the opposition were decimated by defections, while other anti-unionists were persuaded to vacate their seats and allow a government supporter to replace them. The Union passed in June 1800 with few complications in the Commons, and the Irish parliament was finally dissolved in August. One-third of the Irish seats were transferred to the parliament at Westminster, and the later part of 1800 saw an innovative use of a ballot system to choose some of these representatives. The task of representing Ireland in the nineteenth century would fall to these individuals, as the former members of the Irish House of Commons were forced to come to terms with the legacy of the Act of Union.

CHAPTER TEN

Dublin after the Union:
The Age of the Ultra-Protestants,
1801–1822

JACQUELINE HILL

On 19 February 1819, at a meeting of Dublin Corporation, the leading opponent of Catholic emancipation in the Corporation's lower house, John Giffard, proposed a resolution of censure on the lord mayor, Alderman Thomas McKenny. The lord mayor had recently lent his support to an 'aggregate' meeting of Dublin Protestants to petition parliament in favour of Catholic emancipation.[1] In chairing the meeting, according to Giffard, the lord mayor had gone against the advice of his fellow members of the Corporation, with the result that:

> Since the last day they had met here the WORLD WAS TURNED UPSIDE DOWN. Who could have supposed that the Protestant people of this city could be menaced, cajoled, and bullied by a popish rabble! This assembly saw the danger of calling the late aggregate meeting, and did counsel and advise the lord mayor against this meeting . . . which aimed to support the bugbear of a popish supremacy.[2]

Giffard's motion of censure was carried by a two-thirds majority of the 120–member house.

What seems remarkable about Giffard's reaction is not so much the apocalyptic language, or the implication that the 3,000 or so Protestants said to have attended the meeting had somehow been coerced into expressing support for emancipation, but the fact that such a meeting could have been a novelty. Could it really have taken the liberal Protestants of Dublin until 1819 to express their public support for emancipation? Yet, the liberal *Freeman's Journal*, poles apart from Giffard politically, seemed to endorse his assessment of the meeting's significance. On the day of the meeting, held in the Rotunda on 11 February 1819, the newspaper commented that the meeting would be the first of its kind ever held in Ireland: 'the exclusionists' were alarmed, but their cry 'the church in danger' had come too late.

The *Freeman's Journal* was right in its prediction that the day of the 'exclusionists' was nearly over. Although emancipation itself was still a decade away and opposition to emancipation was to persist – Dublin Corporation, for instance, was to remain as staunchly opposed as before – during the 1820s, the Catholic question was to be transformed by the rise of the Catholic Association. Moreover, the granting of emancipation, following so soon after the repeal in 1828 of the Test and Corporation Acts, would sound the death-knell of 'the Protestant constitution in church and state', which had retained such a hold on constitutional thinking in Britain and Ireland since the Revolution of 1688–89.[3] However, John Giffard's preoccupation with the link between church and state was less about constitutional abstractions than about the future of Protestants in Ireland and here his apocalyptic forecast was not altogether wrong. While the passing of Catholic emancipation undoubtedly owed much to liberal Protestant support, once the goal had been achieved the advancing O'Connellite juggernaut did not wait for Protestant backing before hastening to proclaim the next objective: the repeal of the Union. The days when Protestants as a body – liberal or otherwise – could, as it were, speak for Ireland, were numbered.

THE ULTRA-PROTESTANTS

This essay considers the wholly disproportionate influence of a small number of individuals in helping to form and express organised opinion both in Dublin and beyond in the first two post-union decades. These were individuals opposed to Catholic emancipation, not just vaguely but passionately. The description 'ultra-Protestants' is not ideal but, for the period in question, it is difficult to find a better one. The party label 'Tory', although occasionally used by contemporaries, had lost much of the specificity it had enjoyed between the 1670s and the 1760s, while 'Conservative' as a party name was current only from the 1830s. The term 'loyalist' has something to recommend it, at least in suggesting a strong attachment to the link with Britain. All these individuals fit well into the category of 'loyalists' in the context of the 1798 Rebellion. But others felt a similar attachment, without necessarily sharing the same passionate commitment to the Protestant constitution and Protestant control of all areas of Irish political life. The historian of what he calls 'reaction' in Britain in the early nineteenth century, James J. Sack, has acknowledged the problem, and he adopted the label 'right-wing' to describe such hard-liners.[4] But this fails to highlight the particular concerns of the Irish supporters of the status quo. 'Ultra' (sometimes 'ultra-loyalist' or 'ultra-Protestant') has the advantage of being a contemporary term, and it also suggests something of the intensity that drove these individuals.[5] The other feature that distinguished those under consideration here is that they were unionists.

Who were these people? The first point to note about these individuals in the context of early-nineteenth-century Dublin is that they were fairly few in number. The Act of Union was deeply unpopular in the capital, as G.C. Bolton has pointed out, and this extended to Protestants as well as Catholics.[6] Expressions of positive enthusiasm for the Union during the period in question are difficult to find. It is perhaps significant, then, that while those under consideration all had Dublin addresses during this period, they all also had links to other parts of Ireland. One notable figure was Sir Richard Musgrave (?1757–1818).[7] Originally from County Waterford, Musgrave had represented Lismore in the pre-union Irish parliament. He had acquired a national profile, thanks primarily to his account of the 1798 Rebellion, *Memoirs of the different rebellions in Ireland* of 1801, which had run into three editions by 1802. While it still remains in many respects a valuable record for the progress of the Rebellion, the account was slanted by the author's determination to see Catholic priests behind almost every sinister development in the 1790s and before. He gave his vote for the Union in 1800 and obtained the lucrative post of collector of the Dublin city excise. He subsequently resided in Dublin.

Another such figure was Dr Patrick Duigenan (1735–1816). Duigenan was born into a Catholic farming family in County Leitrim, but was educated by a Church of Ireland clergyman and had joined the established church. He qualified as a barrister and obtained a position in the court of admiralty in 1790. He also became Professor of Feudal and English Law in the University of Dublin. He advanced in church circles, becoming judge of the consistorial court in Dublin. During the 1790s, he represented first Old Leighlin and then Armagh in the Irish parliament and was a prominent spokesman for a legislative union during the debates of 1799 and 1800. He was subsequently rewarded with a commissioner's post for distributing borough compensation after the Union had come into operation and, some years later, was made a member of the Irish privy council. Unlike Musgrave, he served in the United Kingdom parliament (continuing to represent Armagh) where he became notorious for his opposition to Catholic emancipation. Outside parliamentary terms, he too resided in Dublin.[8]

Less well known, but even more influential in Dublin civic circles, was John Giffard (1746–1819). At the time of the Union, he was a life-member of the lower house of Dublin Corporation, having served as sheriff in 1793–94, during which time he had proved to be a scourge of the United Irishmen. His social origins were sufficiently obscure for contemporary critics, of whom he had many, to manufacture all sorts of lurid tales about his background. In fact, he was the son of John Giffard, a Devonshire attorney who had come to

Ireland in the 1740s and married a widow named Dorcas Murphy, daughter of Arthur Murphy of Oulartleigh, County Wexford. John Giffard senior had been disinherited, while still a child, of extensive lands in north Devonshire. For their part, the Murphys of Oulartleigh, who by the eighteenth century were Protestants, claimed descent from the MacMurrough kings of Leinster. The product of this union was John Giffard. His parents died when he was a child, leaving him to be raised by Irish relatives and benefactors, especially the barrister Ambrose Hardinge. Having to make his own way in the world, the young Giffard was apprenticed to a Dublin apothecary and subsequently represented his guild on Dublin Corporation. He married into another Wexford family, the Mortons of Ballynaclash. At first, he was inclined to take an opposition stand in city politics, but he subsequently displayed some support for the government side and obtained a post in the customs; for a time he also acted as a reporter of Irish parliamentary debates. He took over the editorship of *Faulkner's Dublin Journal* in 1788, which subsequently became notorious for its attacks on the moré advanced patriots. Giffard's government contacts initially rendered him unpopular in Dublin Corporation circles and it was not until the political climate had become more polarised that he gained sufficient votes in the Corporation's lower house to allow the aldermen to select him as sheriff in 1793.[9]

Jonah Barrington credited Giffard with having created the term 'Protestant ascendancy'. The origins of this term have received considerable attention from scholars in recent years without producing any evidence to substantiate Barrington's claim; but the concept certainly suited Giffard's politics.[10] During the 1790s, he acted as a go-between for Dublin Castle and some of its spies and became a captain in the Dublin city militia. Of the three men noticed so far, Giffard suffered most during the period of the 1798 Rebellion. His youngest son, Lieutenant William Giffard of the 82nd regiment, was killed on the outbreak of rebellion in May 1798; he had been aboard the mail coach from Limerick to Dublin that was stopped by the rebels in Kildare town. Among Giffard's relations by marriage the deaths during the Rebellion apparently ran into double figures; they included a brother-in-law who died in Wexford gaol, and Captain Daniel Ryan, a nephew of Giffard's wife, who died during the arrest of Lord Edward Fitzgerald.[11]

If Musgrave, Duigenan and Giffard were connected by having some sort of government position and by being among the first supporters of legislative union, they also had something else in common. They were all early and highly placed members of the Orange Order. Shortly after the passing of the Union, Musgrave became treasurer to the Grand Lodge of Ireland, Duigenan grand secretary, and Giffard by 1806 was deputy grand master. Giffard's son Hardinge, a barrister, is credited (together with Samuel

Montgomery) with drawing up the rules for the Grand Lodge on its removal to Dublin in 1798.[12] The new rules superseded the various county codes and thus brought greater cohesion to the movement; they were also made public, which served to counter some of the more lurid reports as to what the Orange Order's rules were. As Hereward Senior has pointed out, from that time on the Grand Lodge formed the nucleus of a national movement.[13] It was also becoming more socially and politically respectable. In 1798, government had displayed de facto toleration of Orange auxiliaries to help counter rebellion and, in 1801, George Ogle of Bellvue, County Wexford, MP for Dublin city, was made grand master, taking over from Thomas Verner of Armagh.[14]

ULTRA-PROTESTANT ACTIVITIES

During the first post-union decade, the political climate was generally favourable to those whose outlook was both unionist and ultra-Protestant. The king, whose role as a national symbol during wartime had become very important, remained strongly opposed to Catholic emancipation: this led to the resignation of Pitt in 1801 and inhibited other ministers who might have supported emancipation. For a brief period, in 1806–07, a pro-emancipation ministry, 'the ministry of all the talents', was in place and some attempts were made to oust ultra-Protestants from the Irish magistracy, but the ministry did not hold power long enough to achieve much.[15] The Catholic leadership, meanwhile, pursued the emancipation goal in a low-key and spasmodic fashion and were only slowly realising the potential of enhancing their claims by stressing their contribution to the war effort and especially military manpower. War with France had resumed, after a lull, in 1803.[16]

Yet, even before the Union came into operation, one effect of the 1798 Rebellion had been to reinforce confessional divisions between the largely Catholic militia and the largely Protestant yeomanry. During its early phase in 1796–97 the Dublin yeomanry had admitted significant numbers of Catholics, but this practice appears to have faded after the Rebellion. The Dublin yeomanry prided themselves particularly on having prevented the United Irishmen capturing Dublin in 1798 and using the capital as a springboard to take control of the country at large. Robert Emmet's Rebellion of 1803, together with the end of the peace of Amiens, reinforced the case for maintaining and increasing yeomanry numbers; and despite the fact that Emmet and Thomas Russell were Protestants the essence of the threat still seemed to lie in Catholic numbers and real or possible Catholic disaffection. Thus, there was little disposition to challenge those who argued that only Protestants could be fully loyal citizens and hence only Protestants could be trusted in the yeomanry. Protestant traditions of self-defence were reinforced as links between the yeomanry and the Orange Order were strengthened. Protestants might be increasingly aware of the growth of Catholic numbers, but through the yeomanry and the Order, with its military-style anniversary parades, they could maintain some sense of security.[17]

What is also noteworthy about this period is the survival into the immediate post-union years of much former deference. Dublin Corporation was already beginning to experience chronic financial difficulties, but this was not yet public knowledge and there was still a lingering legacy of prestige accruing from the Corporation's former role as a bastion of the patriot opposition. For instance, the Corporation was still charging and also collecting tolls from country people coming into the city to sell their goods: during the first post-union decade revenue from such tolls was running at peak eighteenth-century levels.[18] Moreover, the Irish economy was reasonably buoyant, which meant that the Union did not come under sustained attacks on economic grounds.

In general, therefore, down to 1810 the ultra-Protestants had little need to exert themselves unduly. This was a period in which even pro-Catholic newspapers such as the *Freeman's Journal* could refer approvingly to King William III (admittedly, as a champion of religious freedom and the scourge of Louis XIV) and the lord lieutenant and state officials continued to take part, down to 1805, in the annual procession to King William's statue in College Green on the anniversary of the latter's birthday, 4 November.[19] The Williamite military victories were celebrated by Orangemen, but without apparently causing very much tension or comment.

During this period, however, the ultra-Protestants did make some contributions to the cause of unionism. One of these was to cast doubt on the achievements of the Irish parliament. This was significant because the memory of that parliament was held in high esteem by Dubliners; this was the case even among many Dublin Orangemen, whose three lodges in January 1800 had defied the advice of the Grand Lodge not to pronounce publicly for or against the Union.[20] In the debates on the Union, Duigenan had begun the process by pouring scorn on the much vaunted 'independence' of the Irish parliament in the period after 1782. He was especially dismissive of the claim, advanced by Henry Grattan, that the Irish crown and parliament were sovereign, imperial authorities in their own right.[21] For his part, Musgrave in the *Memoirs of the different rebellions* described the Irish parliament, at least down to 1782, as a cipher for British government decisions.[22] John Giffard's contribution was somewhat different. In Dublin Corporation and in the columns of the *Dublin Journal*, he eulogised the Union and emphasised the benefits it was likely to bring: capital investment, social tranquillity and protection from French revolutionary principles.[23]

However, the main preoccupation of all three men was the Catholic question. Even though emancipation was not actively pursued in parliament for most of the first post-union decade, the ultra-Protestants helped to set the terms of the debate when it did arise. In the *Memoirs of the different rebellions* Musgrave played down the role of Protestants among the leading United Irishmen and stressed the popish character of the Rebellion, highlighting the sufferings of Protestants at the hands of the rebels and hammering home his theme that success for the rebels would have meant the extirpation of Irish Protestants. This he attributed, not to any innate malevolence of the Catholic people, but to the tenets of the Catholic Church and the influence wielded by the priests over their flocks. The underlying message, which had a particular resonance as long as the country was involved in war, was that only Protestants could be fully loyal to king and constitution. Even before the appearance of Musgrave's work, Hardinge Giffard had contributed to the Ulster Protestants' growing disenchantment with revolutionary action by circulating in Ulster sworn statements from those who claimed to have information about the circumstances of the killing of Protestants at Scullabogue, County Wexford, during the 1798 Rebellion.[24] The unyielding message was reinforced in parliament by Dr Duigenan, who drew on 'old Whig' arguments to sustain his view that the Catholic religion was incompatible with the civil and religious liberties enjoyed by Protestants.[25] As for John Giffard, he continued to propagate these themes in Dublin Corporation and in the *Dublin Journal*. He extolled the yeomanry as having been instrumental in saving Ireland from the rebels in 1798 and countered any suggestion that the yeomanry should be disbanded. He also challenged the claim of the Catholic Church to be the ancient religion of Ireland; according to him, the claim was vitiated by the church's obedience to a foreign power.[26] Moreover, around 1807–08, when the Grand Orange Lodge in Ireland was not very active, Giffard was one of the main points of contact with the Orange Order in Britain. The Rev Ralph Nixon of Manchester, who was the driving force behind the formation in 1808 of a British Grand Lodge, corresponded with Giffard and visited his house in Dublin to learn more about Irish Orangeism.[27]

Between 1810 and 1812 the wider political climate began to change. During 1810, a serious economic depression and high wartime taxes combined to produce the first significant movement in Dublin for repeal of the Union. This was an essentially Protestant phenomenon, led and backed by merchants and artisans, which gathered considerable momentum in the capital during the summer of 1810. The issue was set to be raised in parliament when George III succumbed to the hereditary illness that had first raised the question of a regency in 1788–89. On that occasion, the king had recovered, but this time he did not, and the Prince of Wales became regent early in 1811. Faced with what amounted to a constitutional crisis, the Protestants of Dublin were not inclined to press the matter and risk destabilising Anglo-Irish relations.[28] Significantly, the regent was regarded as a likely supporter of Catholic emancipation. The prospect of this was enhanced when a government was formed in 1812 under Lord Liverpool in which emancipation was left an open question. All this encouraged a new push for emancipation from Catholics – now being orchestrated by Daniel O'Connell – and their liberal Protestant supporters. In June 1812, a motion for an inquiry into Catholic claims passed the House of Commons, though it failed in the Lords. The hostile response of the Irish executive to the activities of the Catholic Board has been noted; but less attention has been paid to the reaction of ultra-Protestants.[29]

Faced with these new challenges, the ultra-Protestant unionists mounted a strong response. On the issue of union itself, economic conditions made it difficult to maintain the same optimistic tone that had characterised their attitude in the early years. In the *Dublin Journal,* Giffard took the line that the economic difficulties were only temporary and that wartime taxes were a necessary evil to be endured for the sake of defeating the French. In Dublin Corporation, he and his small band of unionist supporters urged fellow members to recall that the choice for Ireland lay between the Union and the pikes of the United Irishmen.[30]

In response to the new round of petitions for emancipation presented to parliament in 1811 and 1812, Giffard used Dublin Corporation, the *Dublin Journal* and personal contacts, to organise a national counter-petitioning movement. There had been signs that Protestant support for emancipation was growing and one of the main aims of the counter-petitioning drive in 1812 was to scotch the suggestion that Irish Protestants in general were favourable to emancipation.[31] According to Giffard, the campaign to oppose 'the clamorous demands of popery' won the backing of most public bodies in the country. In Dublin alone, Giffard claimed to have obtained 18,000 signatures, over one-third of them being subscribed in the *Dublin Journal* office.[32] If this was a correct estimate, it represented the bulk of adult male Protestants in the capital. The campaign culminated in Wexford town with Giffard attending a county meeting organised with the help of Archibald Jacob of Enniscorthy, who as a magistrate and yeoman had been one of the most active and hated opponents of the United Irishmen.[33] Along with Hunter Gowan, James Boyd and Hawtrey White, Jacob had been proclaimed an outlaw by the short-lived republican government of Wexford in June 1798. Subsequently, Jacob was among those who established a tradition of commemorating the Rebellion with an annual march to Vinegar Hill and he

retained much support among Protestants in his community.[34] With
memories of the Rebellion still fresh ('The bridge spoke with eloquence
more than human'), Giffard subsequently noted of this Wexford meeting that
everything had been carried according to his wishes.[35]

ORANGEISM

Meanwhile, the Orange Order, which had maintained a low profile during
the period when its values were in the ascendant, redoubled its efforts to
maintain the anniversary celebrations which had become so symbolic of the
self-reliance traditions of Irish Protestants. With the withdrawal from 1806 of
the lord lieutenant and state officials from the celebration of King William's
birthday, it seemed all the more important to ensure the elaborate decoration
of William's statue in Dublin's College Green on anniversary occasions. The
proceedings on these occasions were extensively publicised in the *Dublin Journal*,
and attracted open criticism from Catholics, who sensed that the wider
political climate was changing in their favour.[36] Links with Orange lodges in
England were further cultivated, though it appears that this was something
of a mutual development. A central figure here was John Giffard, who used
his contacts with the British royal family to advance links between Irish and
British Orangeism and to win patronage for the Order at the highest level.

The origins of Giffard's royal contacts are not known, but they appear to
date from 1805. That year saw the presentation to parliament of the first
Catholic petition for emancipation since the Union. It was defeated by large
majorities in both houses in May, but the fact that it was presented at all
aroused the indignation and anxiety of the ultras. In Dublin Corporation,
Giffard helped initiate a counter-petition. He also pressed for an address of
thanks to the duke of Cumberland, fifth son of George III, whose speech in
the House of Lords defending the existing constitution in church and state
had stressed the fact that his family had been called to the throne to protect
that constitution.[37] Cumberland subsequently agreed to the Corporation's
request to supply a portrait of himself to be hung in the Mansion House.[38]
His defence of church and state was also noticed by the University of Dublin,
which elected him its chancellor in December 1805 to succeed his uncle, the
duke of Gloucester, who had died in August of that year.[39]

However, Giffard's actions did not please the government, which, while
constrained by the king's opposition to emancipation, had no wish to see a
strong counter-demonstration that would risk turning Catholic disappointment
into resentment. When, despite warnings, Giffard persisted in pressing on with
the Corporation petition, the lord lieutenant, the earl of Hardwicke, made a
public gesture of disapproval by dismissing Giffard from his post in the
customs, worth £700 per year.[40]

Giffard's dismissal came to the attention of the king, who made enquiries about him to Archbishop Charles Agar; Agar spoke in the warmest terms of Giffard's loyalty and dedication to the royal service.[41] At some point before 1811, Giffard met the king and probably some of the royal dukes, including Cumberland (the latter, together with the duke of York, made representations which led to him being restored to his post in 1808).[42] Giffard drew on these connections when, in 1811, he was asked by Rev Nixon of Manchester to use his influence with Cumberland to persuade him to become 'Grand Orange Master of the empire'.[43] Giffard duly made the approach, only to be informed that, although the duke approved of the principles of the Order, it was not then expedient for him to accept the proposal. However, by 1813, Cumberland had changed his mind. News of his acceptance was conveyed to Dublin in March 1813 by the lord mayor, Orangeman Alderman Abraham Bradley King, who had travelled to London to present another of the Corporation's anti-emancipation petitions.[44] Giffard then had the task (requiring 'much delicacy and some address') of persuading George Ogle, the Irish Grand Master, and Colonel Taylor, his English counterpart, to stand down in the duke's favour. This involved trips to Wexford and Manchester, but was successfully accomplished. But, before Cumberland could be invested the war against Napoleon took a new turn and the duke set off for the continent,[45] leaving the Orangemen to substitute for him the duke of York, who was also known for his ultra-Protestant views.[46] It is not clear from Giffard's correspondence whether the duke of York, having agreed to accept the office, was actually invested, but it appears that he was drawn into British Orangeism at this time.[47] Giffard himself took the opportunity while visiting London for these purposes in May–June 1813 (Duigenan was also present) of initiating several noblemen and gentry into the movement and issuing warrants for several new lodges.[48]

DECLINE

The years 1812–13 marked the high point of Dublin ultra-Protestantism. So exultant was Giffard about the achievements in fostering the Orange Order and its attendant values in England and Ireland that he told his son that, not only were the chances of emancipation gone, but the issue had shifted: the question now was, he thought, whether the existing rights enjoyed by Catholics should be reconsidered.[49] Dr Duigenan spoke in similar terms in 1812 when, during a parliamentary debate on a motion for emancipation, he asserted that the Protestants of Ireland were able, at any time, without assistance from Britain, 'to keep them [the rebels] down'.[50] Developments in Catholic politics played into the ultras' hands. When, in 1813, Dr Thomas

Dromgoole, a prominent member of the Catholic Board, made a speech claiming that the Protestant religion was a mere innovation and bore the marks of impending ruin, there was a predictable outcry. According to the *Dublin Journal*, the Catholics were showing their true colours, and Sir Richard Musgrave brought out a pamphlet on the subject.[51]

However, fortunes were changing for the ultra-Protestants and for the institutions that sustained them. In 1814, Dublin Corporation's growing financial problems were highlighted when the treasurer defaulted on over £40,000. It was not coincidental that it was shortly after this revelation that O'Connell made his comment about 'the beggarly Corporation of Dublin', which on 1 February 1815 led to the duel between himself and a Corporation member, John Norcot D'Esterre, in which D'Esterre was killed.[52] The wartime agricultural boom, with its attendant high prices for Irish agricultural produce, was coming to an end and, during 1813, a campaign on the part of country people against paying tolls to the Corporation got under way. Within five years, the Corporation's income from tolls of some £4,000 per year had collapsed irreversibly.[53]

Meanwhile, the Catholic Board had distanced itself from Dr Dromgoole and, by 1816, had revived its parish organisations in Dublin. O'Connell also boldly announced in 1813 that the board would henceforth patronise only goods of Irish manufacture. Hitherto, Dublin Corporation had been a leading patron of this cause and O'Connell's statement represented a clear challenge to the Corporation. The Catholics were going to be the people who mattered economically in Ireland.[54]

As for the Orange Order, the final stages of the Napoleonic wars witnessed signs that even those who had earlier defended the institution were becoming doubtful about its links with the army. Questions were beginning to be asked in parliament and what had hitherto been one of the strengths of Orangeism now became a liability. In 1814, the Order showed its sensitivity to such criticism when it followed the example set the previous year by the English Grand Lodge and dropped its controversial 'conditional' oath, by which members pledged loyalty to the king 'being Protestant'.[55] When, during a new push for emancipation in 1819, Giffard tried to repeat his 1812 success by getting Protestant signatures to an anti-emancipation petition, he incautiously allowed copies of the petition to be left at the military barracks. This produced an official instruction forbidding soldiers to sign.[56] By this time the war was over and policing in Ireland was undergoing a transformation, first with the beginnings of the peace preservation force in 1814 and subsequently with the establishment of the county constabulary in 1822. The yeomanry, with its Orange links, became relegated to what their historian calls 'a third-line defence force'.[57]

The Williamite celebrations, so important in the post-1810 revival of Orangeism, also incurred growing criticism from Catholics and liberal Protestants. They generated greater sectarian tension and often open hostilities. In Dublin, the climax came in 1822 with the notorious bottle riot at a Dublin theatre in which, following a ban on the decoration of King William's statue on 4 November, local Orangemen staged a demonstration against a pro-emancipation lord lieutenant, Lord Wellesley. This led to a permanent ban on the decoration of the College Green statue on anniversary occasions, and effectively ended the practice whereby lower-class Dublin Protestants, despite their numerical inferiority, periodically asserted their dominance in the capital.[58] In 1825, the Unlawful Societies Act was passed, aimed at curbing the activities of large organisations dedicated to changing the law, notably the Orange Order and the Catholic Association.[59] The Grand Orange Lodge formally dissolved itself, thus bringing to an end (for a time) its role in maintaining links between rich and poor Protestants. The bottle riot was also of great symbolic importance, allowing Catholics to claim that they, rather than the ultra-Protestants, were the only genuine loyalists.[60]

CONCLUSION

By 1825, Musgrave, Duigenan and Giffard were all dead, but they had played an important part in post-union Irish and British politics. They had, for instance, praised the Union, partly for its importance to Protestant security, but also in less defensive terms. Admittedly, the portrayal of the Union's economic benefits must within a few years have rung hollow with Dublin's artisan and labouring community, for whom the pre-union days quickly became suffused with a golden glow. But the suggestion that union would bring a wider perspective to matters of foreign policy and Ireland's place in the world was reflected in contemporary press coverage of the Napoleonic wars and Ireland's contribution to the British military effort. It would take time for the Union to become popular among Protestants, particularly among Dublin Protestants, but some of the foundations were laid by Giffard in Dublin Corporation and in the *Dublin Journal*.[61]

Far more important, however, was the fact that these men had given expression to the sense of Protestant insecurity generated by the Rebellions of 1798 and 1803, heightened by demographic evidence of an ever-increasing imbalance in Protestant–Catholic numbers. Such expression was both rhetorical and practical. Rhetorically, it took the form of anti-popery and defence of the link between church and state. The bluntness and vehemence with which these views were articulated, the periodic scares about Catholic plots, and the tendency to dwell on what might have seemed obsolete points of Catholic theology, makes it easy to dismiss such views as merely bigoted and alarmist.[62] This fails to take into account the historical provenance of the idea of the Protestant constitution in church and state, so closely associated with 'old Whig' values of liberty, which during this period still carried conviction for many in Britain as well as Ireland.[63] However, the vehemence needs to be understood primarily as a reflection of the uncertainty and insecurity among a particular section of Irish Protestants – the middling ranks – especially in Leinster and Munster. While the challenge of a rising Catholic population was universal, in Connaught the smallness of Protestant numbers had suggested the need for some sort of accommodation with Catholics as early as the eighteenth century.[64] In Ulster the issue had arisen only in certain localised areas. But in Leinster and Munster the middle order of Protestants were under threat from changing patterns of land tenure (the disappearance of middlemen leases), changing conditions of work for artisans, growing competition from imports and disrupted relations with Catholic neighbours following the Rebellion. All this was giving rise among such Protestants to high levels of emigration.[65] Those who remained felt all the more exposed because of the presence of comparatively large numbers of middle-class Catholics, ready and anxious to make their way into all levels of Irish public life, with the backing of an increasingly vigorous and assertive Catholic church.

In practical terms, the main contribution of these ultra-Protestants lay in their active support for the Orange Order, especially for the Grand Lodge, the importance of which was that it served as a link between all classes of Protestant. By means of writings, speeches and political activities, they also made a significant impact in Britain, where they contributed to reviving an anti-Catholic strain in 'right-wing' thought.[66] Moreover, they were active in fostering ties with British Orangeism and, particularly, in winning patronage for Orangeism in aristocratic and royal circles. The connection with royalty was not merely of symbolic importance. Monarchy was still an integral part of politics: it has recently been pointed out that the 1807 general election was fought essentially on the issue of the royal prerogative,[67] and throughout this period and for the duration of the emancipation campaign several of the royal dukes became important political players (on both sides).[68] Although none of the three men discussed here survived into the decade that was to be so crucial for Catholic emancipation, Giffard at least left a legacy in the shape of his younger son, Stanley Lees Giffard, whose career in British journalism helped perpetuate the cause of Orangeism and the Protestant constitution.[69] In these ways the Dublin ultra-Protestants made an enduring contribution to fostering closer ties between Ireland and Britain, even if these were hardly of the kind that Pitt had in mind when he introduced the Act of Union.

CHAPTER ELEVEN

Completing the Union?
The Irish Novel and the Moment
of the Union

CLAIRE CONNOLLY

According to Walter Scott, writing in 1829 in the 'General preface' to his works, the fictions of Maria Edgeworth 'may be truly said to have done more towards completing the Union, than perhaps all the legislative enactments by which it has been followed up'.[1] This essay examines the role played by fiction in lending shape and meaning to Ireland's post-1801 relationship with Britain and offers a new reading of the relationship between the Act of Union and novels usually thought to impart its political message and even attempt its 'completion'. Focusing on emblematic moments in key post-Union fictions and steering a course between literature and history, it argues that early nineteenth-century Irish fiction affords an immediate and sometimes dizzyingly close-up perspective on the political spectacle of Union, and that this near-focus on the event itself has been ignored by critics eager to take the long view of its effects.

1829: BETWEEN HISTORY AND LITERATURE

Among the 'legislative enactments' which Scott saw as falling short of fiction in 'completing the Union' were the Roman Catholic Relief Acts of 1828 and 1829. These government measures effected the repeal of the Test and Corporation Acts that had secured Protestant dominance in public life. Rather than aiming at the completion of the Union, however, emancipation was approved because of the immediate threat of an Irish Catholic being elected into parliament; a response to what Thomas Bartlett described as Daniel O'Connell's realisation that '[e]mancipation would never be granted: it could only be taken'.[2] The victory of Henry Villiers Stuart, a liberal Protestant who stood in the Catholic interest in the 1826 general election, sounded the warning bell and was soon followed up by O'Connell's victory in the Clare by-election of 1828. Seen through government eyes, and understood as a political gesture in its own moment, emancipation took pointed aim against mass political mobilisation in Ireland.

Scott was unlikely to oppose the policies of the ruling Tory party with whom he was allied closely, but his preference for Edgeworth's novels over Wellington and Peel's parliamentary measures probably reflects a personal and even instinctive distrust of Roman Catholics: according to Scott's son-in-law John Gibson Lockhart, 'no man [more] disapproved of Romanism as a system of faith and practice than Sir Walter always did'.[3] Lockhart further reported how Scott

> on all occasions expressed manfully his belief, that the best thing for Ireland would have been never to relax the strictly political enactments of the penal laws, however harsh these might appear. Had they been kept in vigour for another half century, it was his conviction that popery would have been all but extinguished in Ireland.[4]

The problems of 'popery' aside, 1829 marked what Peter Garside has called 'a watershed in the production of fiction in Britain'.[5] It saw 'the first clear realization of an extensive middle-class market',[6] as well as being remembered in literary history as the moment at which Walter Scott ('the Great Unknown' for much of the preceding decades) put aside the pseudonym of the 'Author of Waverley' and revealed himself to the public in the 'General Preface' to the *Magnum opus* edition of his novels. In the process, Scott assembled the rudiments of a theory of historical fiction. This fictional philosophy, in which appeasement and accommodation form central planks, provides an important context within which to read his praise of Edgeworth. Ina Ferris has shown how Scott's 1829 championing of Edgeworth sounded quite a different note to his earlier praise of her writing. In the final chapter to *Waverley*, published in 1814 (entitled 'A postscript, which should have been a preface'), Scott recounted how reading 'the admirable Irish portraits drawn by Miss Edgeworth' helped shape his own decision to write historical fiction.[7] Ferris elaborates on the difference between these two, on the face of it equally respectful and admiring, takes on Edgeworth, arguing that '[w]here the novel itself had stressed her innovative role in undermining standard modes of cultural representation, the late preface sets her up as the model of the politics of conciliation that always attracted Scott.'[8]

UNFINISHED BUSINESS: NOVELS AND THE UNION

Scott's analysis of Edgeworth draws on a widespread contemporary tendency to describe the Union between Great Britain and Ireland as incomplete and in need of some supplementary or auxiliary measures. The resumption of the war with France and the resurfacing of the United Irish threat in the shape of Emmet's Rebellion of 1803 sharpened this sense of insufficiency. By the 1820s, the efforts of the Catholic Association gave concrete shape and form to the many expressions of discontent as to the shortcomings of the 1801 settlement. Although the efforts of the Catholic Association may not have given rise to the repeal movement in quite as smooth a transfer of political energies as once was thought, there were, none the less, key connections between the two campaigns to be explained by something more than the driving force of Daniel O'Connell's personality. The twin movements for emancipation and repeal reawakened old grievances and acted as fresh irritants on injuries still raw from a sense of the Union as violation and betrayal. In leaving open the Catholic question, the Act of Union had exposed, or even inflicted, a gaping wound on the very British body politic it had helped, in part, to invent.

The anonymous author of an 1805 pro-Catholic pamphlet described the frustrations of early nineteenth-century Irish Catholics, insisting that the Union would stand or fall on the basis of its insinuated promises: 'There was an implied stipulation, if there were not an express one, to harmonise the country, and render the Union the basis of a settlement, else it was a dangerous and unprofitable intrigue, and the vast detail of its expenses and compensations, incurred without any adequate benefit.' In other words, the failure of the Union to deliver on its unwritten promises meant it was inherently unable to supply what the same pamphleteer called 'resources for attachment'. [9] Instead it came to resemble a crude piece of state machinery, too clumsy and creaking to be effective. One of the mock playbills circulated as part of the anti-Union campaign invited onlookers to 'the royal circus near College Green', to witness 'a grand display of the new political steam engine; or, civilising machine, for Britainizing the wild Irish. After which there will be a harsh concert of woeful and detrimental music.' [10] Thomas Moore supplied a further metaphor, describing the Union legislation as not only maladroit but monstrous, 'like Frankenstein's ghastly patch-work'. [11]

LITERARY UNIONISM

Yet to demonstrate that 'the politics of conciliation' were temperamentally Scott's rather than Edgeworth's, or to show how appeasement was always haunted by the ghosts of past history, is not to deny the influence of his observation, or the extent to which a version of it still dominates contemporary critical debates. Scott's judgement on Edgeworth has been lifted out of its particular context and recycled as a judgement on early nineteenth-century Irish writing in English more generally, leading to a view of Ireland as recalcitrant, resistant to some narrative modes and only diagnosable within what Seamus

Deane (referring to W.B. Yeats) memorably described as 'the pathology of literary unionism'.[12]

In the general introduction to the *Field Day anthology*, Deane turns to 'reconciliation' as a 'key term' in Irish debates from the end of the eighteenth century. He locates Charlotte Brooke's 1789 *Reliques of Irish poetry* as a turning point in Irish writing, after which '[c]ultural reconciliation appeared to be a necessary prelude to political reconciliation'. The Act of Union, then, was to be implemented via the good offices of culture, in the form of acts of translation like Brooke's; to be followed up by aesthetic projects which attempted to create a union of hearts and minds between Ireland and Britain. 'However', Deane continues, cultural reconciliation was not to be: 'a series of catastrophic political developments – the French Revolution, the rise of the United Irishmen, the 1798 Rebellion and the Act of Union in 1800 – deferred the realisation of this ambition.'[13]

Against an image of culture as striving to catch up with the Union, its efforts repeatedly and disastrously wrecked by stormy events, this essay poses an alternative picture. It replaces such a distinction between creaky unionist plots and the irrepressible, organic forces of cultural nationalism. What follows is an argument for reading Irish fiction in tandem with the kind of detailed historical exploration of the Union now under way. Rather than seeing novels as 'completing' the Union, what is proposed is an attempt to engage with Irish fiction in all its shadowy complexity: there are union novels, but they take their place alongside 1798 novels, repeal novels and fictions of Catholic emancipation. Rather than depicting the Union as a substantial and undisputed fact sitting on the horizon of early nineteenth-century Irish expectations, it shows how the fictional focus often falls on the Act, rather than the fact of Union.

It is near impossible to strip away accretions of hindsight – the consequences of the Union have seen to that – but it is at least possible to try to read the Union as an event in its own moment. Discussing Maria Edgeworth's *The absentee* (1812), W.J. McCormack has observed how the text can be described as a union novel in two distinct ways. As a novel which depicts 'Ireland under the Union', *The absentee* testifies to the Union's status as *longue durée* or enduring fact of history. But *The absentee* is also a 'post-Union' fiction in the sense that it was published in 1812, a dozen years after the act had been passed.[14] It is this latter, stricter and more materialist, sense of union which is employed in this essay, in the belief that the relationship between politics and culture must sometimes be sought for in specific public content rather than reduced to preordained notions of political tendencies.

The novel, as 'a "syncretic" or "problem-solving" genre',[15] is thought generally to carry the imaginative and ideological weight of union, proposing specific narrative solutions to the early nineteenth-century political puzzle of Anglo-Irish relations. In literary history, Irish novelists are forever arguing and apologising; defending, explaining, rationalising and resolving, treating of Ireland and, in the process, transforming the country into an object of knowledge to be surveyed by the 'British', or perhaps English, reader. The national tale in particular, with its intertwined plots of travel and love, is seen as a conduit for a harmonising impulse in Anglo-Irish relations. To put this differently: early nineteenth-century Irish novels are thought to participate in a liberal vision of Ireland, itself understood as 'the history of a consolidated effort, frustrated by prejudice but implacable in its direction, to recruit Irish Catholics into the Union with the help of the Irish Catholic Church while appeasing the endless fears and bigotries of Irish Protestants'.[16] The best that can be hoped for in this account is increased understanding and tolerance between the two countries involved.

For Deane, again the most authoritative and convincing spokesperson for this view, this metanarrative manifests itself in literature as allegory, which does little more than lend formal structure and some of the tricks of the novelist's trade to a set of stereotypical assumptions about Irish national character. This is a persuasive argument. It is difficult, for example, to counter Deane's analysis of the retrograde ideology of national character or to disagree with him about its dismayingly long hold on the imperial imagination. He even allowed for the dialogic form of literature, which transformed the Burkean narrative of increasing tolerance into 'a rational account that is constantly threatened by the competition of irrational energies'.[17]

This last observation in particular stands as an apposite summary of the current critical consensus on Maria Edgeworth's *Castle Rackrent*, a text now usually thought of in terms of just such a 'competition' between a rational frame of reference (the notes and glossary) and an energetic, even insurgent, peasant voice (the first person narrative of family steward Thady Quirke). But in Deane's account even this dialogic contest becomes stultifying, at best formulaic and at worst (again in the case of Edgeworth) masquerading as analysis when 'its real achievement was to have produced an analgesic version of the question of Anglo-Irish relations.'[18]

As the example of *Castle Rackrent* should suggest, however, the 'competition' of voices, which is indeed characteristic of post-union Irish fiction, does not occur within a sealed-off, smooth and secure literary space. The form of the novel is shaken up by the internal dialogic contests taking place, and this dialogism has external as well as internal effects: the novel cannot withstand such a battering from within without showing some bumps and bruises on its exterior. Such formal innovations as *Castle Rackrent*'s mixture of narrative frames, experiments with epistolary form and third-person narratives, the interpolated manuscripts of many national tales, and indeed the national tale itself, are evidence of fiction registering political conflict at the level of genre. What follows is an attempt to introduce a focus on genre into the study of Irish fiction and its relation to the Union.

THE SHADOW OF THE UNION

Whether it numbed the pain of that event or not, fiction was indeed present as the Union was born. The pamphlet war which preceded and sustained the parliamentary debates relied on an armoury of fictional methods and techniques.[19] There is no denying that the form of the Irish novel marshalled fresh energy and momentum about this time. Indeed, many describe *Castle Rackrent* as the first genuine Irish novel. The years immediately after the Union saw a marked rise in the production of Irish fiction and, despite much of it being published in London, it is possible to identify a distinct body of novels that take Ireland as their theme, or feature Irish politics, landscape, dialect or characters prominently.[20] Joep Leerssen captured the confluence of political event and fictional form well, when he described the novel as 'a genre which was adopted by Irish authors under the very shadow of the Union'.[21]

In the context of an interpretation such as mine, situated at it is between the formal rigours of literary criticism and the demands of historical detail, what does it mean for a particular genre to be espoused 'under the shadow' of an historical event? Can history be captured in silhouette? Literary critics should concede that, while novels can capture strong shapes or the outline of historical events, they may not prove faithful to the dim flickers of detail. From a literary point of view, however, it is possible to show how history's long shadow can obscure or even eclipse the specificity of fictional forms, and it is to this aspect of the Irish novel I now wish to turn.

In 1800, the novel was a relatively new (or novel) cultural form, with little by way of cultural prestige attached to it. The eighteenth-century achievements of Samuel Richardson, Henry Fielding and Frances Burney had yet to be celebrated as high culture. Moreover, the close association of novels with Jacobinism and such 1790s radicals as Mary Wollstonecraft and William Godwin saw the genre 'struggling to regain respectability' in the early years of the nineteenth century, potentially becoming stranded in the receding tide of revolution.[22] The novel's reputation was certainly not secure until at least the 1830s, a development closely linked to the elevation of Walter Scott to the ranks of literary heavyweight.

From the eighteenth century onwards, the novel seemed to have the power to adumbrate or shadow forth new futures. This generic pliancy and even plasticity appealed particularly to cultural outsiders of all sorts: women writers, who for a brief but heady moment dominated fiction writing between the 1790s and 1820; as well as those seeking out modes of giving expression to non-metropolitan political identities, notably the case in Ireland, Scotland and, to a lesser extent, Wales.[23] It is helpful here to note Katie Trumpener's account of the development of the novel across the British Empire in the period of Romanticism. Surveying these years, Trumpener notices the new prominence of the national tale, which she described as 'a genre developed in Ireland, primarily by women writers, over the decade preceding the publication of *Waverley*.'[24] Where Leerssen had Irish writers 'adopting' the novel genre, Trumpener assigns them a more dynamic role in developing and expanding a new and ultimately influential literary form. Trumpener signals the special importance of women writers in this process, paying particular attention to Maria Edgeworth and Sydney Owenson, but also to their neglected forebear, the Waterford-born, popular, Gothic novelist Regina Maria Roche.

Mapping Leerssen and Trumpener's observations on to one another underlines the importance of plotting political, cultural and literary events side by side as the defining co-ordinates of nineteenth-century Irish fiction. The Irish novel should be read in relation to the Act of Union with Great Britain, certainly. Of equal importance, however, is the uneven nature of generic development, the contemporary dominance of women writers, especially the reputation of Maria Edgeworth, and the impact of Walter Scott's *Waverley* (1814), which latched on to and redirected many of the trends initiated by Edgeworth and Owenson. There are some rough edges in this layering of interpretative frames, but such a critical quadrant has the advantage of making visible the interpenetration of cultural and political modes of apprehending Ireland's entry into the Union. Reading literary production and political debate as interwoven in this way itself underpins a picture of nineteenth-century Ireland as the scene of competition between cultural and political acts of imagination, a tension which can be read as both specifically Irish and as belonging more generally to a contest between Romantic and Enlightenment modes of thought.

Distinguishing between possible approaches to reading relations between fiction and politics from the eighteenth century onwards, William B. Warner has warned against the kind of narrow literary history which 'turns the strife of history into a repertoire of forms'. Warner's strictures remind us that the novel is not static, and that form as well as content takes shape according to the pressure of events. Warner is suspicious of 'the way in which antagonistic historical strife becomes sedimented in one complex, ambivalent cultural object: "the novel"', and is keen to avoid the kind of critical practice which treats the institution of the novel as somehow self-evident and transparent.[25] As Harriet Guest has argued, eighteenth- and early nineteenth-century novels 'themselves participate in debates that cut across genres; they assume readers who are also immersed in periodical literature, in poetry, in histories, readers who discuss plays and parliamentary debates, who perform music, and peer into the windows of print shops'.[26]

Post-union Ireland and Britain provide ample evidence that readers may have had matters other than fictional on their minds, and testifiy too to these 'debates that cut across genres'. George III is said to have read *Castle Rackrent* with relish, observing on completing it 'What, what — now I know something of my Irish subjects'. It is tempting to speculate on what part reading *Castle Rackrent* might have played in forming the king's opinions on the undesirability of Catholic emancipation. Perhaps his decision to impose a royal veto at the last moment is evidence that the danger posed by the Quirkes was felt to be a real one, and that George III was an early proponent of the text's post-colonial tendencies. While the king was thus engaged, his prime minister was said to favour Sydney Owenson's fictions, and especially her novel of religious intolerance *The novice of Saint Dominick*. The critic John Wilson Croker recorded his outrage at hearing a rumour 'That the late Mr. PITT occupied the last hours of his life in reading Miss Owenson's admirable novel of *The novice of Saint Dominick*'.[27] Meanwhile Lord Castlereagh not only read Owenson's novels but 'had been favoured with hearing some of the m[anu]s[cript] [of *The Missionary*] read aloud' to him by the author herself, whom he had met at the home of her patrons, the Abercorns. So impressed was Castlereagh, that he 'offered to take Miss Owenson to town in his chariot, and to give a rendezvous to her publisher in his own study'. Her *Memoirs* record how Stockdale, the publisher in question, 'was naturally impressed by the environments, which gave him a higher opinion of Miss Owenson's genius than he had felt before. The opportunity to make a good bargain was grasped by Miss Owenson, Lord Castlereagh himself standing by whilst the agreement was signed.'[28]

As these examples suggest, the interpenetration of politics and culture could be playful, diverting and often enigmatic. Consider one exemplary instance of the part played by the Union debates in early nineteenth-century Irish culture – a short satirical notice that appeared in the *Dublin Evening Post* of 21 December 1807, detailing the private theatricals 'in preparation at the houses of the following nobility and gentry' for Christmas of that year. The newspaper sedately reports on the latest trend in home entertainment: 'Private theatricals, we understand, by fashionable report, will be the leading feature of the approaching festivities'. The tone is mock-serious and soon gives way to gossipy and malicious examples of these supposed 'theatricals'.[29] Among the fashionable homes listed is that of the recently widowed Lady Clare where, reportedly, a performance entitled *Cease your funning* was to be presented alongside *The Ephesian matron* and *The Irish widow*. The name of

Lady Clare's late husband, John FitzGibbon, earl of Clare, might have brought the Union to mind, but the allusion here is more pointed. 'Cease your funning' is a reference to an early anti-union pamphlet, published in 1799 as a riposte to the government-sponsored *Arguments for and against an union*. Both *The Ephesian matron* (by Isaac Bickerstaffe) and *The Irish widow* (attributed to David Garrick) were eighteenth-century plays revolving around merry widow figures, hinting, perhaps, at Lady Clare's less than secluded widowhood and rumours of her adulteries.[30] Maria Edgeworth described her as 'a painted – made up – vulgar thoroughgoing woman of the world'.[31] The circuit of reference is completed by William Drennan, who speculated in a letter to his sister Martha McTier that the character of the racy and rouged-up Lady Delacour in Edgeworth's novel of fashionable life *Belinda* was based on the glamorous Anne FitzGibbon.[32]

Belinda, published in 1801, returns us to the moment of union. Yet, as a novel set entirely in England and with only one marginal and incidental Irish character, it is usually read in terms of femininity and the private world of courtship and marriage, an aspect of Edgeworth's interests difficult to relate to her explicitly Irish experiences. Different kinds of objection have been raised to reading her *Patronage* (1814) in Irish terms, but it is useful to consult the most recent edition of the text which reminds us that Edgeworth introduced Irish lawyer Charles Kendal Bushe into the fiction in the form of an idealised lord chief justice. Bushe was the probable author of the above-mentioned *Cease your funning*, and as such forms part of the web of reference and allusion that reconnects Edgeworth's 'English' fictions to *Castle Rackrent*, a text included by W.J. McCormack alongside such pamphlets as *Cease your funning* in his bibliography of the debate on the Union.[33]

Just as Drennan's suggestion opens *Belinda* up to the Union, a later novel of fashionable life, Edgeworth's *Manoeuvring* (1812) can also be seen to relate to the same political moment. In its original version (as a draft called first 'Mrs Beaumont' and then 'Plain sailing'), *Manoeuvring* features a rough-and-ready naval officer whom family members recognised immediately as Admiral Thomas Pakenham, an uncle of Lord Longford. The similarities were so visible and the depiction so close to caricature that Edgeworth accepted family counsel and cut the character altogether for fear of offending the Longfords, neighbours of the Edgeworths on the Longford/Westmeath border. The most recognisable aspect of the presentation related to the Union, specifically to Pakenham's bullying and press-ganging of voters in the Irish House of Commons, which Richard Lovell Edgeworth had witnessed and abhorred.[34] Admiral Pakenham's house was, like Lady Clare's, featured in the *Dublin Evening Post* skit on private theatricals; there the entertainment was to consist of 'The tars progress, Neptune deposed and Britannia victorious'.

The above examples suggest just how porous the novel was at its boundaries; a result of its relative generic openness and lack of cultural prestige. Further evidence of this generic receptiveness to immediate political context may be adduced from correspondence between Lady Granard and Denys Scully. In 1799, Lady Granard wrote to her friend Scully, acknowledging receipt of two recent anti-union pamphlets he had sent her. The daughter of the social leader of the Irish Whigs, Lady Moira, Lady Granard belonged to a liberal Protestant circle that was loosely united in opposition to the Union. She reported to Scully that she was 'infinitely pleased & gratified' by what she read but in doing so was cautious as to how she identified the pamphlets. The letter in fact does not mention the Union debates, but instead refers covertly to 'the two novels you sent me': 'If you can get copies of them do get two more, for a friend of mine in England who loves foolish books as well as I do – & keep them 'till you hear again from me which shall be very soon.'[35] In a postscript to a letter to Scully written the next day (and presumably conveyed to him by more secure means), Lady Granard explained how 'I wrote you a few lines by post to acknowledge the receipt of the pamphlets by post, stiling them novels'.[36]

In a culture where union pamphlets could, even if only rhetorically, assume the guise of novels, it is hardly surprising that novels themselves did not scruple to offer an analysis of the Union. John Banim's novel, *The Anglo-Irish of the nineteenth century* (1828), attempts to define what Terry Eagleton has glossed as 'the grammar of Anglo-Irish relations'.[37] During a set-piece conversation witnessed by the novel's protagonist Gerald Blount, the leading political figures of the 1820s discuss 'the present unhappy state of Ireland'. Present in this *roman-à-clef* are 'the Secretary', a thinly disguised John Wilson Croker; Mr Grady, who according to John Kelly was based on George Croly, editor of *The Guardian*; and a range of fictional figures whom Kelly connected to William Magee, Thomas Crofton Croker and the Rev Richard Pope.[38] Mr Grady sets out his political views, and is countered by the antagonistic Croker:

> 'The first point is *this*,' remarked Mr. Grady, composing a *leader* — 'what is the cause of the unhappy state of Ireland? Why is she the only uncivilized portion of the three kingdoms? After more than seven hundred years of identity with this country —'
> 'Not identity, Grady; that almost makes you speak a paradox,' said the Secretary.
> 'Connexion, Sir?'
> 'No.'
> 'Then, Sir, conjunction?'
> 'Not even that, unless you mean our grammatical anomaly, a disjunctive conjunction'

Grady's views, tagged here as the threadbare and clichéd stuff of popular journalism ('composing a *leader*'), meet the cutting cynicism of Croker's more nuanced linguistic analysis. In the same novel, Gerald, in the context of an argument with a thinly disguised Lord Castlereagh character, insists that an implicit promise of Catholic emancipation had been part of the 1801 settlement but is warned by the cool statesman that the words of the Act of Union 'may *seem* to *imply* many meanings'.[39]

Maria Edgeworth and her father Richard Lovell Edgeworth remarked on how the 'passion and prejudice' of politics press down on language in Ireland. Their *Essay on Irish bulls* (1802) observes how, in the immediate aftermath of 1798, not only the resources of the law but those of language itself had been abused: 'many *cant* terms have been brought into use, which are not yet to be reckoned amongst the acknowledged terms of the country'.[40] Alongside examples of these 'party barbarisms in language' the Edgeworths presented the reported conversation of Phelim O'Mooney, 'the Irish Incognito' who, in the disguise of 'John Bull', sets off to England in search of a rich wife.[41] Fortified by a bet with his brother and boasting no obvious 'brogue', he feels sure he can avoid the (in this case entirely correct) English suspicion of Irish fortune hunters. As John Bull, O'Mooney tries to avoid discovery by eschewing such recognisably Irish habits as offering hospitality, evincing enthusiasm and having eggs for breakfast.

Arriving in Deal, he goes to the Custom House where he sees and, more importantly, hears a 'red hot-countryman of his own' in loud dispute over some Irish poplin. When caught with contraband goods, 'the Hibernian fell immediately upon the Union, which he swore was disunion, as the custom-house officers managed it'.[42] Sir John Bull observes this dispute with a cool disinterest that serves to conceal his nationality initially: 'from his quiet appearance and deportment, the custom-house officers took it for granted that he was an Englishman'. The Edgeworths presented John Bull/O'Mooney's reaction in free indirect style, a discursive resource they deployed in order to investigate the psychic strains incurred in acting like an Englishman:

> He was in no hurry, he begged *that* gentleman's business might be settled first; he would wait the officer's leisure, and as he spoke he played so dextrously with half-a-guinea between his fingers as to make it visible only where he wished. The custom-house officer was his humble servant immediately; but the Hibernian would have been his enemy, had he not conciliated him by observing, 'that even Englishmen must allow there was something very like a bull in professing to make a complete identification of the two kingdoms, whilst, at the same time, certain regulations continued in full force to divide the countries by art, even more than the British channel does by nature.'[43]

Phelim O'Mooney/John Bull is involved here in a delicate balancing act, a reflection perhaps on the possibility of the 'British' identity that Ireland under the Union might have been expected to achieve. His reference to the legal articles regarding trade remind us that the Union was, after all, a measure designed to regulate parliamentary representation and commercial exchange, rather than a manifesto for cultural change. The example, however, shows how difficult it is (and perhaps was) to distinguish between the limited legislative intent of the Act and the rhetoric accompanying it, which bore much larger questions of identity, sameness and difference along in its tide. The suggestion here is that these contradictory impulses resulted in a union that is a species of Irish bull: there is 'something very like a bull in professing to make a complete identification of the two kingdoms, whilst, at the same time, certain regulations continued in full force to divide the countries'.

Significantly, Britishness here is the product of disguise, a linguistic costume that proves all too easy to penetrate. Phelim O'Mooney/John Bull continues to speak 'plausibly' and 'candidly and cooly on Irish and English politics', only to give himself away in a manner which belongs precisely to the moment of the Union debates. The characters present begin to discuss John Foster, the last Speaker of the Irish House of Commons and a leader of the anti-unionists. In joining in the general praise of 'a distinguished patriot of his country', Phelim (for it is he who speaks now), 'in the height of his enthusiasm, inadvertently called him *the Speaker.*' He repeats 'the Speaker — *our* Speaker!' Patrick Geoghegan has recorded how William Wilberforce had 'mockingly referred to Foster as "Mr Spaker"', and it seems safe to assume the Edgeworths are signalling both a vowel sound and a fondness for Foster (an old school friend of Richard Lovell Edgeworth) that instantly divulge O'Mooney's nationality.[44]

'WHAT A PICTURE!': THE SPECTACLE OF THE UNION

Early nineteenth-century Irish novelists had frequent recourse to disguise as a plot device, using it to screen the potentially offensive Englishness of travellers newly arrived in Ireland. Their true identity is made visible in other ways, however, often ironically evinced in an attitude toward Ireland that treats the country involuntarily as a picturesque sight: 'What a picture!', sighs the young English hero of Lady Morgan's *The wild Irish girl* on first glimpsing Connemara and the Castle of Inismore.[45]

Ireland is presented here in explicitly picturesque terms, in the eighteenth-century sense of framing a sight as a picture. A scene early in Morgan's novel *Florence Macarthy* (1818) frames the passing of the Union as itself part of a scene that catches the curiosity of two travellers newly arrived in Dublin. As with *The wild Irish girl*, the travellers of this later novel conceal their true backgrounds and go under assumed names. The younger of the two is Lord Fitzadelm, an absentee returning to his estates and travelling under the name Mr De Vere. He has taken passage on a ship captained by 'the Commodore' who, as General Fitzwalter, is returning from leading a brigade in the South American wars against the Spanish, and who is discovered at the end of four volumes to be the rightful heir to Fitzadelm's estate. Walking in the direction of their hotel in Sackville Street under the direction of a Dublin guide, the two men pass 'through that line of the Irish metropolis, which brings within the compass of a *coup d'œil* some of the noblest public edifices and spacious streets to be found in the most leading cities of Europe.'[46] The narrative frames the cityscape as an image, caught within the 'compass of a *coup d'oeil*'. The scene's painterly aspect is underlined by being static: 'All, however, was still, silent, and void.'[47]

This first sight of the Parliament House and Trinity College is framed, the visual experience directed and managed by their Irish guide. As the men view the sights, their tour guide watches them, 'his eye furtively glancing on them'. He darts ahead mentally, scheming so as to set up their next vantage point, and contriving to make the sudden onset of architectural grandeur seem effortless:

> and when they reached that imposing area, which includes so much of the architectural elegance and social bustle of Dublin, the area flanked by its silent senate-house, and commanded by its venerable university, he paused, as if from weariness, leaned his burthen against the college balustrade, and drew upon the attention of the strangers (who also voluntarily halted to look around them, by observing, as he pointed to the right, 'That's the ould parliament-house, sir.'[48]

Thus manoeuvred to confront this spectacle, the travellers respond in highly conventional manners. Their field of vision is structured not only by the efforts of their guide, but is also organised according to visual codes provided by the travellers' own expectations and education. The younger of the two men, De Vere, is a practised picturesque tourist, in search of visual novelty (the conclusion to the novel sees him departing for a tour of the North Pole) and committed to a self-conscious and highly staged practice of looking. In the novel's opening scenes, as their ship sails into Dublin Bay, De Vere searches through his copy of Spenser's *View of the present state of Ireland* for the famous description of Ireland's natural fecundity; challenged by his companion to put by his book and look around him, he responds nonchalantly that he prefers to see places through the 'prismatic hues' of books.[49]

Thus, De Vere's immediate reaction to the former parliament building is to aestheticise and apostrophise it:

> It is a beautiful thing of its kind . . . Beautiful, even *now*, entire and perfect
> in all its parts, what will it be centuries hence, touched by the consecrating
> hand of time, when its columns shall lie prostrate, its pediments and
> architraves broken and moss-grown, when all around shall be silence and
> desolation?[50]

His companion, freshly returned from the South American wars of
liberation, indulges in prolepsis of a more directly political kind. He prefers
to think of how 'some American freeman', 'the descendant of some Irish
exile, may voluntarily seek the bright green shores of his fathers, and, in this
mouldering structure, behold the monument of their former degradation.'[51]
The references here to exile and to Ireland's 'bright green shores' contain
echoes of United Irish discourse and remind readers that the aesthetic vision
of ruin, silence and desolation conjured up by the two men might have
material meanings.

   The novel as a whole endorses a political diagnosis, providing several set
pieces in the opening Dublin scenes showing the grisly effects of the Union. A
place of political decay and economic decline, Morgan's fictional Dublin closely
resembles the highly coloured images conjured up by anti-union propagandists
and politicians, and fulfils dire predictions like the following, found in many
forms in song sheets and speeches: 'British gentlemen, providores of
amusement, and eminent for the exhibition of wild-beasts, rare shows, &c., &c
. . . may occasionally condescend to visit the mouldring remnant of the Irish
metropolis, to divert the melancholy of its desponding inhabitants.'[52]

   Picking up on the anti-union discourse in the novel, one British reviewer
asked incredulously whether Lady Morgan really 'should seriously suppose
that the Rebellion in ninety-eight was promoted by Mr. Pitt to bring about
the Union, or that the Union itself is the cause of the typhus fever which has
raged in Ireland ever since the failure of the crops in 1816'. The same *Anti-
Jacobin* reviewer quoted as evidence of Morgan's excesses the following
speech made by Lady Clancare, the heroine of the novel:

> Repeal the Act which banished our landlords, and exhausts the country of
> its revenue and resources, and then disease will disappear, with the want
> that fosters it. People will die, to be sure, and of typhus fever sometimes;
> but it will no longer be to Ireland what the yellow fever is to the West
> Indies, or the plague to Constantinople.[53]

Commenting on these scenes, the reviewer for the *Edinburgh Monthly Review*
observed that Morgan's depiction of Dublin life would be 'unrivalled', if only

> she had not resolved to make all her pictures subservient to the
> development of political opinions; an endeavour by which she not only

continually destroys the illusions of her descriptions, but adds to the vexation of the reader, by shewing her distrust of his ability to draw those inferences from her statements which she intends to convey.[54]

Part of the problem here is Lady Clancare herself: a writer of national tales who, in the novel, waged a successful war against a thinly veiled John Wilson Croker (appearing in the novel as Counsellor Con Crawley); the character is a composite of opinions and experiences which would have been instantly recognisable as Morgan's own. If the authorial self-portrait is in part responsible for breaking the rules of graceful fictional illusion, however, it may well be the Union that 'continually destroys the illusions' of naturalistic description and vexes the reader. Associated with ruin and decay, the Union is cast in terms that place it on the side of non-naturalistic representation, or that which challenges smooth aesthetic categorisation.

It is useful here to return briefly to *The wild Irish girl*, and its earlier deployment of a traveller's first reaction to the striking features of Dublin's 'splendid and beautiful public structures'.[55] Set in the 1790s (but written post-union) the College Green area is described as small but perfectly formed, a miniature London with no nearby gin shops or poor houses to distract the eye from the harmoniously grouped public buildings. Soon after taking in this scene, from which only the surrounding 'vice, poverty, idleness, and filth' distract, the hero of *The wild Irish girl* crosses a bog in Connemara, 'whose burning surface, heated by a vertical sun, gave me no inadequate idea of *Arabia deserta*'.[56] It is possible to see how the terms of these twin accounts are transformed into the Dublin of *Florence Macarthy* where the city is both splendid and deserted, its grandeur now an effect of rather than a distraction from the prevailing emptiness: 'All, however, was still, silent, and void.'

Such accounts of College Green, the houses of parliament and Trinity College are of course the stuff of travel literature and the descriptions of Dublin as a deposed capital seem almost instantly clichéd. Just as travellers, both fictional and real, recorded the beauties of Dublin Bay repeatedly, so the ill effects of the Union were systematically noted in novels from 1801 on. The fact that these two tropes can sit side by side in the same novel (as they do, for example, in *The absentee* and in *Florence Macarthy*) suggests how the discourses of prestige and poverty are related: Ireland's natural beauties and its economic decay compete for narrative space in the novels of the immediate post-union period, as if no one were quite sure yet which was the more compelling.

To return to Morgan's travellers, their sightseeing tour into the imaginary architectural future evokes a specific drawing by James Malton, the famous recorder of images of eighteenth-century Dublin. Morgan's methods approximate in narrative terms to the visual strategies of James Malton's *capricci*, 'An imaginary view of the Parliament House, Dublin, in decay'. In

1801, Malton produced twin drawings depicting the parliament building in College Green as it was and will be after the Union. The first shows the immense pillars of the building's portico overlooking tiny figures, who are busy, peaceful and apparently prosperous. In the second drawing, a mirror image of the first, ragged men make their way among crumbling masonry and mossy pillars, and a broken pediment looms ominously overhead.

Unlike Malton's more familiar images of classical order, the clutter and disarray of this second drawing encode a proto-romanticism very similar to Morgan's own project. Ruins operate here as an index of cultural value, encoding an appeal to some future appreciation of a once great civilisation: the glory that was Dublin. In *Florence Macarthy* too, the depiction of parliament's picturesque decay encodes a claim to cultural authority, even as it charts the erosion of political power. Its political charge is intensified via a reference to Constantin François de Volney's *Ruins of empire* and what Kevin Whelan called its 'resolutely anti-colonial politics'.[57] De Vere imagines 'some future Volney of the Ohio or Susquehannah upon the shores of this little Palmyra, and he may surmise and wonder, may dream his theories, and calculate his probabilities; and, bending over these ruins, may see the future in the past, and apostrophize the inevitable fate of existing empires.'[58]

In evoking the ubiquitous eighteenth-century spectacle of the decline of empires, Morgan connected the travellers' perspective of Dublin not only to the writings of Volney, but also to the historical philosophy of Edward Gibbon's *The history of the decline and fall of the Roman Empire*. Gibbon presented Rome's fall as 'the natural and inevitable effect of immoderate greatness'; a failure consequent on its earlier successes: 'prosperity ripened the principle of decay; the causes of destruction multiplied with the extent of conquest; and as soon as time or accident had removed the artificial supports, the stupendous fabric yielded to the pressure of its own weight.'[59] Read alongside Gibbon, Morgan can be seen to predict the ruin not so much of Dublin as of Britain, or rather the British Empire into which Ireland had been incorporated by the Union.

This rather lofty cultural analysis is not however the dominant one in the novel, which prompts a different kind of reading. The interpretation favoured by the narrative is not developed via the travellers and their premonitions, but rather takes shape in the margins of their vision and in the hands of their Dublin guide. Having framed this scene for the men's viewing pleasure, his voice guides readers away from their self-important suggestions as to the distant future and towards a reading of the Union as proximate political event. His reaction to College Green is at once less self-conscious and more ironic than theirs: telling the travellers that the parliament building is now a bank, he comments darkly that 'it cost a power of money to make *it what it is.*' The Union is presented as an event occurring within very recent memory, and he points out gleefully the lamp-post from which he had pelted stones at the pro-union MPs ('the thieves that sould us fairly', he calls them) on 'the night of the UNION'.[60]

In deflating what Katie Trumpener described as the 'aesthethiquarian' aspect of the discussions, the Irishman brings the spectacle of 'the ould parliament-house' and the grand warnings as to the corruption of empires to bear on immediate Irish realities.[61] With what looks like a high degree of narrative design, he misunderstands their talk of ruins entirely and assumes they are referring to the Union and the kind of 'decline-speak' widely associated with its passing into law:

> 'Why, then, long life to your honours,' added the guide, who, with the subtlety incidental to his class and country, drew ingenious, and sometimes exact conclusions, from very scanty premises, and who believed that the strangers were predicting the ruin of Ireland from the event of the Union (an event execrated by all the lower orders of the country). 'Why, then, long life to your honors, it's true for you; and was said long ago, that after the Union, the grass would grow high in Dublin streets; and would this day, plaze God, only in respect of the paving board, that be's rippin' up the streets, and layin' down the streets, from June to August, just for the job, by Jagurs.'[62]

In interpreting this talk of ruins in strictly materialist terms, the corruption is revealed to be that of Dublin Corporation, notorious in this period for its 'jobbing' ways, and the mouldering structures become legible as poorly paved city streets. The Dublin guide pricks the bubble of the travellers' inflated language and bears witness to the rawness of recent history.

A GREAT BEAST

To describe the Union in these terms is to introduce, as the novelists of the early nineteenth century did, the language of sensibility into the analysis of politics. A 1790s poem by Thomas Dermody contrasts real to 'seeming' sensibility by analogy with ruins:

> So, some old column, mould'ring in decay,
> Shines, with a gilded outside, on the way,
> But lean'd on, by some wretch, immediate falls,
> And tumbling, bears along, a weight of walls,
> Which o'er the ground, in awful ruin spread,
> Heaps stones and rubbish on his hapless head.[63]

Here, mouldering columns are the stuff of stagey and showy sensibility, contrasted with a sublime or 'aweful' decline, a devastation which defies description.

The heroine of Charles Robert Maturin's novel, *Women*, published in the same year (1818) as *Florence Macarthy*, walks these same Dublin streets in search of a sublime wretchedness to match her own misery. Returning to her native city in a spirit of deep despair, Zaira, an Irish woman turned continental actress, finds Dublin eerily elegant, beautiful but barren:

> it is the lifeless beauty of a cor[p]se; and the magnificent architecture of its public buildings seems like the skeleton of some gigantic frame, which the inhabiting spirit has deserted; like the vast structure of the bones of the Behemoth, which has ceased to live for ages, and round whose remains modern gazers fearfully creep and stare. We can bear the ruins of a city long deserted by human inhabitants, but it is awful to observe the inhabitants stealing from a city whose grandeur they can no longer support.[64]

Maturin collapsed the temporal distance between the political and aesthetic meanings of ruin and depicted Dublin as the wreckage of a living city. Absenteeism ('the inhabitants stealing from a city') here assumes a quasi-supernatural air. *Women* ends in a whirl of death and destruction, with only Zaira surviving 'the tempest of grief'.[65]

In this vision of Dublin as broken and monstrous, Maturin began to frame as an image the empty space left by the Union, creating the outline of a new cultural analysis. By the time the hero of John Banim's *The Anglo-Irish of the nineteenth century* undertakes what is by now a familiar novelistic walk around these same city streets, barrenness has been transmuted into a less troubling beauty. Noting how Dublin's public buildings 'group together, and make pictures together' in the most pleasing way, Gerald declares 'very beautiful, Dublin . . . very beautiful, I admit.'[66] In the context of a novel published on the eve of Catholic emancipation and featuring a hero who is lovingly educated into the necessity for Catholic suffrage, this claim shows how the proper traveller's response to Dublin can be a product of political change.

As a 'sight', picturesque or otherwise, the Union thus exists primarily as an absence rather than a presence. The novels of early nineteenth-century Ireland inscribe this absence repeatedly, depicting the skeletal emptiness of post-union Ireland. In the process, however, they begin to fill in this hollowed-out space, mustering a new and potent sense of cultural purpose amidst the political ruins. These past-oriented cultural politics are now more commonly associated with rural rather than urban wastelands, but in the years immediately after the passing of the Union, city and country both seemed enticingly empty, deserted and yet rich in possibility.

After the Union there was a newly introspective interest in definitions of Irishness, in which the novel played a significant part. This interest drew on eighteenth-century antiquarianism, made newly available, as it is cited in novels like *The wild Irish girl*, *Florence Macarthy* and *The absentee*. These were themselves satirised by Thomas Moore's *Captain Rock*. Antiquarianism encodes a claims to cultural value via the discourse of origins; in more strictly narrative terms, however, it also delivers the ability to dissolve time frames and fracture teleology, bringing in found manuscripts, bundles of old letters and annalistic accounts.

Novels transformed what may be described as the 'decline-speak' of numerous anti-union speeches and pamphlets into the material of a new cultural analysis of Ireland, which in turn gave rise to innovations in culture. But it would be wrong to see the early years of the nineteenth century as progressing smoothly towards cultural nationalism. Rather, an incipient interest in a cultural conception of identity and the beginning of the long backward look existed in counterpoint with the tendency to conceive of Ireland in terms of recent and pressing political trauma. The genre of the novel is the bearer of this latter message, although it contains within itself the possibility of the former. Ironically, the novel was ultimately to lose out, forced to cede its place of privilege to poetry and the lyric.

Andrew Blair Carmichael, a lawyer and associate of the Irish Whigs, wrote a long satirical poem about the Union entitled *The seven thieves* (1807) which, in a note, asks readers to '*reflect* on the miserable change in our golden prospects since this CURSE, like Lear's, has blasted our beautiful City —

> Into her womb convey'd sterility,
> And dried up in her the Organs of Increase?[67]

By reading Dublin as Shakespeare's blasted heath, even in such resolutely negative terms, Carmichael participated in this wider remaking of the meanings of Ireland's political ruin. But it is worth remembering that *The seven thieves* takes more specific aim against the day-to-day management of Irish life, especially the government's fondness for 'trundling out the military on every occasion': 'Heaven help us!', he wrote, 'they order those matters in England without them.'[68] In the poem, a present and immediate sense of the Union as a crime committed in broad daylight co-exists and competes with the new 'decline-speak'; both contribute to and help shape a new language in which the incompleteness of the Union could be diagnosed and discussed.

Appendices

1. MEMBERS OF THE IRISH HOUSE OF COMMONS
22 JANUARY 1799

Source: HC
B. = Borough.   C. = County.

Name	Constituency	Union position
Acheson, Archibald	C. Armagh	Anti-union
Alcock, Henry	B. Fethard (Co. Wexford)	
Alcock, William Congreve	City Waterford	Anti-union
Alexander, Henry	City Londonderry	Union
Alexander, Robert	B. Newtownards	Union
Annesley, Richard	B. Blessington	Union
Archdall, Colonel Mervyn	C. Fermanagh	Anti-union
Archdall, Richard	B. Killibegs	Union
Armstrong, William Henry	B. Wicklow	
Babington, David	B. Ballyshannon	Anti-union
Bagwell, John	C. Tipperary	Anti-union
Bagwell, William	B. Rathcormack	Anti-union
Bailey, William	B. Augher	Union
Ball, John	C. and Town of Drogheda	Anti-union
Barrington, Jonah	City Clogher	Anti-union
Barry, John	B. Newtownlimavady	
Beresford, Colonel Marcus	B. Swords	Union
Beresford, John	B. Coleraine	Union
Beresford, John	C. Waterford	Union
Beresford, John Claudius	City Dublin	Anti-union
Bingham, John	B. Tuam	Union
Blackwood, Sir James Stevenson	B. Killyleagh	
Blackwood, Sir John*	B. Killyleagh	
Blake, Joseph Henry	C. Galway	Union
Blakeney, Colonel William	B. Athenry	Union
Blakeney, Theophilus	B. Athenry	
Blaquiere, Sir John	B. Newtownards	Union
Bligh, Thomas	B. Athboy	
Botet, Anthony	B. Tulsk	Union
Boyd, James	Town Wexford	Union
Boyle, Charles	Town Charleville	

→

Name	Constituency	Union position
Boyle, Lord Viscount	C. Cork	Union
Brooke, Henry Vaughan	C. Donegal	
Browne, Arthur	University of Dublin	Anti-union
Browne, Denis	C. Mayo	Union
Bruce, Stewart	B. Lisbourne	Union
Bunbury, George	B. Gowran	
Burdett, George	B. Gowran	Union
Burgh, Thomas	City Clogher	Union
Burton, Francis Nathaniel	C. Clare	Union
Burton, William	C. Catherlogh	Anti-union
Butler, James	C. Kilkenny	Union
Butler, Sir Richard	C. Catherlogh	
Cane, James	B. Ratoath	Anti-union
Carew, Robert Shapland	City Waterford	
Carroll, Ephraim*	B. Bannow	
Castlereagh, Viscount	C. Down	Union
Caulfeild, Lord Viscount	C. Armagh	Anti-union
Cavendish, George	B. Cavan	Union
Cavendish, Sir Henry	B. Lismore	Union
Chinnery, Broderick	Town Bandon Bridge	Union
Clements, Lord Viscount	C. Leitrim	Anti-union
Coddington, Henry	B. Dunleer	Anti-union
Cole, Lieutenant Colonel Galbraith Lowry	B. Enniskillen	Anti-union
Cole, Lord Viscount	C. Fermanagh	Anti-union
Conolly, Thomas	C. Londonderry	Union
Cooke, Edward	B. Old Leighlin	Union
Cooper, Joshua Edward	C. Sligo	Anti-union
Coote, Charles Henry	Queen's County	Union
Coote, General Eyre	B. Maryborough	
Cornwall, Robert	B. Enniscorthy	Union
Corry, Isaac*	B. Newry	Union
Corry, Lord Viscount	C. Tyrone	Anti-union
Cotter, Rogerson	Town Charleville	Union
Cotter, Sir James Laurence	B. Castlemartyr	Union
Creighton, Abraham	B. Lifford	Anti-union
Creighton, John	B. Lifford	Anti-union
Crookshank, George	B. Belfast	Anti-union
Crosbie, James	C. Kerry	
Crosbie, William Arthur	B. Trim	Union
Crowe, Robert	B. Philipstown	Anti-union
Daly, Denis Bowes	King's County	Anti-union
Daly, St George*	Town Galway	Union
Dawson, Arthur	B. Banagher	Anti-union
Dawson, Richard	C. Monaghan	Anti-union
Dobbs, Francis	B. Charlemont	Anti-union
Duigenan, Patrick	B. Armagh	Union

→

Name	Constituency	Union position
Dunbar, George	B. Thomastown	
Edgeworth, Richard Lovell	B. St Johnstown (Co. Longford)	Anti-union
Egan, John	B. Tallagh	Anti-union
Elliot, William	B. Saint Canice alias Irishtown	Union
Eustace, Major General Charles	B. Fethard (Co. Wexford)	Union
Evans, George	B. Baltimore	Anti-union
Falkiner, Frederick John	C. Dublin	Anti-union
Ferguson, Andrew	City Londonderry	
Fetherstone, Sir Thomas	C. Longford	
Fitzgerald, James	B. Kildare	Anti-union
Fitzgerald, Lord Charles	B. Ardfert	Union
Fitzgerald, Maurice	C. Kerry	Union
Fitzgerald, Robert Uniacke	C. Cork	Union
Fortescue, Sir Chichester	B. Trim	Union
Fortescue, William	B. Monaghan	
Fortescue, William Charles	C. Louth	Anti-union
Forward, William	B. St Johnstown (Co. Donegal)	Union
Foster, John	C. Louth	Anti-union
Foster, Thomas Henry	B. Dunleer	Anti-union
Fox, Luke*	B. Clonmines	
Freke, Sir John	B. Baltimore	Anti-union
French, Arthur	C. Roscommon	Anti-union
Gahan, Daniel	B. Wicklow	
Galbraith, James	B. Augher	Union
Gore, William	B. Carrick	Anti-union
Gorges, Hamilton	C. Meath	Anti-union
Grady, Henry Deane	City Limerick	Union
Hamilton, Alexander	B. Belfast	Anti-union
Hamilton, Arthur Cole	B. Enniskillen	Anti-union
Hamilton, Hans	C. Dublin	Anti-union
Handcock, William	B. Athlone	Anti-union
Hardinge, Richard	Town Middleton	
Hardman, Edward	C. and Town of Drogheda	Anti-union
Hardy, Francis	Manor Mullingar	Anti-union
Hare, Richard	B. Athy	Union
Hare, William	B. Athy	Union
Hatton, George	B. Lisbourne	
Henniker, Bridges	B. Kildare	Union
Hoare, Sir Joseph	B. Askeyton	Anti-union
Hobson, John	B. Cloghnikelty	
Holmes, Peter	Manor Doneraile	Union
Hopkins, Sir Francis	B. Kilbeggan	Anti-union
Howard, Hugh	B. St Johnstown (Co. Donegal)	Union
Howard, Hugh	B. Athboy	
Hunt, Sir Vere	B. Askeyton	
Hutchinson, Francis Hely	B. Naas	Union
Hutchinson, John Hely	City Cork	Union

→

Name	Constituency	Union position
Irvine, Henry	B. Tulsk	
Jackson, George	C. Mayo	Union
Jackson, George	B. Randalstown	
Jephson, Denham	Town Mallow	Union
Jocelyn, John	B. Dundalk	Union
Johnson, Robert	B. Hillsborough	Union
Jones, Theophilus	C. Leitrim	Union
Jones, Walter	B. Coleraine	Union
Kavanagh, Thomas*	City Kilkenny	Union
Keane, John	Town Youghal	Union
Kearney, James	B. Thomastown	Union
Keatinge, Maurice	C. Kildare	
Kemmis, Henry	B. Tralee	Union
King, Charles	B. Belturbet	Anti-union
King, Gilbert	B. Jamestown	Anti-union
King, Henry	B. Boyle	Anti-union
King, John	B. Jamestown	Anti-union
King, Robert	B. Boyle	Anti-union
Kingsborough, Lord Viscount	C. Roscommon	Anti-union
Knott, William	B. Taghmon	Union
Knox, Andrew	B. Strabane	
Knox, Charles*	B. Dungannon	
Knox, Francis	B. Philipstown	Anti-union
Knox, George	University of Dublin	Anti-union
Knox, James	B. Taghmon	Union
La Touche jnr., David	B. Newcastle	Anti-union
La Touche, David	B. Newcastle	
La Touche, John	B. Harristown	Anti-union
La Touche, John	C. Kildare	Anti-union
La Touche, Robert	B. Harristown	Anti-union
Lambart, Gustavus	B. Kilbeggan	
Langrishe, Sir Hercules	B. Knocktopher	Union
Lee, Edward	B. Dungarvon	Anti-union
Leigh, Robert	Town New Ross	
Leslie, Charles Powell	C. Monaghan	Anti-union
Lighton, Sir Thomas	B. Carlingford	Anti-union
Lindsey jnr., Thomas	B. Castlebar	Union
Lindsey, Thomas	B. Castlebar	Union
Loftus, Lord Viscount	C. Wexford	
Loftus, Major General William	B. Bannow	
Longfield, Captain John	B. Ballynakill	Union
Longfield, John	Town Mallow	Union
Longfield, Mountifort	City Cork	Union
Lysaght, Joseph*	City Cashel	
Lyttleton, George Fulk	B. Granard	
Macartney, Sir John	B. Naas	Anti-union
Magenis, Richard	B. Carlingford	

→

Name	Constituency	Union position
Mahon, Ross	B. Granard	Union
Martin, Richard	B. Laneborough	Union
Mason, John Monck	B. Saint Canice alias Irishtown	Union
Massey, Hugh Dillon	C. Clare	Union
Mathew, Lord Viscount	C. Tipperary	Anti-union
Mathew, Montague	B. Ballynakill	
Maxwell, Lord Viscount	C. Cavan	Anti-union
McClelland, James	B. Randalstown	Union
McDonnell, Charles	B. Rathcormack	
McNamara, Francis	B. Killibegs	Union
McNaughton, Edmund Alexander	C. Antrim	Union
Metge, John	B. Tallagh	Anti-union
Monck, William Domville Stanley*	B. Newborough	alias Gorey
Monsell, William	B. Dingle-Icouch	Anti-union
Montgomery, Alexander	C. Donegal	Anti-union
Montgomery, William	B. Hillsborough	
Moore, Arthur	B. Tralee	Anti-union
Moore, Lorenzo	B. Ardfert	Union
Moore, Nathaniel Montgomery	B. Strabane	
Moore, Stephen	B. Kells	Union
Moore, Stephen	B. Clonmel	
Morres, Lodge	B. Dingle-Icouch	Union
Musgrave, Sir Richard	B. Lismore	Union
Nesbit, Thomas	B. Cavan	Union
Nevill, Richard	Town Wexford	Anti-union
Newcomen, Sir William Gleadowe,	C. Longford	Union
Newenham, Thomas	B. Clonmel	Anti-union
O'Brien, Sir Edward	B. Ennis	Anti-union
O'Callaghan, Robert William	Town Bandon Bridge	Anti-union
O'Donnell, Colonel Hugh	B. Donegal	Anti-union
O'Donnell, James Moore	B. Ratoath	Anti-union
O'Hara, Charles	C. Sligo	Anti-union
Odell, Lieutenant Colonel William	C. Limerick	Union
Ogle, George	City Dublin	Anti-union
Oliver jnr., Silver	B. Killmallock	
Oliver, Charles Silver	B. Killmallock	
Ormsby, Charles Montague	B. Duleek	Union
Osbourne, Charles	B. Carysfort	Union
Osbourne, Henry*	B. Carysfort	Anti-union
Pakenham, Thomas	B. Longford	Union
Parnell, Henry	B. Maryborough	
Parnell, Sir John	Queen's County	Anti-union
Parsons, Sir Laurence	King's County	Anti-union

Name	Constituency	Union position
Pelham, Thomas	B. Armagh	
Pennefather, Richard	City Cashel	
Plunket, William Conyngham	B. Charlemont	Anti-union
Ponsonby, George	Town Galway	Anti-union
Ponsonby, John Brabazon	B. Dungarvon	
Ponsonby, Major William	B. Fethard (Co. Tipperary)	Anti-union
Ponsonby, William Brabazon	C. Kilkenny	Anti-union
Power, Richard	C. Waterford	Anti-union
Prendergast, Thomas	B. Cloghnikelty	
Preston, John	B. Navan	Anti-union
Preston, Joseph	B. Navan	Anti-union
Prittie, Henry Sadlier	B. Catherlogh	
Ram, Abel	C. Wexford	Anti-union
Reilly, John	B. Blessington	
Richardson, Sir William	B. Ballyshannon	Anti-union
Roche, Sir Boyle	B. Old Leighlin	Union
Rochfort, Gustavus	C. Westmeath	Anti-union
Rochfort, John Staunton	B. Fore	Anti-union
Ross, Robert* (d. 1799)	B. Newry	
Rowley, Clotworthy	B. Downpatrick	
Rowley, Clotworthy	C. Meath	
Rowley, Josias	B. Downpatrick	
Rowley, Samuel Campbell	Town Kinsale	
Rowley, William	Town Kinsale	
Rutledge, Robert	B. Duleek	Union
Ruxton, William	B. Atherdee	Anti-union
Sandford, George*	B. Roscommon	
Sandford, Henry Moore	B. Roscommon	Union
Saunderson, Francis	C. Cavan	Anti-union
Savage, Francis	C. Down	Anti-union
Sentleger, Barry Boyle	Manor Doneraile	Anti-union
Shee, Sir George	B. Knocktopher	Union
Skeffington, Henry	B. Antrim	Union
Skeffington, William John	B. Antrim	Anti-union
Smyth, William	B. Donegal	Union
Smyth, William	C. Westmeath	Anti-union
Sneyd, Nathaniel	B. Carrick	Anti-union
St George, Sir Richard Bligh	B. Athlone	Anti-union
Stanley, Edmund	B. Laneborough	Union
Stannus, Thomas	B. Portarlington	Anti-union
Staples, John	C. Antrim	Union
Stewart, Henry*	B. Longford	Anti-union
Stewart, James	C. Tyrone	Anti-union
Stewart, John	B. Bangor	Union
Straford, Benjamin O'Neale	B. Baltinglass	Anti-union
Stratford, John	B. Baltinglass	
Stratton, John	B. Dundalk	Union

Name	Constituency	Union position
Synge, Francis	B. Swords	
Taylor, Colonel Robert	B. Kells	Anti-union
Taylor, John	B. Fethard (Co. Tipperary)	
Tighe, Henry	B. Innistioge	Anti-union
Tighe, William	B. Innistioge	Anti-union
Toler, John	B. Newborough alias Gorey	Union
Tottenham, Charles	Town New Ross	Union
Tottenham, Ponsonby	B. Clonmines	Union
Townsend, John	B. Castlemartyr	Union
Townsend, Thomas	B. Belturbet	Anti-union
Trench, Frederick	B. Portarlington	Union
Trench, General Eyre Power	B. Newtownlimavady	
Trench, Richard	C. Galway	Anti-union
Tydd, Sir John	B. Fore	
Tyrone, Earl of	C. Londonderry	Union
Uniacke, Robert	Town Youghal	Union
Vandeleur, John Ormby	B. Ennis	Union
Vereker, Lieutenant Colonel Charles	City Limerick	Anti-union
Verner, James	B. Dungannon	Union
Waller, John	C. Limerick	Anti-union
Ward, Robert	B. Bangor	
Welch, Patrick	B. Callan	
Wemyss, James	City Kilkenny	Union
Westby, Nicholas	C. Wicklow	
Westenra, Henry	B. Monaghan	Union
Whaley, Thomas	B. Enniscorthy	Union
Wilson, Ezekiel Davys	C. and Town of Carrickfergus*	Anti-union
Wolfe, John	B. Catherlogh	
Woodward, Benjamin Blake	Town Middleton	Union
Wynne, Owen	B. Sligo	Anti-union
Wynne, Robert*	B. Sligo	
Yelverton, Walter	B. Tuam	Union

Only 293 of the 300 seats in the Irish House of Commons were filled when parliament met on 22 January 1799. Of these MPs 112 were anti-union, while 110 supported the measure. This left 83 who did not vote, or were undecided. Not all of the 222 who had a position on the union voted at each division. The largest division was on 24 January on a motion for deleting the union paragraph of the king's address. This was defeated by 109 votes to 104. Adding the two tellers to each side this gives a total of 111 to 106 [this excludes the anti-union Speaker, John Foster].

2. MEMBERS OF THE IRISH HOUSE OF COMMONS 1800

Source: HC
B. = Borough.   C. = County.
Bold = Indicates that the MP sat for the same constituency between 22 January 1799 and 7 June 1800.
* = subsequently vacated seat.   [. . .] = date he entered the House of Commons.

Name	Constituency
Acheson, Archibald	C. Armagh
Alcock, William Congreve	City Waterford
Aldridge, Robert*	B. Carysfort
Alexander, Dupre [3 February 1800]	B. Newtownards
Alexander, Henry	City Londonderry
Alexander, Robert*	B. Newtownards
Annesley, Richard [8 May 1800]	Town Middleton
Annesley, Richard*	B. Blessington
Annesley, Richard* [3 February 1800]	City Clogher
Archdall, Colonel Mervyn	C. Fermanagh
Archdall, Richard	B. Killibegs
Armstrong, William Henry	B. Wicklow
Babington, David	B. Ballyshannon
Bagwell, John	C. Tipperary
Bagwell, Richard	City Cashel
Bagwell, William	B. Rathcormack
Bailey, William	B. Augher
Balfour, Blayney Townley [5 February 1800] (King died)	B. Belturbet
Ball, Charles [29 March 1800]	City Clogher
Ball, John	C. and Town of Drogheda
Barrington, Jonah*	City Clogher
Barry, John	B. Newtownlimavady
Beresford, Colonel Marcus	B. Swords
Beresford, John	B. Coleraine
Beresford, John	C. Waterford
Beresford, John Claudius	City Dublin
Bingham, John*	B. Tuam
Blackwood, Hans*	B. Killyleagh
Blackwood, Sir James Stevenson	B. Killyleagh
Blake, Joseph Henry	C. Galway
Blakeney, Colonel William*	B. Athenry
Blakeney, Theophilus*	B. Athenry
Blaquiere, Sir John	B. Newtownards
Bligh, Edward [3 February 1800) (Howard died)	B. Athboy
Bligh, Thomas	B. Athboy
Botet, Anthony*	B. Tulsk
Boyd, James*	Town Wexford
Boyle, Charles*	Town Charleville
Boyle, Lord Viscount	C. Cork

Name	Constituency
Brooke, Henry Vaughan	C. Donegal
Browne, Arthur	University of Dublin
Browne, Denis	C. Mayo
Bruce, Stewart	B. Lisbourne
Bunbury, George*	B. Gowran
Burdett, George	B. Gowran
Burgh, Thomas [19 February 1800]	B. Fore
Burgh, Thomas*	City Clogher
Burke, Michael [8 May 1800]	B. Athenry
Burrowes, Colonel Thomas [12 May 1800]	B. Longford
Burrowes, Peter [3 February 1800]	B. Enniscorthy
Burton, Francis Nathaniel	C. Clare
Burton, William	C. Catherlogh
Bushe, Charles Kendall [15 January 1800]	B. Donegal
(O'Donnell died)	
Butler, James	C. Kilkenny
Butler, Sir Richard	C. Catherlogh
Cane, James	B. Ratoath
Carew, Robert Shapland	City Waterford
Casey, Thomas [15 January 1800]	B. Killmallock
Castlereagh, Viscount	C. Down
Cavendish, George	B. Cavan
Cavendish, Sir Henry	B. Lismore
Chinnery, Sir Broderick	Town Bandon Bridge
Clements, Lord Viscount	C. Leitrim
Coddington, Henry*	B. Dunleer
Cole, Lieutenant Colonel Galbraith Lowry*	B. Enniskillen
Cole, Lord Viscount	C. Fermanagh
Conolly, Thomas*	C. Londonderry
Cooke, Edward	B. Old Leighlin
Cooper, Joshua Edward	C. Sligo
Coote, Charles Henry	Queen's County
Coote, General Eyre*	B. Maryborough
Cope, Robert Camden [15 January 1800]	C. Armagh
Cornwall, Robert*	B. Enniscorthy
Corry, Isaac	B. Newry
Corry, Lord Viscount	C. Tyrone
Cotter, Rogerson	Town Charleville
Cotter, Sir James Laurence	B. Castlemartyr
Cradock, Major General John Francis [19 May 1800]	B. Thomastown
Cradock, Major General John Francis*	Town Middleton
Creighton, Abraham	B. Lifford
Creighton, John	B. Lifford
Crookshank, George	B. Belfast
Crosbie, James	C. Kerry
Crosbie, William Arthur	B. Trim
Crowe, Robert*	B. Philipstown →

Name	Constituency
Cuffe, James [3 February 1800]	B. Tulsk
Dalway, Noah [15 January 1800]	C. and Town of Carrickfergus
(M. of Donegal replaced)	
Daly, Denis Bowes	King's County
Daly, St George	Town Galway
Darby, Verny [8 May 1800]	B. Gowran
Dawson, Arthur	B. Banagher
Dawson, Richard	C. Monaghan
Dennis, John [24 February 1800]	B. Clonmel
Dick, Quentin [12 February 1800]	B. Dunleer
Dobbs, Francis	B. Charlemont
Duigenan, Patrick	B. Armagh
Dunbar, George*	B. Thomastown
Dunne, Colonel Edward [10 February 1800]	B. Maryborough
Edgeworth, Richard Lovell	B. St Johnstown (Co. Longford)
Egan, John	B. Tallow [Tallagh]
Elliot, William	B. Saint Canice alias Irishtown
Eustace, Major General Charles	B. Feathard [Fethard] (Co. Wexford)
Eustace, Major Henry [3 February 1800]	B. Clonmines
Evans, George	B. Baltimore
Falkiner, Frederick John	C. Dublin
Ferguson, Andrew	City Londonderry
Fetherstone, Sir Thomas	C. Longford
Fitzgerald, James	B. Kildare
Fitzgerald, Lord Charles	B. Ardfert
Fitzgerald, Maurice [12 February 1800]	C. Kerry
Fitzgerald, Robert Uniacke	C. Cork
Forestcue, Faithful [3 February 1800]	B. Monaghan
Fortescue, Chichester [3 February 1800]	B. Hillsborough
(Montgomery died)	
Fortescue, Sir Chichester	B. Trim
Fortescue, William Charles	C. Louth
Fortescue, William*	B. Monaghan
Forward, William* [3 February 1800]	B. St Johnstown (Co. Donegal)
Foster, John	C. Louth
Foster, Thomas Henry	B. Dunleer
Fox, Luke	Manor Mullingar
Freke, Sir John	B. Baltimore
French, Arthur	C. Roscommon
Galbraith, James	B. Augher
Gardiner, Lieutenant General William [8 May 1800]	B. Thomastown
Gardiner, Lieutenant General William* [3 February 1800]	City Clogher
Gore, William [3 February 1800]	B. Carrick
Gorges, Hamilton	C. Meath
Gould, Thomas [5 February 1800]	B. Kilbeggan

Name	Constituency
Grady, Henry Deane	City Limerick
Grattan, Henry [15 January 1800] (Gahan died)	B. Wicklow
Gregory, William [3 February 1800]	B. Portarlington
Hamilton, Alexander*	B. Belfast
Hamilton, Arthur Cole	B. Enniskillen
Hamilton, Hans	C. Dublin
Handcock, Richard [30 May 1800]	B. Athlone
Handcock, William	B. Athlone
Hardman, Edward	C. and Town of Drogheda
Hardy, Francis	Manor Mullingar
Hare, Richard	B. Athy
Hare, William	B. Athy
Hatton, George	B. Lisbourne
Henniker, Bridges	B. Kildare
Herbert, Richard Townsend [3 February 1800]	B. Granard
Hoare, Edward*	B. Banagher
Hoare, Sir Joseph	B. Askeyton
Hobson, John	B. Cloghnikelty
Holmes, Peter	Manor Doneraile
Hopkins, Sir Francis*	B. Kilbeggan
Howard, Hugh	B. St Johnstown (Co. Donegal)
Hume, William Hoare	C. Wicklow
Hunt, Sir Vere	B. Askeyton
Hutchinson, Francis Hely [3 February 1800]	B. Naas
Hutchinson, Major General John Hely	City Cork
Irvine, Henry	B. Tulsk
Jackson, George	B. Randalstown
Jackson, George	C. Mayo
Jephson, Denham	Town Mallow
Jocelyn, John	B. Dundalk
Johnson, Robert [3 February 1800]	B. Philipstown
Johnson, William	B. Roscommon
Jones, Theophilus	C. Leitrim
Jones, Walter	B. Coleraine
Keane, John	Town Youghal
Kearney, James*	B. Thomastown
Keatinge, Maurice	C. Kildare
Kemmis, Henry	B. Tralee
King, Colonel Robert [15 January 1800]	B. Boyle
King, Gilbert	B. Jamestown
King, Henry	B. Boyle
King, John	B. Jamestown
King, John [29 March 1800]	City Clogher
Knott, William	B. Taghmon
Knox, Andrew	B. Strabane
Knox, Francis*	B. Philipstown
Knox, George	University of Dublin →

Name	Constituency
Knox, James	B. Taghmon
La Touche jnr., David	B. Newcastle
La Touche, David	B. Newcastle
La Touche, John	B. Harristown
La Touche, John	C. Kildare
La Touche, Robert	B. Harristown
Lake, General Gerard [15 January 1800]	B. Armagh
Lambart, Gustavus	B. Kilbeggan
Langrishe, Sir Hercules*	B. Knocktopher
Lee, Edward	B. Dungarvon
Leigh, Francis [3 February 1800]	Town Wexford
Leigh, Robert	Town New Ross
Leslie, Charles Powell	C. Monaghan
Lighton, Sir Thomas	B. Carlingford
Lindsey jnr., Thomas	B. Castlebar
Lindsey, Thomas*	B. Castlebar
Loftus, Lord Viscount	C. Wexford
Loftus, Major General William*	B. Bannow
Longfield, Captain John	B. Ballynakill
Longfield, John	Town Mallow
Longfield, Mountifort* [3 February 1800]	City Cork
Luttrell, Henry*	B. Clonmines
Lyttleton, George Fulk*	B. Granard
Macartney, Sir John	B. Naas
MacLean, Joseph [3 February 1800]	B. Bannow
Magenis, Richard	B. Carlingford
Mahon, James [3 February 1800]	B. Philipstown
Mahon, Ross	B. Granard
Mahon, Stephen* [12 May 1800]	B. Knocktopher
Mahon, Thomas [15 January 1800]	C. Roscommon
Martin, Richard	B. Laneborough
Mason, John Monck	B. Saint Canice alias Irishtown
Massey, Hugh Dillon	C. Clare
Mathew, Lord Viscount	C. Tipperary
Mathew, Montague*	B. Ballynakill
Maxwell, Lord Viscount	C. Cavan
May, Edward [3 February 1800]	B. Belfast
McClelland, James	B. Randalstown
McDonnell, Charles	B. Rathcormack
McNamara, Francis	B. Killibegs
McNaughton, Edmund Alexander	C. Antrim
Metge, John	B. Tallow [Tallagh]
Miller, George [3 February 1800]	B. Castlebar
Monsell, William*	B. Dingle-Icouch
Montgomery, Alexander	C. Donegal
Moore, Arthur	B. Tralee
Moore, John	B. Newry

→

Name	Constituency
Moore, Lorenzo*	B. Ardfert
Moore, Nathaniel Montgomery	B. Strabane
Moore, Stephen	B. Clonmel
Moore, Stephen	B. Kells
Moore, William*	B. St Johnstown (Co. Longford)
Morres, Lodge	B. Dingle-Icouch
Mullins, William Townsend [10 February 1800]	B. Dingle-Icouch*
Musgrave, Sir Richard	B. Lismore
Mussenden, Daniel [4 March 1800]	B. Killyleagh
Needham, William [8 May 1800]	B. Athenry
Nesbit, Thomas	B. Cavan
Nevill, Richard	Town Wexford
Newcomen, Sir William Gleadowe	C. Longford
Newenham, Thomas*	B. Clonmel
Nugent, Major General George [3 March 1800]	Town Charleville
O'Brien, Sir Edward	B. Ennis
O'Callaghan, Robert William	Town Bandon Bridge
O'Donnell, James Moore	B. Ratoath
O'Hara, Charles	C. Sligo
Odell, Lieutenant Colonel William	C. Limerick
Ogle, George	City Dublin
Ormsby, Charles Montague [3 February 1800]	B. Duleek
Ormsby, John Mason	B. Newborough alias Gorey
Osbourne, Charles	B. Carysfort
Osbourne, Henry [3 February 1800]	B. Enniskillen
Pakenham, Edward*	B. Longford
Pakenham, Thomas	B. Longford
Parnell, Henry	B. Maryborough
Parnell, Sir John	Queen's County
Parsons, Sir Laurence	King's County
Pennefather, Richard	City Cashel
Pepper, Thomas [3 February 1800]	B. Kells
Plunket, William Conyngham	B. Charlemont
Ponsonby, George	Town Galway
Ponsonby, John Brabazon	B. Dungarvon
Ponsonby, Major William	B. Fethard (Co. Tipperary)
Ponsonby, William Brabazon	C. Kilkenny
Power, Richard	C. Waterford
Prendergast, Thomas	B. Cloghnikelty
Preston, John	B. Navan
Preston, Joseph	B. Navan
Prior, Thomas [13 March 1800]	B. Bannow
Prittie, Henry Sadlier	B. Catherlogh
Quin, Sir Richard [15 January 1800]	B. Killmallock
Ram, Abel	C. Wexford
Reade, George Harrison* [3 February 1800]	B. Feathard [Fethard] (Co. Wexford)

Name	Constituency
Reilly, John	B. Blessington
Reilly, William Edmund [3 February 1800]	B. Hillsborough
Richardson, Sir William	B. Ballyshannon
Roche, Sir Boyle	B. Old Leighlin
Rochfort, Gustavus	C. Westmeath
Rochfort, John Staunton	B. Fore
Rowley, Clotworthy	B. Downpatrick
Rowley, Clotworthy	C. Meath
Rowley, Josias	B. Downpatrick
Rowley, Samuel Campbell	Town Kinsale
Rowley, William	Town Kinsale
Rutledge, Robert	B. Duleek
Ruxton, William	B. Atherdee
Ruxton, William Parkinson	B. Atherdee
Sandford, Henry Moore	B. Roscommon
Saunderson, Francis	C. Cavan
Saurin, William [3 February 1800]	B. Blessington
Savage, Francis	C. Down
Savage, James	B. Callan
Sentleger, Barry Boyle	Manor Doneraile
Sharkey, Richard Fortescue	B. Dungannon
Shaw, Robert [3 February 1800]	B. St Johnstown (Co. Longford)
Shaw, Robert*	B. Bannow
Shee, Sir George [3 February 1800]	B. Knocktopher
Singleton, Mark [5 February 1800]	B. Carysfort
Skeffington, Henry	B. Antrim
Skeffington, William John	B. Antrim
Smyth, William	B. Donegal
Smyth, William	C. Westmeath
Sneyd, Nathaniel*	B. Carrick
St George, Sir Richard Bligh*	B. Athlone
Stanley, Edmund	B. Laneborough
Stannus, Thomas*	B. Portarlington
Staples, John	C. Antrim
Staples, Thomas* [18 March 1800]	B. Knocktopher
Stewart, Charles William [29 May 1800]	C. Londonderry
Stewart, Charles William* [18 March 1800]	B. Thomastown
Stewart, James	C. Tyrone
Stewart, John	B. Bangor
Straford, Benjamin O'Neale	B. Baltinglass
Stratford, John	B. Baltinglass
Stratton, John	B. Dundalk
Synge, Francis	B. Swords
Talbot, John* [11 February 1800]	B. Ardfert
Talbot, William	City Kilkenny
Taylor, Colonel Robert*	B. Kells
Taylor, John	B. Fethard (Co. Tipperary)

Name	Constituency
Tighe, Henry	B. Innistioge
Tighe, Robert [3 February 1800]	B. Carrick
Tighe, William	B. Innistioge
Toler, John	B. Newborough alias Gorey
Tottenham, Charles	Town New Ross
Tottenham, Ponsonby	B. Clonmines
Townsend, John★ [3 February 1800]	B. Castlemartyr
Townsend, Thomas	B. Belturbet
Trench, Charles [15 January 1800]	B. Newtownlimavady
Trench, Frederick	B. Portarlington
Trench, Frrancis [21 March 1800]	B. Ballynakill
Trench, Richard	C. Galway
Tydd, Sir John★	B. Fore
Tyrone, Earl of	C. Londonderry
Uniacke, Robert★ [3 February 1800]	Town Youghal
Vandeleur, John Ormby★ [5 February 1800]	B. Ennis
Vereker, Lieutenant Colonel Charles	City Limerick
Verner, James	B. Dungannon
Vesey, George [17 February 1800]	B. Tuam
Waller, John	C. Limerick
Walsh, David [vacated 1 March 1800]	B. Ballynakill★
Ward, Robert	B. Bangor
Welch, Patrick	B. Callan
Wemyss, James	City Kilkenny
Westby, Nicholas	C. Wicklow
Westenra, Henry	B. Monaghan
Whaley, Thomas	B. Enniscorthy
Wilson, Ezekiel Davys	C. and Town of Carrickfergus★
Wolfe, John	B. Catherlogh
Woodward, Benjamin Blake	Town Middleton
Wynne, Owen	B. Sligo
Wynne, William	B. Sligo
Yelverton, Walter [17 February 1800]	B. Tuam

3. IRISH MPS IN THE HOUSE OF COMMONS OF THE UNITED
KINGDOM 1801

Source: HC
B. = Borough   C. = County

Name	Constituency	Union position
Acheson, Archibald	C. Armagh	Anti-Union
Alcock, William Congreve	City Waterford	Union*
Alexander, Henry	City Londonderry	Union
Archdall, Colonel Mervyn	C. Fermanagh	Anti-Union
Bagwell, John	C. Tipperary	Union*
Bagwell, Richard	City Cashel	Union*
Bagwell, William	B. Clonmel	Union*
Beresford, John	C. Waterford	Union
Beresford, John Claudius	City Dublin	Anti-Union
Boyle, Lord Viscount	C. Cork	Union
Brooke, Henry Vaughan	C. Donegal	Anti-Union
Browne, Denis	C. Mayo	Union
Burton, Francis Nathaniel	C. Clare	Union
Burton, William	C. Catherlogh	Anti-Union
Butler, James	C. Kilkenny	Anti-Union*
Butler, Sir Richard	C. Catherlogh	Anti-Union
Castlereagh, Viscount	C. Down	Union
Chinnery, Sir Broderick	Town Bandon Bridge	Union
Clements, Lord Viscount	C. Leitrim	Anti-Union
Cole, Lord Viscount	C. Fermanagh	Anti-Union
Cole-Hamilton, Arthur	B. Enniskillen	Anti-Union
Cooper, Joshua Edward	C. Sligo	Anti-Union
Coote, Charles Henry	Queen's County	Union
Cope, Robert Camden	C. Armagh	Union
Corry, Isaac	B. Dundalk	Union
Corry, Lord Viscount	C. Tyrone	Anti-Union
Crosbie, James	C. Kerry	Union
Dalway, Noah	C. and Town of Carrickfergus	Anti-Union
Daly, Denis Bowes	King's County	Anti-Union
Daly, St George	Town Galway	Union
Dawson, Richard	C. Monaghan	Anti-Union
Duigenan, Patrick	B. Armagh	Union
Falkiner, Frederick John	C. Dublin	Anti-Union
Fetherstone, Sir Thomas	C. Longford	Anti-Union
Fitzgerald, Maurice	C. Kerry	Union
Fitzgerald, Robert Uniacke	C. Cork	Union
Fortescue, William Charles	C. Louth	Union*
Foster, John	C. Louth	Anti-Union
French, Arthur	C. Roscommon	Anti-Union
Gleadowe, Sir William	C. Longford	Union
Gore, Arthur	C. Donegal	No vote
Gorges, Hamilton	C. Meath	Anti-Union

42   anti Union   20
            Union   21
            No vote   1

Name	Constituency	Union position
Grady, Henry Deane	City Limerick	Union
Hamilton, Hans	C. Dublin	Anti-Union
Handcock, William	B. Athlone	Union*
Hardman, Edward	C. and Town of Drogheda	Anti-Union
Hatton, George	B. Lisburn	Union
Hill, Sir George Fitzgerald	C. Londonderry	Union
Hume, William Hoare	C. Wicklow	Anti-Union
Hely-Hutchinson, John	City Cork	Union
Jackson, George	C. Mayo	Union
Jones, Theophilus	C. Leitrim	Union
Jones, Walter	B. Coleraine	Union
Keane, John	Town Youghal	Union
Keatinge, Maurice	C. Kildare	Union
Knox, George	University of Dublin	Union*
Knox, John	B. Dungannon	No vote
La Touche, John	C. Kildare	Anti-Union
Lee, Edward	B. Dungarvon	Anti-Union
Leigh, Francis	Town Wexford	Union
Leigh, Robert	Town New Ross	Union
Loftus, Lord Viscount	C. Wexford	Union
Longfield, John	Town Mallow	Union
Longfield, Mountifort	City Cork	Union
Mahon, Thomas	C. Roscommon	Union
Martin, Richard	C. Galway	Union
Massey, Hugh Dillon	C. Clare	Union
Mathew, Lord Viscount	C. Tipperary	Anti-Union
May, Edward	B. Belfast	Union
McNaughton, Edmund Alexander	C. Antrim	Union
Moore, Arthur	B. Tralee	Anti-Union
Moore, John	B. Newry	Anti-Union
O'Hara, Charles	C. Sligo	Anti-Union
Odell, Lieutenant Colonel William	C. Limerick	Union
Ogle, George	City Dublin	Anti-Union
Parnell, Sir John	Queen's County	Anti-Union
Parsons, Sir Laurence	King's County	Anti-Union
Ponsonby, William Brabazon	C. Kilkenny	Anti-Union
Power, Richard	C. Waterford	Anti-Union
Prittie, Henry Sadlier	B. Catherlogh	Union
Ram, Abel	C. Wexford	Union*
Rochfort, Gustavus	C. Westmeath	Anti-Union
Rowley, Clotworthy	B. Downpatrick	Anti-Union
Rowley, Clotworthy	C. Meath	Anti-Union
Rowley, William	Town Kinsale	Anti-Union
Saunderson, Francis	C. Cavan	Anti-Union
Savage, Francis	C. Down	Anti-Union

→

45   anti Union   20
      Union   24
      No Vote   1

Name	Constituency	Union position
Smyth, William	C. Westmeath	Anti-Union
Sneyd, Nathaniel	C. Cavan	Anti-Union
Staples, John	C. Antrim	Union
Stewart, Charles William	C. Londonderry	Union
Stewart, James	C. Tyrone	Anti-Union
Talbot, William	City Kilkenny	Unknown
Trench, Frederick	B. Portarlington	Union
Trench, Richard	C. Galway	Union
Vandeleur, John Ormby	B. Ennis	Union
Waller, John	C. Limerick	Anti-Union
Westenra, Warner William	C. Monaghan	Anti-Union
Wynne, Owen	B. Sligo	Anti-Union

* = These MPs changed sides; either from Union to Anti-union (1), or Anti-union to Union (7).

12

anti-Union 6
Union 5
Unknown 1

Notes

INTRODUCTION

1 Bolton, *Union*.
2 James Kelly, 'The origins of the Irish Act of Union: an examination of unionist opinion in Britain and Ireland, 1650–1800', *Irish Historical Studies*, 25 (1987), pp. 236–63; Jim Smyth, '"Like amphibious animals": Irish Protestants, ancient Britons, 1691–1707', *Historical Journal*, 36 (1993), pp. 785–96.
3 David Wilkinson, '"How did they pass the Union"? Secret service expenditure', *History*, 82 (1997), pp. 223–51.
4 Geoghegan, *Union*.
5 'The British-Irish Union of 1801', *Transactions of the Royal Historical Society*, 6th series, 10 (2000), pp. 165–408.
6 Dáire Keogh and Kevin Whelan (eds), *Acts of Union: the causes, contexts and consequences of the Act of Union* (Dublin, 2001).
7 Daniel Mansergh, '"As much support as it needs": Social clas and regional attitudes to the Union', *Eighteenth-Century Ireland*, 15 (2000), pp. 77–97.

CHAPTER ONE

1 Jonah Barrington, *Rise and fall of the Irish nation* (Paris, 1833). See also note 47 below.
2 T. Dunbar Ingram, *A history of the legislative union of Great Britain and Ireland* (London, 1887).
3 Bolton, *Union*.
4 Geoghegan, *Union*; David Wilkinson, 'How did they pass the Union: secret service expenditure in Ireland 1799–1804', *History*, 82 (1997), pp. 223–51; I.R. MacBride, *Scripture politics: Ulster Presbyterianism and Irish radicalism in the late eighteenth century* (Oxford, 1998), p. 231.
5 See James Kelly, 'Popular politics in Ireland and the Act of Union', *Transactions of the Royal Historical Society*, 6th series, 10 (2000), pp. 259–88; S.J. Connolly, 'Aftermath and adjustment' in W.E. Vaughan (ed.), *A New History of Ireland* (Oxford, 1989), v, pp. 1–23.
6 Patrick Duigenan's, *An impartial history of the late Rebellion in Ireland and of the Union between Great Britain and Ireland in three parts* (London, 1800) was not a history in the formal sense of the term. Rather, it was a 'collection of the author's works on the late Rebellion of Ireland and the necessity of an incorporating union' (p.iii) repackaged to appeal to an English audience.

7   Fitzgerald contrived unsuccessfully from his position as MP for Ennis (1802–08, 1812) to advance his object of a high office in the law. He expressed a wish in 1806 to be made master of the rolls in Ireland, and sought later to promote the ambitions of his son, William Vesey, who reciprocated by seeking a peerage for his father (Arthur Aspinall (ed.) *The correspondence of George, Prince of Wales* (7 vols., London, 1963–69), iv, 1822, v, 2003; R.G. Thorne (ed.), *The history of parliament: the House of Commons 1790–1820* (5 vols., London, 1986), iii, pp. 751–2; Barrington, *Rise and fall*, p. 416n).

8   Barrington, *Memoirs*.

9   H.B. Staples, *The Ireland of Sir Jonah Barrington* (London, 1968), pp. xvi–ii; Webb, *Irish Biography*; DNB. The existing literature on Barrington's relationship with the Irish administration is inconsistent. As well as the sources cited above, see Robert Welch (ed.), *Oxford companion to Irish literature* (Oxford, 1996), p. 35; S.J. Connolly (ed.), *Oxford companion to Irish history* (Oxford, 1998), p. 39.

10 Charles Coote, *History of the Union of the Kingdoms of Great Britain and Ireland* (London, 1802), *passim*, especially pp. 18, 21, 289, 295, 510.

11 H.E.G. Rope, 'An English historian of Ireland: Francis Plowden', *Irish Monthly*, 47 (1919), pp. 552–62; Donal Macartney, 'The writing of history in Ireland 1800–30', *Irish Historical Studies*, 10 (1957), pp. 352, 355; Addington to Abbot, 30 August 1801 in HMC, *Fourth Report* (London, 1874), appendix, p. 345; DNB, i, pp. 315–16; Connolly (ed.), *Companion*, p. 446.

12 Francis Plowden, *A postliminous preface to the historical review of the state of Ireland* (2nd ed., Dublin, 1804), pp. 21–3.

13 Ibid., pp. 1–34; Addington to Abbot, 30 November 1801 in HMC, *Fourth report*, appendix, p. 345.

14 Plowden, *A postliminous preface*, pp. 27–9, 33.

15 Ibid.

16 Ibid., pp. 34–55.

17 Francis Plowden, *An historical review of the state of Ireland from the invasion of that country under Henry II to its union with Great Britain on the first of January 1801* (2 vols., London, 1803). The edition used here is that published in five volumes in Philadelphia in 1805–06: v, p. 72.

18 Ibid. v, pp. 81, 83, 85.

19 Francis Plowden, *The history of Ireland from the Union with Great Britain* (3 vols., Dublin, 1811), i, pp. 136–9.

20 Brian MacDermot (ed.), *The Catholic question in Ireland and England 1798–1822: the papers of Denys Scully* (Dublin, 1988), pp. 70, 207, 318.

21 Plowden, *Historical review*, v, pp. 85, 90.

22 Ibid., p. 91.

23 Ibid., p. 117 n.

24 Ibid., pp. 100–01, 104.

25 Ibid., pp. 91–176, 183–207.

26 Ibid., pp. 218–29, 239.

27 Grattan's re-entry to the Irish House of Commons and speech against the Union dominates the account provided of the key debate of 15 January 1800 (Ibid., pp. 239–77 *passim*).

28 Ibid., pp. 239–324 *passim*. The quotes are from pp. 277, 312. In this context, his reference to the earl of Clare's disposition to cast 'obloquy upon his country' is a further example of his critical capacity (ibid, pp. 280–82).

29 Ibid., pp. 280–82.

30 Ibid., pp. 87–9, 138.

31 Ibid., pp. 179–81.

32 Ibid., p. 234.

33 Ibid., pp. 235, 237–8, 239.

34 Ibid., i, p. 3n, v, p. 324.

35 Macartney, 'The writing of history', p. 355, citing *Edinburgh Review*, v, p. 154.

36 Grattan to Plowden, 23 December 1803, Fitzwilliam to Plowden, 25 September 1803 (National Archives, Frazer Papers), cited in Kevin Whelan, *The tree of liberty* (Cork, 1996), p. 148.

37 James Kelly, 'Conservative political thought in late eighteenth-century Ireland' in S.J. Connolly (ed.), *Political ideas in eighteenth-century Ireland* (Dublin, 2000), pp. 215–9.

38 Plowden, *A postliminous preface*, p. 3; Sir Richard Musgrave, *Strictures upon an historical review of the state of Ireland by Francis Plowden* (London, 1804), p. 7.

39 Musgrave, *Strictures*, pp. 173–4.

40 Plowden, *Historical Review*, i, p. 4n; Francis Plowden, *An historical letter . . . to Sir Richard Musgrave* (London and Dublin, 1805); Francis Plowden, *An historical letter to the Rev Charles O'Conor* (London, 1812), pp. i–ii.

41 William Wenman Seward, *Collectanea politica, or the political transactions of Ireland from the accession of George the III to the present time . . .* (3 vols., Dublin, 1804), iii, p. 475 ff.

42 Stephen Barlow, *The history of Ireland from the earliest period to the present time . . .* (2 vols., London, 1814), ii, pp. 293–311, especially pp. 307, 312–3.

43 J.R. Hill, *From patriots to unionists: Dublin civic politics and Irish Protestant patriotism, 1660–1840* (Oxford, 1997), pp. 265–70.

44 Oliver MacDonagh, *Daniel O'Connell: the emancipist 1830–47* (London, 1989), chapter 2.

45 *Repeal of the Union: report of the debate in the House of Commons on Mr O'Connell's motion . . . April 1834* (London, 1834), pp. 11–24 *passim*.

46 Significantly, O'Connell requested P.V. Fitzpatrick in February and early April 1834 to send him copies of Plowden and Barrington. See M.R. O'Connell (ed.), *Correspondence of Daniel O'Connell* (8 vols., Dublin, 1973–80), v, no. 2043, 2059.

47 Plowden, *Historical Review*, v, 101, 177; as footnote 8.

48 Barrington, *Rise and fall of the Irish nation* (Paris, 1833); idem, *Memoirs of Ireland; comprising secret records of the National Convention, the Rebellion and the Union; with delineations of the principal characters connected with these transactions* (2 vols., London, 1835); *The Rise and fall of the Irish nation* (Dublin, 1843); *The rise and fall of the Irish nation: a full account of the bribery and corruption by which the Union was carried; the family histories of the members who voted away the Irish parliament with an extraordinary black list of the titles, places and pensions which they received for their corrupt votes* (Dublin, 1868). More generally, see G.C. Bolton, 'The Anglo-Irish and the historians, 1830–1980' in Oliver MacDonagh, *et al.* (eds), *Irish culture and nationalism 1750–1950* (London, 1983), p. 241.

49 Barrington, *Fall and rise*, p. 479. All quotations are from the 1833 edition.

50 Ibid., pp. 388, 479.

51 Ibid., pp. 380–83.
52 Ibid., pp. 384–94, 409.
53 Ibid., pp. 397, 421–4.
54 Ibid., pp. 429–36.
55 Ibid., pp. 430, 437–50.
56 Ibid., pp. 451–62, 480–94.
57 Ibid., p. 461.
58 Ibid., pp. 458–9; Henry Grattan Junior, *Memoirs of the life and times of the Rt Hon Henry Grattan* (5 vols., London, 1839–46).
59 Grattan, junior, *Life of Grattan*, iv, 430; v, p. 3; Barrington, *Fall and rise*, p. 380.
60 Grattan, junior, *Life of Grattan*, v, pp. 2–5.
61 Ibid., p. 6.
62 Ibid., pp. 8, 10, 12, 188–96.
63 Ibid., pp. 49, 50.
64 Ibid., pp. 14, 17, 18–21, 27–8, 41–46.
65 Ibid., pp. 51, 56, 58, 60.
66 Ibid., p. 68.
67 Ibid., p. 65 ff.
68 R.M. Martin, *Ireland before and after the Union* (3rd ed., London and Dublin, 1848), p. 35.
69 Ibid., pp. 11–15.
70 Ibid., pp. 16–23.
71 Ibid., pp. 24–33.
72 [William O'Neill Daunt], *Catechism of the history of Ireland, ancient and modern* (Dublin, 1844)
73 *New and popular history of Ireland; from the beginning of the Christian era to the present time* (3 vols., London, 1851), ii, pp. 61–2, iii, p. 133.
74 Marquess of Londonderry (ed.), *Memoirs and correspondence of Viscount Castlereagh* (4 vols., London, 1848–49); Sir Charles Ross (ed.), *Correspondence of Charles, 1st Marquess Cornwallis* (3 vols., London, 1859); William Beresford (ed.), *Correspondence of the Rt Hon John Beresford* (2 vols., London, 1854); Duke of Buckingham (ed.), *Memoirs of the courts and cabinets of George III* (4 vols., London, 1852–3).
75 Goldwin Smith, *Irish history and character* (Oxford and London, 1862).
76 Patrick O'Kelly, *History of Ireland since the expulsion of James II* (Dublin, 1855), pp. 308–12.
77 John Mitchel, *The history of Ireland from the Treaty of Limerick to the present time being a continuation of the history of the Abbé MacGeoghegan* (Glasgow, 1869), pp. 39–80.
78 Bill Kirwin, 'The radical youth of a conservative: D'Arcy McGee and Young Ireland', *The Canadian Journal of Irish Studies*, 10 (1984), pp. 51–62.
79 Thomas D'Arcy McGee, *A popular history of Ireland from the earliest period to the emancipation of the Catholics* (2 vols., New York, 1863), ii, pp. 727–34.
80 Ibid., ii, pp. 734–46.
81 R.F. Foster, *The story of Ireland: an inaugural lecture delivered before the University of Oxford on 1 December 1994* (Oxford, 1995), pp. 8–9.
82 A.M. Sullivan, *The story of Ireland* (new ed., Dublin and London, 1894), pp. 522–32.
83 James Anthony Froude, *The English in Ireland* (3 vols., London, 1881), iii, pp. 545–55.

84 W.E. Hume-Williams, *The Irish parliament from the year 1782 to 1800* (London, 1879), pp. 86–7, 96.

85 Alvin Jackson, 'Unionist history, I', *Irish Review*, 7 (1989), p. 61; T. Dunbar Ingram, *A history of the legislative union of Great Britain and Ireland* (London, 1887); Donal Macartney, *W.E.H. Lecky, historian and politician, 1838–1903* (Dublin, 1994), pp. 148–8, 245n79; Dunbar Ingram, *The legislative union*, pp. v–vii. Ingram later achieved a measure of fame when he differed with W.E.H. Lecky, whom he accused of accepting 'every utterance . . . from an anti-English source'.

86 Dunbar Ingram, *The legislative union*, pp. 36–7, 77–81.

87 Ibid., pp. 5–16, 24–35, 38–44, 45–51.

88 Ibid., pp. 56–77.

89 Ibid., pp. 83–108.

90 Ibid., pp. 111–27.

91 Ibid., pp. 139–62.

92 Ibid., p. 163.

93 Ibid., pp. 178–231 *passim*.

94 Macartney, *Lecky*, pp. 140, 243n25; Patrick Maume, *The long gestation: Irish nationalist life 1891–1918* (Dublin, 2000), pp. 235–6. MacNeill's most famous work to date was *The Irish parliament, what it was and what it did* (London, 1885).

95 J.G. Swift MacNeill, *How the Union was carried* (London, 1887), pp. 1–3.

96 Ibid., pp. 7–78, especially pp. 35, 42, 70.

97 Ibid., pp. 93–152 *passim*.

98 Ibid., p. 125.

99 Justin Huntley McCarthy, *Ireland since the Union: sketches of Irish history from 1798 to 1886* (London, 1887), p. 57.

100 Obituary of W.F. Dennehy, *Irish Book Lover*, 9 (1917–18), p. 111; Richard Hayes, *Guide to Irish civilisation: articles in Irish periodicals* (9 vols., Boston, 1970), iv, p. 71; W.F. Dennehy, *The story of the Union, told by its plotters* (Dublin, 1891).

101 Dennehy, *The story of the Union*, pp. 2, 3, 8, 42, 86, 20, 38.

102 Ibid., pp. 15, 69 and *passim*.

103 Ibid., pp. 35, 90.

104 Ibid., p. 118.

105 Ibid., pp. 52, 91, 123.

106 Ibid., p. 132.

107 W.E.H. Lecky, *History of England in the eighteenth century* (8 vols., London, 1878–90). The Irish aspects were extracted and published separately as *History of Ireland in the eighteenth century* (5 vols., London, 1892). All quotations are taken from this edition.

108 Macartney, *Lecky*, chapter 4–6 *passim*.

109 Lecky, *History of Ireland*, v, p. 422.

110 Ibid., pp. 120–422 *passim*.

111 One result of his researches reported by Lecky (*Ibid.*, p. 354n1) was that the nationalist claim that 707,000 people signed petitions against the Union was based on a misprinting of the 107,000 people that put their names to the opposition petition campaign in 1800. The 3000 people who signed pro union petitions in 1800 against which this is counterpoised is misleading since it does not include the many more that signed pro-union addresses in 1799.

112 John Roche Ardill, *The closing of the Irish parliament* (Dublin, 1907).

113 Emily Lawless, *Ireland* (3rd ed., London, 1923), pp. 370–76.

114 George Sigerson, 'Last sessions of parliament – the Union' in R. Barry O'Brien (ed.), *Two centuries of Irish history 1691–1870* (2nd ed., London, 1907), pp. 171, 174, 180, 185, 198; *The last independent parliament of Ireland* (Dublin, 1918), pp. 136–83 *passim*.

115 Robert Dunlop, *Ireland: from the earliest times to the present day* (Oxford, 1922), pp. 160–61.

116 Edmund Curtis, *A history of Ireland* (London, 1936), pp. 345–52.

117 Stephen Gwynn, *The history of Ireland* (Dublin and London, 1923), pp. 414–8.

118 George Creel, *Ireland's fight for freedom* (New York and London, 1919), p. 94; Charles Johnston and Carita Spencer, *Ireland's story: a short history of Ireland* (Boston, New York, Chicago, 1912), pp. 283–92; T.A. McEvoy (ed.), *A course of lectures on Irish history* (Worcester, Mass., 1915), pp. 125–6.

119 Dunlop, *Ireland*, p. 159; Curtis, *Ireland*, p. 345.

120 E.A. D'Alton, *History of Ireland from the earliest times to the present day* (London [ca 1910]), v, pp. 81, 86, 91. D'Alton was equally anxious to absolve the Catholic clergy from the hostile criticism of Grattan. To this end, he argued that the 'great mass' of Catholics was 'indifferent to the question of Union' and that Grattan's censure that the bishops were 'a band of prostituted men engaged in the service of government' was 'unjust' (pp. 94, 96).

121 M.J. McKenna described Castlereagh as 'cold-blooded, stony-hearted, Catholic-hating, self-destroying' ('The Catholic Emancipation period', in McEvoy (ed.), *A course of lectures*, p. 130); P.S. O'Hegarty, *A history of Ireland under the Union 1801 to 1922* (London, 1952), p. 4.

122 Seumas MacManus, *A short story of the Irish race* (2 vols., Dublin, nd), ii, pp. 77–81; John Waldron, *Ireland: an historical review* (Dublin, 1958), p. 32; Mary Hayden and G.A. Moonan, *A short history of the Irish people* (new ed., Dublin, 1960), pp. 402–10; James Carty, *A class book of Irish history* (London, 1955), pp. 117–21; Christopher Preston, *A school history of Ireland* (Dublin, [1955]), pp. 91–3; I.J. Herring, *History of Ireland* (2nd ed., Belfast, 1947).

123 Sir James O'Connor, *History of Ireland 1798–1924* (2 vols., London, 1925), i, pp. 107–37 *passim*.

124 Lord Ashbourne, *Pitt: some chapters in his life and times* (London, 1898), chapter 9.

125 C.L. Falkiner, *Studies in Irish history and biography* (London, 1902), chapter 3.

126 Goldwin Smith, *Irish history and the Irish question* (London, 1905), pp. 148–57.

127 J.R. Fisher, *The end of the Irish parliament* (London, 1911), pp. 273–307.

128 R.B. McDowell, *Irish public opinion 1750–1800* (London, 1944), chapter 13.

129 J.C. Beckett, *The making of modern Ireland, 1603–1923* (London, 1966), chapter 14 *passim*.

130 See, for example, R.B. McDowell's review in *Irish Historical Studies*, 15 (1966–67), pp. 492–3.

131 Bolton, *Union*, *passim*.

132 R. Dudley Edwards, *A new history of Ireland* (Dublin, 1972), pp. 153–4; Connolly (ed.), *The Oxford companion to Irish history*, p. 565.

133 Though he cited Bolton favourably, Patrick O'Farrell maintained that 'the Union was an urgent and naked assertion of British power in what seemed an emergency situation' (*Ireland's English question: Anglo-Irish relations 1534–1970* (London, 1971), p. 67.

134 Edith Mary Johnston, *Ireland in the eighteenth century* (Dublin, 1974), pp. 192–3; R.B. McDowell, 'The Protestant nation, 1775–1800' in T.W. Moody and F.X. Martin (eds.), *The course of Irish history* (Cork, 1984), pp. 246–7.

135 See, for example, T.E. Hachey et als, *The Irish experience: a concise history* (London and New York, 1996), pp. 50–51.

136 Roy Foster, *Modern Ireland 1600–1972* (London, 1989), p. 284.

137 R.B. McDowell, *Ireland in the age of imperialism and revolution 1760–1801* (Oxford, 1979), chapter 19.

138 See A.P.W. Malcomson's review in *English Historical Review*, 96 (1981), pp. 154–6.

139 G.C. Bolton, 'Some British reactions to the Irish Act of Union', *Economic History Review*, 2nd series, 18 (1965), pp. 367–75; Hereward Senior, *Orangeism in Ireland and Britain 1795–1836* (London, 1966), chapter 5.

140 James Kelly, 'The origins of the Act of Union: an examination of unionist opinion in Britain and Ireland, 1650–1800', *Irish Historical Studies*, 25 (1988), pp. 236–63.

141 H.L. Calkin, 'For and against an union', *Eire-Ireland*, 13 (1978), pp. 22–33; John Biggs Davison and George Chowdharay-Best, *The cross of St Patrick: the Catholic unionist tradition in Ireland* (Bourne End, 1984), chapter 6.

CHAPTER TWO

1 The author is indebted to Patrick Geoghegan and James Kelly for their help in developing the ideas within this article. Sandra Hynes deserves thanks for reading an early draft.

2 See J.G.A Pocock, 'The Atlantic archipelago and the war of the three kingdoms' in Brendan Bradshaw and John Morrill (eds.), *The British problem c.1534–1707: state formation in the Atlantic archipelago* (London, 1996), pp. 172–91. See also John Robertson, 'Empire and union: two concepts of the early modern political order', pp. 3–36, in which multiple monarchy is subsumed into the broader category of confederation that includes the United Provinces and was later used to articulate opposition to the Anglo-Scottish Union of 1707.

3 This categorisation is offered in Anthony Pagden's survey of early modern political thought concerning empire, *Lords of all the world: ideologies of empire in Spain, Britain and France* (London, 1995).

4 Sarah Barber, 'Scotland and Ireland under the Commonwealth: a question of loyalty' in Steven G. Ellis and Sarah Barber (eds.), *Conquest and union: fashioning a British state, 1485–1725* (London, 1995), pp. 195–221.

5 This thesis is most vividly applied in the work of Nicholas Canny; particularly, 'Identity formation in Ireland: the emergence of the Anglo-Irish,' in Nicholas Canny and Anthony Pagden (eds), *Colonial identity in the Atlantic world, 1500–1800* (New Jersey, 1987), pp. 159–212 and idem, 'The marginal kingdom: Ireland as a problem in the first

British empire' in Bernard Bailyn and Philip D. Moran (eds), *Strangers within the realm: cultural margins of the first British empire* (London, 1991), pp. 33–66. See also, Anthony Carty, *Was Ireland conquered? International law and the Irish question* (London, 1996).

6 William Molyneux, *The Case of Ireland . . . truly stated*, J.G. Simms (ed.) (Dublin, 1977).

7 Ibid., p. 35. See Jacqueline Hill, 'Ireland without union: Molyneux and his legacy' in John Robertson (ed.), *A union for empire: political thought and the British Union of 1707* (Cambridge, 1995), pp. 271–96.

8 Jonathan Swift, 'The story of the injured lady' in Jonathan Swift, *Prose works*, Temple Scott (ed.) (12 vols., London, 1905), vii, pp. 93–104.

9 Ibid., p. 97.

10 On the legacy of Scottish economic development in the seventeenth century, see Christopher A. Whatley, *Scottish society, 1707–1830: beyond Jacobitism, towards industrialisation* (Manchester, 2000), pp. 16–47.

11 For an interesting reconsideration of the significance of this scheme, see David Armitage, 'The Scottish vision of empire: intellectual origins of the Darien venture' in Robertson (ed.), *A union for empire*, pp. 97–118.

12 G.S. Pryde (ed.), *The treaty of Union of Scotland and Ireland* (London, 1950), p. 84.

13 On the varied motives and responses to the Union of 1707, see John R. Young, 'The parliamentary incorporating Union of 1707: political management, anti-unionism and foreign policy' in T.M. Devine and J.R. Young (eds), *Eighteenth-century Scotland: new perspectives* (East Lothian, 1999), pp. 24–52.

14 Pryde (ed.), *The treaty of Union*, p. 83.

15 Ibid., p. 83.

16 Ibid., p. 84.

17 Ibid., p. 98.

18 Ibid., p. 95.

19 Ibid., p. 105.

20 See John Robertson, 'Andrew Fletcher's vision of union' in Roger Mason (ed.), *Scotland and England 1286–1815* (Edinburgh, 1987), pp. 203–25.

21 Andrew Fletcher, *An account of a conversation*, in *Political works*, John Robertson (ed.) (Cambridge, 1997), pp. 175–215.

22 Ibid., p. 210.

23 Ibid., p. 214.

24 Ibid., p. 213.

25 Robert Burns, 'Such a parcel of rogues in a nation,' in Robert Burns, *The Canongate Burns: the complete poems and songs of Robert Burns*, Andrew Noble and Patrick Hogg Scott (eds.) (Edinburgh, 2001), p. 394.

26 William Ferguson, *Scotland's relations with England: a survey to 1707* (Edinburgh, 1977).

27 See P.W.J. Riley, *The Union of England and Scotland* (Manchester, 1978), pp. 256–73 and appendix B.

28 Young, 'The parliamentary incorporating Union of 1707', pp. 43–6.

29 On the context of these early union debates, see Allan Macinnes, 'Union failed, union accomplished: the Irish union of 1703 and the Scottish union of 1707' in Dáire Keogh and Kevin Whelan (eds), *Acts of Union: the causes, contexts and consequences of the Act of Union* (Dublin, 2001), pp. 67–94.

30 Report by Robert Molesworth on Act of Union, 11 October 1703, *Journal of the Irish House of Commons*, vol. ii, part i, p. 333. This speech was reported back to Nottingham by Southwell on 15 October, writing that: 'On Monday 11, Mr. Molesworth made the report from the Committee of the State of the Nation; the substance of which was that the constitution had been mightily shaken by the late method of proceedings in the Trustee Act, and by exercising martial law upon the English Act. Some other things are there enumerated and it concluded with desiring to be restored to their ancient privileges or else to be united to England. Further consideration was postponed.' Edward Southwell to Nottingham, Dublin, 15 October 1703, *Calendar of State Papers Domestic, 1703–4*, p. 156.

31 Francis Annesley to William King, in HMC, *Second Report* (London, 1871), appendix, p. 244.

32 Henry Grattan, 'Speech dated 22 February 1782' in Henry Grattan, *The speeches of the Rt Hon Henry Grattan*, D.O. Madden (ed.) (Dublin, 1874), p. 68.

33 Ibid., pp. 68–9.

34 Motion proposed by Henry Grattan, 22 February 1782, in *Journal of the Irish House of Commons*, vol. x, part i, pp. 306–7.

35 Ibid., p. 307.

36 Wolfe Tone, 'An address to the people of Ireland' in Thomas Bartlett (ed.), *Life of Theobald Wolfe Tone by his son* (Dublin, 1998), p. 703.

37 For an example of similar thinking by a contemporary with reference to the American crisis, see Edmund Burke, 'Conciliation with America' in Edmund Burke, *Pre-revolutionary writings*, Ian Harris (ed.) (Cambridge, 1993), pp. 206–69.

38 Geoghegan, *Union*, pp. 10–2.

39 T.M. Devine, *The Scottish nation: 1700–2000* (London, 1999), p. 4.

40 James Kelly, 'Public and political opinion in Ireland and the idea of an Anglo-Irish union, 1650–1800' in D. George Boyce and Robert Eccelshall and Vincent Geoghegan (eds), *Political discourse in seventeenth- and eighteenth-century Ireland* (Basingstoke, 2001), pp. 110–41.

41 See Patrick M. Geoghegan, 'An act of power and corruption: the Union debate', *History Ireland*, 8, no. 2 (2000), pp. 22–6 for a recent reassessment.

42 40 George III, c. 38, article one.

43 Ibid., article two.

44 Ibid., article three.

45 Ibid., article six.

46 Ibid., article eight.

47 Ibid., article five.

48 Linda Colley, *Britons: forging a nation 1707–1837* (London, 1994); see also Ian McBride and Tony Claydon (eds), *Protestantism and national identity* (Cambridge, 1998), *passim*.

49 On the Presbyterians see Ian McBride, '"When Ulster Joined Ireland": anti-popery, Presbyterian radicalism and Irish republicanism in the 1790s', *Past and Present*, 157 (1997), pp. 63–93 and idem, *Scripture Politics: Ulster Presbyterianism and Irish radicalism in the late eighteenth century* (Oxford, 1998), pp. 165–206.

50 Sean Connolly, *Religion, law and power* (Oxford, 1992) pp. 263–313. See also Charles Ivor McGrath, 'Securing the Protestant Interest: the origins and purpose of the penal laws of 1695' in *Irish Historical Studies*, 30 (1996–7), pp. 25–46.

51 For a full delineation of this structure, see Patrick M. Geoghegan, 'The Catholics and the Union', *Transactions of the Royal Historical Society*, 6th series, 10 (2000), pp. 243–58.

52 Geoghegan, *Union*, pp. 156–91.

53 By the 1770s, the Hanoverian monarchy was secure in Scotland and the economic benefits of Scotland's attachment to England and empire were becoming evident. See, T.C. Smout, 'Where had the Scottish economy got to by the third quarter of the eighteenth century?' in Istvan Hont and Michael Ignatieff (eds), *Wealth and virtue* (Cambridge, 1983), pp. 45–72.

CHAPTER THREE

1 This essay draws on my '"This famous island set in a Virginian sea": Ireland in the British Empire, 1690–1800' in Peter Marshall (ed.), *The Oxford history of the British Empire* (Oxford, 1998), pp. 253–75; and my 'Britishness, Irishness and the Act of Union' in Dáire Keogh and Kevin Whelan (eds), *Acts of Union: the causes, contexts and consequences of the Act of Union* (Dublin, 2001), pp. 243–58.

2 See especially, Theobald Wolfe Tone, *Spanish War!* in Thomas Bartlett (ed.), *Life of Theobald Wolfe Tone by his son* (Dublin, 1998), pp. 265–77,

3 This is the argument advanced in Thomas Bartlett, *Fall and rise of the Irish nation: the Catholic question, 1690–1830* (Dublin, 1992), pp. 82–6.

4 For the origins of the Union see James Kelly, 'The origins of the Act of Union: an examination of unionist opinion in Britain and Ireland, 1650–1800', *Irish Historical Studies*, 25 (1988), pp. 236–63. During the Cromwellian period there had actually been a union, but only republicans thought well of Cromwell the king-killer, and the memory of his experiment of 1653 had been largely suppressed.

5 Carysfort to Grenville, 15 August 1798, HMC, Dropmore, iv, p. 280.

6 Pitt's speech, 23 January 1799 in *Parliamentary history of England*, xxxiv, pp. 242–9.

7 [Lord Hillsborough?], *A proposal for uniting the kingdoms of Great Britain* (Dublin, 1751, reprinted, 1800).

8 See A.P.W. Malcomson, *John Foster, the politics of the Anglo-Irish ascendancy* (Oxford, 1978), pp. 367–9.

9 See the various essays in John Robertson (ed.), *A union for empire: political thought and the British Union of 1707* (Cambridge, 1995).

10 *A report of the debate in the House of Commons of Ireland . . . 22 and 23 January 1799 on the subject of an Union* (Dublin, 1799), p. 2.

11 Ibid., p. 44.

12 Ibid., p. 14.

13 *The substance of Mr. William Smith's speech on the subject of a legislative union . . . delivered in the House of Commons on Thursday 24 January 1799* (Dublin, 1799), p. 3.

14 *Speech of the Rt Hon William Pitt . . . Thursday 31 January 1799* (London, 1799), pp. 31, 34, 43.

15 *Substance of the speech of the Rt Hon Henry Dundas . . . Thursday, 7 February 1799* (London, 1799), p. 17.

16 *Pro and con: being an impartial abstract of the principal publications on the subject of a legislative union . . .* (Dublin, 1800), pp. 6, 10.

17 *The speech of Lord Minto in the House of Peers, 11 April 1799 . . . respecting an Union* (London, 1799), pp. 50, 109, 113–4, 117.

18 Archibald Redfoord, *Union necessary to security, addressed to the loyal inhabitants of Ireland* (Dublin, 1800), pp. 34, 67, 69.

19 Anon., *The necessity of an incorporate union between Great Britain and Ireland proved from the situation of both kingdoms* (Dublin, 1799), p. 54.

20 An Orangeman, *Union or not?* (Dublin, 1799), p. 37.

21 Anon., *Verbum sapienti: or a few reasons for thinking that it is imprudent to oppose and difficult to prevent the projected Union* (Dublin, 1799), pp. 7, 8, 14.

22 Anon., *A reply to the memoire of Theobald McKenna Esq on some questions touching the projected Union of Great Britain and Ireland* (Dublin, 1799), p. 18.

23 Anon., *A reply to the gentleman who has published a pamphlet entitled "Arguments for and against an union"* (Dublin, 1799), p. 18; for Flood's fate see, *An answer to a pamphlet entitled the speech of the earl of Clare on the subject of a legislative union* (Dublin, 1800), p. 34.

24 Charles Ball, *An union neither necessary nor expedient for Ireland* (Dublin, 1798), p. 7.

25 Anon, *A reply to the gentleman who has published a pamphlet entitled "Arguments for and against an union"* (Dublin, 1799), p. 18.

26 Rev Denis Taaffe, *The probability, causes, and consequences of an union between Great Britain and Ireland discussed* (Dublin, 1798), p. 29.

27 *Speech of the Rt Hon John Foster, Speaker . . . delivered in committee, 17 February 1800* (Dublin, 1800), pp. 38, 42.

28 Mathew Weld, *No union, being an appeal to Irishmen* (Dublin, 1798), p. 18.

29 Anon., *A reply to the memoire of Theobald McKenna Esq. on some questions touching the projected Union of Great Britain and Ireland* (Dublin, 1799), p. 35

30 Charles Ball, *An union neither necessary nor expedient for Ireland* (Dublin, 1798), p. 53.

31 George Knox, member for Phillipstown, King's county, recalled Grattan's peroration but it was not followed up: *A report of the debate in the House of Commons of Ireland . . . 22 and 23 January 1799* (Dublin, 1799), p. 44.

32 A.T. Singleton to Maurice Fitzgerald, 13 April 1830, PRONI, T3075/13/47; S.B. Cook, '"The Irish Raj": social origins and careers of Irishmen in the Indian civil service, 1855–1914', *Journal of Social History*, 20 (1987), pp. 507–29.

CHAPTER FOUR

1 Although the term 'Anglican' was invented by Edmund Burke and is therefore strictly anachronistic for most of the period under review, it is the most accurate and readily understood term available to describe the intellectual and theological outlook of all those churches which grew from the Henry VIII's schism from Rome.

2 William King, *State of the Protestants of Ireland under the late King James's government* (Dublin, 1692). For a biography of King, see Philip O'Regan, *Archbishop William King*

and the constitution in church and state (Dublin, 2000). Sir Richard Musgrave, *Memoirs of the different rebellions in Ireland from the arrival of the English; also a particular detail of that which broke out the XXIII day of May MDCCXCVIII; with the history of the conspiracy which preceded it, and the characters of the principal actors in it. To this is added a concise history of the Reformation in Ireland and considerations on the means of extending its advantages therein.* (Dublin, 1802).

3 William King, *Europe's deliverance from France and slavery: a sermon, preached at St Patrick's Church, Dublin, on 16th of November 1690, before the right honourable the lords justices of Ireland. Being the day of thanksgiving for the preservation of his majesty's person, his good success in our deliverance and his safe and happy return into England* (Dublin & London, 1691) (TCD call no. 47 h. 134).

4 Ibid., p. 2.

5 Ibid.

6 J.C.D. Clark, *English society 1688–1832* (Cambridge, 1985).

7 Ibid., p. 124.

8 For a discussion of the development of the doctrine of the ancient constitution see J.G.A. Pocock, *The ancient constitution and the feudal law* (London, 1974).

9 William King, *State of the Protestants of Ireland*, pp. 1–2.

10 Richard Tuck, *Natural rights theories: their origin and development* (Cambridge, 1979), pp. 58–81.

11 Patrick Kelly, 'Nationalism and the contemporary historians of the Jacobite war in Ireland' in Michael O'Dea and Kevin Whelan (eds.), *Nations and nationalism, France, Britain, and Ireland in the eighteenth-century context*, Studies in Voltaire and the Eighteenth Century, 335 (Oxford, 1992), p. 91.

12 DNB.

13 The *State of the Protestants of Ireland* was printed eleven times by 1770; London, 1691; London, 1692 (2nd, 3rd, & 4th edn); Dublin, 1713; London, 1713 (abstract); Dublin, 1724; Dublin, 1730; London, 1745; London, 1746; and Cork, 1768. See Patrick Kelly, 'William Molyneux and the spirit of liberty in eighteenth-century Ireland', *Eighteenth-century Ireland*, 3 (1988), p. 136n12.

14 Steven Pincus, 'Popery, trade, and universal monarchy', *English Historical Review*, 107 (1992) pp. 1–28.

15 James Kelly, 'Public and political opinion in Ireland and the idea of an Anglo-Irish Union, 1650–1800' in D. George Boyce, Robert Eccleshall and Vincent Geoghegan (eds), *Political discourse in seventeenth- and eighteenth-century Ireland* (Basingstoke, 2001) pp. 115–21.

16 Jonathan Swift, 'The story of the injured lady' in Jonathan Swift, *Prose works*, Temple Scott (ed.), (12 vols., London, 1905), vii, pp. 93–104.

17 Sir John Temple, *The Irish rebellion* (London, 1646).

18 J.C. Beckett, *The making of modern Ireland, 1603–1923* (London, 1981) pp. 75–87.

19 T.C. Barnard, 'The uses of 23 October 1641 and Irish Protestant celebrations', *English Historical Review*, 106 (1991), pp. 889–920.

20 Temple, *The Irish rebellion*, preface.

21 Ibid.

22 Ibid., p. 2.

23 Ibid., pp. 2–3.

24 Ibid., pp. 4–6.

25 Ibid., p. 7.

26 Ibid., pp. 76–8.

27 Musgrave, *Memoirs* pp. 199–210. For a general context see Jim Smyth, 'Anti-Catholicism, conservatism, and conspiracy: Sir Richard Musgrave's *Memoirs of the different rebellions in Ireland*', *Eighteenth-century Life*, 22 (1998), pp. 64–65.

28 Musgrave, *Memoirs*, p. 203.

29 Ibid.

30 Ibid., p. 206.

31 Ibid.

32 Ibid.

33 Ibid., p. 4.

34 Ibid., p. 5. Troy and Hussey, both contemporary Catholic bishops, were accused of promoting a religion sympathetic to rebels and republicans.

35 Musgrave, *Memoirs*, p. 5.

36 Ibid.

37 Ibid., p. 6.

38 Ibid., pp. 10–11.

39 Ibid.

40 Ibid., pp. 11–13.

41 Ibid., p. 14.

42 Ibid., pp. 18–20.

43 David Hayton, 'Did Protestantism fail in the eighteenth-century Ireland? Charity Schools and the enterprise of religious and social reformation, c. 1690–1730' in Alan Ford, James McGuire and Kenneth Milne (eds), *As by law established: The Church of Ireland since the Reformation* (Dublin, 1995), pp. 120–35.

44 Sean Connolly, *Religion, law, and power* (Oxford, 1992) *passim*

45 Musgrave, *Memoirs*, p. 206.

46 Geoghegan, *Union, passim.*

CHAPTER FIVE

1 Clare to Auckland, 3 July 1798, quoted in Bolton, *Union*, p. 60.

2 For a full account see I.R. McBride, *Scripture politics: Ulster Presbyterians and Irish radicalism in the late eighteenth century* (Oxford, 1998).

3 Geoghegan, *Union*, p. 37

4 T. Dunbar Ingram, *A history of the legislative union of Great Britain and Ireland* (London, 1887), p. 18.

5 Ibid., p. 118.

6 J.R. Fisher, *The end of the Irish parliament* (London, 1911), p. 224. See also Thomas MacKnight, *Ulster as it is* (2 vols., London, 1896), i, 23.

7 Ibid., pp. 274–5. Neilson is said to have made known his support for the Union in a letter to his wife written whilst in prison in Fort George; the story was then passed on to Richard Madden by Neilson's daughters forty years later: see R.R. Madden, *The United Irishmen, their lives and times* (3 series, 7 vols., London, 1842–46), 2nd ser., i, p. 247. Madden suggested that the letter was written to please the prison authorities. For Rowan see ibid., iii, p. 41.

8 Bolton, *Union*, pp. 129–30, 135–42

9 For attendance at Dungannon see *Belfast News-Letter*, 5–8 March 1793.

10 Hereward Senior, *Orangeism in Ireland and Britain 1795–1836* (London, 1966), pp. 133–4.

11 Bolton, *Union*, pp. 129–30.

12 James G. Patterson, 'Continued Presbyterian resistance in the aftermath of the Rebellion of 1798 in Antrim and Down', *Eighteenth-Century Life*, 22,3 (1998), pp. 45–61.

13 Ibid., p. 48.

14 James Hamilton junior to the marquess of Abercorn, 22 January 1800, PRONI, Abercorn Papers, D/623/A/92/4.

15 Londonderry to Castlereagh, 10 December 1798, *Castlereagh corr.*, ii, pp. 39–40.

16 Cornwallis to Gosford, 31 October 1799, PRONI, Gosford papers, D/1606/225A.

17 Henry Alexander to Castlereagh, 7 October 1799, Edward Littlehales to Castlereagh, 9 October 1799, PRONI, Castlereagh Papers, D/3030/1005, 1006.

18 Robert Bradshaw to Castlereagh, 13 January 1800, *Castlereagh corr.*, iii, pp. 224–5.

19 Quoted in Ingram, *History of the legislative union*, p. 118.

20 Hamilton to Abercorn, 15 October 1799, PRONI, Abercorn Papers, D/623/A/9/1120.

21 Bruce to Castlereagh, 9 April 1800, *Castlereagh corr.*, iii, pp. 266–9; Robert Black to Castlereagh, 26 April 1800, ibid., pp. 287–91.

22 *Records of the General Synod of Ulster from 1691 to 1820* (3 vols., Belfast, 1890–99), iii, pp. 208–212.

23 Ibid., p. 221.

24 Richard Musgrave, *Memoirs of the different rebellions in Ireland* (Dublin, 1801), pp. 80, 111, 124, 178, 181, 557.

25 William Parnell, *An enquiry into the causes of popular discontents in Ireland by an Irish country gentleman* (Dublin, 1805), p. 29.

26 For a full list of ministers and probationers suspected of involvement in the Rebellion see *Scripture politics*, pp. 232–6, but note that Dickson, listed on p. 234 with the Presbytery of Killileagh, had moved to Bangor. Gowdie (or Goudy) was most likely acting as a schoolmaster, like many of the young licentiates who had not yet been installed in a congregation. He does not appear in the records of the Synod, though his execution is recorded in the *Belfast News-Letter*, 26 June 1798.

27 *Records of the General Synod of Ulster*, iii, p. 222.

28 Ibid., pp. 221, 223.

29 Black to Bruce, 14 October 1804, 27 November 1804, 15 February 1805, PRONI, T/3041/1/E47, E49/E51; quotation from E49. On Shaw see also *Analytical review of a pamphlet lately published by a person styling himself the Rev Robert Black, D.D. in a series of letters: by an elder* (Belfast, 1813), pp. 40–1.

30 Thomas Bartlett (ed.), *Life of Theobald Wolfe Tone by his son* (Dublin, 1998), p. 145; Thomas Ledlie Birch, *Physicians languishing under disease* (Belfast, 1796), p. 41.

31 W.S. Dickson, *A narrative of the confinement and exile of William Steel Dickson* (Dublin, 1812), p. 28.

32 Robert Black, *Substance of two speeches, delivered in the General Synod of Ulster at its annual meeting in 1812* (Dublin, 1812), p. 61; but see also William Steel Dickson, *Retractions; or, a review of, and reply to, a pamphlet, entitled, Substance of two speeches* (Belfast, 1813), pp. 30–2.

33 J.W. Kernohan, *The parishes of Kilrea and Tamlaght O'Crilly: a sketch of their history, with an account of Boveedy congregation* (Coleraine, 1912), pp. 39–40.

34 Classon Porter, *Congregational memoirs of the Old Presbyterian Congregation of Larne and Kitwaughter* (Larne, 1929), pp. 75–6.

35 Dickson, *Narrative*, pp. 279–80.

36 *Records of the General Synod of Ulster*, iii, p. 302.

37 Dickson, *Narrative*, p. 2.

38 *Records of the General Synod of Ulster*, iii, p. 399.

39 See Classon Porter, *Irish Presbyterian biographical sketches* (Belfast, 1883), pp. 5–9.

40 *The Down squib book* (Belfast, 1831), p. 61.

41 Dickson, *Narrative*, p. 226.

42 Ibid., p. 182.

43 William Campbell, 'History of the Presbyterians in Ireland' unpublished Ms in the Presbyterian Historical Society of Ireland, Belfast, pp. 100–1.

44 McBride, *Scripture politics*, pp. 172–3.

45 *Belfast News-Letter*, 22–25 January 1793.

46 See Ian McBride, 'The harp without the crown: republicanism and nationalism in the 1790s' in Sean Connolly (ed.), *Political ideas in eighteenth-century Ireland* (Dublin, 2000), pp. 159–84.

47 *Observations upon the oath of allegiance, as prescribed by the enrolling act. Addressed to the inhabitants of the north of Ireland* (Dublin, 1797), p. 5. See also [William Sampson], *Advice to the rich* (Belfast, 1796), p. 19; James Hamilton junior to Abercorn, PRONI, Abercorn Papers, D623/A/89/21; unsigned petition by the inhabitants of Ballydally and Ballindrum [1796–8], PRONI, Abercorn Papers, D/1449/12/292; Thomas Pelham to Chichester Skeffington, 4 January 1797, PRONI, Foster-Massarene Papers, D/562/301; Haliday to Charlemont, 28 January, 1797, HMC, *Charlemont MS*, ii, pp. 293–4.

48 *Belfast News-Letter*, 13 March 1797. Italics added.

49 See the association entered into by the inhabitants of the parish of Newtownards, Co. Down, November 1796, PRONI, D/1494/2124; Hamilton to Abercorn, 4 April 1797, PRONI, Abercorn Papers, D/623/A/89/21.

50 Martha McTier to William Drennan, 13 January [1797], in Jean Agnew (ed.), *The Drennan – McTier letters* (3 vols., Dublin, 1998–9), ii, 285.

51 Report of a United Irish meeting at Armagh, 29 May 1798, PRO, HO 100/77 l.44.

52 Madden, *United Irishmen*, 3rd ser., i, p. 260.

53 [Samuel McSkimmin] 'Secret history of the Irish insurrection of 1803', *Fraser's Magazine*, 14/83 (1836), p. 554.

54 *McComb's guide to Belfast, the Giant's Causeway, and the adjoining districts of the counties of Antrim and Down, with an account of the battle of Ballynahinch* (Belfast, 1861), pp. 130–1.

55 James Hope, quoted in Madden, *United Irishmen*, 3rd ser., i, p. 222.

56 For examples see W.S. Smith, *Memories of '98* (Belfast, 1895).

57 Porter, *Irish Presbyterian biographical sketches*, p. 19.

58 R.M. Young, *Ulster in '98: episodes and anecdotes* (Belfast, 1893), p. 17.

59 R.L. Marshall, 'Maghera in '98', in S.S. McFarland, *Presbyterianism in Maghera: a social and congregational history* (Maghera, 1985), pp. 174–8.

60 R.F.G. Holmes, *Henry Cooke* (Belfast, 1981), p. 4.

61 Michael Durey, *Transatlantic radicals and the early American republic* (Kansas, 1997), pp. 44–5.

62 Castlereagh to Portland, 3 June 1799, PRO, HO 100/87 ll. 5–7.

63 Quoted in Allan Blackstock, *An ascendancy army: the Irish yeomanry, 1796–1834* (Dublin, 1998), p. 211.

64 White to Joy, 23 October 1801, Linenhall Library, Belfast, Joy Mss., 13.

65 Haliday to Castlereagh, 26 August 1798, NAI, Rebellion Papers, 620/4/29/29.

66 Downshire to Portland, 13 July 1798, KAO, Camden Papers, U840/C196/1/2 (copy in PRONI, T2627).

67 McClelland to Redesdale, 9 August 1803, PRONI, Redesdale Papers, T3030/9/12

68 George Vaughan Hart to Sir Edward Littlehales, 29 August 1803, NAI, SOC 1025/34.

69 Cupples to Rev Mr Archer, 14 September 1803, NAI, Rebellion Papers, 620/11/158.

70 [Henry Joy, ed.], *Historical collections relative to the town of Belfast* (Belfast, 1817), p. xvn.

71 A.F. Blackstock, 'The origin and development of the Irish yeomanry, 1796–c. 1807' (PhD thesis, Q.U.B., 1993), pp. 382, 399, 435.

72 Allan F. Blackstock, '"A dangerous species of ally": Orangeism and the Irish yeomanry', *Irish Historical Studies*, 30 (1997), pp. 393–405.

73 See the testimony of the Quaker James Christie before the Select Committee on Orangeism, 1835, quoted in D.W. Miller (ed.), *Peep O'Day Boys and Defenders: selected documents on the County Armagh disturbances 1784–96* (Belfast, 1990), p. 116.

74 Rev Edward Hudson to Charlemont, 6 October 1798, HMC *Charlemont Mss.*, ii, p. 336.

75 'Declaration and resolutions of the Society of United Irishmen of Belfast', reprinted in Bartlett (ed.), *Life of Tone*, p. 298.

76 See e.g. *Belfast News-Letter*, 5–8 January 1790, 26 February–2 March 1790, 7–11 January 1791, 25–9 March 1791, 17–20 May 1791.

77 'Presbyter' [Henry Henry], *An illustrative of the present critical state of the Synod of Ulster* (n. pl., 1802), pp. 25–7.

78 Linda Colley, *Britons: forging the nation 1707–1837* (London, 1992), p. 312.

79 Quoted in R.B. McDowell, *Irish public opinion, 1750–1800* (London, 1944), p. 255.

80 William Drennan, *A protest from one of the people of Ireland, against an union with Great Britain* (Dublin, 1800), pp. 5–6.

81 McBride, 'Harp without the crown', esp. pp. 169–72.

82 William Percy, *Irish salvation promulged* [sic]; *or, The effects of an union with Great Britain, candidly investigated* (Belfast, 1800), p. 10. The author, presumably, was an Episcopalian, but the intended audience appears to have been the old Presbyterian radicals.

CHAPTER SIX

1 Thomas Goold, *An address to the people of Ireland on the subject of the projected Union* (Dublin, 1799), p. 74.

2 [Edward Cooke], *Arguments for and against an union between Great Britain and Ireland, considered* (Dublin, 1798), p. 57. For the attribution to Cooke see DNB, iv, pp. 1004–5; W.J. McCormack, *The pamphlet debate on the Union between Great Britain and Ireland, 1797–1800* (Dublin, 1996), p. 9.

3 J.C. Beresford to Lord Castlereagh, 19 December 1798, in *Castlereagh corr.*, ii, p. 51.

4 Denis Taaffe, *The probability, causes, and consequences of an union between Great Britain and Ireland, discussed: with strictures on an anonymous pamphlet, in favour of the measure, supposed to be written by a gentleman high in office* (Dublin, 1798). On Taaffe's involvement in the United Irish movement, see DNB, xix, p. 284.

5 J.C. Beresford to Lord Castlereagh, 19 December 1798, in *Castlereagh corr.*, ii, p. 51.

6 Tom Bartlett (ed.), *Life of Theobald Wolfe Tone by his son* (Dublin, 1998), p. 39.

7 Quoted in *Castlereagh corr.*, i, p. 155.

8 See W.J. McCormack, *The pamphlet debate on the Union between Great Britain and Ireland, 1797–1800* (Dublin, 1996); see also R.B. McDowell, *Irish public opinion, 1750–1800* (London, 1944), pp. 243–60.

9 William Drennan to William Bruce, ? August 1785 (PRONI, D/553/45).

10 Marianne Elliott, *Wolfe Tone: prophet of Irish independence* (London, 1989), p. 64. See also the well known letter on separation of Tone to Thomas Russell of 9 July 1791 in T.W. Moody, R.B. McDowell, and C.J. Woods (eds), *The writings of Theobald Wolfe Tone, 1763–98* (Oxford, 1998), i, pp. 104–6.

11 *Idem sentire, dicere, agere*, NAI, Rebellion Papers, 620/19/24, folio 3. For the attribution to Drennan see William Drennan to Samuel McTier, November 1791 in D.A. Chart (ed.), *The Drennan letters* (Belfast, 1931), pp. 64–5; Alexander Knox, *Essays on the political circumstances of Ireland, written during the administration of Earl Camden with an appendix containing thoughts on the will of the people* (Dublin, 1799), p. 138; A.T.Q. Stewart, "'A stable unseen power': Dr William Drennan and the origins of the United Irishmen' in John Bossy and P.J. Jupp (eds), *Essays presented to Michael Roberts* (Belfast, 1976), pp. 80–92.

12 *The speech of Edward Sweetman captain of a late independent company, at a meeting of the freeholders of the country of Wexford convened by the sheriff on September 22* (Dublin, 1792), p. 8. For the affiliation of Sweetman see R.B. McDowell, 'The personnel of the Dublin Society of United Irishmen', *Irish Historical Studies*, 2 (1940) p. 49. The argument used by Sweetman had been advanced already in Edmund Burke's 'Letter to Sir Hercules Langrishe' published in February 1792 see R.B. McDowell (ed.), *The writings and speeches of Edmund Burke* (Oxford, 1991), ix, pp. 631–2.

13 *United Irishmen of Dublin to the friends of the people, at London, 26 October 1792*, in Society of United Irishmen of Dublin, *'Let the nation stand'* (Dublin, 1794), p. 29. The text was written by Drennan, see William Drennan to Samuel McTier, 30 October 1792, in *The Drennan letters*, p. 93.

14 See James Kelly, 'The origins of the Act of Union: an examination of unionist opinion, 1650–1800', *Irish Historical Studies*, 25 (1987) pp. 236–3.

15 William Drennan to Samuel McTier, 26 March 1793, in *The Drennan letters*, p. 145.

16 William Drennan to Samuel McTier, 16 March 1795, in *The Drennan letters*, p. 226.

17 *Speech of Arthur O'Connor, Esq in the House of Commons of Ireland, Monday, May 4, 1795, on the Catholic bill* (Dublin, 1795), p. 31.

18 [William Sampson], *An advice to the rich by an independent country gentleman, pointing out the road to security and peace* (Dublin, 1796), p. 15. Sampson himself claimed to be the author of this work in his *Memoirs of William Sampson* (New York, 1807), p. 344.

19 Edmund Burke to S. Span, 23 April 1778, in T.W. Copeland (ed.), *The correspondence of Edmund Burke* (10 vols., Cambridge, 1958–1978), iii, p. 432; Edmund Burke to Lord Edward Fitzwilliam, ca. 26 September 1794, in *The correspondence of Edmund Burke*, viii, p. 20; see also J. Conniff, 'Edmund Burke's reflections on the coming revolution in Ireland', *Journal of the History of Ideas*, 47 (1986), pp. 37–59.

20 William Drennan to Mrs McTier, 9 September 1796, in *The Drennan letters*, p. 239.

21 *An advice to the rich*, p. 15; *Memoirs of William Sampson*, p. 344.

22 William Drennan to Martha McTier, 15 October 1798, in *The Drennan letters*, p. 279.

23 *An advice to the rich*, p. 20.

24 [W.J. MacNeven], *An argument for independence, in opposition to an union addressed to all his countrymen by an Irish Catholic* (Dublin, 1799), p. 14.

25 Samuel Neilson to Miss Bryson, 21 July 1799, Fort George, Scotland, quoted in R.R. Madden, *The United Irishmen*, 4th series, 2nd edition (London, 1860), pp. 105–6.

26 *The second part of Taaffe's reflections on the Union* (Dublin, 1799), p. 15.

27 *Pitt's union* (Dublin, 1799), p. 10. For the attribution to MacNeven, see W.J. McCormack, *The pamphlet debate*, p. 68.

28 *Speech of the Rt Hon William Pitt, in the House of Commons, Thursday 31 January 1799* (London, 1799), pp. 64–6.

29 Henry Maxwell, *Essay towards an union of Ireland with England* (London, 1703), pp. 17–18.

30 As has been shown by Jim Smyth, Thomas Bartlett and David Hayton among others, the pro-union option was part of the difficult process of adopting an Irish identity by those Anglo-Irish that 'like amphibious animals' were considered English in Ireland and Irish in England: Jim Smyth, '"Like amphibious animals": Irish Protestants, ancient Britons, 1691–1707', *Historical Journal*, 36 (1994) pp. 785–97; idem, 'Anglo-Irish unionist discourse, c. 1656-1707: from Harrington to Fletcher', *Bullán*, 2 (1995), pp. 17–34; David Hayton, 'Anglo-Irish attitudes: changing perceptions of national identity among the Protestant ascendancy in Ireland, c.1690–1750', *Studies in Eighteenth Century Culture*, 15 (1988), pp. 5–31; Thomas Bartlett, '"A People made rather for copies than originals": the Anglo-Irish, 1760–1800', *The International History Review*, 12 (1990), pp. 11–25.

31 *Union or not? By an Orangeman* in *Tracts on the subject of an union between Great Britain and Ireland* (11 vols., Dublin, 1799), ii, p. 29.

32 *Speech of the Rt Hon William Pitt, in the House of Commons, Thursday 31 January*, p. 12. On the link of providence and deliverance in Irish Protestant mentality, see Ian McBride, *The siege of Derry in Ulster Protestant mythology* (Dublin, 1997), pp. 12–13, 32.

33   *Speech of the Rt Hon William Pitt, in the House of Commons, Thursday 31 January,* pp. 33–64; William Pitt to Lord Westmorland, 18 November 1792, quoted in Gerard O'Brien, *Anglo-Irish politics in the age of Grattan and Pitt* (Dublin, 1987), p. 163.

34   *Arguments for and against an union between Great Britain and Ireland, considered,* pp. 27, 30.

35   Richard Musgrave to T. Percy, 15 January 1799 (NLI, Ms 4157). On this point see also William Petty, 'Of reconciling the English and Irish and reforming both nations' (1686); E. Fitzmaurice, *The life of William Petty* (London, 1895), p. 144.

36   *Speech of the Rt Hon William Pitt, in the House of Commons, Thursday 31 January,* p. 6.

37   Ibid., pp. 3, 4, 11.

38   *Arguments for and against an union between Great Britain and Ireland, considered,* p. 7.

39   Thomas Goold, *Vindication of the Rt Hon Edmund Burke's Reflections on the coming revolution in France. In answer to all his opponents* (Dublin, 1791), p. 37.

40   *Speech of the Rt Hon William Pitt, in the House of Commons, Thursday 31 January 1799,* pp. 64–6.

41   Ibid., p. 33.

42   *Arguments for and against an union between Great Britain and Ireland, considered,* p. 11.

43   Ibid., p. 12.

44   Ibid., p. 27.

45   Ibid., p. 59.

46   William Drennan, *A letter to the Rt Hon William Pitt* (Dublin, 1799), p. 34. See also William Drennan to Mrs McTier, 10 October 1796, in *The Drennan letters,* p. 243.

47   *Idem sentire, dicere, agere,* NAI, Rebellion Papers, 620/19/24, folio 3.

48   Theobald Wolfe Tone, *Spanish war! An enquiry how far Ireland is bound, of right, to embark in the impending contest on the side of Great Britain. Addressed to the members of both houses of parliament* (Dublin, 1790).

49   W.J. MacNeven (ed.), 'Introduction' in *Pieces of Irish history, illustrative of the conditions of the Catholics of Ireland: of the origins and progress of the political system of the United Irishmen; and their transaction with the Anglo-Irish government* (New York, 1807), p. xix.

50   William Drennan, *A letter to the Rt Hon William Pitt,* p. 46. Another United Irishmen, Thomas Ledlie Birch wrote wishing the institution of 'a congress, consisting of delegates from the different states of Europe, to act as arbitrators in settling the disputes between the several nations, and so put an end to the havok and desolation of war', see the letter from Saintfield, in *Northern Star,* 25 June 1795.

51   Arthur O'Connor, *Defence of the united people of Ireland,* London (Dublin, 1799), p. 12. The book contains the conclusions of Arthur O'Connor's *The state of Ireland, to which are added his addresses to the electors of County Antrim* (London, 1798).

52   Arthur O'Connor, *Defence of the united people of Ireland,* pp. 11–12.

53   Rev Dr Troy to Lord Castlereagh, 24 December 1798, in *Castlereagh corr.,* ii, p. 61. Further examples of this approach are in Catholic writings and in Orange propaganda: see Theobald M'Kenna, *A memoire on some questions respecting the projected Union of Great Britain and Ireland* (Dublin, 1799); *Union or not? By an Orangeman* in *Tracts on the subject of an union between Great Britain and Ireland,* ii, pp. 20–1; *A letter to Theobald M'Kenna, esq the Catholic advocate in reply to the calumnies against the Orange institution,* by an Orangeman, (Dublin, 1799).

54 [W.J. MacNeven], *An argument for independence, in opposition to an union addressed to all his countrymen by an Irish Catholic*, p. 32.

55 'The Society of the United Irishmen of Dublin to the Irish nation', 25 January 1793, in *Let the nation stand*, p. 59.

56 *United Irishmen of Dublin to the Friends of the People, at London*, 26 October 1792, p. 28.

57 Quoted in J.C. Beckett, *The making of modern Ireland* (London, 1966), p. 236.

58 Denis Taaffe, *The probability, causes, and consequences of an union*, pp. 20–1.

59 Ibid., p. 38.

60 Ibid., p. 39.

61 William Drennan, *A letter to the Rt Hon William Pitt*, p. 40.

62 See for instance: *The second part of Taaffe's reflections on the Union*, pp. 24–5.

63 [William Sampson], *An advice to the rich*, p. 37.

64 [W.J. MacNeven], *An argument for independence, in opposition to an union addressed to all his countrymen by an Irish Catholic*, p. 47.

65 'Address from the Society of United Irishmen in Dublin, to the delegates for promoting a reform in Scotland', 23 November 1792, in *Let the nation stand*, p. 38.

66 On United Irishmen on Orangeism see the *Northern Star*, 15 July 1796; B. Clifford (ed.), *The causes of the Rebellion in Ireland and other writings by Rev Thomas Ledlie United Irishmen* (Belfast, 1991), p. 99; Tone, *Life*, pp. 596–7; [William Sampson], *A view of the present state of Ireland with an account of the origin and progress of the disturbances in that country; and a narrative of facts addressed to the people of England, by an observer* (London, 1797), p. 6; O'Connor, *The state of Ireland*, p. 29; O'Connor, *Address to the electors of County Antrim*, 22 October 1796, in *The state of Ireland*, page not numbered corresponding to p. 111; Denis Taaffe, *Observations, occasioned by the alarm of an invasion, propagated by authority. Addressed to the people of Ireland by an Irish Volunteer* (Dublin, 1796), p. 14; Denis Taaffe, *The probability, causes, and consequences of an union between Great Britain and Ireland, discussed*, pp. 26–7 and p. 29; Thomas Russell, *A letter to the people of Ireland on the present situation of the country* (Belfast, 1796), p. 9. See also the following handbills: VINCENT, *TO THE PEOPLE OF IRELAND*, Dublin, 7 April 1798 (NAI, Rebellion Papers, 620/36/145); *Orangemen triumphant!!!* (Ibid., 620/54/60); *Invocation to discord*, 26 April 1797 (Ibid., 620/29/320); *The Orangeman's conversion, founded on a true story* (Ibid., 620/54/69); *Countrymen, Orange and Green awake-arouse-unite* (NAI, Rebellion Papers, 620/51/3).

67 [William Ogilvie], *Protestant ascendancy and Catholic emancipation reconciled* (Dublin, 1800) in *Tracts on the subject of an union between Great Britain and Ireland*, ix, pp. 75–85.

68 *TO THE PEOPLE* (NAI, Rebellion Papers, 620/7/74/12).

69 W. Todd Jones, *A letter to the societies of the United Irishmen of the town of Belfast upon the subject of certain apprehensions which have arisen from proposed restoration of the Catholic rights* (Dublin, 1792), p. 37.

70 William Drennan, *A letter to his excellency Earl Fitzwilliam, lord lieutenant, &c of Ireland* (Dublin, 1795), pp. 11–12.

71 Thomas Russell, *A letter to the people of Ireland on the present situation of the country*, pp. 2–3.

72 Adam Smith, *An inquiry into the nature and causes of the wealth of nations* (3 vols., Oxford, 1993), iii, p. 461. This opinion was also restated in the twentieth century by a rather less impartial observer, William Monypenny, who claimed during the Home Rule debate that 'the only hope for unity for the Irish was the Union with Great Britain': W.F. Monypenny, *The two Irish nations: an essay on home rule* (London, 1913), pp. 67–8.

73 *Idem sentire, dicere, agere*, NAI, Rebellion Papers, 620/19/24, folio 1.

74 VINCENT, *TO THE PEOPLE OF IRELAND*, Dublin 7 April 1798, NAI, Rebellion Papers, 620/36/145.

75 See for the expression: Henry Dundas to Adam Smith, 30 October 1779, in Ernest Campbell Mossner and Ian Simpson Ross (eds), *The correspondence of Adam Smith* (Oxford, 1987), p. 240.

76 William Drennan to Mrs McTier, 11 January 1800, in *The Drennan letters*, p. 295.

77 William Drennan, *A protest from one of the people of Ireland against an union with Great Britain* (Dublin, 1800), p. 7. For similar arguments see [William Sampson], *A view of the present state of Ireland* (Dublin, 1797), p. 6; O'Connor, *The state of Ireland* (Dublin, 1798), p. 29; T.L. Birch, *The causes of the Rebellion in Ireland and other writings* (London, 1812), p. 29.

78 I would like to thank Dr James Quinn for his steady support and helpful criticism.

CHAPTER SEVEN

1 Cornwallis to Portland, 25 January 1799, *Cornwallis corr.*, iii, p. 51.

2 Beresford to Auckland , 6 February 1799, *Beresford corr.*, ii, p. 209.

3 Cornwallis to Portland, 28 June, 8, 24 July 1798, *Cornwallis corr.*, ii, pp. 357, 359–60, 372–4; *Cornwallis corr.*, iii, p. 62.

4 Earl of Carysfort to Grenville, 15 August 1798, Buckingham to Grenville, 15 September 1798, HMC *Dropmore Mss,* iv, pp. 280, 315.

5 Cornwallis to Portland, 28 June, 8 July 1798, *Cornwallis corr.*, ii, pp. 357, 360.

6 Cornwallis to Pitt, 20 July 1798, *Cornwallis corr.*, ii, p. 367.

7 Cornwallis to Portland, 16 September 1798, *Cornwallis corr.*, ii, pp. 406–7.

8 Cornwallis to Pitt, 25 September 1798, *Cornwallis corr.*, ii, p. 416; Cornwallis to Ross, 8 November 1798 *Cornwallis corr.*, ii, p. 431.

9 Bolton, *Union*, p. 71.

10 Cornwallis to Ross, 26 December 1798, *Cornwallis corr.*, iii, p. 24; Castlereagh to Portland, 5 January 1799, *Cornwallis corr.*, iii, pp. 30–3.

11 Cooke to Auckland, 26 January 1799, BL, Auckland Papers, Add Ms 34455.

12 Duigenan to Castlereagh, 20 December 1798, *Castlereagh corr.*, ii, p. 53; *Auckland papers*, iv, pp. 67, 70, 71, 80, 82–5 and Auckland to John Beresford, Beresford to Auckland, 31 January, 6 February 1799, *Beresford corr.*, ii, pp. 206, 208–11; for further criticisms of Cornwallis by Cooke see Cooke to Auckland, 30 October 1798, PRONI Sneyd Papers, T3229/2/40, and 2 November 1798, BL Add Ms 34455, ff 26–8.

13 Despite the success of the government's campaign of pacification there were still those who thought that union was being brought forward too quickly, See, for example, Lord de Clifford to Townshend, 23 July 1799, *Castlereagh corr.*, ii, pp. 356–8.

14 Castlereagh to Elliot, 9 November 1798, cited in Bolton, *Union*, pp. 71–2.

15 Cornwallis to Pitt, 25 October 1798, Cornwallis to Portland, 26 July 1798, *Cornwallis corr.*, ii, pp. 372–4, 425; Cooke to Wickham, 28 July 1798, *Cornwallis corr.*, ii, p. 378; Cornwallis to Ross; 26 July 1798, *Cornwallis corr.*, ii, p. 374; Cooke to General Nugent, 12 August 1798, PRONI, Nugent Papers, D272/40.

16 Cornwallis to Portland, 28 February 1799, *Cornwallis corr.*, iii, p. 70; Marianne Elliott, *Wolfe Tone: prophet of Irish independence* (London, 1989), p. 397.

17 Duke of Leinster to Castlereagh, 16 January 1799, *Castlereagh corr.*, ii, p. 115.

18 Patrick Duigenan to Castlereagh, 20 December 1798, *Castlereagh corr.*, ii, p. 53; Buckingham to Grenville, 26 September 1798, HMC, *Dropmore Mss*, iv, p. 324.

19 Buckingham to Grenville, 2 October 1798, HMC, *Dropmore Mss*, iv, p. 333.

20 Earl of Carysfort to Grenville, 15 August 1798, HMC, *Dropmore Mss*, iv, p. 280.

21 Buckingham to Grenville, 16 October 1798, HMC, *Dropmore Mss*, iv, p. 321.

22 Cornwallis to Pitt, 1 November 1798, *Cornwallis corr.*, ii, p. 429; Cornwallis to Ross, 23 November 1798, *Cornwallis corr.*, ii, p. 445.

23 Cornwallis to Ross, 21 January, 28 January 1799, *Cornwallis corr.*, iii, pp. 39–40, 56.

24 Cornwallis to Ross, 8 November 1798, *Cornwallis corr.*, ii, p. 431.

25 Bolton,*Union*, p. 108.

26 Castlereagh to Portland, 16 January 1799, *Castlereagh corr.*, ii, pp. 142–3; Castlereagh to Sylvester Douglas, 4 February 1799, *Castlereagh corr.*, ii, p. 160.

27 Castlereagh to Portland, 25 January, February 1799, *Castlereagh corr.*, ii, pp. 133, 149–53.

28 Cooke to Auckland, 27 October 1798, PRONI, Sneyd Papers, T3229/2/37.

29 Cornwallis to Portland, 23 January, 24 May 1799, *Cornwallis corr.*, iii, pp. 45–6, 101–2.

30 Castlereagh to Portland, 3 June 1799, *Castlereagh corr.*, ii, p. 327.

31 Cornwallis to Portland, 26 Jan. 1799, *Cornwallis corr.*, iii, p. 52.

32 Castlereagh to Portland, 20 July 1799, *Castlereagh corr.*, ii, pp. 354–5; Cornwallis to Ross, 19 June 1799, *Cornwallis corr.*, iii, p. 104.

33 Cornwallis to Portland, 20 July 1799, *Castlereagh corr.*, ii, p. 352, 13 August 1799, *Cornwallis corr.*, iii, pp. 121–2, 22 October 1799, *Cornwallis corr.*, iii, p. 140.

34 Foster to Sheffield, 8 December 1799, quoted in A.P.W. Malcomson, *John Foster: the politics of the Anglo-Irish ascendancy* (Oxford, 1978), p. 224.

35 Bolton, *Union*, p. 156.

36 Cornwallis to Ross, 2 July 1799, *Cornwallis corr.*, iii, p. 111.

37 Cornwallis to Portland, 22 June 1799, *Cornwallis corr.*, iii, p. 105.

38 Cornwallis to Portland, 26 Jan. 1799, *Cornwallis corr.*, iii, p. 52; Cooke to W. Wickham, 12 April 1799, *Cornwallis corr.*, iii, pp. 86–7; Cornwallis to Ross, 2 July 1799, *Cornwallis corr.*, iii, p. 111.

39 Cornwallis to Pitt, 8 October, 17 October 1798, *Cornwallis corr.*, ii, pp. 418, 420–1.

40 Cornwallis to Pitt, 25 September 1798, *Cornwallis corr.*, ii, p. 416.

41 Cornwallis to Ross, 15 November, 30 September 1798, *Cornwallis corr.*, ii, pp. 436, 416–17, 416.

42 Cornwallis to Ross, 15 November 1798, *Cornwallis corr.*, ii, p. 436.

43 Cornwallis to Portland, 5 December 1798, *Castlereagh corr.*, ii, p. 36.

44 Cornwallis to Ross, 24 July 1798, *Cornwallis corr.*, ii, p. 371.

45 Allan Blackstock, *An ascendancy army: the Irish yeomanry 1796–1834* (Dublin, 1998), pp. 181–6; Hereward Senior, *Orangeism in Ireland and Britain, 1795–1836* (London, 1966), pp. 126–7; Castlereagh to Portland, 2 January 1799, *Castlereagh corr.*, ii, p. 81; Cornwallis to Portland, 16 January 1799, PRO, HO 100/85 l.87.

46 Cornwallis to Ross, 13 February 1800, *Cornwallis corr.*, iii, p. 189; Portland to Cornwallis, 17 February 1800, *Castlereagh corr.*, iii, p. 241.

47 Cornwallis to Portland, 30 January 1799, *Cornwallis corr.*, iii, p. 58; Cornwallis to Portland, 29 March 1799, *Cornwallis corr.*, iii, p. 83.

48 Beresford to Auckland, 25 January 1799, *Beresford corr.*, ii, p. 198.

49 Cornwallis to Portland, 19 October 1799, *Cornwallis corr.*, iii, pp. 137–8.

50 Cornwallis to Portland, 14 August 1799, *Cornwallis corr.*, iii, p. 122; see also Cornwallis to Portland, 22 September 1799, *Cornwallis corr.*, iii, p. 133; Beresford to Auckland, 25 January 1799, *Beresford corr.*, ii, p. 198.

51 Bolton, *Union*, pp. 166–7, 173.

52 Ibid.

53 W.E.H. Lecky, *A history of Ireland in the eighteenth century* (5 vols., London, 1892), v, p. 298.

54 Geoghegan, *Union*, pp. 87, 108, 128–9.

55 Cornwallis to Ross, 20 May 1799, *Cornwallis corr.*, iii, p. 100; see also Cornwallis to the bishop of Lichfield and Coventry, 11 October 1798, *Cornwallis corr.*, ii, p. 419; Cornwallis to Ross, 15 April, 8 June, 28 December 1799, *Cornwallis corr.*, iii, pp. 89, 102, 153.

56 Cornwallis to Ross, 8 June 1799, *Cornwallis corr.*, iii, p. 102.

57 Bolton, *Union*, p. 206.

58 Lecky, *Ireland*, v, 343.

59 Cornwallis to Ross, 18 May 1800, *Cornwallis corr.*, iii, p. 235; Cornwallis to Portland, 18 February, 5 March 1800, *Cornwallis corr.*, iii, pp. 195, 203–4.

60 Cornwallis to Ross, 28 December 1799; Henry Alexander to Thomas Pelham, 15 January 1800, *Cornwallis corr.*, iii, pp. 153, 161.

61 Auckland to Beresford, 15 February 1800, *Beresford corr.*, ii, p. 244.

62 Cornwallis to Ross, 7 June 1800, *Cornwallis corr.*, iii, pp. 249–50.

63 Clare to [Auckland], 2 April 1800, PRONI T3456/1; see also Col. Maitland to William Huskisson, 14 May 1800, *Cornwallis corr.*, iii, pp. 234–5, for praise of Cornwallis's handling of the Union.

64 Cooke to King, 7 June 1800, *Cornwallis corr.*, iii, p. 250.

65 Bolton, *Union*, p. 87; 'Project for the representation of Ireland in the imperial parliament' in *Castlereagh corr.*, iii, p. 56.

66 *Dublin Evening Post*, 18 May 1797.

CHAPTER EIGHT

1 See James Kelly, 'The historiography of the Act of Union', above.

2 Henry Grattan junior., *Memoirs of the life and times of the Rt Hon Henry Grattan* (5 vols., London, 1839–46), v, p. 50.

3 Perhaps the best example is T. Dunbar Ingram, *A history of the legislative union of Great Britain and Ireland* (London, 1887), especially pp. 107–8.

4 The best example of this is Bolton, *Union*.

5 Addressed more fully in James Kelly, 'Public and political opinion in Ireland and the idea of an Anglo-Irish union, 1650–1800' in D. George Boyce, Robert Eccleshall and Vincent Geoghegan (eds), *Political discourse in seventeenth- and eighteenth-century Ireland* (Basingstoke, 2001), pp. 110–41.

6 Kevin Whelan, *The tree of liberty* (Cork, 1996), pp. 155–67; *Beauties of the press* (London, 1798), p. 341; more generally see Manuela Ceretta, above.

7 Welsford to Portland, 22 September 1799, NLS, Minto Papers, Ms 1195 ff 13–4; see also Cornwallis to Lichfield, 27 April 1799 in *Cornwallis corr.*, iii, p. 93. The situation may have been different in Ulster. On this see Hamilton to Abercorn, 10 December 1798 in G.H. Gebbie (ed.), *An introduction to the Abercorn letters* (Omagh, 1972), p. 207; Hudson to Charlemont, 9 March 1799 in HMC, *Charlemont*, ii, p. 347.

8 Lord to Lady Minto, 23 May 1797 in Countess of Minto (ed.), *Life and letters of Sir Gilbert Elliot, first earl of Minto* (3 vols, London, 1874), ii, p. 394; Jonah Barrington, *Rise and fall*, p. 434; J.W. to Cornwallis, 6 February 1798 in *Cornwallis Corr.*, ii, p. 349.

9 James Kelly, *Henry Grattan* (Dundalk, 1993), pp. 35–6.

10 Musgrave to Percy, 28 January, 11 February 1799, NLI, Musgrave Papers, Ms 4157 ff 1, 19.

11 Pitt to Camden, 11 June 1798, KAO, Camden Papers, U840/O195/7.

12 Castlereagh to Camden, 9 July [1798], KAO, Camden Papers, U840/C98/2.

13 *Dublin Evening Post*, 13 October, 8 November; Garthstone to Paget, 26 October 1798 in Lord Hylton (ed.), *The Paget brothers* (London, 1918), pp. 12–13.

14 *Dublin Evening Post*, 13, 17 October; *Freeman's Journal*, 8 November; Tighe to Ponsonby, November in G.H.Bell (ed.), *The Hamwood papers* (London, 1930), p. 304; Musgrave to Percy, 16 November 1798, NLI, Musgrave Papers, Ms 4157 ff 102–12.

15 Charlemont to Parsons, 16 October, NLI, Rosse Papers, Ms 13840/4; James Kelly, '"A genuine Whig and Patriot": Lord Charlemont's political career' in Michael McCarthy (ed.), *Lord Charlemont and his circle* (Dublin, 2001), p. 36; Parsons to Charlemont, 5 November, Stewart to Charlemont, 12 December 1798 in HMC, *Charlemont*, ii, pp. 337–8, 342.

16 *Freeman's Journal*, 1 December; Castlereagh to Fitzgerald, 21 November, Castlereagh to Longueville, 28 November in *Castlereagh corr.*, ii, pp. 10, 31–2; Cornwallis to Pitt, 1, 27 November in *Cornwallis Corr.*, ii, pp. 427–8, 448–51; Musgrave to Percy, 30 November 1798, NLI, Musgrave Papers, Ms 4157 f. 103.

17 Musgrave to Percy, 30 November 1798, 15 January 1799, NLI, Musgrave Papers, Ms 4157 ff 103, 7.

18 Cooke to Castlereagh, 9 November, Castlereagh to Wickham, 19 November in *Castlereagh corr.*, i, p. 432, ii, pp. 8–9; Patrick to James Clancy, 31 October, NLI, Clancy Papers, Ms 20626; Elliot to Elliot, 19 November 1798 in *Minto letters*, iii, pp. 27–8.

19 Cooke to Auckland, 27 October 1798 in A.P.W. Malcomson (ed.), *Eighteenth-century Irish official papers in Great Britain, vol 2* (Belfast, 1990), p. 298.

20 *Dublin Evening Post*, 28 November 1798.

21 See Portland to Cornwallis, 23 November, Castlereagh to Wickham, 23 November in *Cornwallis corr.*, ii, pp. 440, 443–4; Geoghegan, *Union*, chapter 2 *passim*.

22 Musgrave to Percy, 6 December, NLI, Musgrave Papers, Ms 4157 f. 81; Patrick to James Clancy, 24 November 1798, NLI, Clancy Papers, Ms 20626.

23 Barrington, *Rise and fall*, pp. 383–6; M'Clelland to Corry, 9 December, Cooke to Castlereagh, 16 December in *Castlereagh corr.*, ii, pp. 37–9, i, pp. 343–4; *Dublin Evening Post*, 11 December; Patrick to James Clancy, 11 December 1798, NLI, Clancy Papers, Ms 20626.

24 As note 23; Cooke to Auckland, 30 October 1798 in Malcomson (ed.), *Irish official papers*, ii, p. 299.

25 Patrick to James Clancy, 11 December 1798, NLI, Clancy Papers, Ms 20626.

26 Cooke's pamphlet elicited some thirty replies, mostly hostile, in the space of six weeks. They are listed in Francis Plowden, *An historical review of the state of Ireland* . . . (5 vols, Philadelphia, 1805–06), v, pp. 86–7n.

27 Cooke to Auckland, 30 October in Malcomson (ed.), *Irish official papers*, ii, p. 299; *Dublin Evening Post*, 22 December 1798.

28 James Kelly, 'Conservative Protestant political thought in late eighteenth-century Ireland' in S.J. Connolly (ed.), *Political ideas in eighteenth-century Ireland* (Dublin, 2000), pp. 215–19; idem, '"We were all to have been massacred": Irish Protestants and the experience of rebellion' in Thomas Bartlett, *et al.* (eds), *The 1798 Rebellion: a bicentennial perspective* (Dublin, forthcoming); idem, 'Popular politics in Ireland and the Act of Union', *Transactions of the Royal Historical Society*, 6th series, 10 (2000), pp. 259–87.

29 Beresford to Castlereagh, 12 December, Duigenan to Castlereagh, 20 December 1798 in *Castlereagh corr.*, ii, pp. 41–3, 52–3.

30 As note 29; Cornwallis to Ross, 12 December in *Cornwallis corr.*, iii, p. 16; Cooke to Castlereagh, 18 December in *Castlereagh corr.*, ii, pp. 47–8; *Dublin Evening Post*, 20 December and December-January 1798–99; *Freeman's Journal*, 10 January 1799; CARD, xv, pp. 80–1; W.J. Battersby, *The repealer's manual or the Union reconsidered* (Dublin, 1837), pp. 331–51.

31 Kelly, 'Popular politics and the Act of Union', pp. 265–68.

32 Ibid., pp. 268–9.

33 Ibid., pp. 269–70.

34 Hardy to Charlemont, 6 November 1798 in HMC, *Charlemont*, ii, p. 338.

35 James Kelly, *Prelude to Union: Anglo-Irish politics in the 1780s* (Cork, 1992).

36 The initial sounding made by the administration indicated that a substantial number of peers and MPs were well disposed; NLI, Union Correspondence, Ms 887 ff 23–32.

37 Castlereagh to Portland, 21 January 1799 in *Castlereagh corr.*, ii, p. 126.

38 Cornwallis to Portland, 5 January in *Cornwallis corr.*, iii, pp. 30–1; Cornwallis to Portland, 11 January, Camden to Castlereagh, 14 January, Castlereagh to Portland, 21 January 1799 in *Castlereagh corr.*, ii, pp. 89–90, 111–12, 126.

39 Cornwallis to Portland, 11 January, Camden to Castlereagh, 15 January in *Castlereagh corr.*, ii, pp. 89–90, 111–12; Castlereagh to Portland, 13 January, Ely to [ ], 7 January, Cornwallis to Ely, 13 January, Cornwallis to Portland, 16 January in *Cornwallis corr.*,

iii, pp. 36–7, 38; Howard to Forward, 8 January, NLI, Wicklow Papers; *Dublin Evening Post*, 17 January; *Freeman's Journal*, 17 January; Musgrave to Percy, 15 January 1799, NLI, Musgrave Papers, Ms 4157 ff 7–8.

40 38 Geo. III, chap 36

41 *A report of the debate in the House of Commons of Ireland on Tuesday and Wednesday the 22nd and 23rd January 1799 on the subject of an union* (Dublin, 1799), pp. 3–4; 38 Geo.III, chap 36; Castlereagh to Camden, 9 July, 4 October, KAO, Camden Papers, U840/C98/2, 3; Camden to Castlereagh, 31 August, [ ], 25 September, 11, 27 October, 4 November, Pelham to Castlereagh, 13 September, 2 November, Marshall to Castlereagh, 26 October, Elliot to Castlereagh, 27 October, Cornwallis to Castlereagh, 8 November, Castlereagh to Portland, 15 November 1798 in *Castlereagh corr.*, i, pp. 324–5, 344, 375–8, 391, 411–2, 419–21, 424, 428, 444.

42 *A report of the debate in the House of Commons . . .* , p. 4.

43 Ibid., p. 11.

44 Ibid., pp. 4–91 *passim*.

45 *Dublin Evening Post*, 24 January; Fitzgerald to Malone, 23 January, Folger Library, Malone Papers; Cornwallis to Portland, 23 January 1799 in *Cornwallis corr.*, iii, pp. 40–5.

46 Musgrave to Percy, 24/25 January 1799, NLI, Musgrave Papers, Ms 4157 ff 23–4; *A report of the debate in the House of Commons of Ireland on the 24th, 25th, 26th and 28th of January, 1799 on the subject of an union* (Dublin, 1799), p. 94.

47 *A report of the debate . . . on 24th . . . January . . .* , pp. 95–154; Musgrave to Percy, 24/25 January NLI, Musgrave Papers, Ms 4157, ff 23–4; Cornwallis to Portland, 25 January 1799 in *Cornwallis corr.*, iii, pp. 47–50.

48 *A report of the debate . . . on 24th . . . January . . .* , p. 155; Barrington, *Rise and fall*, pp. 420–3; *Dublin Evening Post*, 26 January; Cornwallis to Portland, 25 January 1799 in *Cornwallis corr.*, iii, pp. 47–50.

49 Barrington, *Rise and fall*, pp. 423–4; Cornwallis to Portland, 25 January 1799 in *Castlereagh corr.*, ii, pp. 130–2.

50 Cornwallis to Portland, 25 January in *Castlereagh corr.*, ii, pp. 130–2; Cornwallis to Portland, 28, 30 January 1799 in *Cornwallis corr.*, iii, pp. 53–6, 58.

51 Castlereagh to Portland, 28 January, Castlereagh to Portland, 4 February 1799 in *Castlereagh corr.*, ii, pp. 143, 160.

52 Musgrave to Percy, 24 January, 7, 20 February 1799, NLI, Musgrave Papers, Ms 4157 ff 5, 13, 9.

53 Portland to Cornwallis, 26 January in *Cornwallis corr.*, ii, pp. 134, 137; Musgrave to Percy, 28 January 1799, NLI, Musgrave Papers, Ms 4157 f. 1.

54 *Dublin Evening Post*, 24, 26, 29 January; Cornwallis to Portland, 25 January in *Cornwallis corr.*, iii, p. 51; Charlemont to Haliday, 25 January in HMC, *Charlemont*, ii, p. 344; Musgrave to Percy, 5 February 1799, NLI, Musgrave Papers, Ms 4157 f. 11.

55 Kelly, 'Popular politics and the Act of Union', pp. 271–2.

56 Charlemont to Haliday, 2 February, Hudson to Charlemont, 3 February in HMC, *Charlemont*, ii, pp. 345–6.

57 Wickham to Castlereagh, 24 January in *Cornwallis corr.*, iii, p. 53; Musgrave to Percy, 7 February 1799, NLI, Musgrave Papers, Ms 4157 f. 13.

58 Camden to Clare, 8 February 1799, KAO, Camden Papers, U840/0183/13.

59 Portland to Castlereagh, 29 January 1798 in *Castlereagh corr.*, iii, pp. 145–6.

60 Cornwallis to Ross, 28 January, 13 February, in *Cornwallis corr.*, ii, pp. 56, 59–60; Castlereagh to Portland, 9 February in *Castlereagh corr.*, ii, pp. 170–1; *Dublin Evening Post,* 14 February 1799; Geoghegan, *Union*, p. 74.

61 Cornwallis to Portland, 23, 28 February 1799 in *Cornwallis corr.*, iii, pp. 62, 68–70.

62 Clare to [Camden], 16 February 1799, KAO, Camden Papers, U840/C103.

63 *Dublin Evening Post,* 7 March 1799.

64 Castlereagh to Portland, 14 April 1799 in *Castlereagh corr.*, ii, p. 273.

65 Cooke to Wickham, 12 April, Cornwallis to Portland, 13 April, Cornwallis to Ross, 15 April in *Cornwallis corr.*, iii, pp. 86–7, 89; Castlereagh to Portland, 12, 14 April in *Castlereagh corr.*, ii, pp. 269–70, 273–5; Buckingham to Grenville, 12 April in HMC, *Charlemont*, ii, pp. 349, 351; Cleaver to Egremont, 17 April 1799, Petworth House, Egremont Papers.

66 Fitzgerald to Malone, 1 March 1799, Folger Library, Malone Papers.

67 *Dublin Evening Post,* 6 April; *Freeman's Journal,* 2 May 1800.

68 Barrington, *Rise and fall*, p. 431.

69 Shannon to Camden, 17 February, KAO, Camden papers, U840/081/7; Pelham to Minto, 22 February, NLS, Minto Papers, Ms 11195 f. 3; Castlereagh to Portland, 27 March 1799 in *Castlereagh corr.*, ii, p. 240.

70 Kelly, 'Popular politics and the Act of Union', pp. 274–9; Cornwallis to Dundas, 14 March in *Cornwallis corr.,* iii, p. 77; Cooke to Camden, 7 May, KAO, Camden papers, U840/081/3; Welsford to Minto, 29 April, Elliot to Minto, 23 May, NLS, Minto Papers, Ms 11195 ff 9–10, MS 11229 ff 152–3; Alexander to Castlereagh, 28 March in *Castlereagh corr.*, ii, p. 242; Hill to Barnard, 22 May 1799 in A. Powell (ed.), *Barnard letters 1778–1824* (London, 1928), p. 107.

71 Charlemont to Haliday, 10 May, Charlemont to Hartley, 14 May 1799 in HMC, *Charlemont*, ii, pp. 351–2.

72 Barrington, *Rise and fall*, p. 435.

73 Cornwallis to Ross, 13 February 1799 in *Cornwallis corr.*, iii, pp. 59–60; Barrington, *Rise and fall*, p. 435.

74 Barrington, *Rise and fall*, pp. 429, 436; Musgrave to Percy, 20 February, 7 July, NLI, Musgrave Papers, Ms 4157 ff 9, 17; Burke to Castlereagh, 16 April 1799 in *Castlereagh corr.*, ii, pp. 275–7.

75 Fitzgerald to Malone, 17 May, Folger Library, Malone Papers; *Dublin Evening Post,* 16, 18, 23 May; Cornwallis to Ross, 29 March, 24 May 1799 in *Cornwallis corr.*, iii, pp. 82–3, 101.

76 Elliot to Minto, 23 May 1799, NLS, Minto Papers, Ms 11229 ff 152–3.

77 See, generally, Geoghegan, *Union*, chapter 4; for growing support see Cornwallis to Ross, 19 June, Cornwallis to Portland, 22 June in *Cornwallis corr.*, iii, pp. 103–6; Shannon to Boyle, 22 July 1799 in E. Hewitt (ed.), *Lord Shannon's letters to his son* (Belfast, 1983), p. 207.

78 For which see Kelly, 'Popular politics and the Act of Union', pp. 276–9.

79 Elliot to Minto, 23 May, Douglas to Minto, 17 September, NLS, Minto Papers, Ms 11229 f. 152, Ms 11130 f. 98; Kelly, 'Popular politics and the Act of Union', pp. 279–80. As well

as Minto, the 'Union or separation' argument featured in pamphlets by Thomas Brooke Clarke and Josiah Tucker; it also featured in the resolutions approved by pro-union interests. See King's County, for example; *Dublin Evening Post*, 11 May 1799.

80 Kelly, 'Popular politics and the Act of Union', pp. 277–8; Cornwallis to Ross, 2 July 1799 in *Cornwallis corr.*, iii, p. 111.

81 Cornwallis to Ross, 2 July, 22 September in *Cornwallis corr.*, iii, pp. 111, 133; Douglas to Minto, 15 September, NLS, Minto Papers, Ms 11130 f. 97; Troy to Marshall, 12 October in *Castlereagh corr.*, ii, pp. 420–1; Musgrave to Percy, 7, 15, 25 July 1799, NLI, Musgrave Papers, Ms 4157 ff 17, 47, 27.

82 *Dublin Evening Post*, 6, 11, 15 June, 4, 6, 16 July, 13 August, 1, 3 October; *Freeman's Journal*, 15 June 1799.

83 *Dublin Evening Post*, 27 July, 3, 8, 27 Aug., 5, 14 September, 10, 29 October 1799.

84 CARD, xv, 115; *Freeman's Journal*, 20 July; Castlereagh to Portland, 20 July 1799 in *Castlereagh corr.*, ii, pp. 353–4.

85 *Dublin Evening Post*, 14, 24 October, 9, 14 November; Elliot to Castlereagh, 17, 19 October 1799 in *Castlereagh corr.*, ii, pp. 428, 431–2.

86 Elliot to Castlereagh, 19 October in *Castlereagh corr.*, ii, pp. 431–2; *Dublin Evening Post*, 12, 14, 30 November, 14 December; *Freeman's Journal*, 19 December 1799.

87 *Dublin Evening Post*, 26 November; *The Constitution, or Anti-Union*, 9 December and December–January *passim*; John Carr, *The stranger in Ireland* (London, 1806), p. 220; Lees to Auckland, 20 December 1799 in Malcomson (ed.), *Irish official papers*, ii, p. 303.

88 *Dublin Evening Post*, 31 December 1799, 2, 4, 7, 9, 14, 16, 18 January; *The Constitution, or Anti-Union*, 14, 16 January 1800; Gebbie (ed.), *Abercorn letters*, p. 210.

89 Bradshaw to Castlereagh, 13 January 1800 in *Castlereagh corr.*, iii, pp. 224–5.

90 Cooke to Auckland, 12 December, Castlereagh to Auckland, 13 December, Beresford to Auckland, 18 December, Lees to Auckland, 20 December 1799 in Malcomson (ed.), *Irish official papers*, ii, pp. 301–3; Cornwallis to Ross, 4 January 1800 in *Cornwallis corr.*, iii, p. 157.

91 Alexander to Pelham, 15 January, Cornwallis to Ross, 16 January, Cornwallis to Portland, 16 January in *Cornwallis corr.*, iii, pp. 161, 163–5; Barrington, *Rise and fall*, pp. 453–7; Cooke to Auckland, 16, 18 January 1800 in Malcomson (ed.), *Irish official papers*, ii, p. 304.

92 Barrington, *Rise and fall*, p. 441; Copies of printed circular and petition, 20, 29 January, Cooke to Auckland, 18, 20 January, Castlereagh to Auckland, 25 January, PRONI, Sneyd Papers, T3229/2/55, 56, 52, 54; Castlereagh to Portland, 20, 27 January, Castlereagh to King, 25 January in *Cornwallis corr.*, iii, pp. 166–7, 170–1, 173; Grattan junior, *Life of Grattan*, v, p. 70; *The Constitution, or Anti-Union*, 21 January 1800.

93 Cooke to Auckland, 18, 20 January in Malcomson (ed.), *Irish official papers*, ii, pp. 304, 305; Castlereagh to King, 25 January, Castlereagh to Portland, 29 January 1800 in *Cornwallis corr.*, iii, pp. 170, 174; Grattan junior, *Life of Grattan*, iv, pp. 70–2. Foster was reputedly 'enraged' at the appearance of 'green ribbands with "Grattan and Foster, the friends of the people" for the motto.' *Irish official papers*, ii, p. 305.

94 Castlereagh to Portland, 20 January, Cornwallis to Ross, 21 January in *Cornwallis corr.*, iii, pp. 166–8; Cooke to Auckland, 20 January 1800 in Malcomson (ed.), *Irish official papers*, ii, p. 305; Grattan junior, *Life of Grattan*, iv, pp. 66–7.

95 See *Dublin Evening Post*, January-February; *The Constitution or Anti-Union*, January–February 1800.

96 Castlereagh to Portland, 29 January 1800 in *Cornwallis corr.*, iii, p. 174. Curran did not secure a seat (as MP for Banagher) until May.

97 *Dublin Evening Post*, 23 January; Cornwallis to Lichfield, 24 January 1800 in *Cornwallis corr.*, iii, p. 169; CARD, xv, 127–8, 135–9.

98 The resolutions of the various guilds and corporations (merchants, cutlers and stationers, chandlers, barbers and surgeons, goldsmiths, hosiers, tailors, butchers, joiners, weavers, carpenters, saddlers and upholsterers, shoemakers, bricklayers and plasterers, smiths, coopers) are printed in Battersby, *Repealer's manuel*, pp. 334–50; J.R. Hill, *From patriots to unionists* (Oxford, 1997), pp. 260–1; Beresford to Auckland, 20 January 1800, PRONI, Sneyd Papers, T3229/2/53.

99 One noteworthy exception was the Roman Catholics of Limerick who resolved at a general meeting on 23 January that a union must bring 'ruin and degradation to a country, which since the glorious epoch of 1782 has been rapidly improving in commerce, manufacturers, industry and population'; *Dublin Evening Post*, 28 January 1800.

100 Cornwallis to Ross, 31 January, 4 February in *Cornwallis corr.*, iii, pp. 175, 177; *Freeman's Journal*, 16 January 1800; Kelly, 'Popular politics and the Act of Union', p. 283.

101 Cornwallis to Portland, 4 February, Cornwallis to Ross, 13 February in *Cornwallis corr.*, iii, pp. 178–9, 189.

102 Cornwallis to Portland, 6, 12, 15, 18 February in *Cornwallis corr.*, iii, pp. 181, 186–7, 193–6; Cooke to Grenville, 18 February 1800 in HMC, *Fortescue*, vi, pp. 136–7; Beresford to Auckland, 18 February 1800 in Malcomson (ed.), *Irish official papers*, ii, p. 307.

103 Cornwallis to Ross, 22, 25 February 1800 in *Cornwallis corr.*, iii, pp. 198–200.

104 Cooke to Grenville, 22, 25, 29 February 1800 in HMC, *Fortescue*, vi, pp. 139, 145, 149.

105 *Dublin Evening Post*, 25 January, 1, 4, 6,11, 13, 25, 27 February, 4, 8, 20 March, 3, 19 April 1800.

106 *Dublin Evening Post*, 1, 4, 6, 13, 15, 18, 20, 22, 27 February By 7 March, the number of county petitions had risen to 26 (*Cornwallis corr.*, iii, p. 205).

107 Cornwallis to Portland, 5 March in *Cornwallis corr.*, iii, pp. 202–4; Cooke to Grenville, 5 March 1800 in HMC, *Fortescue*, vi, 152.

108 *Dublin Evening Post*, 1, 6, 15, 22, February; *Freeman's Journal*, 8 March 1800.

109 Cooke to Grenville, 1, 5, 21 March in HMC, *Fortescue*, vi, pp. 150, 152, 170–1; Cornwallis to Portland, 22, 26 March in *Cornwallis corr.*, iii, pp. 215–7; Castlereagh to Rose, 7 March 1800 in *Castlereagh corr.*, iii, p. 251.

110 Castlereagh to King, 27 February, Cornwallis to Ross, 28 February, Cornwallis to Portland, 22 March in *Cornwallis corr.*, iii, pp. 200–1, 201–2, 214–5; *Freeman's Journal*, 18 March; *Dublin Evening Post*, 6, 22 March 1800.

111 Cornwallis to Portland, 11, 12, 14, 22, 24, 28 March in *Cornwallis corr.*, iii, pp. 210–15, 219–20, 222–3; Cooke to Grenville, 5, 10, 14, 15, 21, 22, 24, 28 March in HMC, *Fortescue*, vi, pp. 152, 159–60, 162–3, 170–1, 172, 173, 187.

112 Cornwallis to Portland, 22 March in *Cornwallis corr.*, iii, p. 217; Cooke to Castlereagh, 5 April 1800 in *Castlereagh corr.*, iii, p. 261.

113 *Dublin Evening Post*, 3, 10, 15, 17, 19, 29 April, 3, 13, 15, 22 May; F.H. Tuckey, *The county and city of Cork remembrancer* (Cork, 1837), pp. 213–4; Cornwallis to Ross, 22 April, 2 May 1800 in *Cornwallis corr.*, iii, pp. 229–30.

114 Cornwallis to Portland, 20 May in *Cornwallis corr.*, iii, p. 236; CARD, xv, p. 159; *Dublin Evening Post*, 10, 12, 17, 21, 28 June. 1800.

115 *Freeman's Journal*, 31 May–5 June; Cornwallis to Portland, 9 June in *Cornwallis corr.*, iii, p. 251; Barnard to Barnard, 12 June in Powell (ed.), *Barnard letters*, p. 122; *Freeman's Journal*, 19 June 1800.

116 Molyneux to Morgan, 24 December 1822 in G.N. Nuttall-Smith, *The chronicles of a puritan family in Ireland* (Oxford, 1923), p. 92; Francis Plowden, *A postliminous preface to the historical review of the state of Ireland* (Dublin, 1804), pp. 27–9.

CHAPTER NINE

1 John O'Keeffe, *Recollections* (2 vols., London, 1826), i, p. 262.

2 *The College Green statue: a masque* in Adelaide O'Keeffe (ed.), *O'Keeffe's legacy to his daughter* (London, 1834), pp. 390–3.

3 A.P.W. Malcomson, 'The parliamentary traffic of this country' in Thomas Bartlett and D.W. Hayton (eds.), *Penal era and golden age* (Belfast, 1979), p. 140.

4 'Points to be considered with a view to an incorporating union of Great Britain and Ireland', Cambridge University Library, Add. Ms 6958, f. 3,700.

5 Pitt to Auckland, 14 August 1798, PRONI, T3229/2/35.

6 Either Carrickfergus or Drogheda, if Pitt was including the other in his calculations of 'thirty-three counties'.

7 Bolton, *Union*, p. 86; Sheffield to Auckland, 13 November 1798, BL, Auckland Papers, Add. Ms 34455, f. 34.

8 See Bolton, *Union*, p. 87.

9 This was Arthur Gore, MP for County Donegal. In his obituaries it was claimed that he never actually attended either House of Commons, but this was an exaggeration.

10 Based on the lists of John Roche Ardill, *The closing of the Irish parliament* (Dublin, 1907), pp. 91–101.

11 John Gilbert, *A history of the city of Dublin* (3 vols., Dublin, 1978), iii, pp. 177–8.

12 Based on the *Journals of the House of Commons of the kingdom of Ireland*, 1799–1800. There were some changes after the final Union debate on 7 June 1800 but these have not been included in these calculations. Luke Fox has not been included because he switched seats in January 1799 in suspicious circumstances. Only members who sat for the same seat 1799–1800 are included in the total of 225.

13 Barrington, *Memoirs*.

14 Ardill, *The closing of the Irish parliament*.

15 For example, it lists Thomas Burgh (Clogher City) as voting for the Union on 5 February 1800. Burgh had in fact vacated the seat in January. It also lists Charles Ruxton as voting against the Union on the same occasion but he had vacated his seat

the previous year. There are numerous other errors contained in the lists, but it is still a useful, if tainted, source.

16 Bolton, *Union,* p. 164.

17 Geoghegan, *Union.*

18 Bolton, *Union,* p. 169.

19 See R.G. Thorne (ed.), *History of Parliament, The Commons, 1790–1820* (5 vols., London, 1986).

20 Bolton, *Union* p. 170.

21 Bolton's twelve names are: Arthur Browne (University of Dublin); James Cane (Ratoath); Abraham Creighton (Lifford); John Creighton (Lifford); William Gore (Carrick); William Handcock (Athlone); Richard Nevill (Wexford Town); John Preston (Navan); Abel Ram (County Wexford); Thomas Stannus (Portarlington); Benjamin O'Neale Stratford (Baltinglass); Richard Trench (County Galway).

22 To Bolton's list can be added the following eight MPs: John Bagwell (County Tipperary); William Bagwell (Rathcormack); William Charles Fortescue (County Louth); George Knox (University of Dublin); Alexander Hamilton (Belfast Borough); William Monsell (Dingle); John Reilly (Blessington); Gustavus Rochfort (County Westmeath).

23 See Thorne, *The Commons.*

24 Malcomson, 'The parliamentary traffic', p. 158.

25 Ibid., pp. 159, 153.

26 Debate on 23 January 1799, p. 3.

27 T.W. Moody et al (eds), *A new history of Ireland* (Oxford, 1984), ix, pp. 534–5.

28 Some other boroughs did fall vacant but, as they were not filled until 1800, they will be included in that section.

29 Bolton, *Union,* pp. 95–6n5.

30 Barrington, *Memoirs,* ii, pp. 377–8.

31 Ibid., p. 336.

32 Ibid., p. 370.

33 Information about Stewart in G.D. Burtchaell, *Genealogical memoirs of the members of parliament for the county and city of Kilkenny* (Dublin, 1888), p. 194. I would like to thank Mr James McGuire for his assistance with this paper.

CHAPTER TEN

1 An aggregate meeting is a public meeting, open to all, as opposed to what was still the norm at this time, a meeting confined to those groups with political rights, freemen, freeholders, etc.

2 *Freeman's Journal,* 20 February 1819; CARD, xvii, p. 261.

3 See G.F.A. Best, 'The Protestant constitution and its supporters, 1800–1829', *Transactions of the Royal Historical Society,* 5th series, 8 (1958), pp. 105–27; J.C.D. Clark, *English society 1688–1832* (Cambridge, 1985), pp. 383–93.

4 For party labels see Robert Blake, *The conservative party from Peel to Churchill* (London, 1972), pp. 6–9; John Wolffe, *The Protestant crusade in Great Britain 1829–1860* (Oxford, 1991), p. 22; James J. Sack, *From Jacobite to Conservative: reaction and orthodoxy in Britain, c. 1760–1832* (Cambridge, 1993), pp. 1–6, and chapters three and four.

5 See, e.g., Barrington, *Recollections*, pp. 154, 158.

6 Bolton, *Union*, p. 130.

7 For Musgrave, see DNB (which erroneously depicts him as an anti-unionist), and the Foreword by David Dickson to the 4th edn of Musgrave's *Memoirs of the different rebellions in Ireland*, Steven W. Myers and Delores E. McKnight (eds) (Fort Wayne, 1995).

8 See DNB; Jacqueline Hill, 'The legal profession and the defence of the *ancien régime* in Ireland, 1790–1840' in Daire Hogan and W.N. Osborough (eds.), *Brehons, serjeants and attorneys* (Dublin, 1990), pp. 181–209; pp. 183–97.

9 For Giffard see the obituary in *Gentleman's Magazine*, 89 (1819), pp. 481–4; A.H. and E. Giffard, *Who was my grandfather? A biographical sketch* (London, 1865). I am grateful to Sir Richard Aylmer for bringing this work to my attention. See also Brian Inglis, *The freedom of the press in Ireland 1784–1841* (London, 1954); Gerard O'Brien, 'An account of a debate in the Irish parliament, 1787', *Analecta Hibernica*, 33 (1986), pp. 131–98; Jacqueline Hill, *From patriots to unionists: Dublin civic politics and Irish Protestant patriotism* (Oxford, 1997), part II.

10 Barrington, *Recollections*, p. 154. See also, Jacqueline Hill, 'The meaning and significance of "Protestant Ascendancy", 1787–1840' *Ireland under the Union: proceedings of the second joint meeting of the Royal Irish Academy and the British Academy* (Oxford, 1989), pp. 1–22; James Kelly, 'Eighteenth-century ascendancy: a commentary', *Eighteenth-Century Ireland*, 5 (1990), pp. 173–87.

11 *Gentleman's Magazine*, 89 (1819) p. 483.

12 *Report from the select committee appointed to inquire into the nature, character, extent and tendency of Orange lodges, associations or societies in Ireland*, HC, 1835 (377) xv, appendix no. 3; R.M. Sibbett, *Orangeism in Ireland and throughout the empire* (2 vols., London, n.d.), i, pp. 367, 440.

13 Hereward Senior, *Orangeism in Ireland and Britain, 1795–1836* (London and Toronto, 1966), pp. 76, 91.

14 Ibid., p. 143.

15 See Allan Blackstock, *An ascendancy army: the Irish yeomanry, 1796–1834* (Dublin, 1998), pp. 281–2.

16 Ibid., pp. 282–3; Thomas Bartlett, *The fall and rise of the Irish nation: the Catholic question, 1690–1830* (Dublin, 1992), pp. 323–6.

17 Blackstock, *Ascendancy army*, pp. 270–85; Thomas Bartlett, 'Militarisation and politicisation in Ireland, 1780–1820' in L.M. Cullen *et al.* (eds), *Culture et pratiques politiques en France et en Irlande xvie–xviiie siècle* (Paris, 1990), pp. 125–36.

18 Jacqueline Hill, 'The shaping of Dublin government, 1690–1840' in Peter Clark and Raymond Gillespie (eds), *Two capitals: London and Dublin* (Cambridge, 2002).

19 See, e.g., *Freeman's Journal*, 5 November 1803.

20 Sibbett, *Orangeism*, i, p. 445; Senior, *Orangeism*, p. 133.

21 Patrick Duigenan, *Speech . . . in the Irish House of Commons, 5 February 1800 on the subject of an incorporating union between Great Britain and Ireland* (London, 1800), pp. 3–8.

22 Richard Musgrave, *Memoirs of the different rebellions in Ireland*, 2nd ed. (Dublin, 1801), p. 206.

23 See e.g., *Dublin Journal*, 1 January 1801; 2 January 1802.

24 *Report, Orange lodges*, HC, 1835 (377), xv, p. 82. The Scullabogue atrocity is well contextualised by Daniel Gahan in *The people's rising: Wexford, 1798* (Dublin, 1995), chapter nine.

25 *Hansard's parliamentary debates*, 1st ser., iv, pp. 869–902 (13 May 1805).

26 See, e.g, *Dublin Journal*, 2 January, 8 May 1802; Sibbett, *Orangeism*, ii, p. 108.

27 Giffard to A.H. Giffard, 10 June 1813, in Giffard, *Who was my grandfather?* p. 82. The first Orange lodge in England was in the Lancashire militia (see Senior, *Orangeism*, pp. 151–4).

28 Hill, *From patriots to unionists*, pp. 266–70.

29 W.E. Vaughan (ed.), *A new history of Ireland* (Oxford, 1989), pp. 45–56.

30 Journal of Sheriffs and Commons, 1804–12 (Dublin Corporation Archives, C1/JSC/9, ff. 190v–191; *Dublin Journal*, 21 July 1810.

31 CARD, xvi, p. 325.

32 Giffard to A.H. Giffard, [24 December] 1812, 10 June 1813, in Giffard, *Who was my grandfather?* pp. 74, 82. See also CARD, xvi, p. 353.

33 Giffard to A.H. Giffard, [24 Dec.] 1812, in Giffard, *Who was my grandfather?* p. 74.

34 For Jacob, see Daniel Gahan, *The people's rising: Wexford, 1798* (Dublin, 1995); Kevin Whelan, 'Politicisation in County Wexford and the origins of the 1798 Rebellion' in Hugh Gough and David Dickson (eds), *Ireland and the French Revolution* (Dublin, 1990), pp. 156–78; and for unsuccessful efforts by the 'talents' ministry to remove him from command of his local yeomanry corps, see Blackstock, *Ascendancy army*, pp. 281–2.

35 Giffard to A.H. Giffard, [24 December] 1812, in Giffard, *Who was my grandfather?*, p. 74.

36 See, e.g., *Dublin Journal*, 14 July 1807.

37 CARD, xv, pp. 404, 413–15; Anthony Bird, *The damnable duke of Cumberland* (London, 1966), pp. 73–4.

38 CARD, xv, p. 415, xvi, p. 30.

39 Bird, *Damnable duke of Cumberland*, p. 74.

40 Inglis, *Freedom of the press*, p. 113; Senior, *Orangeism*, p. 178.

41 Giffard to A.H. Giffard, 10 June 1813, in Giffard, *Who was my grandfather?*, p. 85; Gillard to his wife, 3 September 1805 (Halsbury papers in possession of Lady Clare Lindsay, Beer Hackett, Dorset, Box 100/6B). For Agar (archbishop of Dublin, 1801–9), an early opponent of emancipation and supporter of legislative union, see A.P.W. Malcomson, *Archbishop Charles Agar: churchmanship and politics in Ireland, 1760–1810* (Dublin, 2002).

42 Giffard to A.H. Giffard, 10 June 1813, in Giffard, *Who was my grandfather?*, p. 82; R. Nixon to J. Giffard, 11 February 1811, *Report from the select committee . . . on Orange institutions in Great Britain and the colonies*, HC, 1835 (605), xvii, appendix 21, p. 177; Senior, *Orangeism*, p. 180.

43 Giffard to A.H. Giffard, 10 June 1813, in Giffard, *Who was my grandfather?*, pp. 82–3; Nixon to Giffard, 11 February 1811, *Report . . . on Orange institutions in Great Britain*, HC, 1835 (605), xvii, appendix 21, p. 177.

44 CARD, xvi, p. 415; Giffard to A.H. Giffard, 10 June 1813, in Giffard, *Who was my grandfather?*, p. 82.

45 Giffard to A.H. Giffard, 10 June 1813, in Giffard, *Who was my grandfather?*, p. 82; Bird, *Damnable duke of Cumberland*, p. 108. Bird seems to be mistaken in supposing that Cumberland had been elected grand master of Orange lodges in 1807 (p. 82).

46 Giffard to A.H. Giffard, 10 June 1813, in Giffard, *Who was my grandfather?*, pp. 82–4.

47 Senior, *Orangeism*, p. 166. Senior comments that the exact relationship of the duke of York with the Orange Order at this time is not known, though it was probably close. The evidence from Giffard's correspondence suggests that at the least he became a member (see Giffard's comments at the 'great satisfaction' expressed by Manchester Orangeism to whom Giffard reported the outcome of his dealings with the duke in London: Giffard to A.H. Giffard, 10 June 1813, in Giffard, *Who was my grandfather?*, pp. 84–5).

48 Giffard to A.H. Giffard, 10 June 1813, in Giffard, *Who was my grandfather?*, pp. 83–4.

49 Giffard to A.H. Giffard, 28 January 1812, in Giffard, *Who was my grandfather?*, p. 71.

50 Quoted in Blackstock, *Ascendancy army*, p. 286.

51 *Dublin Evening Post*, 11 December 1813; Richard Musgrave, *Observations on Dr Dromgoole's speech delivered in the Catholic board on the 8th of December 1813*, 2nd ed. (Dublin, 1814) (advertised in *Dublin Journal*, 12 July 1814).

52 Hill, *From patriots to unionists*, p. 357.

53 Hill, 'The shaping of Dublin government', pp. 157–8.

54 *Dublin Evening Post*, 30 December 1813 (but see also ibid., 8 March 1814); *Freeman's Journal*, 6, 13 July 1813.

55 Senior, *Orangeism*, pp. 192, 298.

56 *Freeman's Journal*, 1 March 1819.

57 Blackstock, *Ascendancy army*, pp. 249, 262–3.

58 Jacqueline Hill, 'National festivals, the state and 'Protestant ascendancy' in Ireland', *Irish Historical Studies*, 24 (1984), pp. 30–51.

59 6 Geo. IV, c. 4 (9 March 1825).

60 Hill, *From patriots to unionists*, p. 329.

61 Inglis argues that the *Dublin Journal* under Giffard's proprietorship was a commercial failure (*Freedom of the press*, p. 155), but Giffard himself indicates that between 1812 and 1815 the paper was making a modest profit (Giffard to A.H. Giffard, 28 January 1812; 1 January 1815, in Giffard, *Who was my grandfather?*, pp. 71, 91).

62 See, e.g., Giffard to A.H. Giffard, 5 June 1814, in Giffard, *Who was my grandfather?*, p. 88.

63 See Best, 'Protestant constitution', pp. 107–9.

64 David Dickson, '"Centres of motion": Irish cities and the origins of popular politics' in Cullen et al (eds.), *Culture et pratiques politiques*, pp. 109–10.

65 Kerby Miller, 'No middle ground: the erosion of the Protestant middle class in southern Ireland during the pre-famine era', *Huntingdon Library Quarterly*, 49 (1986), pp. 295–306.

66 Sack, *From Jacobite to Conservative*, pp. 99, 240; Wolffe, *Protestant crusade*, pp. 22–4.

67 Wolffe, *Protestant crusade*, p. 25.

68 The dukes of Clarence, Kent, and Sussex were all inclined to the Whig side in politics (Bird, *Damnable duke of Cumberland*, p. 75).

69 Sack, *From Jacobite to Conservative*, p. 71.

CHAPTER ELEVEN

1 Walter Scott, 'General preface' [1829], *Waverley; or, 'tis sixty years since* [1814] (Oxford, 1989), p. 352. A glance at my footnotes will indicate my indebtedness to recent work by Jacqueline Belanger and Peter Garside. As colleagues they have been generous in giving advice and, along with David Skilton, have helped make Cardiff a very good place to ask questions about nineteenth-century fiction.

2 Thomas Bartlett, *The fall and rise of the Irish nation: the Catholic question, 1690–1830* (Dublin, 1992), p. 334.

3 J.G. Lockhart, *The life of Sir Walter Scott* (London, 1937), p. 477.

4 Ibid., p. 477. Lockhart argued however that once measures for Catholic relief had been passed, Scott lent them his support: 'he thought that, after admitting Romanists to the elective franchise, it was a vain notion that they could be permanently or advantageously debarred from using that franchise in favour of those of their own persuasion' (Ibid., p. 477). The context for these observations is a visit paid by Scott to Ireland. While there he met with warm welcome almost everywhere but in Kerry and Lockhart recounted 'the refusal of a Roman Catholic gentleman, named O'Connell, who kept stag-hounds near Killarney, to allow of a hunt on the upper lake, the day he visited that beautiful scenery. This he did, as we were told, because he considered it as a notorious fact, that Sir Walter Scott was an enemy to the Roman Catholic claims for admission to seats in parliament'. (Ibid., pp. 476–7). This was John O'Connell, the brother of Daniel O'Connell MP.

5 Peter Garside, 'The English novel in the Romantic era', in Peter Garside and Rainer Schöwerling (eds.), *The English novel 1770–1829: a bibliographical survey of prose fiction published in the British Isles, ii: 1800–1829* (Oxford, 2000), p. 102.

6 Ibid., p. 102.

7 Scott, *Waverley*, p. 341.

8 Ina Ferris, *The achievement of literary authority: gender, history and the Waverley novels* (London, 1991), p. 107.

9 *An abstract of the arguments on the Catholic question* (London, 1805), pp. 14–15.

10 Playbill advertising 'At the Royal Circus near College-Green for the benefit of Mrs Britain on Wednesday February 5 will be performed a grand serio-comic pastichio called the "Rape of Ierne, or fidelity betrayed"' [Dublin, 1800]. Cambridge University Library: Hib.o.800.1.

11 [Thomas Moore], *Memoirs of Captain Rock, the celebrated Irish chieftain, with some account of his ancestors, written by himself* (London, 1824), pp. 321–2.

12 Seamus Deane, 'Heroic styles the tradition of an idea', *Ireland's Field Day*, Field Day Theatre Company (London, 1985), pp. 45–58.

13 Seamus Deane, 'General introduction' in Seamus Deane (ed.), *The Field Day anthology of Irish writing* (3 vols., Derry, 1991), i, pp. xix–xxvi (p. xxvi).

14 'The Edgeworths and the Union'. Paper presented at the Conference of Irish Historians in Britain, Sussex University, April 2000.

15 Ros Ballaster, 'Women and the rise of the novel: sexual prescripts', in Vivien Jones (ed.), *Women and literature in Britain, 1700–1800* (Cambridge, 2000), pp. 197–216 (p. 200).

16 Seamus Deane, *Strange country: modernity and nationhood in Irish writing since 1790* (Oxford, 1997), p. 20.

17 Ibid., p. 20.

18 Ibid., p. 30.

19 See Claire Connolly, 'Writing the Union', in Dáire Keogh and Kevin Whelan (eds.), *Acts of Union: the causes, contexts and consequences of the Act of Union* (Dublin, 2001), pp. 171–86.

20 For a listing, see Jacqueline Belanger, 'Some preliminary remarks on the production and reception of fiction relating to Ireland, 1800–1829', *Cardiff Corvey: reading the Romantic text*, 4 (2000). Online: http://www.cf.ac.uk/encap/corvey/articles/cc04_n02.html. Date accessed: 15/7/02.

21 Joep Leerssen, *Remembrance and imagination: patterns in the historical and literary representation of Ireland in the nineteenth century* (Cork, 1996), pp. 38–9.

22 Garside, 'The English novel in the Romantic era', p. 40.

23 Ibid., p. 74 for statistical evidence.

24 Katie Trumpener, *Bardic nationalism: the Romantic novel and the British Empire* (Princeton, 1997), p. 131.

25 William B. Warner, *Licensing entertainment: the elevation of novel reading in Britain, 1684–1750* (London, 1998), p. 40.

26 Harriet Guest, *Small change: women, learning, patriotism, 1750–1810* (London, 2000), p. 15.

27 *Freeman's Journal*, 17 January 1807. For an analysis of this claim, see Claire Connolly, '"I accuse Miss Owenson": *The wild Irish girl* as media event', in Anne Fogarty (ed.), *Colby Quarterly*, special issue on 'Irish women novelists, 1800–1940', 36 (2000), pp. 98–115.

28 *Lady Morgan's memoirs: autobiography, diaries and correspondence*, William Hepworth Dixon (ed.) (2 vols., London, 1863), i, p. 424.

29 *Dublin Evening Post*, 21 December 1807, p. 2.

30 See Ann C. Kavanaugh, *John FitzGibbon, earl of Clare: Protestant reaction and English authority in late eighteenth-century Ireland* (Dublin, 1997), p. 203.

31 Quoted in ibid., p. 392.

32 William Drennan to Martha McTier, Belfast, 11 November 1801; quoted in Jean Agnew (ed.), *The Drennan-McTier letters: ii, 1794–1801* (Dublin, 1999), p. 737. Drennan wrote: 'By the bye, we began a novel yesterday called *Belinda* by Miss Edgeworth in which there are portraits drawn with a masterly hand, as far as we have gone – Lady Delacour (perhaps Lady Clare) is done in high style. This Miss Edgeworth is a genius, and if she wrote *Castle Rackrent* and this novel, few in the present day can surpass her.'

33 W.J. McCormack, *The pamphlet debate on the Union between Great Britain and Ireland, 1797–1800* (Dublin, 1996), p. 34.

34 Marilyn Butler and Claire Connolly, 'Introductory note', Maria Edgeworth, *Manoeuvring and Vivian*, *The novels and selected works of Maria Edgeworth* (12 vols., London, 1999), iv, p. xix.

35 Lady Granard to Suffolk Street, 7 February 1799, quoted in Brian MacDermot (ed.), *The Catholic question in Ireland and England, 1798—1822: the papers of Denys Scully* (Dublin, 1988), p. 26.

36 Ibid., p. 27.

37 Terry Eagleton, *Heathcliff and the great hunger: studies in Irish culture* (London, 1995), p. 125.

38 John Kelly, 'Introduction' in John Banim, *The Anglo-Irish of the nineteenth century* [1828] (3 vols., Oxford, 1997), i, p. 150.

39 Ibid.

40 Maria Edgeworth and Richard Lovell Edgeworth, *An essay on Irish bulls*, *The novels and selected works of Maria Edgeworth* (12 vols., London, 1999), i, p. 84.

41 Ibid., p. 85.

42 Ibid., p. 138.

43 Ibid.

44 Geoghegan, *Union*, p. 45.

45 Sydney Owenson [Lady Morgan], *The wild Irish girl* [1806], Claire Connolly and Stephen Copley (eds.) (3 vols., London, 2000), i, p. 48.

46 Lady Morgan, *Florence Macarthy: an Irish tale* [1818] (4 vols., London, 1979), i, p. 46.

47 Ibid.

48 Ibid., pp. 46–7.

49 Ibid., p. 14.

50 Ibid., p. 49.

51 Ibid., p. 50.

52 'The Union, a lyric canto appointed to be sung or said in all meeting houses' [Dublin, 1798]. British Library: 1325.g.15(8).

53 Review of *Florence Macarthy*, *Anti-Jacobin Review*, 55 (1819), pp. 509–21 (p. 517).

54 Review of *Florence Macarthy*, *Edinburgh Monthly Review*, 1 June 1819, pp. 655–62 (p. 656). Jacqueline Belanger has argued that reviews of *Florence Macarthy* constitute a turning point in the British critical reception of Irish writing, registering (even as they criticise) an inescapably political dimension. See Jacqueline Belanger, 'Educating the reading public: British critical reception of the works of Maria Edgeworth and Lady Morgan', unpublished PhD Thesis, University of Kent, 1999, p. 197.

55 Owenson, *The wild Irish girl*, p. 15.

56 Ibid., p. 22.

57 Kevin Whelan, 'Foreword: writing Ireland, reading England', in Owenson [Lady Morgan], *The wild Irish girl*, pp. ix–xxiv (p. xviii).

58 Morgan, *Florence Macarthy*, i, pp. 49–50.

59 Edward Gibbon, *The history of the decline and fall of the Roman Empire* [1776–78], David Wormsley (ed.), 4 vols (Harmondsworth, 1995), iii, p. 509.

60 Morgan, *Florence Macarthy*, i, p. 47.

61 Trumpener, *Bardic nationalism*, p. 144.

62 Morgan, *Florence Macarthy*, i, pp.50–1.

63 'On sensibility without feeling', *Poems, consisting of essays, lyric, elegaic &c., by Thomas Dermody, written between the 13th and 16th year of his age* (Dublin, 1792), p. 63. Dermody, a promising young writer who died young was befriended by Robert Owenson and became a childhood friend of Sydney Owenson and her sister Olivia, to whom he dedicated a sonnet.

64 Charles Robert Maturin, *Women; or pour et contre* [1818] (3 vols., London, 1979), iii, p. 295.

65 Ibid., p. 407.

66 [Banim], *The Anglo-Irish of the nineteenth century*, ii, p. 178.

67 [Andrew Blair Carmichael], *The seven thieves, in six books, by the author of The metropolis* (Dublin, 1807), pp. 72–3n.

68 Ibid., pp. vi, viii.

Contributors

THOMAS BARTLETT is professor of Modern Irish History at University College, Dublin. He has written numerous works including *The fall and rise of the Irish nation* (1992). He recently edited a military history of Ireland, and the life of Theobald Wolfe Tone.

MICHAEL BROWN is a lecturer in Modern Irish History at University College, Dublin. He is the author of *Francis Hutcheson in Dublin, 1719–30* (Dublin, 2002) and the co-editor, with Stephen H. Harrison, of *The medieval world and the modern mind* (2000). He is writing a study on the Irish Enlightenment.

MANUELA CERETTA lectures in Turin University. She has translated into Italian and edited Theobald Wolfe Tone's *An argument on behalf of the Catholics of Ireland* (1998) and has published a book on the political thought of the United Irishmen, entitled *Nazione e popolo nella rivoluzione irlandese* (1999).

CLAIRE CONNOLLY lectures in English literature and Cultural Criticism at Cardiff University. She has edited Maria Edgeworth's *Letters for literary ladies* (1993), as well as *Ormond, Manoeuvring* and *Vivian* for the Pickering and Chatto Tales and Novels of Maria Edgeworth. With Stephen Copley, she has published an annotated edition of Sydney Owenson's *The wild Irish girl* (2001). She is currently writing a cultural history of the novel in Irish romanticism.

PATRICK M. GEOGHEGAN is a lecturer in the Department of Modern History in Trinity College Dublin. He is the author of *The Irish Act of Union: A study in high politics* (Dublin, 1999) and his separate biographies of Lord Castlereagh and Robert Emmet have recently been published.

JACQUELINE HILL is a lecturer at the Department of History, NUI Maynooth. She is the author of *From patriots to unionists: Dublin civic politics and Irish*

Protestant patriotism (Oxford, 1997), and the editor (with Colm Lennon) of *Luxury and austerity* (Dublin, 1999). She is currently working on the careers of Charles Lucas (1713–1771) and John Giffard (1746–1819).

JAMES KELLY is head of the Department of History at St. Patrick's College, Drumcondra. He has written widely on the eighteenth century and among his recent publications are a biography of Henry Flood, and a history of duelling. His most recent book is *Gallows speeches from eighteenth-century Ireland* (Dublin, 2001).

IAN MCBRIDE is a lecturer in the Department of History, King's College London. He is the author of *The siege of Derry in Ulster Protestant mythology* (1997) and *Scripture politics: Ulster Presbyterians and Irish radicalism in the late eighteenth century* (1998), and co-editor, with Tony Claydon, of *Protestantism and national identity: Britain and Ireland, c.1650–c.1850* (1998).

JAMES QUINN is executive editor of the Royal Irish Academy's *Dictionary of Irish Biography*. He has published several articles on radical movements in eighteenth- and nineteenth-century Ireland, and a biography of the United Irishman, Thomas Russell, *Soul on Fire: a life of Thomas Russell* (Dublin, 2002).

JOSEPH RICHARDSON received his doctorate from NUI, Maynooth for a study of Archbishop William King. He is the author of articles on Irish religious thought in the eighteenth century and is currently working on an intellectual history of Irish Anglicanism.

Index

A proposal for uniting the kingdoms of Great Britain, 53

Abbott, Henry (chief secretary), 8

Abercorn, John James Hamilton, 1st marquess of, 72

Abercromby, General Sir Ralph, 99

Acts of parliament
  Declaration of the Kingdom of Ireland (1541), 38, 43, 50
  Declaratory Act (1720), 43, 44, 62
  Catholic Relief Act (1793), 24, 48, 52
  Catholic Relief Act (1828, 1829), 157
  Place Act (1793), 115, 134
  Place Act (1798), 115, 137–9
  Poynings' Law, 38, 43, 44, 62, 66
  Repeal of Corporation Act (1828), 157
  Repeal of Test (1828), 157
  Union, Act of (1800): bicentenary, 2, 36
  Catholics and, 11, 17, 21, 25, 28, 49, 68, 90–1, 120, 125
  historiography, 3, 5–36, 69, 93, 108
  opposition to, 108–28
  'pamphlet war', 111, 112
  Presbyterians and, 3, 68–83
  Union representation, 129–33
  Union parliament 1799–1800, 133–43
  United Irishmen and, 84–94
  terms of, 46–7
  Unlawful Societies Act (1825), 155
Acts of Union: the causes, contexts and consequences of the Act of Union, 2

Addington, Henry, 7–9, 11

Africa, 54

Agar, Charles, archbishop of Cashel, 68, 153

Aldermen of Skinner's Alley, 112

Aldridge, Robert MP, 139

Amiens, peace of, 148

Ancien régime, 66, 82

ancient constitution, 59

Anglicans, 48, 49, 60, 62, 63, 64, 65, 67

Anglicanism, 3, 58, 61, 62, 64, 65, 66

Anglo-Scottish Union (1603), 39

Anglo-Scottish Union (1707), 2, 3, 8, 37, 39–42, 43, 45, 46, 53, 61, 82, 130

Anne, Queen, 39, 59

Annesley, Francis, 43

Annesley, Richard MP, 140, 142, 143

Anti-Jacobin, 170

Anti-Union, 122, 123

Antrim, County, 70, 71, 72, 73, 76, 77, 78, 79, 81

Archer, Thomas, 71

Ardee, County Louth, 133

Ardill, John Roche (historian), 30–1, 135
  The closing of the Irish parliament, 135
  Forgotten facts of Irish history, 31

Armagh, County, 70, 73, 75, 113, 134, 146

Armagh outrages, 93

Asia, 54

Ashbourne, Edward Gibson, 1st Lord (historian), 33
  Pitt: some chapters in his life and times, 33

Athboy, 134

Athenry, 136

Auckland, William Eden, 1st Lord Auckland, 106

Bagwell, John MP, 136

Bagwell, Richard MP, 136

Bagwell, William MP, 132, 136
Ball, John MP, 113
Ball, Charles MP, 57, 140–1
Ballymena, 78
Ballymoney, 71
Ballynahinch, battle of, 74, 78, 81
Baltimore, 79
Bank of Ireland, 133
Banim, John, 166–7, 174
    The Anglo-Irish of the nineteenth century,
      166, 174
Bannagher, King's County, 133
Barber, Rev Samuel, 73
Barlow, Stephen (historian), 12–13
    History of Ireland, 12
Barnard, Toby (historian), 61
Barrington, Jonah, 3, 5, 6, 7, 10, 14–17,
    18–19, 21, 22, 23, 24, 25, 26, 30, 31,
    109, 111, 115, 116, 119, 120, 121, 135,
    136, 139, 140, 142, 147
    Historic anecdotes and secret memoirs of
      the legislative union, 7, 14, 135, 140
    Rise and fall of the Irish nation, 5, 14
Bartlett, Thomas (historian), 157
Bayly, Christopher (historian), 2
Beckett, J.C. (historian), 34
    The making of modern Ireland,
      1603–1923, 34
Belfast, 2, 72, 75, 76, 77, 79, 82
Belfast Academical Institution, 75
Belfast, Frederick Richard Chichester, 1st
    earl of, 133
Belfast News-letter, 74, 77, 81
Belfast Society, 80
Belturbet, 134
Beresford, John, 21, 28, 96, 97, 99, 103,
    124
Beresford, John Claudius MP, 84, 112,
    115
Beresford, Henry de la Poer, earl of
    Tyrone, 15, 115, 137
Bicheno, James, 81
Bickerstaffe, Isaac, 165
    The Ephesian matron, 164–5
Biggs-Davison, John, 36

Birch, Rev Thomas Ledlie, 73, 74, 79
Black, Rev Robert, 73, 74, 75, 76, 77
Blackstock, Allan (historian), 80
Blackwood, Sir John MP, 134
Blakeney, William MP, 136
Blaquiere, Sir John MP, 10
Blessington, County Wexford, 143
Bolton, G.C. (historian), 1, 3, 4, 6–7, 34–5,
    36, 69, 70, 71, 101, 104, 135, 136, 137,
    139, 146
    The passing of the Irish Act of Union, 1,
      69, 104
Bonaparte, Napoleon, 81, 153
Boyd, James, 151
Boyne, Battle (1690), 58, 62, 66
Brehon laws, 64
Brest, 71
Bristol, 41
British Critic, 12
British Empire, 3, 7, 8, 9, 11, 24, 32, 46,
    49, 50, 51, 53, 54, 55, 56, 57, 66, 88, 89,
    90, 95, 105, 114, 163, 172
Brooke, Charlotte, 160
    Reliques of Irish poetry, 160
Brothers, Richard, 81
Broughshane, 78
Browne, James MP, 116
Bruce, Rev. William, 72, 74, 76, 77
Buckingham, George Nugent-Temple-
    Grenville, 1st marquess of, 11, 21, 99,
    130
Burgh, Thomas MP, 140
Burke, Edmund, 55, 84, 86
Burnet, Gilbert, 60
Burney, Frances, 162
Burrowes, Peter, 111, 123
Burton, William MP, 137
Bushe, Charles Kendal MP, 14, 97, 111,
    133, 165
    Cease your funning, 164–5
Butler, James MP, 136

Calcutta, 23
Calkin, Homer (historian), 36
Callan, County Kilkenny, 133, 139

Camden, Charles Pratt, 1st Earl, 70, 115, 138

Cameron of Glasgow (publishers), 22

Cameronians, 42

Campbell, Rev. William, 76

Campbell of Cessnock, 42

Canada, 51

Cannosa, 64

Carmichael, Andrew Blair, 175
    The seven thieves, 175

Carrickfergus, 79, 130, 131, 133

Carty, James (historian), 32
    Class-book of Irish history, 32

Carysfort, 139

Castlereagh, Robert Stewart, 2nd Viscount, 3, 15, 16, 19, 21, 22, 26, 28, 31, 32, 33, 34, 52, 53, 71, 73, 76, 79, 80, 84, 95, 96, 98–100, 105–7, 109, 110, 115, 116, 118–19, 123, 125, 131, 138, 164, 167
    Castlereagh correspondence, 141

Carlow, County, 113, 137

Catholic Association, 145, 155, 159

Catholic Board, 151, 154

Catholic emancipation, 2, 7, 8, 9, 13, 25, 48, 49, 57, 65, 73, 76, 77, 79, 82, 85, 86, 91, 92, 102, 144, 145, 146, 148, 150, 151, 152, 154, 156, 157, 158, 160, 164, 167, 174

Catholic Whiggery, 49

Catholicism, 61, 62, 64, 65, 66, 150

Cavan, County, 70, 126

Cavendish, Sir Henry, 116

Charlemont, James Caulfeild, 1st Earl, 70, 110, 113, 117, 119, 120, 126, 134

Charlemont, Francis William Caulfeild, 2nd Earl, 111, 113, 123

Charles I, 61

Charles II, 60

Chester, 41

Chowdharay-Best, George, 36

Church of Ireland, 22, 31, 146

civil society, 41

Clare, Anne FitzGibbon, Lady, 164–5

Clare, John FitzGibbon, earl of, 15, 19, 22, 33, 68, 69, 83, 91, 95, 97, 98, 102, 106, 165

Clark. J.C.D. (historian), 59

Cleaver, Euseby, bishop of Ferns, 119

Clonmel, County Tipperary, 132

Clonmines, County Wexford, 139

Clogher borough, County Tyrone, 140–1, 143

Coleraine, 72

College Green, 10, 82, 129, 149, 152, 155, 159, 171, 172

Colley, Linda (historian), 48, 81

Common law, 40, 47

Confederation of Kilkenny, 61

Connaught, 156

Connemara, 168, 171

Conolly, Thomas, 54

Cooke, Edward, 15, 28, 84, 87, 88, 89, 91, 92, 95, 97, 98, 100, 106, 110, 111, 112, 114, 125
    Arguments for and against an union, 97, 112, 165

Cooke, Henry, 78

Coote, Sir Charles, 7, 10
    History of the Union of Great Britain and Ireland, 7

Cork city, 41, 131

Cork, County, 113, 126, 132, 141, 143

Cornwallis, Charles, Lord, 3, 15, 21, 23, 25, 26, 52, 53, 69, 71, 72, 79, 95–9, 101–7, 115, 116, 118, 120, 121, 126, 136, 138, 141
    Cornwallis correspondence, 21

corruption, 2, 5, 6, 7, 14, 16, 18, 19, 21, 25, 27, 28, 29, 31, 32, 33, 34, 35, 42, 46, 99, 104, 133, 135, 136, 137, 140, 173

Corry, Isaac, 124, 132

counter-insurgency, 78

Cradock, Major General John Francis MP, 141, 143

Craig, Rev Alexander, 73

Creel, George (historian), 32

Croker, John Wilson, 164, 166, 167, 171

Croker, Thomas Crofton, 166

Croly, George, 166
Cuddy, Billy, 78
Cullen, L.M. (historian), 2
Cumberland, Prince Ernest Augustus,
    Duke of, 152–3
Cuming, Rev. Thomas, 73, 74
Cupples, Dr Snowden, 80
Curtis, Edmund (historian), 31, 32
Curran, John Philpot MP, 97, 111, 123,
    126

D'Alton, E.A. (historian), 32
D'Arcy McGee, Thomas, 21–2
    Popular history of Ireland, 22
Darien scheme, 39
Deane, Seamus, 159–60, 161
    Field Day anthology of Irish writing,
    160
Defenders, 20, 108
Dennehy, W.F. (historian), 27–9
    The story of the Union told by its plotters,
    28
Dennis, John, MP, 132
Dermody, Thomas, 173
Derry, County, 70, 71, 72, 73, 79–80, 141
Devonshire, 41
D'Esterre, John Norcot, 154
Dickson, George, 71
Dickson, William Steel, 73–6, 79
    *A narrative of the confinement of William
    Steel Dickson*, 75
Dobbs, Francis MP, 110, 111, 115, 116
Donegal, County, 26, 70, 122, 132, 134
Donegal, Arthur Chichester, 1st marquess
    of, 133
Donegore, 75
Douglas, Sylvester (chief secretary), 54
Down, County, 70, 71, 73, 74, 75, 76, 77, 78,
    79, 125, 138
Downshire, Wills Hill, 1st Marquess, 70,
    103, 104, 114, 123, 124
Doyle, William MP, 133
Doyle, William (historian), 2
Drennan, Dr William, 81–3, 85, 86, 87, 90,
    92, 93, 94, 165

Idem sentire, dicere agere, 85, 90
    A letter to the rt. hon. William Pitt, 92
Drogheda, 113, 130, 131
Drumgoole, Dr Thomas, 153–4
Dublin, 2, 4, 13, 14, 21, 41, 43, 48, 51, 63,
    66, 78, 81, 86, 97, 98, 100, 106, 108,
    111, 112, 113, 117, 121, 122, 124, 126,
    129, 131, 132, 133, 144–56, 168–75
Dublin bar, 95, 111
Dublin bay, 169, 171
Dublin Castle, 3, 22, 35, 52, 71, 76, 79, 84,
    95, 97–107, 108, 110, 122, 124, 127,
    136, 137, 140, 143, 147
Dublin Corporation, 112, 121, 124, 144,
    145, 146, 147, 149, 150, 151, 152, 154,
    173
Dublin, County, 112, 126
Dublin Evening Post, 110, 112, 117, 121,
    164, 165
Dublin Journal, 147, 149, 150, 151, 152,
    154, 155
Duigenan, Patrick, MP, 97, 112, 146, 147,
    149, 150, 153, 155
Dunbar George MP, 141
Dundalk, 132
Dundas, Henry, 54
Dungannon, 132, 139
Dungannon Convention (1793), 70, 74
Dunlop, Robert (historian), 31, 32
Duquery, William MP, 111
Durey, Michael (historian), 79

Eagleton, Terry, 166
East India trade, 53
Edgeworth, Maria, 157–61, 163, 165, 167
    The Absentee, 160, 171, 175
    Belinda, 165
    Castle Rackrent, 161–2, 164, 165
    Essay on Irish bulls, 167–8
    Manoeuvring, 165
    Patronage, 165
Edgeworth, Richard Lovell, 116, 165, 167,
    168
Edinburgh, 39, 40, 42
Edinburgh Review, 11, 170

Egypt, 81
elections, by-
  Clare, 157
  Newry, 119
  Galway, 119
  Co Londonderry, 127
Elibank, Lord, 42
Elizabeth I, 37
Ely, Charles Tottenham, 1st marquess of, 114, 139
Eighteenth-Century Ireland, 2
English attitudes to Irish, 56
Enlightenment, 81, 82, 89, 163
Enniscorthy, 136, 151
Enniskillen, Lord, 97
Erastianism, 65
Europe, 50, 53, 54, 59, 65, 80, 89, 169
evangelicalism, 83
Exeter, 41

Falkiner, Caesar Litton (historian), 33
Fermanagh, County, 70, 122, 126
Ferguson, William, 42
Ferris, Ina, 158
Fielding, Henry, 162
Fingal, Earl, 102
Fisher, J.R. (historian), 33, 34, 69, 76
  The end of the Irish parliament, 69
Fitzgerald, Lord Edward, 147
Fitzgerald, James (prime serjeant), 6, 19, 100, 116, 117,118–9
Fitzwilliam, William Wentworth-Fitzwilliam, 2nd Earl, 12, 27, 86, 87, 99, 102
Fletcher, Andrew of Saltoun, 41–2
  Account of a conversation, 41
Fleming, Robert, 81
Flood, Henry, 56
Forbes, Lord, 42
Fort George, 73, 74, 87
Foster, Speaker John, 19, 56, 68, 70, 97, 99, 101, 104, 105, 113, 114, 117, 118, 119, 120, 123, 126, 168
Foster, Roy (historian), 35
Fox, Luke MP, 139

France, 7, 20, 21, 24, 48, 51, 54, 56, 59, 60, 71, 73, 81, 82, 89, 96, 97, 148, 159
free trade, 39, 46
French Revolution, 66, 69, 80, 84, 160
Freeman's Journal, 144–5, 149
Froude, James Anthony (historian), 23, 29

Gahan, Daniel MP, 134
Galloway, 41
Galway city, 113
Galway, County, 122
Gardiner, Lieutenant General William MP, 140, 141
Garside, Peter, 158
Garrick, David, 165
  The Irish widow, 164–5
Geoghegan, Patrick (historian), 2, 49, 67, 69, 104, 168
  The Irish Act of Union: a study in high politics, 1798–1801, 2
George I, 59
George III, 2, 9, 48, 49, 52, 126, 150–51, 164
Gibbon, Edward, 172
  The history of the decline and fall of the Roman Empire, 172
Giffard, John, 83, 144–7, 149–55
Giffard, Ambrose Hardinge, 147, 150
Giffard, Stanley Lees, 156
Giffard, Lieutenant William, 147
Glasgow, 22, 42
Gloucester, Prince William Frederick, 6th duke of, 152
Glorious Revolution (1688–90), 45, 59, 60, 85, 145
Godwin, William, 162
Goldsmith, Oliver, 7
  History of England, 7
Goodwin, Christopher, 81
Goold, Thomas MP, 84, 89, 123
Gordon, James Bentley, 84
  History of the Rebellion: Ireland in 1798, 84
Gore, Arthur MP, 132
Gorey, 139

Gowan, Hunter, 151
Gowdie, Robert, 73
Graham, Watty, 78
Grand Orange Lodge of England, 150, 154
Grand Orange Lodge of Ireland, 71, 125, 147–50, 155, 156
Granard, Lady Selina Frances, 166
Grattan, Henry, 11, 14, 17, 19, 22, 26, 27, 44, 57, 83, 86, 105, 109, 122, 123, 124, 126, 129, 149
Grattan, Henry junior (MP and historian), 17–19, 20, 21, 22, 23, 27, 28, 31, 108
	Life, 21
Grattan's parliament, 44, 83
Gray, Bessie, 78
Great Reform Bill (1832), 14
Gregory VII, Pope, 64
Gregory, William MP, 132
Grenville, William Wyndham, 1st Lord, 130, 132
Grey, Charles, 1st Lord, 14, 19
Grotius, Hugo, 60, 66
	De jure belli et pacis, 60
Guardian, 167
Guest, Harriet, 163–4
Gwynn, Stephen, 31–2
	History of Ireland, 32

Haliday, Dr Alexander, 76, 79
Hanover, 44
Hardman, Edward MP, 113
Hardwicke, earl of, 152
Hardy, Francis MP, 113, 115, 133
Harlow, V.T. (historian), 50
Hart, Brigadier General, 80
Hazlitt, William, 129
Henry II, emperor, 64
Henry VIII, 38
Hillsborough, 134
Historical Manuscripts Commission, 33
History, 1
Hoare, William MP, 133
Home Rule, 23, 29, 57, 69

Hope, James, 78
Howard, Hugh MP, 134
Hull, Rev James, 73
Hume-Williams, W.E. (historian), 23
Hussey, Thomas, 64

India, 51, 96
industrialisation, 83
informers, 75
Ingram, T. Dunbar (historian), 6, 23–8, 29, 30, 33, 69, 76
	A history of the legislative union of Great Britain and Ireland, 23, 26, 69
Innocent II, Pope, 64
Interregnum, 37–8
Inverness, 41
Irish Catholic, 27
Irish Free State, 32
Irish trade, 53, 57

James II, 58, 59, 60
Jacob, Archibald, 151
Jacobinism, 75, 81, 162
Jacobins, 52
Jacobite, 40, 42, 59
Jesuit Order, 8
Johnson, William MP, 139
Johnston, Charles (historian), 32
Johnston, E.M. (historian), 35
Journal of the Irish House of Commons, 42–3, 134
Joy, Henry, 77, 79, 80
Jupp, Peter (historian), 2
Jurieu, Pierre, 81

Kearney, James MP, 141
Kelburne, Rev Sinclare, 73
Kelly, James (historian), 2, 61
Kelly, John, 166
Kelly, Patrick (historian), 60
Kenmare, Valentine Browne, earl of, 29, 102
Keogh, Dáire (historian), 2
Kildare, 147
Kilkenny city, 132

Kilkenny, County, 125, 133, 136
Killyleagh, 134
Kilrea, 74
King, Abraham Bradley (alderman), 153
King, Charles MP, 134
King, John MP, 140, 141
King, Archbishop William, 3, 42, 43,
   58–61, 62, 63, 64, 65, 66
   State of the Protestants of Ireland, 58, 59,
   60, 61
King's County, 113, 126, 133
King's Inns, 26
Kingsborough, Lord Viscount, 134
Knights of the Black Garter, 71
Knox, John MP, 132

Lake, General Gerard, 77, 141
Larne, 74, 79
LaTouche, James Digges, 112
Lawless, Emily (writer), 31
Lecky, W.E.H. (historian), 29, 30, 31, 32,
   34, 105
   *History of England in the Eighteenth
   Century*, 29
   Leaders of public opinion, 29
Leerssen, Joep (historian), 162, 163
Lees, John, 122
legislative independence, 7, 13, 16, 18, 20,
   23, 24, 45, 51, 52, 58, 63, 64, 66, 83,
   103, 108, 110, 122, 149
Leinster, 147, 156
Leinster, James Fitzgerald, 2nd duke of
   Leinster, 99
Leitrim, County, 122, 146
Leslie, Charles Powell MP, 134
Limavady, 72
Limerick city, 147
Limerick, County, 122
Lisburn, 73, 80
Lismore, 146
Liverpool, Charles Jenkinson, 1st Earl,
   130
Liverpool, Robert Banks Jenkinson, 2nd
   Earl, 151
Lockhart, John Gibson, 158

London, 7, 14, 18, 41, 44, 48, 49, 51, 56,
   63, 67, 98, 102, 106, 107, 108, 117, 132,
   153, 162, 171
Londonderry, Earl of, 71
Londonderry city, 41, 77, 80
Longford, County, 125, 126, 133, 139, 165
Longford, Lord, 165
Lords of the Articles, 45
Louis XIV, 60, 66, 149
Louth, County, 113, 125, 133
Love, Christopher, 81
loyalism, 81, 98, 145–7
Lucas, Charles, 44
Luttrell, Henry Lord Carhampton, MP,
   139–40

McCarthy, Justin Huntley (historian), 27,
   28
McCavery, Trevor (historian), 2
McClelland, James, 79
McComb, William, 78
McCormack, W.J., 160, 165
McCracken, Henry Joy, 78
MacDonagh, Peter (historian), 2
McDowell, R.B. (historian), 34, 35
   *Ireland in the age of imperialism and
   revolution*, 35
MacGeoghegan, Abbé, 21
   History of Ireland, 21
McKenna, M.J. (historian), 32
McKenny, Thomas (alderman), 144
MacMurrough, Dermot, 62, 147
MacNeven, William James, 84, 87, 90–1,
   92
McNeill, J.G. Swift (historian), 26–7, 29
   How the Union was carried, 27
McTier, Martha, 77, 165
Magee, William, 166
Maghera, 78
Magill, Rev Robert, 78
Malcomson, A.P.W. (historian), 2, 130
Malton, James, 171–2
Manchester, 150, 153
Mansergh, Daniel (historian), 2
Mansion House, Dublin, 152

Martin, R.M., 20, 21
    Ireland before and after the Union, 20
Maturin, Charles Robert, 174
    Women, 174
Maxwell, Henry, 88
Mayo, County, 125
Meath, County, 113, 125
Metge, John MP, 133
Middleton, County Cork, 143
Miles, Rev John, 73
militia, 78, 103, 147
Minto, Gilbert Elliot, 1st Lord, 54–5
Mitchel, John, 21
Moira, Lady, 166
Moira, Francis Rawdon, 2nd earl of, 27
Molesworth, Robert, 1st Viscount, 42–3
Molyneux, Capel MP, 121, 126, 127
Molyneux, William, 38
    Case of Ireland . . . truly stated, 38
Monaghan, County, 70, 122, 134
Montgomery, Samuel, 147–8
Montgomery, William MP, 134
Moore, Arthur, MP, 10, 19, 116
Moore, John MP, 132
Moore, Samuel, 80
Moore, Stephen MP, 132
Moore, Thomas, 159, 175
    Captain Rock, 175
Monaghan, County, 113
Monro, Henry, 78
Mullingar Manor, County Westmeath,
    133, 139
Munster, 25, 121, 140, 156
Murphy, Dorcas, 147
Murphy, Arthur, 147
Musgrave, Sir Richard, 3, 8, 12, 20, 58, 61,
    62, 63–5, 66, 67, 73, 81, 88, 110, 111,
    117, 146, 147, 149–50, 154, 155
    Memoirs of the different rebellions in
        Ireland, 8, 58, 63, 65, 73, 81, 146,
        149–50
Mysore Wars, 96

Namier, Lewis (historian), 35
Napoleonic Wars, 13, 154, 155

nationalists / nationalism, 5, 6, 17, 19, 21,
    22, 23, 24, 25, 27, 29, 30, 33, 34, 42, 49,
    108, 129, 160, 175
natural law, 59, 60
Neilson, Samuel, 70, 87
New York, 22
Newry, 132, 134, 139
Nixon, Rev Ralph, 150, 153
Northern Star, 73, 81
Northern Whig, 69
Norwich, 41
Nugent, General George, 71, 141

Ó Tuathaigh, Gearóid, 2
O'Beirne, Bishop Thomas Lewis, 28
O'Brien, Gillian (historian), 2
O'Connor, Arthur, 86, 87
O'Connor, Sir James (historian), 32–3
O'Connell, Daniel, 11, 13–14, 15, 25, 27,
    49, 125, 151, 154, 157, 159
O'Donnel, Hugh MP, 134
O'Donnell, James Moore MP, 116
O'Hagan, Thomas, 27
O'Keeffe, John, 129
O'Kelly, Patrick (historian), 21
O'Neill Daunt, William (historian), 21
    Catechism of the history of Ireland, 21
oath of allegiance, 77
Ogilvie, William MP, 92
Ogle, George MP, 70, 115, 148, 153
Old Lighlin, 146
Orange Order, 4, 28, 36, 63, 70, 71, 72, 80,
    112, 125, 147–50, 152–6
Orangemen, 9, 11, 22, 55, 71, 80, 84, 92,
    94, 88, 149, 155
Orange parades, 93
Ormonde, earl of, 132
Ormsby, John Mason MP, 139
Osborne, Thomas MP, 121
Oulartleigh County Wexford, 147
Owen, John, 81
Owensen, Sydney, Lady Morgan, 163, 164,
    168, 170, 171, 172
    Florence Macarthy, 168–9, 170, 171, 172,
        174, 175

Memoirs, 164

The missionary, 164

The novice of Saint Dominick, 164

The wild Irish girl, 168, 171, 175

Paine, Thomas, 45

Pakenham, Edward MP, 139

Pakenham, Admiral Thomas, 165

Pale, the, 61

Panama, 39

Paris, 14

parliament (British), 20, 40, 54, 55, 65, 92,
    130, 131, 132, 146, 151, 152, 154

parliament (English), 38

parliament (Irish), 3, 4, 7, 14, 16, 17, 18, 19,
    22, 24, 25, 26, 30, 31, 32, 33, 43, 44, 50,
    51, 52, 54, 55, 56, 65, 81, 85, 86, 92, 101,
    103, 105, 107, 111, 114, 123, 127–30,
    132, 133, 134, 143, 169

    House of Commons, 3, 16, 18, 19, 20,
        32, 43, 44, 45, 50, 68, 86, 91, 95, 97,
        98, 99, 100, 101, 105, 106, 107, 109,
        116, 118, 119, 120–6, 129, 130, 131,
        133–42, 149, 165, 168

    House of Lords, 2, 18, 44, 50, 68, 75,
        95, 116, 126

    legislative output, 45

    membership, 1799–1800, 133–5

    representation, 129–30

parliament (Scottish), 41

parliamentary reform, 69

Parnell, Sir John, 70, 100, 113, 114, 116,
    117

Parsons, Lawrence, 110, 113, 116, 122

Patriots, 44, 109–28

patronage, 5, 10, 18, 21, 26, 31, 34, 35, 57,
    66, 100, 104, 108, 127, 135, 143, 156

Patterson, James (historian), 71

Peden, Alexander, 81

Peel, Robert MP, 158

Pelham, Thomas (chief secretary), 115,
    138

Percy, William, 82

    Irish salvation, 82

Pery, Edmund Sexten Pery, 1st Lord, 110,
    114

Pincus, Steven (historian), 60

Pitt, William, 2, 15, 17, 21, 31, 32, 33, 34, 35,
    45, 48, 49, 51, 52, 53, 54, 86, 87, 88, 89,
    92, 96, 102, 106, 109, 113, 117, 118, 126,
    130, 148, 156, 164, 170

Plowden, Francis (historian), 7–12, 13, 15,
    16, 21, 31, 127

    Historical review, 9, 11, 12

Plunket, William Conyngham MP, 14, 19,
    97, 110, 111, 115

Pocock, J.G.A. (historian), 2

Ponsonby, George MP, 16, 19, 25, 109,
    111, 115, 116, 118, 119, 120, 125,
    137–8

Ponsonby, William Brabazon, 123

Pope, Rev Richard, 166

Portaferry, 74

Portarlington, 132

Portarlington, Lord, 137

Porter, Rev James, 73, 74, 75, 78

    Billy Bluff, 74

Portland, William Henry Cavendish-
    Bentinck, 3rd duke of, 106, 117, 118

Presbyterian Church of Scotland, 41

Presbyterians, 3, 42, 49, 50, 61, 68–81

    Presbyterian clergy and 1798, 72–3

    Presbytery of Antrim, 72, 73

    Presbytery of Bangor, 73

Presbyterianism, 39, 40, 73, 76

Protestant ascendancy, 9, 12, 24, 70, 71,
    91, 92, 94, 95, 106, 112, 147

Protestants, 24, 25, 28, 33, 40, 48, 50, 53,
    55, 56, 57, 60, 61, 62, 70, 81, 85, 89, 95,
    97, 99, 103, 112, 127, 135, 141, 145,
    146, 147, 148, 150, 152, 153, 155, 156,
    161

Protestantism, 3, 24, 46, 59, 91

public opinion, 2, 19, 30, 35, 36, 69, 70,
    101, 102, 103, 106, 110, 111, 122, 126

Queen's College, Belfast, 23

Queen's County, 113

Queensbury, James Douglas, 3rd
    Marquess, 42

rebellion
    1641 rising, 61, 62, 65
    1798 Rebellion, 3, 7, 9, 20, 29, 31, 32,
        48, 52, 63, 66, 68, 69, 70, 71, 73, 74,
        75, 76, 77, 78, 79, 81, 89, 96, 98,
        103, 108, 112, 145, 146, 147, 148,
        150, 151, 152, 155, 160, 170
    Emmet's (1803), 79, 148, 155, 156, 159
Redfoord, Archibald, 55
Reformation, 64
Regency (1811), 151
Regency crisis (1788–89), 52, 118, 150
regium donum, 73, 74, 75
repeal, 13, 49, 57, 127, 150–1, 159
republicanism, 77, 78, 79, 82, 88
Restoration (1660), 39, 60
Richardson, Samuel, 162
Robinson, Nicholas, 2
Roche, Regina Maria, 163
Roman Catholics, 3, 7, 8, 9, 10, 11, 12, 16,
        17, 19, 20, 22, 24, 25, 33, 48, 50, 51, 57,
        61, 64, 66, 67, 68, 69, 70, 73, 79, 80, 84,
        89, 90, 91, 99, 102, 121, 122, 125, 135,
        136, 146, 148, 151, 152, 154, 155, 156,
        158, 159, 161
    and the Empire, 57
    Protestant attitude to, 64–5
    Relief, 48, 52, 147
    Roman Catholic Church, 21, 150, 156,
        161
Roman law, 40, 47
Romantic nationalism, 19, 81, 82, 163
Rome, 81
Roscommon, County, 121, 126, 134,
    139
Royal College of Maynooth, 48
Royal Irish Academy, 2
Rowan, Hamilton, 70
Russell, Thomas, 93, 148
Ruxton, Charles MP, 133
Ryan, Captain Daniel, 147

Sack, James J. (historian), 145
Sacramental test, 72, 157
Saintfield, County Down, 74
Sampson, William, 86, 87
    Advice to the rich, 86, 87
Saurin, William, 111, 121
Savage, James MP, 139
Scotland, 38, 39, 40, 41, 42, 43, 46, 47, 49,
    61, 82, 87, 163
    see Anglo-Scottish Union (1707)
Scott, Sir Walter, 157, 158, 159, 162, 163
    Waverley, 158, 163
Scullabogue, County Wexford, 150
Scully, Denys, 166
Second Keady, County Armagh, 75
Secret service accounts, 2, 46, 133, 135
Senior, Hereward (historian), 36, 148
Seven Years War (1756–63), 51
Seward, William Wenman, 12
    Political transactions of Ireland, 12
Shannon, Richard Boyle, 2nd Earl, 68
Sharkey, Richard Fortescue MP, 139, 132
Shaw, Rev Nathaniel, 74
Shaw, Robert MP, 139
Sheridan, Richard Brinsley, 19, 27, 55
Sheffield, John Baker-Holroyd, 1st Lord,
    130, 131
Sigerson, George, 31
Sligo, County, 126
Smith, Adam, 93
    *Inquiry into the nature and causes of the
        wealth of nations*, 93
Smith, Goldwin (historian), 21, 27, 33
    Irish history and the Irish question, 33
Smith, William, 54
Smyth, Jim (historian), 63
Smyth, Rev John, 74
Sophia, electress of Hanover, 40
South American wars, 169, 170
Spenser, Edmund, 169
    View of the present state of Ireland, 169
Squadrone, 42
St Johnstown, County Longford, 133, 139
St Patrick's Cathedral, 58

Sterling [Stirling], 41

Stewart, Charles William MP, 141

Stewart, James MP, 110

Strabane, County Tyrone, 72,

Stuarts, 37, 40, 41

   see Charles I, Charles II, James II,
     Anne

Sullivan, A.M., 22

   The Nation, 22

   The Story of Ireland, 22

Sweetman, Captain Edward, 85

Swift, Jonathan, 38–9, 43, 61

Swords, County Dublin, 112

Synod of Ulster, 72–6, 79

Taaffe, Denis, 56, 84, 87, 91–2

Talbot, William, 132

Tallagh, County Waterford

Taylor, Colonel, Grand Master of English
   Orangemen, 153

Temple, Sir John, 3, 61–2, 63, 64, 65

Texel, 71

Thomastown, County Kilkenny, 139,
   140–3

Tipperary, County, 78, 122

Toler, John, 138

Tone, Theobald Wolfe, 45, 51, 54, 55, 74,
   77, 84, 85, 90, 98

   Address to the people of Ireland, 45

To the Friends of the People at London, 86

Tories, 59

Tory Party, 145, 158

Townsend, Rev James, 74

Transactions of the Royal Historical Society, 2

Trench, Fredrick MP, 132

Trinity College, University of Dublin, 23,
   85, 112, 130, 131, 133, 146, 152, 169,
   171

Troy, John Thomas, Catholic archbishop
   of Dublin, 64, 90, 102

Trumpener, Katie, 163, 173

Tudors, 38, 82

Tyrone, County, 70, 122, 140–1, 143

Tyrone, Lord, 2

Ulster, 25, 61, 69, 70, 76, 77, 78, 79, 80,
   113, 121, 150, 156

Ulstermen, 63

ultra-Protestants, 4, 97, 145, 148, 149, 150,
   151, 153–6

unionists / unionism, 5, 19, 23, 24, 26, 29,
   30, 33, 36, 70, 82, 84, 105, 108, 145,
   148, 149

United Irishmen, 3, 20, 32, 45, 47,
   70, 74–80, 82, 84–94, 96, 97,
   98, 108, 109, 146, 148, 150,
   151, 159, 160

   propaganda and political ideas on
    union, 84–94, 170

United States of America, 51, 53, 54, 73,
   78, 79, 80, 89, 103

Verner, Thomas, 148

Villiers Stuart, Henry, 157

Vinegar Hill, 96, 151

Volney, Constantin François de, 172

   Ruins of empire, 172

Volunteers, 69, 70, 80, 102–3

Wales, 38, 163

Warden, Rev David Bailie, 73

Warner, W.B., 163

Waterford, County, 133, 146

Wellesley, Richard, 2nd Earl, 155

Wellington, Arthur Wellesley, 1st Duke
   of, 158

Westby, Nicholas MP, 132

Westmeath, County, 113, 122, 125, 133,
   139, 165

Westminster, 10, 19, 39, 43, 46, 47, 48, 56,
   61, 65, 117, 131, 132, 143

Wexford, 2, 20, 69, 80, 81, 84, 139, 143,
   147, 148, 150, 151–3

Wicklow, 132, 133, 134, 141

Wilberforce, William, 168

Wilkinson, David, 1

Whaley, Thomas 'Buck' MP, 136

Whelan, Kevin (historian), 2, 172

Whig Club, 76, 109

Whigs (English), 59
Whigs (Irish), 11, 73, 79, 109–28, 137, 166, 175
White, Hawtrey, 151
White, John Campbell, 79
Whiteboys, 20
Whitehall, 99, 105, 106, 138
Widows' Fund, 74
William III, 59, 149
  commemoration of, 152, 155

Wollstonecraft, Mary, 162
Worrall, Rev James, 74, 79

Yeats, W.B., 160
yeomanry, 3, 14, 77, 80, 81, 103, 111, 123, 148, 149, 150, 151, 154
York, 41
York, Duke of, 153
Yorkshire, 41
Young Irelanders, 17, 21